English Sou

D0568544

For my mother and father

English Sound Structure

John Harris

BLACKWELL
Oxford UK & Cambridge USA

Copyright © John Harris 1994

The right of John Harris to be identified as author of this work has been asserted in accordance with the Copyright, Designs and Patents Act 1988.

First published 1994

Blackwell Publishers
108 Cowley Road
Oxford OX4 1JF
UK

238 Main Street
Cambridge, Massachusetts 02142
USA

All rights reserved. Except for the quotation of short passages for the purposes of criticism and review, no part of this publication may be reproduced, stored in a retrieval system, or transmitted, in any form or by any means, electronic, mechanical, photocopying, recording or otherwise, without the prior permission of the publisher.

Except in the United States of America, this book is sold subject to the condition that it shall not, by way of trade or otherwise, be lent, resold, hired out, or otherwise circulated without the publisher's prior consent in any form of binding or cover other than that in which it is published and without a similar condition including this condition being imposed on the subsequent purchaser.

British Library Cataloguing in Publication Data
A CIP catalogue record for this book is available from the British Library.

Library of Congress Cataloging-in-Publication Data
Harris, John, 1954–
English sound structure / John Harris.
p. cm.
Includes bibliographical references and index.
ISBN 0–631–18261–6. –ISBN 0–631–18741–3 (pbk.)
1. English language – Phonology. I. Title.
PE 1133.H365 1994 421.5–dc20 93–44174 CIP

Typeset in 10 on 12 ½ pt Sabon
by Pure Tech Corporation, Pondicherry, India
Printed and bound in Great Britain by
Hartnolls Limited, Bodmin, Cornwall
This book is printed on acid-free paper

Library
University of Texas
at San Antonio

Contents

3 Melody   90

4 Licensing   148

Note on Transcription

The alphabetic system of phonetic transcription followed in the book is essentially that used in most generative treatments of English, although somewhat modified in the direction of the International Phonetic Association model. In running text, forms cited in normal spelling are enclosed in angled brackets, e.g. bɪt ⟨bit⟩.

Vowels

		Front		Non-front	
		Non-round	Round	Non-round	Round
High	tense	i	ü	ɨ	u
High	Lax	ɪ	ü̇		ʊ
Mid	Tense	e	ø	ʌ	o
Mid	Lax	ɛ	œ		ɔ
Low		æ		a	ɒ

Consonants

The phonetic values of the consonant symbols employed in the book are for the most part self-evident. The following particular conventions should be noted:

ʃ voiceless palato-alveolar fricative
ʒ voiced palato-alveolar fricative
č voiceless palato-alveolar affricate
ǰ voiced palato-alveolar affricate
y palatal glide
x voiceless velar fricative
ʍ voiceless labial-velar fricative

Preface

There are two immediate decisions that face anyone setting out to write a book on modern English phonology. One has to do with the nature of the material to be presented: to what extent should it reflect the dialect diversity that is part and parcel of the present-day language? The other concerns the terms within which the material is to be described and analysed: how much discussion should be devoted to the theoretical issues it raises?

Books on the subject tend to fall into one of three categories according to the answers their authors give to these questions. One type is the primarily descriptive textbook which focuses on some standard variety of English, either exclusively or perhaps with some passing acknowledgement of dialect differences. Kenyon's *American Pronunciation* and Jones' *An Outline of English Phonetics* are benchmark examples. Authors of such books are typically not felt to be under much obligation to justify the theoretical assumptions that are implicit in the particular descriptive framework adopted. The second type differs from the first in explicitly concerning itself with theoretical issues but is similar in drawing its data from primarily standard sources. The classic of this genre is Chomsky and Halle's *The Sound Pattern of English*. The third type is usually marketed under the heading of sociolinguistics or dialectology. It differs from the others in giving pride of place to varieties which rarely if ever make it into the standard textbooks but generally shares with the first a lack of interest in phonological theory. The example which offers perhaps the most comprehensive coverage is Wells' *Accents of English*.

Much less common is a type of book that is based on a fourth permutation of answers to the questions posed above – a book in which coverage of a wide range of English varieties, standard and non-standard, is combined with an interest in matters theoretical. The present book is designed to fill that gap. It discusses a range of phonological phenomena drawn from different types of English and, in analysing them, introduces the reader to recent theoretical advances in phonology. This orientation is not born out of a desire merely to analyse dialect material for its own sake, still less out of a belief that such an investigation would be rewarding only for whatever phonological curios it might turn up. The main rationale stems from the strategic importance that studies of dialect variation have assumed in the recent development of linguistic theory.

Linguistic theory of late has witnessed a move away from an emphasis on rule-based analyses of structural differences among and within languages. What has emerged in its place is a framework in which linguistic variation is seen as occurring along a limited number of parameters, in a manner that is determined by universal principles. Where previously a particular phenomenon in a grammar would have been characterized in terms of a language-specific rule, now it is more likely to be treated as one of a fixed number of choices forced on the language system by Universal Grammar. This theoretical development is already well established in syntax and is now beginning to have a significant impact on phonology.

With this shift in theoretical priorities has come a renewed interest in dialect variation. The comparative study of closely related language systems provides a controlled research environment in which individual linguistic variables can be investigated while surrounding variables in the grammar are held constant.

Reflecting these recent developments, this book sets out to use phonological variation within English as a test-bed for the principle-oriented approach. The choice of variables to be analysed is necessarily rather selective and has been determined primarily by matters of theoretical interest. It is thus not part of the brief of the book to provide an exhaustive description of English dialect phonology. Nor is there any reason to say any more about the regional and social distribution of the variables than is minimally necessary to establish the credentials of particular data sets. With a blithe indifference to the social evaluation of phonological differences, the researcher is free to ransack the English data-base for whatever material makes promising grist for the theoretical mill. And the data-base, it has to be said, is pretty comprehensive – in part a reflection of the language's wide geographical dispersion. In fact, a good case can be made for saying that in English we find a hefty sample of the phonological phenomena that are possible in any natural language.

The introductory chapter discusses the place of phonology in generative grammar and briefly reviews the types of phonological regularity that have occupied the attention of researchers over the years. We consider some of the reasons for the flight from earlier rule-oriented analyses of phonological processes. The chapter also seeks to identify the types of phonological phenomena in English that are most likely to provide fruitful material against which to assess the more recent principle-based approach.

Chapter 2 is about how sequences of sounds are organized into syllabic constituents. This level of structure, we will see, has a significant role to play in such phenomena as the relative duration of sounds and the restrictions that are imposed on their ability to occur next to one another. One conclusion of the chapter is that a binary limit is imposed on the number of positions that syllabic constituents can contain.

The next two chapters address a number of fundamental questions about the nature of phonological processes: what is the set of possible processes, where do they occur, and why do they occur where they do? Chapter 3 tackles the first of these issues by considering how the internal make-up of sounds influences their susceptibility to phonological processing. Here we investigate the basic building blocks of sounds, how they are phonetically manifested, and how they are organized within phonological representations.

Chapter 4 seeks to answer the questions of where and why processes occur by establishing an intimate link between the make-up of a sound and its ability to occupy particular positions in syllable structure. We consider evidence supporting the view that relations between adjacent positions are asymmetric. That is, within a domain formed by a pair of positions, one acts as the head. Headedness is observable not only within syllabic constituents but also between them, as well as within wider phonological domains, including the word and the phrase. We will consider arguments in favour of the view that it is these asymmetries that create the conditions for phonological processes to take place. The chapter discusses how headedness as well as the maximal binarity of constituents can be derived from fundamental principles which regulate phonological representations and indeed linguistic structure in general.

Drawing on the theoretical insights reviewed in the first part of the book, chapter 5 presents a detailed analysis of a collection of phenomena related to *r* in English. These illustrate how differences in the realization of a particular sound are directly relatable to the syllabic position it occupies.

Various sections of the book are given over to analyses of data relating to particular phonological variables in English. In each case, the presentation begins with a description of the different manifestations of the variable in a selected number of systems. Discussion of various competing analyses then provides the opportunity to compare rule-oriented and principle-oriented approaches. Each chapter concludes with sets of exercises which can be used in tutorial work. The treatment of this material offers further opportunities to consider the issues discussed in the body of the chapter.

It is my pleasure to thank various colleagues who were prevailed upon to take me quietly on one side in an attempt to talk me out of committing to print the indiscretions of earlier drafts of the book. Three people in particular deserve special commendation for taking on this task – Michael Kenstowicz for his detailed and perspicacious comments, Neil Smith for his patient and thorough reading of several drafts, and Edmund Gussmann for allowing me to drive him up the wall with an early rough cut. Let me be the first to hold up my hand and accept blame for any follies which, for reasons of oversight or sheer bloody-mindedness, I have failed to expunge from the text.

Others who are in a position to call in hefty debts of gratitude include Monik Charette and Eugeniusz Cyran, who provided helpful criticism of various portions of the manuscript. Thanks also to Martine Grice, Phil Harrison and Theo Maniski for saving me from error in a number of places.

Perhaps the biggest IOU is due to the students at University College London who let me try out the book's material on them. There is nothing quite like the justified puzzlement of a captive audience for sending a coursebook author scurrying back to the word-processor. I am also in hock to the numerous participants in other courses where the material was given trial runs, particularly at the Universitat Autònoma de Barcelona, the Eövös Loránd University in Budapest, the Central Institute for English and Foreign Languages in Hyderabad, and the University of Helsinki.

John Harris
London
October 1993

1 Sounds and Words

1.1 Phonology in generative grammar

The capacity to use spoken language boils down to an ability to assign meaning to sequences of speech sounds. It thus involves a harnessing of two different types of knowledge. One interacts with the central conceptual systems and controls how we compute meaning. The other is phonological and regulates the issuing of instructions to the motor-perceptual systems for the purposes of producing and recognizing speech sounds.

These two types of knowledge are usually viewed as being located at separate levels of a **generative grammar** which models linguistic competence: the level of **logical form** (LF) interfaces with the central conceptual systems, while that of **phonetic form** (PF) interfaces with articulation and perception.

The mapping between LF and PF is mediated by **syntax**, which, by drawing on the **lexicon, generates** or defines well-formed sentence structures. The lexicon is the repository of all those properties which are idiosyncratically associated with each word – its meaning, its pronunciation and its syntactic and morphological characteristics.[1]

As depicted in (1), the function of LF and PF is to assign respectively semantic and phonetic interpretations to sentences.

(1)

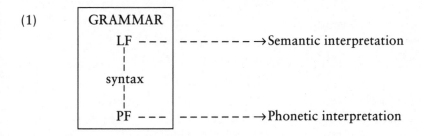

Linguistic semantic interpretation is based on a combination of the lexical meanings of words and the relations these contract with one another in sentences.[2] In somewhat similar fashion, the phonetic interpretation of a sentence makes reference not only to the phonological shape of individual words but also to the phonological effects that result from combining these words in sequence. For reasons to be considered presently, the significance of this point is that phonological facts in the grammar are distributed between the lexicon and PF.

Some aspects of pronunciation are peculiar to individual words and reflect the essential arbitrariness of the sound–meaning pairing.[3] The idiosyncratic nature of such facts is underlined by the observation that the same concept in different languages can be signified by arbitrarily different sound sequences. (Compare, for example, the forms *dʌk*, *kanar* (French) and *letata* (Sesotho) for the notion 'duck'.) Not being subject to any general phonological or other grammatical principles, pronunciation facts of this type have to be listed in the lexicon.

Other properties of pronunciation, however, display regular phonological patterning, in the sense that they are characteristic of particular sound sequences rather than individual words. And not being lexically idiosyncratic, these patterns tend to recur in different languages wherever the relevant sequences occur.

One such pattern involves a process whereby a particular type of sound systematically undergoes a change when it comes to stand next to another particular type of sound. This situation can arise, for example, when two words or morphemes are juxtaposed in a sentence, and the final sound of the first form comes into contact with the initial sound of the second. In the prototypical case, such a process will affect any sequence of morphemes containing the relevant string of sounds. Here are some examples that occur naturally in conversational English:

(2) (a) te[n]   te[m] birds
          ru[n]   ru[m] past   ru[ŋ] clear

     (b) miss [s]   miss you   [ʃ y]
          faze [z]   faze you   [ʒ y]
          get [t]   get your   [č y]
          did [d]   did Eunice   [ǰ y]

     (c) sen[d]   sen[d] Anne   sen[d̸] two
          fin[d]   fin[d] it   fin[d̸] them
          hol[d]   hol[d] on   hol[d̸] tight

The first two examples illustrate processes involving assimilation of place of articulation. In (2a), a word-final alveolar nasal assimilates to the place specification of the consonant at the beginning of the following word. Something similar happens in (2b), where we see how a word-final alveolar obstruent (plosive or fricative) becomes palatalized (to a palato-alveolar) under the influence of a following palatal glide. (2c) is an example of a truncation process; in this case, *d* in a word-final consonant cluster drops when the next word begins with a consonant.

1.2 Phonological phenomena

1.2.1 *Alternations*

The examples in (2) illustrate the point that a morpheme can appear in one of a number of shapes or **alternants**. On the basis of the facts given in (2b), for example, we can identify two alternants associated with the morpheme ⟨miss⟩, namely *mɪs* and *mɪʃ*. To put it somewhat differently, the *s* in ⟨miss⟩ **alternates** with *ʃ*. Two properties of the examples in (2) are worth remarking on. First, the relationship between the alternating sounds can be expressed in phonological terms; *ʃ* in ⟨miss⟩, for example, can be described as a palatalized relative of *s*. Second, the context in which the alternations take place can also be specified phonologically; that is, the selection of alternants is determined by the sounds a morpheme comes into contact with in neighbouring morphemes. These properties are characteristic of a large class of the alternations that are encountered in the world's languages. Not all alternations conform to this pattern, however. In the case of **suppletive** morphology, for example, no phonological connection exists between the different shapes of a morpheme; examples in English include ⟨go–went⟩ and ⟨good–better⟩.

The question now is how alternations are to be represented in the grammar. One possibility might be to list the different alternants of a morpheme in the lexicon. Given that the lexicon is the repository of idiosyncratic information, this would certainly seem to be the appropriate solution for suppletions such as ⟨go–went⟩, since they are by definition peculiar to particular morphemes. However, to treat all alternations in this way would obscure the fact that the majority are not tied to particular morphemes but are instead characteristic of particular sound sequences.

The alternative view is to assume that processes responsible for producing phonologically regular alternations such as those in (2) are represented at PF. This opens the way towards setting up unique phonological representations for each non-suppletive morpheme in the lexicon. The various forms of a regularly alternating morpheme can be derived from a single basic representation by means of processes operating at PF.[4] Take for example the truncation-prone form ⟨send⟩ with its two alternants *send* and *sɛn*. Assuming the lexical representation to be *sɛnd*, as in (3), we can derive *sɛn* by exposing the form to the process of truncation operating in a pre-consonantal context.[5] Pre-vocalically, the final *d* remains intact.

(3)		⟨send (to)⟩	⟨send (it)⟩
	Lexical representation	*sɛnd* (*tü*)	*sɛnd* (*ɪt*)
	Truncation	*sɛn* (*tü*)	
	Alternants	*sɛn*	*sɛnd*

Precisely the same kind of **derivation** can be envisaged for all morphemes in the lexicon that show the same *d*–zero alternation. The general format for a phonological derivation is thus as follows:

(4) Lexical representation
↓
Phonological processes
↓
Derived representation

1.2.2 *Distribution*

Not all phonological regularities involve dynamic alternations such as those represented in (2). Another type takes the form of static patterns which emerge from the phonological shape of morphemes as these are represented in the lexicon. Patterns of this sort govern the **distribution** of sounds in different phonological contexts – that is, the ability of sounds to occur at particular points in phonological strings. To gain some idea of the kind of phenomena that are at issue here, compare the distributions of *t* and *h* in English. Both can occur at the beginning of words (as in ⟨tie, high⟩), but only *t* can appear at the end of words; hence the existence of forms of the type ⟨it⟩ but none of the type *⟨ıh⟩.

Positions in phonological strings vary in the extent to which they can support the distribution of a range of sounds. By way of a more detailed illustration, compare the distributional potential of a position occupied by a single word-initial consonant (C), shown in (5a), with that of the second position in a word-initial *s*-plus-consonant cluster (5b):

(5) (a) Single word-initial C

p pail		*t* tail	*k* kale
b bail		*d* dale	*g* gale
			č chain
			ǰ jail
m mail		*n* nail	
f fail	*θ* thane	*s* sail	*ʃ* shale
v vale	*ð* they	*z* zany	
(*ʍ*) whale		*l* lay	
w wail		*r* rail	*y* Yale
			h hail

(b) C in word-initial *s*C cluster

p spin	*t* sting	*k* skin
m smear	*n* sneer	
w swoop	*l* sloop	(*y*) suit

(Omitted from this display are rare clusters of marginal status, such as in ⟨sphere, svelte, sthenic, vroom⟩. Parentheses indicate a sound or cluster that is dialectally restricted, as in *syu:t* versus *su:t* ⟨suit⟩.) The distributional possibilities are obviously much greater in (5a) than in (5b). To put it differently, the ability of consonants to **contrast** with one another is greater in one context than the other. The presence of a preceding *s* evidently reduces the contrastive potential of the following position. For example, although voiced and voiceless plosives freely occur in a single initial consonant position, this contrast is suspended after *s*.

Now, although distributional facts such as these differ from alternations in that they involve static patterns rather than dynamic changes, they are similar in one important respect: no less than regular alternations, they represent recurrent properties of sound sequences rather than random effects associated with individual morphemes. For this reason, most phonologists are in agreement that the two types of regularity should be represented in the same manner, namely at PF.

Further justification for this decision comes from the finding that, in some cases, what is evidently the same phonological pattern shows up as a dynamic alternation under some circumstances but as a static distributional effect under others. One example involves the palatalization process illustrated in (2b). In some dialects of English, Type A in (6), sequences of an alveolar obstruent followed by a palatal glide occur freely within morphemes. In another type, B in (6), the corresponding morphemes categorically contain palato-alveolar fricatives or affricates. (Other types of dialect show other patterns, including a lack of *y* in certain contexts, as in *tu:n* ⟨tune⟩.[6])

(6) Dialect   A   B
     issue   *isyu:*   *iʃu:*
     tune   *tyu:n*   *ču:n*
     dune   *dyu:n*   *ǰu:n*

The situation in Type-B dialects is that no clusters of alveolar obstruent plus *y* are ever found within the same morpheme. The gap is due to a historical analogue of the palatalization process in (2b), whereby all such sequences were converted into palato-alveolars. In the case of cross-word palatalization, there is alternation evidence in all dialects to support the setting up of lexical representations containing the alveolar-plus-*y* sequence. But no such evidence exists for similar morpheme-internal sequences to be lexically constructed in dialects of Type B. In other words, lexical representations in B have been historically restructured to contain only palato-alveolars in morphemes such as those in (6). This conclusion is buttressed by the observation that the historical C*y* sequences are now merged with original palato-alveolars; hence homophones in B such as ⟨dune = June, deuce = juice⟩.

The distributional gap in Type-B dialects has to be accounted for somehow. We might try to characterize it in terms of a filter statement which bars the occurrence of sequences of alveolar obstruent plus *y* from morpheme-internal contexts. But this would duplicate part of the statement needed to characterize the cross-word palatalization alternation in (2b) and would thus miss an underlying generalization.

A solution which is more economical and at the same time captures the relatedness of the two phenomena in Type-B dialects is to represent them in terms of a single palatalization process. The process will apply in a dynamic fashion in the cross-word context but in a static distributional fashion morpheme-internally. In the latter instance, the process can be said to operate **vacuously**; that is, the lexical representations of the morphemes in question already conform to the output of the process. Viewed in these terms, what we are dealing with is not so much two independent phenomena as a single phenomenon operating in a rather different fashion in different contexts.

1.3 Representation and derivation

1.3.1 *Principles vs. rules*

Having established that PF is the appropriate place to locate the statement of both dynamic and static phonological regularities, the next question is **how** such statements are to be formulated. At one time, devising a notational system for formalizing the statements was taken to be a primary goal of phonological theory. With the benefit of hindsight, this can be seen to be a relatively trivial exercise, influenced as much by typographical considerations as by the ingenuity of the phonologist. What is required is a theory of phonological processing. That is, the goal is to construct a model which generates a set of phonological processes that as closely as possible approximates the set of processes we observe in the world's languages. It is only when embedded in a theoretical matrix that the notational aspect of the research challenge takes on non-trivial significance. The notational system associated with a successful phonological model should be such that it captures only those process-types that actually occur – no more, no less.

The task of building such a model has two main aspects. The **derivational** aspect involves determining the set of operations responsible for mapping lexical phonological representations onto derived representations. Responding to this challenge requires making decisions about such questions as whether and how sounds can be deleted, inserted, or replaced by other sounds. Related to this is the **representational** issue: the manner in which derivational processes function is clearly going to be influenced by the nature of the phonological representations on which they operate. Establishing how one sound might be mapped onto another sound, for example, naturally depends on how we view those sounds as being made up.

Looking back over a generation of research into phonological processing, it is possible to discern a clear shift in emphasis away from the derivational towards the representational aspect of the problem.[7] In earlier models of generative phonology, the prominence given to the former was reflected in the relatively large set of process-types countenanced by the theory as well as in a concentration on how series of processes could interact during the course of derivation. More recent years have seen radical changes in how we view phonological representations. With this has come a growing awareness that the derivational aspect of phonological processing can be greatly simplified by reducing it to a very limited set of primitive operations. The bulk of this book will be taken up with discussing these representational developments. Nevertheless, since much of this progress is to be understood as a reaction against a heavily derivationally weighted approach, it makes sense to have some idea of what earlier generative theory looked like.

Over the years, the main reference point for phonological theorizing has been Chomsky and Halle's *Sound Pattern of English*, published in 1968. The profound influence this book has had on the development of phonological theory is evident in the label **SPE** that has come to be applied to any work carried out within the same general paradigm.

The SPE view of phonology was consistent with contemporary work in generative syntax. All linguistic regularities, whether syntactic or phonological, were characterized by means of rules represented in the grammars of individual languages. Specifically, a grammar was assumed to contain independent components, one dedicated to syntactic rules, the other to phonological rules. The analysis of a given domain of linguistic facts consisted largely in specifying a derivation defined in terms of a set of rules and the manner in which these interact. Rules were assumed to apply in sequence, ordered in relation to one another according to explicit grammar-internal statements.[8]

Rules tended to be quite specific to particular constructions and processes in particular languages. Thus work on English phonology from this period contains references to such rules as Vowel Shift, Velar Softening and Trisyllabic Laxing (on which more in 1.4.2), just as in syntax we find reference to such rules as Passivization, Affix-Hopping and Equi-NP Deletion. The view at this time was that the primary task of linguistic theory was to construct a notational framework for the formulation of rule systems, a framework that would define the set of possible rules.[9]

More recent developments in syntactic theory have seen a sharp move away from this preoccupation with rules and rule ordering. Syntactic representations are now understood as being constructed by very general mechanisms, such as X-bar principles of phrase structure, and as being subject to unordered well-formedness conditions which filter out ungrammatical structures. These conditions are not specific to particular constructions but are formulated in general terms such that they hold of a range of different phenomena. For example, the conditions of subjacency and the Empty Category Principle place constraints on syntactic movement operations and apply to an apparently disparate range of phenomena including passives, dative movement, NP raising and WH-movement.[10] A particular domain of syntactic facts is now more likely to be explained as far as possible by reference to general principles of grammar rather than in terms of rules which are specific to the language under investigation. Thus analytic tasks previously performed by batteries of particular conditions placed on specific rules are now performed by general conditions that hold of language in general.

Even more recently, this line of enquiry has culminated in the conclusion that grammars do not contain an independent syntactic component. Instead, syntax is subsumed under LF.[11] This has the consequence that the only autonomous levels in the grammar are those of LF and PF. The mapping between these two levels is performed by a single universal computation which optimizes the relation between them. According to this view, syntactic differences between languages are restricted to options governing the morphological properties of words in the lexicon.

These developments have been rather slower to catch on in phonological theory. Much current work in phonology seems to acknowledge that a certain amount of language-specific stipulation in the form of rules is inevitable, at least given the present state of our knowledge. Some take this is as an indication that phonology is fundamentally different from syntax and that phonological phenomena are simply not amenable to the same type of principle-based explanations as are available in syntax.[12] Some take the opposite view that all phonological phenomena are ultimately reducible to general principles.[13] It is probably fair to say that many phonologists these days, more often than not implicitly, take up a position somewhere between these two extremes.

The emerging consensus is that a large body of phonological phenomena is indeed susceptible to principled explanation. While there may be disagreements about where the precise boundaries of this corpus lie, there is general recognition that language-specific stipulations should only be resorted to once currently available principled accounts have been exhausted. Persevering with this line of investigation leads to the conclusion that any stipulatory statement of a particular phonological process represents an admission of defeat, but perhaps only a temporary one. The conviction is that future progress will allow such analyses eventually to be replaced by principled solutions. The ultimate goal is a rule-free phonology. Under such a view, grammars do not contain anything resembling a phonological rule component.[14] Instead, derivations run their course in response to quite general constraints. It is in this spirit that the analyses to be offered in this book are formulated.

Much phonological research since the late 1970s has been devoted to the discovery and refinement of principles that can be shown to be active in the organization of phonological systems. More recently there has been some debate about which of these principles are specifically phonological and which are of a more general grammatical nature. An example of the latter type is furnished by principles of X-bar organization which, it has been argued, regulate not only syntactic structure but also the arrangement of phonological strings into syllabic constituents.[15] A number of other principles, methodological as well as theoretical, come up for discussion when we consider some of the problems that led to a rejection of certain aspects of the SPE model of phonological processing.

1.3.2 Linear rules and representations

According to SPE, a phonological representation consists of a string of segments and morpho-syntactic boundary symbols, each segment being characterized as a matrix of features. The features are binary-valued (represented as a distinction between plus and minus) and code information relating to the phonetic interpretation of the segments (voice, coronality, anteriority, height, etc.) and the relations they contract with one another (syllabic status, for example). This arrangement is illustrated by the partial representation of the form ⟨fin⟩ given in (7). (# stands for a word boundary. The dotted lines indicate that a fuller specification of each segment would require the presence of additional features.)

$$
(7) \quad \# \quad
\begin{bmatrix}
- \text{syllabic} \\
- \text{sonorant} \\
+ \text{continuant} \\
- \text{coronal} \\
+ \text{anterior} \\
- \text{voice} \\
\vdots
\end{bmatrix}
\begin{bmatrix}
+ \text{syllabic} \\
+ \text{sonorant} \\
- \text{consonantal} \\
+ \text{high} \\
- \text{back} \\
\vdots
\end{bmatrix}
\begin{bmatrix}
- \text{syllabic} \\
+ \text{sonorant} \\
- \text{continuant} \\
+ \text{coronal} \\
+ \text{anterior} \\
+ \text{nasal} \\
\vdots
\end{bmatrix}
\quad \#
$$

A representation of this type is often described as **linear** in the sense that segments are strung together in a single row, with each feature being uniquely assigned to a particular matrix.

Phonological processes in this framework are represented transformationally by means of rewrite rules which operate on representations of the type illustrated in (7). The general format of such rules is as follows:[16]

(8) (a) A → B/C ___ D

    (b) Structural description: CAD
         Structural change: CBD

The letters here can stand for feature matrices which identify individual sounds or classes of sounds. The arrangement in (8a) specifies that A, the rule's **input**, is rewritten as B, the **output**, in the context of a preceding C and a following D. C and D, either or both of which may be empty, constitute the rule's **environment**. The effect of the rule is to take a string CAD (the rule's structural description in (8b)) and transform it into CBD (the structural change).

To take a concrete example, we can formalize the labial portion of the place-assimilation process illustrated in (2a) in the following terms:

$$
(9) \quad [+ \text{nasal}] \rightarrow [+ \text{labial}]/ \ \underline{\quad\quad} \begin{bmatrix} - \text{syllabic} \\ + \text{labial} \end{bmatrix}
$$

That is, a nasal acquires a labial place of articulation when a labial consonant follows.

The letters A or B in (8a) can also stand for null; C or D can also stand for a morpheme boundary. Where null occupies the input ($\emptyset \rightarrow$ B), the rule is interpreted as inserting a sound. Where the output is null (A $\rightarrow \emptyset$), a deletion process is represented. The truncation process in (2c), for example, is expressed along the following lines:

(10) d → ∅/[− syllabic] ___ # [− syllabic]

In prose, *d* is deleted when preceded by a consonant and followed by a word boundary (#) which is itself followed by another consonant.

There has never been any real doubt about the rewrite rule's ability to represent any observed phonological process. However, it suffers from a number of major and long-recognized flaws. First, it permits the expression of an enormous set of possible processes, the vast majority of which are unobserved in the languages of the world. Second, the model fails to capture significant asymmetries in the distribution of those processes that are attested. Some processes are evidently more favoured or natural than others, in the sense that they show a greater propensity to recur in different grammars. These two points are not likely to be unconnected; so let us consider them in unison.

One aim of early generative theory was to provide a direct correlation between the naturalness of a rule and its formal simplicity. According to this notion, the more natural a process is, the simpler should be the corresponding rule, as gauged by the number of units contained in its structural description and change. It was soon acknowledged, however, that the rewrite-rule model patently failed to measure up to the simplicity criterion.[17]

To illustrate this point, consider just a few of the permutations that can be performed on the place assimilation rule in (9). A rule which specified a nasal as, say, [− labial] as opposed to [+labial] in the context of a following [+labial] constant would be formally just as simple as (9). However, the process it expresses, one of dissimilation, is much less favoured than assimilation. Examples of other rules minimally different from (9) include one which specifies the input nasal as [+labial] in, say, the context of a following vowel, or another which specifies the nasal as [+lateral] before a [+labial] consonant. The latter two examples express processes which are disfavoured to the point of being completely unattested in any natural language. This rather limited illustration points up a very general problem with the rewrite-rule format: for every rule that corresponds to a naturally occurring process, it is possible to formulate an unfortunately large array of minimally distinct rules which express processes that are either heavily disfavoured or downright impossible.

To be fair to proponents of the SPE apprach, this failing was acknowledged from an early date. In response, the sub-theory of **markedness** was proposed, in which a set of universal conventions designated certain features or feature combinations as being unmarked, that is, more favoured than others.[18] Only marked features were then deemed to contribute to a rule's formal complexity. The most highly valued rule would thus be one which contained nothing but unmarked features. A subset of the conventions defined the conditions under which assimilatory rules such as that in (9) were evaluated more highly than disfavoured permutations such as those mentioned in the last paragraph.

The markedness solution was but one of a number of approaches to the central problem of the rewrite-rule model, its capacity for over-generation. Each of these proposals in its own way illustrates a quite general development in the emergence, elaboration and demise of scientific paradigms. As dissatisfaction grows with a particular theory's inability to fit the facts it is intended to explain, the research community is faced with a familiar choice: either it modifies the theory or abandons it altogether. Naturally the former option is likely to be preferred in the absence of a better competing theory. If the model's main flaw is one of excessive generative power, some modifications may amount to no more than patch-up jobs, devised to mask a fundamental design fault. Markedness theory could be said to fulfil this role in relation to rewrite rules.

Suppose, however, that an alternative model becomes available, one which is not afflicted by the expressive exorbitance of its competitor. As it is developed, the new theory may show signs of under-generation. That is, in eschewing generative promiscuity, it may apparently go too far the other way and fail to account for sets of data which its predecessor was able to handle quite comfortably. At this point, there may be some temptation to fall back on the earlier theory and carry on with attempts to reform it. Alternatively, the researcher can persevere with the new model and earmark those areas where it seems to under-generate as problems for future research.

Both orientations are in evidence in current attitudes to linear rewrite rules, sometimes even within the work of the same researcher. Few still assume a full-blooded SPE version of the rewrite-rule model. Some have abandoned it altogether in favour of the more recent principle-based approach briefly reviewed in the last section. Still others implicitly work with some kind of hybrid, reserving the right to invoke SPE-type rules whenever they feel the newer model lets them down through apparent under-generation.

Inherent in the principle-based approach to phonological processing embraced in this book is a well established minimalist methodology, widely assumed in scientific endeavour and based on the following procedure. Given two competing models, begin by preferring the more impoverished. Initially set aside for future investigation any data for which no immediate fit with the model can be found. Only abandon the model if, after persistent disconfirmation, the empirical balance tilts decisively in favour of the more enriched competitor.

Returning to our consideration of the SPE markedness approach, we may note yet another problem: the universal markedness conventions are themselves no less arbitrary than rewrite rules. One convention, for example, identifies front rounded vowels as being more marked than their non-round congeners. This correctly captures the more favoured status of front non-round vowels. But simply stating the asymmetry in these terms provides no explanation of why things should be this way rather than the other way round.

Arbitrariness is in fact one of the inherent weaknesses of the rewrite-rule model which contributes to its over-generating capacity. One of the things an account of a given process has to do before it can be considered non-arbitrary is to establish a direct connection between the process and the context in which it occurs.[19] That is, it should offer an explanation of why a particular process takes place where it does. Rewrite-rule analyses fail on this count for the reason that they provide no formal link between a process and the context in which it occurs. This weakness stems from the representation of the output and environment as independent entities in a rewrite operation. This property of the model contributes to the equal facility with which disfavoured non-assimilatory processes and favoured assimilatory processes can be formulated. Intuitively, features acquired by the input to an assimilation process are somehow 'the same' as features represented in its environment. It is of course possible to declare that rules in which a copy of a feature from the environment appears in the output are more highly valued than rules which manipulate dissimilar features. But the need for such a stipulation amounts to an admission that the rewrite rule fails to capture the intuition directly.

Another arbitrary characteristic of the rewrite-rule format is that it establishes no principled limit on the length of phonological strings that can be referred to in a rule's structural description. With the possibility of including more than one segment or boundary symbol in a rule's environment (as in (10), for example) comes the prediction that the trigger of a process can occur at any distance from the site at which the process takes place. Again this allows for the formulation of a host of rules which express process-types that are unattested in any language. For example: 'delete the third segment in a sequence of seven segments'.

The same kind of criticism was levelled at the use of transformational rules in early generative syntax. In recent times, the response has been to assume that all syntactic operations are subject to the constraining principle of **locality**.[20] That is, a relation of adjacency must exist between two phrase-structure positions before they can participate in a particular syntactic movement. This constraint is now seen as one of the central principles regulating processes in both phonology and syntax. In phonology, the locality principle requires that the target and trigger of a process be adjacent.[21]

Adjacency in phonology, no less than in syntax, cannot be equated with superficial contiguity. That is, in many cases, two positions must be considered adjacent at some level of structure, even though they are superficially separated by other positions. Classic cases of this type include vowel harmony, in which all vowels within a certain span (usually the word) agree with respect to a particular feature, irrespective of the number of intervening consonants that might be present. By the same token, the fact that two positions are superficially contiguous is no guarantee that they are structurally adjacent. Exactly what constitutes adjacency in a phonological representation is one of the main themes running through this book.

Within the SPE framework, it is not at all clear how the locality principle can be applied. Restricting rules to those that refer only to adjacent segments and boundary symbols will certainly exclude environments containing strings of arbitrary lengths, while still allowing for the formulation of local assimilation processes such as that in (9). Unfortunately, however, it will also rule out a significant class of attested processes which do display long-distance effects, such as the vowel-harmony phenomenon just mentioned. This problem stems as much from the linear nature of SPE-type representations as from the rewrite-rule model itself. Intuitively, we would want to say that vowels in a harmonic domain are adjacent at some level that is inaccessible to consonants. But such a level has no formal expression within a representational framework in which sounds are concatenated in a single linear string.

1.3.3 Non-linear representations

Since the late 1970s, research into phonological processing has seen a concerted effort to redistribute the explanatory burden between derivation and representation. By enriching representations, it has proved possible to reduce reliance on potentially arbitrary derivational machinery. There are two main respects in which this development can be seen to yield a more constrained model of derivation. First, the set of formal operations that can be performed on a representation is now deemed to be considerably smaller than at first thought. On current assumptions, there are in fact only two fundamental operations – one which joins together different parts of a representation, and another which sunders them. A further contraction in the role of derivation is achieved if we adopt the simplest possible hypothesis regarding the applicability of phonological processes, namely that they take place freely wherever their conditions are satisfied. Under this view, there is no provision for processes to be arbitrarily prevented from occurring in contexts where they otherwise could; nor is there any mechanism whereby one process could be arbitrarily stipulated as applying before another. These developments, it has to be said, have not been universally taken on board by phonologists. But they remain fundamental to the principle-based research programme.

The move away from derivational concerns would not have proved particularly fruitful, had it only succeeded in simplifying one aspect of the theory at the expense of complicating another. As the focus shifted, so the need to discover general constraints on the shape of representations became all the more pressing. On the success of this enterprise hinges the possibility of reaching a stage where all processes, or at least a substantial proportion of them, can be viewed as necessary consequences of particular conditions prevailing in phonological representations.

This development has indeed enabled some progress to be made on the issues of locality and non-arbitrariness. It is now widely acknowledged that features are arrayed on independent tiers rather than being lumped together in bundles.[22] The synchronization of features belonging to a single segment is expressed by means of association lines, as illustrated in the following rough approximation of the representation corresponding to a labial plosive:

(11) [labial]
         |
       [stop]
         |
       [oral]

During the course of the book, we will examine in more detail the nature of this mode of representation and the evidence supporting it. For the moment, however, let us accept that multi-tiered representations are well motivated and note how they allow us to characterize assimilatory processes in a non-arbitrary fashion.

Allied to the multi-tiered mode of representation is the hypothesis alluded to above, that most if not all phonological processing can be reduced to two primitive operations – the insertion or deletion of association lines.[23] All assimilation processes are represented as line insertion, an operation that permits a single feature to be linked simultaneously to more than one segment. It is this possibility that gives rise to the term **non-linear**, used to describe representations of this type. The place assimilation in (2a), for example, can be characterized in terms of the following representation of a labial nasal-plosive cluster:

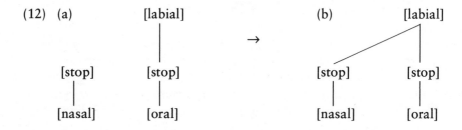

(12) (a) [labial]   →   (b) [labial]

    [stop] [stop]   [stop] [stop]

    [nasal] [oral]   [nasal] [oral]

The homorganicity of the cluster is represented as the insertion of an association line linking the [labial] feature of the plosive to the preceding nasal. The [labial] feature can be said to **spread** from the plosive to the nasal. The advantage of expressing assimilation in this fashion is that it establishes a non-arbitrary relation between the process and its operating context.[24] This it does in the most direct way possible – by identifying the output of the process and the context as one and the same feature, in this case [labial].

The question now is whether, in spite of its non-arbitrariness, the formulation in (12) is any less of a stipulative statement than the rewrite rule in (9). One response has been to assume that spreading is automatic and thus does not need to be represented as a rule operating in individual grammars. According to this view, the operation is universally defined and occurs wherever it can in individual systems, as long as the necessary conditions prevail. One condition involves a locality requirement: the segments participating in the spreading operation must be adjacent. Another involves one segment being specified for a particular feature while the other is not, as depicted in (12a). Automatic spreading will result in the unspecified segment acquiring the missing feature from its neighbour.

For this account to be successful, there needs to be some principled means of determining the directionality of spreading and the contexts within which it does and does not take place. Is spreading always unidirectional, or can it proceed in either direction? What constitutes adjacency for the purposes of spreading? If these questions elicit answers that invoke general principles, rather than language-specific statements, then we are on the way towards providing a non-stipulative account of assimilation and perhaps ultimately of phonological processing in general.

In the succeeding pages, we will consider precise formulations of a number of principles, including those relating to locality and directionality, and consider how they offer answers to the fundamental question of why phonological processes occur where they do.

1.3.4 *Parametric variation*

A major preoccupation of modern linguistics has been the study of **Universal Grammar**.[25] This notion can be understood both as a theory of those universal properties that constrain the form of individual grammars and as an account of the human language faculty in general. Studying individual language systems from this perspective involves distinguishing between a **core**, containing those linguistic traits which reflect systematic properties of Universal Grammar, and a **periphery**, containing traits which display unsystematic or eccentric behaviour. In the latter category belong such syntactic phenomena as one-off idioms and freakish constructions. (An example of the latter in English would be constructions of the type ⟨secretaries general⟩, which fail to conform to the otherwise regular pre-nominal positioning of attributive adjectives.)

At the phonological level, the periphery consists of those idiosyncratic pronunciation properties of individual lexical items that reflect the arbitrariness of the sound–meaning pairing. Included in this category are accidental lexical gaps – phonologically possible forms that happen not to be utilized as lexical addresses in a particular language, such as *blɪk* in English.[26] Some peripheral properties represent historical debris washed up in the lexicon as a result of once-active phonological processes becoming extinct over time. For example, the fact that the dental fricatives of words such as ⟨mother, together, either⟩ are voiced bears witness to a process of inter-vocalic fricative voicing that was once fully productive in Old English. The extinction of this process is evidenced in the considerable number of (mostly borrowed) words in the modern language which contain medial voiceless θ, such as ⟨ether, method, mathematics⟩.

One source of dissatisfaction with earlier generative theory was an inability to provide a principled distinction between core and peripheral facts of grammar. The transformational rule format is unfortunately as adept at characterizing phenomena which recur across different grammars as characterizing those which are peculiar to specific constructions or phonological sequences in particular languages. At the phonological level, this failing is linked to the essentially open-ended nature of the rewrite-rule model. The set of possible phonological processes that can be expressed within this theory is of vast proportions. And this generative excess is compounded by the possibility of stipulating different ordering relations between pairs of rules.[27] As a result, the choice of derivational routes whereby the different shapes of an alternating morpheme can be mapped from a single lexical representation is enormously wide. This arrangement cannot be considered a sound basis for plausible models of phonological acquisition or speech recognition. It would place excessive processing burdens on learners seeking to construct and listeners seeking to recognize lexical representations on the basis of variant phonetic shapes appearing in linguistic input.[28]

The overall effect of the rewrite-rule model is that the set of possible phonological grammars it generates is to all intents and purposes infinite. This prediction fails to tally with the current perception that core phonology is finite. That is, differences among phonological systems occur within fixed bounds laid down by Universal Grammar. The investigative task is to discover where these limits lie and to determine the precise points at which grammars are free to vary.

Variability in core syntax is nowadays characterized in terms of a relatively small number of **parameters**, each of which defines a choice (usually binary) between particular typological characteristics.[29] One well-known example has to do with whether or not a subject pronoun position can be left empty: in languages such as Italian and Spanish it can, in others such as French and English it cannot. The core grammar of a language is now viewed as a collection of specific choices or settings on such parameters.

It is increasingly being acknowledged that cross-grammar variability in core phonology should be conceived of in the same parametric terms.[30] Precisely how much of phonological variation is amenable to this kind of treatment continues to be subject to debate. There seems to be general agreement that certain gross typological differences to do with such dimensions as syllable structure and stress assignment can be characterized in this way. One such parameter determines whether stress prominence is located at the left or the right edge of a rhythmic constituent. At the level of the phonological word, for example, French takes up the right-hand option, while Hungarian opts for the left-hand setting.[31] In chapters 2 and 4, where we examine how phonological strings are organized into syllabic constituents, we will see that the syllable structure of a given language can be defined in terms of a small number of options which determine the shape of different types of constituent. It is now widely recognized that parameterization can and should be extended to phonological processes. For example, the general parameter that regulates the left versus right placement of stress can also be taken to control leftward versus rightward spreading in long-distance harmony processes.

The overall picture that is emerging is one in which Universal Grammar defines rigid limits beyond which it is impossible for individual phonological systems to stray. At the same time, it identifies particular areas where phonological structure is only partially determined; it is at these interstices that differences among core phonological grammars are located.

One of the methodological challenges associated with the parametric research programme is familiar from other fields of scientific enquiry. It concerns the necessity of ensuring that the results of investigating a particular set of data are not contaminated by effects emanating from some related set. For example, before attributing a specific structural difference between two languages to a particular parameter, we need to be sure that the divergence is not simply an incidental reflection of some other entirely independent distinction between the grammars.

To take a concrete example: languages vary in terms of the type of vocalic clusters (vowels and glides) they permit, an effect that is frequently expressed in terms of a parameter regulating the relative **sonority** of neighbouring sounds. (Very crudely, sonority can be understood as the degree of articulatory opening involved in the production of a sound. We will examine the notion in more detail in the next chapter.) In English, the second member of a vowel–vowel or vowel–glide cluster is generally restricted to *u*, *i* and (in some dialects at least) ə, as in the second portion of the diphthongs in ⟨cow, die, fear⟩. Compare this with the situation in Sesotho, a Bantu language spoken in southern Africa, in which sequences of vocalic pairs are more or less unrestricted – hence the occurrence of clusters such as *ai, ae, aɛ, aɔ, ao, au*. The mismatch between the two languages can be described at some level in terms of sonority differences: unlike English, Sesotho apparently imposes no restrictions on the sonority profile of vocalic clusters.

However, to ascribe the divergence directly to a difference in sonority restrictions in this instance would be misguided. The mismatch is in fact a superficial reflection of a more deep-seated difference between the languages which itself involves a parameter that is quite independent of sonority. Each of the English vocalic clusters just described is diphthongal in so far as it is contained within the same syllable. The Sesotho clusters do not qualify as diphthongs in this sense; instead they constitute sequences of separate syllables. (This conclusion is supported by the observation that each vowel in such strings bears a separate tone.) In fact, Sesotho is like many languages in forbidding more than one segment to occupy the **nucleus** of a syllable (that portion most typically occupied by a vowel). The fundamental distinction between Sesotho and English in this matter thus stems from different settings on a parameter which regulates the number of positions permitted to occur in the nucleus.

This example illustrates the pitfalls awaiting the researcher trying to isolate the source of a difference between two languages when more than one parameter is potentially involved. The ideal experimental environment in which to test a particular parametric hypothesis is one where all variables in the data are held constant save the one which is the object of investigation. The varying effects of sonority constraints in vocalic clusters, for example, can be more accurately gauged by comparing languages with like settings on the nuclear parameter just mentioned. The more closely related the two language systems are, the more likely we are to approximate laboratory-like conditions. For this reason much of the work on parametric variation in syntax has taken the form of contrastive studies of genetically related languages. It is in the light of this experimental orientation that comparative dialectology takes on a strategic significance it rarely enjoyed in earlier rule-based approaches to linguistic variation.[32] The considerable degree of structural relatedness that typically unifies dialects of the same language provides a favourable research environment within which to focus on one linguistic variable at a time, while minimizing the danger of contamination from extraneous noise due to other variables. This point provides one of the main motives for the present book's treatment of dialect variation in English.

1.4 Words and roots

1.4.1 *English morphology*

Before proceeding any further with the discussion, we need to come to some decisions about the nature of the data we should be investigating. In particular, it is necessary to establish what kind of phonological phenomena in English are most likely to furnish the relevant material against which to test the validity of the principle-based approach outlined in the last section. This requires us to take account of the manner in which English morphology contributes to the conditions under which phonological phenomena of different types occur.

The phonological phenomena found in any given grammar are not necessarily evenly distributed throughout the morphology. In many languages, including English, different subsets of patterns are observable within different sorts of morphological domains. By way of illustration, compare the phonological behaviour of the prefixes ⟨in-⟩ and ⟨un-⟩. ⟨in-⟩ has a number of alternants, the basic one, *in-*, being evident before vowel-initial stems (as in (13a)) as well as before certain consonants (13b). Before certain other consonants, however, other alternants show up: *im-* before labial plosives (13c), *i-* before liquids (*l* or *r*, as in (13d)) or nasals (13e).

(13) (a) inexcusable, ineligible, inoperative
  (b) inflammable, intrepid, insouciant
  (c) impossible, implicit, imbued
  (d) illegal, irregular, irresponsible
  (e) innocuous, immaterial, immature

Note that, in spite of the spelling, the forms in (13d) and (13e) do not contain geminate (double or long) consonants. That is, a word such as ⟨innocuous⟩ is pronounced ⟨i[n]ocuous⟩ rather than *⟨i[nn]ocuous⟩. This makes this prefix quite different from ⟨un-⟩. If the latter alternates at all, it does so only optionally; the place of articulation of the nasal may be subject to the assimilation process in (2) (as in ⟨u[m]pleasant, u[ŋ]kind⟩). But the most significant difference is that the nasal of ⟨un-⟩, unlike that of ⟨in-⟩, is consistently present. One consequence of this is that the attachment of ⟨un-⟩ to a stem can result in the creation of geminate sequences. Hence forms such as

(14) u[nn]erved, u[un]ecessary, u[un]atural

The different behaviour of ⟨in-⟩ and ⟨un-⟩ illustrates a fundamental distinction between two types of morphology in English. ⟨in-⟩ is representative of what is often referred to as **root-level** affixation, ⟨un-⟩ of **word-level** affixation. Very broadly speaking, different morphological operations are assigned to each of these categories along the following lines:[33]

(15) English morphology
  (a) **Root**-level morphology:
       Affixation: ⟨in-, -ity, -ic, -al, -ory, -ate, -ion, -ant, -th, . . .⟩
       'Strong' verbs/nouns: ⟨blew, brought, sang, feet, mice, ...⟩

  (b) **Word**-level morphology:
       Affixation: ⟨un-, -ed, -(e)s, -ing, -ness, -ly, -ful, -ship, -hood, -ment, . . .⟩
       Compounds, e.g. ⟨cart horse, seagull, blackboard, . . .⟩

(Apart from a handful of largely unproductive Germanic suffixes (including ⟨-th⟩, as in ⟨fifth⟩), root-level affixes are overwhelmingly of Greek or Latinate origin. The 'strong' verb and noun forms are nearly all Germanic. So are the bulk of word-level affixes, although a few Latinate forms (⟨-ment⟩, for example⟩) belong to this group. Certain pairs of root and word affixes are Latinate cognates: compare root-level ⟨su(C)-⟩ (where C stands for some orthographic consonant, as in ⟨suffix, sustain⟩) with word-level ⟨sub-⟩ (as in ⟨subfreezing, subtend⟩). The use of terms such as **Latinate** and **Germanic** in this context is purely descriptive and is not meant to imply that etymological considerations play a synchronic role in lexical organization.)

The root and word categories are distinguished by a collection of semantic, morphological and phonological characteristics. At the semantic level, the meaning of forms derived by means of word-level morphology is typically compositional; that is, the overall meaning can by and large be extrapolated from the component morphemes. This is not necessarily the case with root-level morphology. Compare for example the ⟨in-⟩ and ⟨un-⟩ prefixes already mentioned. ⟨un-⟩ attaches to **free** morphemes – that is, to minimal forms which can stand as words in their own right. Under such circumstances, the reading contributed by ⟨un-⟩ is regularly analysable as negative (as in ⟨unkind⟩) or reversive (as in ⟨untie⟩). In contrast, ⟨in-⟩ is frequently prefixed to **bound** morphemes, forms which do not exist as independent words, such as in ⟨impeach, illusive, imminent⟩.[34] Three basic meanings are usually associated with ⟨in-⟩: negative (as in ⟨inapplicable⟩), intensive or causative (as in ⟨imperil⟩), and directional (as in ⟨immigrate⟩). But there are many words in which the presence of ⟨in-⟩ has no readily identifiable autonomous meaning, including ⟨inane, inveigh, imminent⟩.

Morphologically, some degree of ordering relation evidently exists between the two levels. Root-level affixes can be attached inside other root-level affixes (as in (16a)) or inside word-level affixes (as in (16b)).[35]

(16) (a) nation-al-ity
      (b) nation-al-s
      (c) nation-hood-s
      (d) *nation-hood-al, *nation-s-ity

In contrast, although word-level affixes can be attached inside other word-level affixes (as in (16c)), typically they cannot be attached inside root-level affixes; hence the ungrammaticality of forms such as those in (16d). One way of accounting for this discrepancy has been to view root-level operations as taking place at an earlier stage of morphological derivation than word-level operations.[36] The sequencing generalization is, however, not absolute; a word such as ⟨un-grammatical-ity⟩, for example, evidently involves the attachment of the root-level suffix ⟨-ity⟩ to the word-level-derived form ⟨un-grammatical⟩.[37]

1.4.2 *The phonology of roots and words*

The most consistent differences between English root and word morphology are phonological. That is, there exist sets of phonological phenomena that occur at one level but not the other. Let us first examine examples of root-level alternations that are absent from the word level.

Root-level phenomena are actually of two types: some represent generalizations that extend to morphologically underived forms, while others are peculiar to root morphology. We have already seen one example of the first type in the failure of geminate consonants to appear in forms containing the root prefix ⟨in-⟩. According to one analysis, this reflects the operation of a process of degemination, illustrated in the forms in (17a).[38] This process can be assumed to operate vacuously within underived forms, since they too lack geminates in English. (This is why words borrowed from languages with geminates only ever show short consonants in English. Thus a typically English pronunciation of ⟨spaghetti⟩ lacks the geminate *tt* of Italian.)

(17)　(a) Degemination

i[n]-effectual	i[ɲ]-nocuous
i[m]-probable	i[m̩]-mature

    (b) Closed-syllable shortening

Long VVC	Short VCC
perceive	perceptive
describe	descriptive
reduce	reduction
thieve	theft

The examples in (17b) illustrate another process that is common to root-level morphology and underived forms – so-called closed-syllable shortening.[39] In the next chapter, we will examine the syllabic conditioning of this phenomenon in some detail, but for the time being it is sufficient to note that long vowels before a single final consonant alternate with short before a cluster of two consonants. (Also implicated here is a set of vowel-quality changes, on which more presently.) The same pattern is evident in underived forms; hence the non-existence of sequences such as *-uːkt-*, *-iːpt-*, *-ayft-* within the same morpheme. (That is not to say that such sequences never occur in English. They do, but only when they contain a word-level morpheme boundary, as in *stiːpt* ⟨steep-ed⟩. We will return to this point in 2.4.4.)

Some alternations, on the other hand, are specific to root-level morphology. That is, they involve patterns that generalize neither to underived forms nor to word-level morphology. The examples given in (18) are identified by terms adopted in SPE and still widely used in the literature.

(18) (a) Velar Softening
          electri[k]   electri[s]-ity
          criti[k]   criti[s]-ism
          mysti[k]   mysti[s]-ism

      (b) Spirantization
          pirate   pira[s]-y
          president   presiden[s]-y
          permit   permiss-ive
          conclude   conclus-ive
          corrode   corros-ive
          deride   deris-ive

      (c) Vowel Shift and Trisyllabic Laxing
          veyn vain   *vænɪti* van-ity
          səriːn serene   *sərenɪti* seren-ity
          dɪvayn divine   *dɪvɪnɪti* divin-ity

In Velar Softening (18a), a stem-final *k* alternates with *s* when a root-level suffix beginning with *ɪ* is attached. As shown in (19a), this pattern is not evident in word-level suffixes beginning with the same sound.

(19) (a) panick-ing   *pani[s]-ing
      (b) flight[t]-y   *fligh[s]-y
      (c) might-i-ly   *m[ɪ]t-i-ly
          teeter-ing   *t[ɛ]ter-ing

Neither does Velar Softening extend to *kɪ* sequences within underived forms. Hence the lack of Velar Softening in, say, ⟨king⟩ (*→ *sɪŋ*).

Under Spirantization (18b), stem-final *t/d* alternate with *s* when followed by suffix-initial *ɪ/i*. Compare the alternation-inducing behaviour of the root-level nominalizing suffix ⟨-y⟩ in (18b) with the lack of alternation associated with the word-level adjectival suffix ⟨-y⟩ illustrated in (19b). Like Velar Softening, Spirantization does not manifest itself morpheme-internally; hence ⟨tea⟩ (*→ *siː*), ⟨deem⟩ (*→ *siːm*), for example.

The forms in (18c) illustrate two patterns: Trisyllabic Laxing, in which long (including diphthongal) vowels alternate with short in suffixed forms, and Vowel

Shift, in which the resulting short–long contrast is accompanied by a difference in vowel quality. As shown in (19c), neither of these alternations is evident in forms derived at the word level. Nor do they correspond to any generalization that can be made about underived forms; hence examples such as ⟨salient⟩ (⟨s[ey]lient⟩ not *⟨s[æ]lient⟩) and ⟨lenient⟩ (⟨l[i:]nient⟩ not *⟨l[ɛ]nient⟩).

It is characteristic of specifically root-level alternations of the type illustrated in (18) that they sustain lexical exceptions; the presence of *i:* in both ⟨obese⟩ and ⟨obesity⟩, for example, shows an absence of Trisyllabic Laxing and Vowel Shift. In this respect, root-level generalizations which also hold of underived forms are quite different. Patterns such as those illustrated in (17) are exceptionless.

Nevertheless, in spite of the differences just detailed, there is one significant respect in which the two types of root-level alternations are identical: they faithfully conform to the set of phonological structures associated with underived forms.[40] For example, they introduce no segments not already found in morphologically simple forms. Moreover, as we will see in the next chapter, there exist severe restrictions on the co-occurrence of segment sequences across a root boundary, and these are identical to those operating morpheme-internally. To put it another way, the collection of phonological traits that characterize forms derived by root-level morphology is indistinguishable from that associated with underived forms. The phonological shape of root-derived forms thus provides no clue as to their morphologically complex structure. For example, there is nothing in the phonological shape of root-derived forms such as ⟨dorsal, polar, tonic⟩ which would in principle exclude them from being morphologically simplex words; compare these examples with, say, ⟨morsel, molar, panic⟩. Indeed in many cases, 'strong' root forms are homophonous with unrelated simplex forms; compare ⟨blew–blue, feet–feat, taught–taut⟩.

All this is in stark contrast to word-level morphology, which introduces 'novel' segmental contrasts and segment sequences not found in underived and root-level forms. Most of these patterns word-level morphology shares with phrase and sentence domains. Examples of sound sequences which straddle a word-level morpheme boundary but which are impossible within morphologically simplex or root-derived forms are particularly plentiful in compounds. Here, just as across word boundaries at sentence level, there are no restrictions on the co-occurrence of morpheme-final and following morpheme-initial consonants. Impossible morpheme-internal sequences that occur quite freely within compounds include *p-m*, *v-t* and *θ-b*, illustrated in (20a).

(20)		(a) Compound	(b) Phrase/sentence
	p-m	lap marker	stop me
	v-t	dove tail	live to
	θ-b	moth ball	path belongs

The same freely occurring sequences are evident across words at phrase and sentence level, as the examples in (20b) show.

Moreover it is precisely at word-level morpheme boundaries that we find the gemination effect that is absent from root-level morphology. The gemination associated with ⟨un-⟩, illustrated in (14), is in fact characteristic of the word level in general. Thus, we find geminate *nn* not only in forms such as ⟨u[n-n]atural⟩ but also in suffixed forms such as those in (21a). Indeed any consonant-initial word-level suffix is free to create a geminate, as the forms in (21b) demonstrate.

(21) (a) *nn*   keen-ness, brown-ness
    (b) *ll*   cool-ly, tail-less
        ff   trough-ful
    (c) night time, sack cloth, tail light
    (d) good day, take care, pass slowly

The same phenomenon occurs at compound-internal boundaries, as in (21c), as well as at the phrasal level, as in (21d). Furthermore, whenever intra-compound and morpheme-internal sequences might be expected to coincide, they usually differ with respect to their phonetic realization. A sequence transcribed as *tr*, for example, is pronounced quite differently according to whether or not a word-level morpheme boundary intervenes. A typical pattern is to find a released plosive followed by an aspirated *r* in, say, ⟨nitrate, petrol⟩ but an unreleased stop followed by an unaspirated *r* in, say, ⟨night rate, hat rack⟩.

Although cross-morpheme sequences involving word-level affixes are not totally unrestricted in the way that cross-word sequences are, the possibilities of co-occurrence are nevertheless very much greater than within underived and root-level forms. One of the few restrictions we find holding of word-level suffixes involves the phenomenon of voice assimilation which affects the suffixes ⟨-ed⟩ and ⟨-(e)s⟩. Among the various alternants exhibited by each of these affixes, a voiceless type, *t* or *s*, occurs when the preceding morpheme ends in a certain class of voiceless consonant (as in ⟨hopped, missed, tops, laughs⟩). There are grounds for taking the most widely distributed alternants of these suffixes, *d* and *z* (as in ⟨stayed, days⟩), to be equivalent to their lexical shapes. The voiceless alternants can then be derived by means of an assimilation process.

Apart from this one assimilatory phenomenon, the set of sound sequences occurring across word-level affix boundaries is equivalent to that occurring at the boundaries between words. Many of these sequences, exemplified in (22), are unattested either morpheme-internally or across root-level boundaries.

(22)   (a) Word-affix   (b) Cross-word
t-h   parent-hood   parent who
f-n   stiff-ness   if none
m-l   harm-less   come late

On the other hand, there are some sound sequences which can occur word-internally at the end of roots but which are impossible word-finally. This discrepancy is due to a set of consonant–zero alternations in which the zero form is peculiar to the right edge of the word level. That is, as the following examples (23) illustrate, the consonant in question fails to appear in absolute word-final position (column (ii)) or morpheme-finally before a word-level suffix (iii):[41]

(23)		(i) Root-affix	(ii) Word-final	(iii) Word-affix
(a)	*gn*	si[gn]ature	si~~g~~n	si~~g~~ning
		resi[gn]ation	resi~~g~~n	resi~~g~~ning
(b)	*mn*	da[mn]ation	dam~~n~~	dam~~n~~ing
		conde[mn]ation	condem~~n~~	condem~~n~~ing
		hy[mn]al	hym~~n~~	
(c)	*mb*	bo[mb]ard	bom~~b~~	bom~~b~~er
		cru[mb]le	crum~~b~~	crum~~b~~y

A similar case in point is the cluster *ŋg*. Inside simplex forms, *ŋ* only ever occurs before a velar plosive, at least in most dialects.[42] We thus find it immediately followed by *g*, as in (24a), but not by, say, a vowel, as the ungrammaticality of simplex forms such as those in (24b) demonstrates.

(24) (a)   fi[ŋg]er, a[ŋg]er
      (b)   *fi[ŋ]er, *a[ŋ]er
      (c)   lo[ŋg]-er, stro[ŋg]-er
            (*lo[ŋ]-er, *stro[ŋ]-er)
      (d)   si[ŋ]-er, ba[ŋ]-er
      (e)   lo[ŋ]~~g~~, stro[ŋ]~~g~~, si[ŋ]~~g~~

What is significant is that the distribution of *ŋg* is sensitive to the difference between root-and word-level affixes. This point can be illustrated by comparing two independent suffixes both spelt ⟨-er⟩, the root-level comparative adjectival marker (as in ⟨quick-er⟩), and the agentive nominal marker (as in ⟨fight-er⟩). The distributional pattern found in root-derived forms is identical to that found in simplex forms, as a comparison of (24a) and (24c) shows. In the *ŋg* clusters of such forms, the velarity of the nasal is entirely dependent on the place of articulation of the following plosive, a pattern that is evidently related to the assimilation process already illustrated in (2).

Inside word-derived forms, in contrast, *ŋ* can occur pre-vocalically, including before the agentive suffix, shown in (24d). This pattern is related to the fact that the cluster *ŋg* cannot occur in word-final position, where instead we only find *ŋ*, as in (24e). In the latter context, a potentially present *g* is thus suppressed. In exercise 1 at the end of the next chapter, we will have the opportunity to consider a detailed analysis of these and related facts. For the moment, all we need note are the different influences roots and words exert on the distribution of *ŋ*. The velar nasal cannot occur independently of a following velar plosive unless a word-level morpheme boundary follows, as in (24d, e). A root-level boundary in this context cannot support an immediately preceding ŋ. In this respect, root-derived forms can once again be seen to behave identically to morphologically simplex forms.

1.4.3 *Morphological vs. phonological domains*

The discrepancy in the phonological behaviour of root-level and word-level morphology raises the issue of whether domains that are morphologically and syntactically relevant necessarily coincide with domains that are phonologically relevant. That is, how much morpho-syntactic structure is visible to phonological processes? It is generally agreed that the word in English, irrespective of its internal morphological structure, constitutes a phonological domain. Beyond the word, it is clear that larger phonological domains are defined by phrase and sentence constituents, which play a role in regulating such phenomena as sentence accent and intonation. What is perhaps not so clear, however, is the extent to which it is possible to recognize phonological domains below the level of the word.

Compounding is a relatively straightforward case. Since each component of a compound in English is by definition a word and since the word is well established as a phonological domain, it follows that compounds contain at least as many phonological domains as they contain component words. Thus a form such as ⟨seagull⟩, besides comprising a domain in its own right, also contains two independent sub-domains, ⟨sea⟩ and ⟨gull⟩. The bracketing that this domain structure implies is thus: [[sea] [gull]]. In this respect, the structure of compounds in English can be said to be **analytic** (using this term in a rather specific sense).[43] That is, from the viewpoint of their phonological make-up, they are analysable into more than one domain.

The question is whether affixation also helps define phonologically relevant domains. It is generally agreed that word-level affixes involve analytic structure. This conclusion is consistent with the observations made above about the relatedness of phonological phenomena occurring across internal word-level morpheme boundaries and across full word boundaries. Affixes are not generally assumed to constitute independent domains, however. So a form such as ⟨quick-ly⟩ can be taken to comprise two domains, one formed by the word ⟨quick⟩, the other by the word ⟨quickly⟩; thus [[quick] ly].[44]

To say that a particular phonological string displays analytic structure is to say that it contains a number of sub-strings, each defining an independent domain within which phonological processes can occur without needing to make reference to material from some other domain. This means that, in a form such as [[quick] ly], processes have in principle two opportunities to take place – once within the domain defined by [quick], and again within that defined by [quickly]. In other words, phonological processing has the potential to proceed **cyclically** through successive domains. The form ⟨god-li-ness⟩ presents three cycles: [god], [godly], and [godliness]. ⟨seagull⟩ provides two: an inner cycle, on which [sea] and [gull] are separately processed, and an outer one constituted by [seagull].

In the SPE framework and its closest descendants, rules are individually designated as applying at particular points in cyclic derivation. Some rules, for example, are permitted to reapply during the earliest cycles, while others are held at bay until later cycles. Such stipulations are of course inconsistent with the position that processes take place freely wherever their conditions are met. In a model incorporating the latter principle, all phonological processing proceeds cyclically. That is, each and every domain is individually accessible to each and every process.

Less clear-cut than word-level morphology is the case of root-level affixation. Under one view, the English root defines an independent phonological domain no less than the word. One corollary of this position is that every morphological domain in English constitutes a phonological domain. Nevertheless, the demonstrably different phonological behaviour of root- and word-level morphology has to be accounted for somehow. According to one variant of this approach, known as **Lexical Phonology**, all alternations are characterized in terms of phonological rules, which may apply either within the lexicon (where word formation occurs) or outside the lexicon (where words are concatenated into phrases and sentences).[45] Within the lexicon itself, root-level and word-level alternations are represented in terms of separate strata of rule application. Phenomena such as Velar Softening, Spirantization and Vowel Shift are designated as applying at Stratum 1, while the consonant–zero alternations in (23) are treated in terms of word-final deletion rules assigned to Stratum 2.

Within the context of the present discussion, the significant point about the Lexical Phonology account is the assumption that the root level defines a domain for phonological processing. A root-derived form such as ⟨im-mature⟩ is thus deemed to have the same basic morphological shape as a word-derived form such as ⟨un-nerve⟩, viz. [im [mature]] and [un [nerve]]. What differentiates them is that the former but not the latter is subject to the Stratum-1 phonological rule of degemination. Root-derived [[damn] ation] and word-derived [[damn] ing] are similarly structured, except in this case it is a Stratum-2 rule that distinguishes the two forms, namely consonant-deletion; hence ⟨dam[n]ation⟩ but ⟨dam[n̸]ing⟩.

According to an alternative account, the root level in English does not constitute an independent phonological domain.[46] For reasons to be introduced below and to be expanded on in the following chapters, this is the position adopted in this book. Underlying this view is the assumption that a potential mismatch can exist between domains that are morphologically relevant and those that are phonologically relevant. Thus a root-derived form such as ⟨secrecy⟩ is deemed to be identical to a simplex form such as ⟨lottery⟩ in containing but one phonological domain. In this sense, root-level affixation is considered **non-analytic**; that is, root-derived forms are not phonologically analysable into their component morphemes.

One consequence of this position is that alternations which are restricted to the root-level morphology are not treated in terms of phonological processes. That is, the root-level alternants of a non-suppletive morpheme are not derivable from a common lexical base by means of phonological processes but are listed in the lexicon. The relatedness of such alternants must then be captured by non-phonological means, for example through non-derivational lexical rules or by reference to some notion of proximity in lexical storage.[47] There seems little doubt that alternations such as Velar Softening, Spirantization and Vowel Shift were at one time active phonological processes, either at earlier stages in the history of English or in the languages from which Latinate forms were borrowed. However, according to the non-derivational account of root-level morphology, these processes are extinct in modern English; the alternations they gave rise to are, at least from a phonological viewpoint, no more than historical relics.

The idea that root-level alternants, like morphologically simplex forms, are listed in the lexicon is consistent with the observation that the collections of phonological characteristics associated with the two types of form are indistinguishable. It also squares with the fact that root alternations typically sustain lexical exceptions.

That is not to say that we should ignore root-level patterns altogether. Recall that a subset of such phenomena, those illustrated in (17), clearly correspond to distributional regularities that are also evident in underived forms. Irrespective of whether or not we consider it appropriate to represent these patterns in terms of dynamic processes, there remains the question of how we account for the fact that such generalizations apparently do not hold of the word level. In fact, the bulk of the material to be considered in the next chapter consists of distributional regularities of this sort.

On the other hand we have root-level alternations, such as those in (18), which have very little if anything to do with distributional regularities found in underived forms. There are at least two reasons why phenomena of this sort will barely figure in the following chapters.

For one thing, they are stable across different dialects. This immediately reduces their interest in the context of this book, given the aim of holding minimal distinctions between phonological grammars up to the mirror of a principle-driven theory. Thus, even if morphologically simple and root-derived forms are represented differently in the grammar, this difference is located at a level that is inaccessible to the sorts of phonological phenomena we are interested in here. Where variability is observable at the root level, it is clearly morphological or lexical rather than phonological in nature. (An example is the reduced paradigm of strong-verb morphology evident in many dialects. Compare, say, standard ⟨do–did–done⟩ with non-standard ⟨do–done–done⟩.) This immunity to variability seems to reflect the special status of root-level morphology: it is typically associated with the more learned vocabulary; it is acquired later than word-level morphology; and establishing connections between alternants at this level appears to be influenced by orthographic factors.[48]

There is in fact a rather more mundane reason for not paying too much attention to specifically root-level alternations. They are among the most frequently studied grammatical phenomena in English, and accounts of them are widely available elsewhere in the literature. It would be a pity to devote too much space to them, at the expense of other material which might prove to be of more direct relevance to the concerns of this book. Not that removing root-specific alternations from consideration leaves us scraping the barrel for phonological tit-bits. As I hope to show in the succeeding chapters, the word and phrase domains in English furnish us with a rich seam of data against which to assess theories of phonological processing.[49] Much is still to be learnt about the dialect differences that manifest themselves at these levels.

Exercises

Vowel contrasts

The data Each of the examples below illustrates a particular vowel contrast that occurs in some dialects of English but not in others. In some dialects, for example, the first vowel in ⟨ladder⟩ is different from that in ⟨madder⟩. Each of the contrasts in question may be described as marginal, in the sense that the different vocalic variants are in near-complementary distribution. The only contexts in which the sounds directly contrast turn out to be distinguishable on the basis of morphological structure.

The data are arranged in rows, each containing words which illustrate a particular combination of phonological and morphological contexts.

The task For the time being, we may set on one side the issue of how the qualitative differences between the vowel sounds in each example should be represented. Nor need we be concerned with the issue of whether one vowel in each contrast can or should be derived from the other (or indeed whether both should be derived from some third source).

The focus here is rather on the contexts in which the different vocalic variants occur.

(a) Identify both the phonological and morphological dimensions of the contexts in question.

(b) What do the contrasts reveal about the visibility of different types of morphological domain to patterns of phonological distribution?

I PAUSE–PAWS

In vernacular London English, the nucleus of words such as ⟨paw, sauce, thought, hawk, fawn⟩ typically contains one of two main vowel variants: a centring diphthong ɔə and a closing diphthong ow.[50] (In this dialect, words such as ⟨go, boat, bone⟩ have aw, while those such as ⟨cow, shout, crown⟩ have æw.) The dialect is **non-rhotic**; that is, unlike in rhotic dialects, r is only ever pronounced before a vowel. (More on this in chapter 5.) The quality of the nucleus in words such as ⟨pork, court, born⟩, which are *r*-less in this system but *r*-ful in rhotic dialects, is identical to that in ⟨thought⟩.

1	ow	thought, hawk, broad, board/bawd, pork
2	ow	sauce/source, coarse, pause, gauze
3	ow	yawn, lawn, call, torn, form
4	ɔə	saw/sore, paw/pour/poor, bore
5	ɔə	poorly, sawed, bored, paws/pours, yourn ('yours, your one'), soreness
6	ɔə	door knob, saw-tooth, draw bridge

II MOLAR–ROLLER

Another characteristic of vernacular London English is the occurrence of two qualitatively distinct vowels in the nuclei of words such as ⟨go, boat, bone, foal⟩: *aw* and *ɒw*.[51]

1	aw	go, toe, slow
2	aw	boat, road, slope, soak, brooch
3	aw	loaf, most, both, stove, rose
4	aw	bone, loan, home
5	ɒw	goal, hole, bowl, roll, told, gold, shoulder
6	aw	molar, Roland, cola
7	ɒw	roller, goalie, bowling
8	ɒw	coal effect, pole axe, goal area
9	ɒw	roll about, hole in, shoal of

III DAZE–DAYS

Many varieties of northern Irish English have two vocalic variants in the nuclei of words such as ⟨day, fate, fade, pain⟩: *ɪə* nd *ɛ:*.[52]

1	ɪə	fate, staid, tape, lake, cater, baby
2	ɪə	face, faith, save, daze, lazy, station
3	ɪə	vain, game, fail, Daley
4	ɛ:	day, stay, pay, ray
5	ɛ:	days, stays, stayed, frayed, daily, greyness, playful
6	ɛ:	ray gun, pay cheque, day time
7	ɛ:	pay them, stay behind, pray for

IV LADDER–MADDER

The original set of words that contained historically short stressed *æ* in English includes ⟨bat, bad, pass, man⟩. Many dialects of English bear the marks of a change whereby this vowel has split into two main variants or **reflexes**, one lax, the other tense. **Tensing** is actually a cover-term for a range of developments, common to all of which is an increase in duration. This is typically accompanied by one or more qualitative changes, involving amongst other things the appearance of an off-glide, backing to *a*, or front-raising to *ɛə, eə*, or even higher.[53]

In some dialects, tensing has led to a full-blown split in the original short-*æ* category, the tense reflex merging with back vowels from other historical sources (such as that in ⟨calm, palm⟩). In this case, the result is that a word such as ⟨gas⟩ with *æ* has a different vowel from, say, ⟨pass⟩ with *a*.

In the type of dialect illustrated in the data below, however, the phonological contexts in which the tense and lax reflexes appear remain more or less complementary, the distribution being determined largely by the nature of the following consonant. In its broadest outlines, this pattern is widely represented in a range of dialects spoken in various parts of the eastern United States, southern England, Australia and Ireland, although the precise class of tensing consonants varies from system to system. The particular pattern illustrated here is one that is common to metropolitan New York and Belfast.[54]

æ reflex

1	lax	bat, back, tap, hatch
2	lax	hang, sang
3	tense	bad, lag, dab, badge
4	tense	man, ban, damn, lamb
5	tense	laugh, graph, path, pass, class, gas
6	lax	ladder, wagon, dagger, adder ('snake')
7	lax	manner, panel, panic, damage
8	lax	placid, passage, saffron
9	lax	vanity, sanity, opacity, classical, graphic, pallor
10	tense	madder, dragging, baddie, adder ('one who adds')
11	tense	manning, damning, lambing
12	tense	passer, laughing, classy
13	tense	lag effect, gas emission, lamb enclosure
14	tense	ban it, pass around, bad adjustment

V TIDE–TIED

One characteristic of Lowland Scots and Scottish English is a phenomenon known as Aitken's Law or the Scottish Vowel Length Rule, according to which certain vowels show long and short reflexes in a manner that is determined by the following context.[55] The following Scottish English data illustrate how this pattern affects the three vowel classes represented by words such as ⟨see, feed⟩, ⟨two, food⟩ and ⟨go, road⟩. Scottish English lacks the contrast between *ʊ* (as in ⟨good⟩) and *uː* (⟨food⟩) found in most other types of English.[56]

1	short	feet, keep, leak, peach, meter
		boot, loop, Luke/look, hootch, stupid
		boat, soap, soak, brooch
2	short	feed, greed, league, cedar
		food, rude, good, Cooder
		road, globe, rogue, ogre
3	short	peace, teeth, leash, leaf, recent
		goose, tooth, hoof, lucid
		loaf, dose, both, grocer
4	short	keen, mean, seam, penis
		moon, soon, loom, Souness
		bone, moan, roam, bonus
5	short	feel, wheel, steal, feline, Healy
		tool, fool/full, bullet
		foal, hole, goal, molar
6	long	see, tea, agree
		two, brew, blue
		go, slow, row
7	long	seize, teethe, leave, beaver
		lose, bruise, smooth, move, music
		rose, loathe, rove, Ambrosia
8	long	fear, peer, eerie
		poor, moor, lurid
		door, more, glory
9	long	keys, keyed, agreed, freely, gleeful
		brews, brewed, stewed, truly, blueness
		rows, rowed, slowly, woeful, slowness
10	long	bee line, stew pot, snow drop
11	long	three guitars, two bananas, go behind

The effect of Aitken's Law on the diphthong in words such as ⟨die, fight, line⟩ has additional qualitative consequences: the long reflex is *ay*, while the short is *əy* or the like.

12	əy	fight, ripe, like
		tide, bribe, idle, spider
		rice, life, rifle
		line, time, minor
		file, pilot, Reilly
13	ay	tie, sigh
		rise, lithe, arrive, miser
		tire, biro
14	ay	tied, ties, sighed, dryly, dryness
		tie pin, fly net
		fly beneath, tie down

2 Constituency

2.1 Non-linear phonological representations

This chapter focuses on the question of how sequences of sounds are organized within phonological representations.

The standard SPE response to this question, recall, was to view a representation as consisting of a linear string of segments and morpho-syntactic boundary symbols, each segment being characterized as a matrix of binary-valued features (see 1.3.2). In this type of arrangement, features code two very different sets of facts. One set consists of those aspects of a segment's identity that can be defined in purely phonetic terms. Features of this sort typically have a relatively stable articulatory or acoustic interpretation. They include such categories as [coronal], [continuant], [sonorant] and [high]. Features of the other type are essentially relational or structural in nature, in the sense that they code information about relations between segments within phonological strings; [syllabic], [stress] and [long] are prime examples. There is no such thing as a stable phonetic definition of [long], for instance. The distinction between a [+long] and a [−long] vowel cannot be expressed in terms of absolute temporal values (milliseconds, say); rather it manifests itself as a difference in the relative duration of the two segments when these are compared in identical contexts.

As noted in 1.3.3, the SPE view has since given way to a non-linear conception of phonological representations. One aspect of this is a recognition of the need to keep phonetic and relational information formally distinct. Features, it is now widely assumed, are to be reserved for phonetically definable aspects of representation, while relational aspects are to be characterized in terms of hierarchical structure. The justification for this separation is straightforward: the phonetic and structural aspects are observed to behave independently of one another and are subject to different sets of organizing principles.

In the next chapter, we will consider how the phonetically definable aspects of segments should be characterized. The focus of the present chapter is on two relational dimensions of phonological representations: quantity and constituency. We will review some of the main arguments which support a hierarchical as opposed to a featural characterization of these aspects of phonological structure. At its lowest levels, the phonological hierarchy can be shown to be composed of syllabic constituents into which segment-strings are organized.

One finding that will emerge from our investigation of the phonological hierarchy is that a binary limit imposes itself on the amount of branching structure each constituent can support. One syllabic constituent is the nucleus, corresponding to the vocalic portions of forms such as ⟨say, see, saw⟩ (one nucleus each) and ⟨Betty, city, window⟩ (two nuclei each). Maximal binarity means that the nucleus can contain one or two segments but no more. As illustrated in (1), a one-segment nucleus corresponds to a short vowel (1a), a two-segment nucleus to a diphthong (1b) (or long monophthong). Anything larger than this, such as the ternary-branching structure in (1c), is ill-formed.

(1)   (a) Nucleus   (b) Nucleus   (c) Nucleus
           | / \   / | \
           ɛ   e   y   * e o w

In chapter 4, we will see that the relation between positions within a branching constituent is asymmetric, a property that is reflected in the differing abilities of various segment-types to occupy particular positions.

In this chapter, the coverage of constituency in English phonology is not meant to be exhaustive. In some areas, I present views which synthesize conclusions reached from a variety of theoretical perspectives. In other areas, where two or more currently held views are incompatible, I will present arguments which I feel favour one position over others. In some other cases, the present state of our knowledge does not permit the drawing of any firm conclusions on the superiority of any particular approach. In such cases, I will simply draw attention to problems which for the time being remain unresolved.

2.2 Timing

2.2.1 Introduction

We begin our examination of the phonological hierarchy by considering the dimension of phonological **quantity**. Quantity has to do with the amount of 'space' a segment occupies in a phonological string. Informally, the values on this dimension are often referred to in such terms as **short** versus **long** or **light** versus **heavy**. Like tone or stress, quantity manifests itself phonetically in a relational rather than an absolute manner. A phonologically long segment is realized with relatively greater duration than a short segment appearing under otherwise identical conditions, just as a phonologically high tone is realized on a relatively higher pitch than a low tone in the same context.

The independence of quantity from other dimensions is exemplified in a number of phenomena, two of which we will concentrate on here. One is the widespread process of compensatory lengthening. The other is the Jekyll-and-Hyde-like behaviour of a class of sounds whose quantitative and qualitative properties do not match up.

2.2.2 *Compensatory lengthening*

Compensatory lengthening is the name given to processes in which the loss of a particular segment is compensated for by the lengthening of an adjacent segment in the phonological string. By way of illustration, consider the fate of the voiceless velar fricative *x* in English, specifically as it appears in the historical sequence *ixt*, reflected in the spelling of such words as ⟨right, night, sight, might⟩. Something like the original pronunciation is retained in Scots:

(2)   Scots   English
       nɪxt   nayt, nəyt, . . .   ⟨night⟩
       rɪxt   rayt, rəyt, . . .   ⟨right⟩
       mɪxt   mayt, məyt, . . .   ⟨might⟩

A form in Scots such as *nɪxt* has the same sort of structure as, say, *fɪst* ⟨fist⟩; that is, we find a short reflex of historical *i* followed by a voiceless fricative. In most types of English, however, the velar fricative has been lost from this context, indeed in most cases from all contexts. If all that were involved here were the simple loss of a consonant, we would expect the general English pronunciation of ⟨night⟩ to be something like *nɪt* with a short *ɪ*. Instead, what we get is some kind of diphthongal reflex, as in *nayt, nəyt* or the like. This leads us to conclude that, at some stage in the past, historically *ix* forms must have had a long *iː* nucleus identical to that in words such as ⟨bite, kite⟩ (which never contained the velar fricative).[1] The reasoning behind this conclusion is this: the current diphthongal reflexes illustrated in (2) are the result of the historical Vowel-Shift change briefly mentioned in 1.4.2, and this only affected long vowels. The sequence of events in ⟨night⟩, for example, thus went something like this: *nixt > niːt > nayt*. The first stage in this sequence illustrates the phenomenon of compensatory lengthening.

In linear terms, we could try to account for the pre-Vowel-Shift part of the change by means of two ordered rules. One would lengthen *i* before *x* to produce *nixt > niːxt*. The other would then delete *x*, producing *niːxt > niːt*. Note that these rules have to be ordered. Deletion must not be allowed to apply before lengthening; otherwise it would obliterate the context in which the latter operates.[2] There are at least two problems with this analysis. For a start, there is no historical or comparative dialect evidence to support an intermediate stage in which long *iː* co-existed with *x* in *niːxt.

More seriously from a theoretical point of view, the two-rule account fails to capture the unitary nature of the process. The intuition is that there is an intimate connection between loss of *x* and lengthening of the *i*. It is as though the vowel somehow expands to fill a vacuum created by the disappearance of the consonant. But this connection is not established by the two rules, which are in principle quite independent of one another.[3] Under this analysis, we would expect one or other of the rules to occur independently in other systems. But there is no evidence to indicate that velar fricatives particularly favour vowel lengthening.

The compensatory lengthening that is evident in this and many similar cases in the world's languages illustrates what we might call **quantity stability**. That is, the quantity dimension of a phonological string is in principle capable of remaining stable while the phonetic-quality dimension is in a state of flux. In order to be able to characterize this independent behaviour, we need to represent each dimension on a separate level. The way this notion has been implemented in non-linear theory is to separate quantitative information from other aspects of the representation and deploy it on an independent tier consisting of a sequence of slots or positions. Each position, usually indicated by x, constitutes a bare unit of phonological timing which, since it has no featural content, is often referred to as a **skeletal point**.[4] The term used to describe the level from which quantiative (and, as we will see, other relational) information is absent is the **melodic tier**. (The use of the term **melodic** stems from early non-linear studies of tone languages, in which suprasegmental pitch 'melodies' can be shown to exist independently of non-tonal aspects of a representation.[5]) The synchronization of melodic units with timing positions is indicated by **association lines**, as shown in (3).

(3)   Skeletal tier   x   x   x   x
       Association lines | | | |
       Melodic tier   n   i   x   t

In the normal case, each melodic unit is associated to one timing slot. However, the independence of the skeletal and melodic tiers leaves open the possibility of setting up one-to-many associations. For example, we have the possibility of having a single melodic unit linked to two skeletal points. Since a multiply-linked melodic unit takes up more timing space than a singly-linked one, this arrangement provides us with a straightforward way of representing the contrast between short and long vowels:[6]

(4)   (a) Short vowel   (b) Long vowel

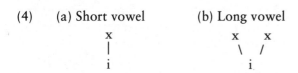

Compensatory lengthening in the *ixt* > *i:t* case can now be accounted for in the following terms. The association between the velar fricative and its skeletal point is severed, as shown in (5a).[7] Then, as shown in (5b), a new association is established between the now vacant slot and *i*. The former operation is known as **delinking**, the latter as **spreading**.[8]

(5)   (a) **Delinking**   (b) **Spreading**

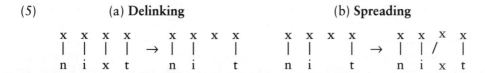

Spreading in this instance results in a doubly-linked *i* which, as we saw in (4b), defines a long vowel.

There are two assumptions that have to be made in order for this account to work. First, the process of delinking a melodic unit from its position is not reversible; that is, a delinked melodic unit does not automatically relink to its original position. Second, for a melodic unit to be realized at the end of a derivation, it must be anchored to a skeletal point.[9] Since the velar fricative in (5b) is unanchored, it fails to be pronounced. The second of these assumptions is derivable from a more general principle which we will discuss in chapter 4.

Like the rule-based linear analysis, the timing-tier account of compensatory lengthening involves two operations, in the latter case delinking and spreading. However, now a clearer connection is established between the two events. The spreading of *i* can only take place as a result of a vacant timing slot having been made available through the delinking of the velar fricative. The notion of quantity stability is captured by the manner in which units on the timing tier are able to ride out changes that affect units on the melodic tier.

In capturing more directly the independence of the quantitative and qualitative dimensions, the non-linear account is superior to the linear. Nevertheless, at least in the form given here, the non-linear analysis cannot yet be considered to have established a causal connection between consonant deletion and compensatory vowel lengthening. To approach that goal requires appeal to be made to certain additional theoretical considerations to be discussed in 2.4 and chapter 4. One problem, already alluded to above, is that delinking and spreading are in principle independent operations. Confirmation of this fact comes from numerous examples where the loss of a consonant is not automatically adjusted for by the compensatory lengthening of a neighbouring segment. A case in point is the truncation of final C*d* clusters in English, discussed in the last chapter. The suppression of *d* in a phrase such as ⟨send two⟩ is not accompanied by the lengthening of, say, the preceding *n*.

Evidently certain specific conditions have to be met before deletion of one segment is counterbalanced by lengthening of another segment. One generalization that can be made about compensatory vowel lengthening, for example, is that it only occurs in systems already possessing long vowels.[10] In a more technical sense to be explained in the succeeding sections, the syllabic nuclei of such systems must be capable of containing two timing slots, something that is by no means true of all languages. This suggests that compensatory vowel lengthening is sensitive to the manner in which skeletal positions are gathered into syllabic constituents.

Related to this is the issue of the directionality of compensatory lengthening. We might ask why it is *i* that spreads in (5b), rather than the following *t*, or indeed even the word-initial *n*. The first of these alternatives in fact corresponds to a real option that is taken up in some languages. For instance, certain Latin two-consonant clusters show up in Italian as geminate (long) segments (e.g. *nokte > notte* 'night'), which can be analysed as a delinking of the first consonant in the cluster accompanied by spreading of the second. Determining whether a particular language is likely to plump for rightward or leftward spreading in such cases again involves making appeal to aspects of phonological constituent structure. However, the other alternative in which some non-adjacent melodic unit spreads into a vacant skeletal slot (for example, the *n* in (5b)) seems on the face of it implausible. In any event, we would want to exclude it on the general theoretical grounds that it contravenes the principle of locality. The question is whether there is anything in the nature of a multi-tiered representation to rule out the crossing of association lines that non-local spreading of this type implies:

(6)

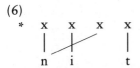

Two properties of non-linear representations express relations that have a direct bearing on this issue: precedence and temporal overlap. Relations of precedence are expressed in the linear order of units on each tier: in (6), $x1 <$ (precedes) $x2 < x3 < x4$ on the skeletal tier, while $n < i < t$ on the melody tier. Each association line meanwhile represents a situation in which the duration of a melody unit overlaps at some point with the duration of the skeletal point to which it is linked. The interaction between these two properties rules out line crossing. It is logically impossible for a melody unit to overlap with two discontinuous skeletal positions while simultaneously maintaining its precedence with respect to a melody unit attached to an intervening position. Inherent in the ill-formed representation in (6) is the contradiction that all of *n* precedes *i* while part of *i* precedes *n*.[11]

2.2.3 Diphthongs and affricates

Let us now take a more detailed look at the bi-linear representation of long versus short vowels shown in (4). A long vowel can have either a monophthongal or a diphthongal quality. The proportion of diphthongs to long monophthongs in English varies from dialect to dialect. Some systems, such as Scottish English, have a full range of long monophthongs (for example in ⟨see, say, Shah, saw, so, too⟩); some have nothing but diphthongal realizations; others fall somewhere in between. From the viewpoint of phonological quantity, however, this variation is insignificant. This is because long vowels in English, irrespective of whether they are monophthongal or diphthongal, belong to a single natural class. The unified nature of the class is revealed in the distributional characteristics of vowels as well as in their participation in particular processes. For example, unlike short vowels, diphthongs and long monophthongs can occur in word-final stressed open syllables. Hence variant forms such as *goː/gow* ⟨go⟩, *seː/sey* ⟨say⟩.[12] Compare these with ungrammatical final-stressed forms with short vowels such as **sɪ, *sɛ*. If we assume that diphthongs (at least of the English type we are concerned with here) occupy two timing slots, it is not difficult to see that the class of long vowels can be distinguished from short on the basis of the skeletal tier. Diphthongs and long monophthongs both occupy two timing slots, short vowels only one:

(7)   (a)   Long   (b) Short
          Monophthong   Diphthong
            x   x   x   x   x
            \ / | | |
             e   e   y   e:

The behaviour of long monophthongs illustrates a class of segments that display a dual identity when viewed in terms of their quantity and quality properties. They are qualitatively simplex but quantitatively complex. These properties are straightforwardly captured in the bi-linear representation shown in (7a). Long e: is simplex from the viewpoint of the melodic tier but complex from the viewpoint of the skeletal tier.

The same type of behaviour is exhibited by 'true' geminate (long) consonants. Such geminates are true in the sense that they contrast lexically with non-geminate (short) consonants, as in Italian *gratto* 'I scratch' versus *grato* 'grateful (masc.)'. 'Fake' geminates are of the type we encountered in 1.4.2; that is, they are pairs of identical consonants which accidentally occur together as a result of the juxtaposition of two morphemes, as in the *nn* of English ⟨un-nerved⟩. For quantitative purposes, true geminates are to two-consonant clusters what long monophthongs are to diphthongs. For example, true geminates count as two consonants for purposes of **syllabification.**

Syllabification has to do with the location of syllable boundaries within polysyllabic strings of segments. In this book, the term will not be used to refer to the sort of activity in which speakers are asked to make judgements about where syllable boundaries lie, for example by getting them to utter polysyllabic words in separate and allegedly syllable-sized chunks. For reasons to be expanded on below, elicitation methods of this type can be quite unreliable. Rather, as the notion is employed here, syllabification is to be established purely on the basis of empirically verifiable phonological evidence. As the discussion unfolds, we will see that syllabification is subject to quite general principles. This raises the question of whether syllable structure is inherently present in phonological representations or is built up from scratch by means of some kind of dynamic algorithm. We will take up this matter in 2.5, once we have had a chance to see what the main principles are. For the time being, we may simply assume that syllable structure is in place and forms a backdrop against which other phonological phenomena are to be examined.

As far as the syllabification of true geminates is concerned, they behave exactly like $VC_i.C_jV$ clusters (where C_i and C_j are different consonants and '.' indicates a syllable boundary). That is, the first part of a geminate in a $VC:V$ sequence closes the first syllable. Returning to the Italian example, we may note that *grat.to* 'I scratch' is syllabified in the same way as a form such as *ven.to* 'wind'. There is plenty of phonological evidence to support this syllabification. In standard Italian, for example, the vowel of an open syllable (that is, one not closed by a consonant) is lengthened when stressed; hence *graːto* 'grateful'.[13] No such lengthening occurs in closed syllables, something which applies as much to geminates as to consonant clusters straddling a syllable boundary (**gratto* 'I scratch', **veːnto*).

The parallelism between clusters and true geminates is straightforwardly captured in terms of their identity on the skeletal tier. Compare the representations in (8) with those in (7).

(8)　(a)　　　　　　　Long　　　　　　　　(b) Short

　　　　　Geminate　　　Cluster

```
       x   x        x   x                 x
        \ /          |   |                 |
         n           n   d                 n
```

Having discussed a configuration in which a single melody unit is linked to two timing slots, we can now consider how the bi-linear approach makes available another possible configuration, one in which the opposite pattern of association prevails – two melody units linked to a single timing slot. This possibility can be exploited in order to characterize another class of dual-identity segments, those which are the converse of geminates in being qualitatively complex but quantitatively simplex. This class is illustrated by the affricates *č* and *ǰ*. As the alternative transcriptions *tʃ* and *dʒ* indicate, an affricate consists of a stop portion followed by a fricative portion and is thus qualitatively similar to any homorganic stop-fricative cluster. (The two types are not necessarily identical, though. Compare the medial consonants of, say, ⟨recharge, catch it⟩ on the one hand with those in ⟨pet shop, cat shit⟩ on the other.[14]) Quantitatively, however, affricates can be shown to line up with simplex consonants rather than with clusters.

We can check the quantitative behaviour of affricates by considering how they interact with stress assignment. The placement of word-stress in English and many other languages is conditioned by the manner in which segments pattern into constituents which, for the time being at least, we can informally label syllables. Specifically, stress in such languages is what is known as **quantity-sensitive**; that is, its appearance on particular syllables in a word is sensitive to whether they are heavy or light. A heavy syllable contains either a long vowel (monophthong or diphthong, which we can symbolize as VV) or a short vowel and a syllable-closing consonant (VC). A light syllable contains a short vowel (V). For the purposes of calculating the weight of a word-final syllable in English (and many other languages), a final consonant is disregarded, a phenomenon known as **extra-metricality** (to be considered in more detail in 2.4.4).[15] Heavy syllables tend to attract stress, a pattern that is evident in English verbs.

The general rule for English verbs is that stress falls on the final syllable if it is heavy; otherwise the penult receives stress. This is illustrated by the following forms:

(9)   (a)   (b)   (c)
      tormént   cajóle   édit
      lamént   maintáin   astónish
      collápse   caróuse   cáncel

In a verb such as ⟨tormént⟩ (9a), with final extra-metrical *t*, the last syllable *men* is heavy and thus receives main stress. Similarly, the final syllable of the forms in (9b) is stressed by virtue of being heavy, in these cases as a result of its containing a long vowel. On the other hand, in ⟨édit⟩ (9c), with extra-metrical *t*, stress falls on the penult, since the final syllable (spelt ⟨di⟩) is light.

We now have a straightforward way of testing the quantity of *č* and *ǰ*. The test involves polysyllabic verbs that end in a short vowel followed by an affricate. If affricates are quantitatively complex, stress should be assigned as in (9a). Only the second (fricative) portion will be extra-metrical, yielding a word-final sequence of the pattern $Vd⟨ʒ⟩_{em}$ (where ⟨ ⟩$_{em}$ indicates extra-metricality). The final syllable will be heavy (closed by the stop portion) and should thus receive final stress. If, on the other hand, we are dealing with a quantitatively simplex consonant, stress should be assigned on a par with the forms in (9c). That is to say, the whole affricate will be extra-metrical, the final syllable will be light, and stress should be penultimate.

We find the answer in (10):

(10)   mánage píllage dámage fórage encóurage

These forms line up with the pattern in (9c). In other words, *ǰ* behaves like a final simplex consonant.[16]

In order to express the notion that affricates are qualitatively complex but quantitatively simplex, we can represent them in terms of a **contour** structure: that is, one in which two melodic units are linked to a single skeletal position, as depicted in (11).

(11)   x
          / \
         t   ʃ

(Like **melody**, the term **contour** is borrowed from non-linear analyses of tone. A contour tone consists of two level tones attached to a single tone-bearing unit (typically a vowel). A falling pattern, for example, is represented as a High tone followed by a Low.)[17]

We can now assume that extra-metricality operates on the skeletal level, rather than on the melodic level:

(12)   x   x   x   x   ⟨x⟩$_{em}$
       | | | | / \
       m   æ   n   ɨ   d ʒ   ⟨mánage⟩

In this way, we capture the fact that, in spite of their phonetically dynamic nature, affricates function exactly like simplex consonants for quantitative purposes. In (12), the whole of the affricate is extra-metrical, with the result that the final syllable is light and thus fails to attract stress.

In the SPE framework, it was difficult to capture the dual identity of sounds which display a mismatch between their quantitative and qualitative properties. One linear way of characterizing what we now think of as contour segments was in terms of a feature such as [delayed release] for affricates. This arrangement correctly identified such segments as quantitatively simplex, but at the expense of introducing dynamic feature definitions. These were anomalous in a framework in which quality features otherwise described steady-state phonetic characteristics ([coronal], [labial], [high], for instance).[18] One way of avoiding this anomaly would be to split the representation of such sounds into two matrices, each containing a steady-state feature which specified the beginning and end points of the dynamic articulation. In the case of affricates, for example, this would mean [−continuant] for the stop-closure matrix followed by [+continuant] for the fricative-release matrix. Unfortunately, the two-matrix treatment suggests that affricates should behave quantitatively like two-consonant clusters, which, as our brief review of the stress facts indicates, is incorrect.

By splitting the quantity dimension off from other aspects of the representation, we avoid being caught between two stools in this way. As our discussion of compensatory lengthening revealed, the move also allows us to account for quantity stability in a straightforward manner. Furthermore, the non-linear treatment of quantity has an important theoretical consequence for the representation of suprasegmental phenomena in general. In a linear framework, any feature is in principle capable of being implicated in stress assignment. In natural language, however, the only systems in which stress is partly or wholly dependent on aspects of segmental structure are those described as quantity-sensitive. In SPE terms, as we will see in a moment, this is reflected in the incorporation in stress-assignment rules of features such as [long] or [tense] or those needed to characterize the contrast between C and V. But, according to the internal logic of the framework, we should not be surprised to encounter systems in which stress placement is sensitive to any feature or feature combination – [low], [continuant], or [glottal suction], say. Significantly, robust evidence supporting the existence of such systems is hard to come by.

With the abandonment of featural representations of the quantity dimension, we now have the possibility of greatly restricting the predictive power of the stress-handling component of the theory. We can now assume that stress placement is completely blind to the featural make-up of segments. Instead only structural aspects of the representation can be scanned by stress processes. So far the only structural dimension I have attempted to formalize in any way is the skeletal tier. Informally, however, I have been referring to the role of syllabic structure in quantity-sensitivity. This indicates that positions on the skeletal tier are not concatenated in linear sequence but are gathered into constituents. It is to the issue of how this notion is formalized that we now turn.

2.3 Phonological constituent structure

2.3.1 Introduction

The notion most familiarly applied to the constituent dimension of phonological representations is the syllable. The concept has a long history in phonological scholarship, although within generative theory it has not always been as firmly established as in other traditions. In SPE, the nearest we get to its recognition is in the feature [syllabic], designed primarily to characterize the contrast between, for example, vowels ([+syllabic]) and glides ([–syllabic]). From the early 1970s onwards, however, the pivotal role of constituency in phonological structure has come to be acknowledged more and more in generative theory.[19] Today there is near-universal agreement that syllabic structure is an integral part of phonological representations. However, it would be fair to say that there remains less than general agreement about the precise nature of that structure.

In the following sections, we will consider some of the arguments which suggest that certain types of phonological phenomena are more adequately characterized in terms of constituent structure than in terms of linear segmental strings. The evidence is of three main types, involving the statement of (a) suprasegmental patterns; (b) phonotactic constraints (i.e. constraints on the combinability of segments in sequence); and (c) the domains in which certain segmental processes operate. The focus of this chapter is on the first two types of evidence, but at various points I will make reference to the third. Actually, most of the arguments based on the evidence to be reviewed below turn out to support the existence of phonological constituency rather than the notion syllable *per se*.

2.3.2 Stress and constituency

In our discussion of English verb stress, we have already begun to see the role played by constituent structure in suprasegmental processes. In order to illustrate the superiority of a constituent-based treatment of stress over a linear account, we will now look at the phenomenon of quantity-sensitivity in more detail.

Consider the following facts relating to primary stress placement in a large class of English nouns:[20]

(13)	(a)	(b)	(c)	(d)
	ballóon	horízon	agénda	cínema
	domáin	aróma	veránda	análysis
		muséum	amálgam	América
		aréna	uténsil	Cánada

Let us try to characterize the general pattern that is evident in these forms in linear terms. In each column of (13), the stressed vowel (underlined in (14)) is located in the following respective contexts:

(14)　(a)　<u>VV</u> (C)]_N: stress the rightmost vowel if it is long, regardless of whether or not the noun ends in a consonant.

　　　(b)　<u>VV</u> (C) V (C)]_N: stress the penultimate vowel if it is long and is followed by zero or more consonants followed by a short vowel, regardless of whether or not the noun ends in a consonant.

　　　(c)　<u>V</u> C C V (C)]_N: stress the penultimate vowel if it is followed by two consonants followed by a short vowel, regardless of whether or not the noun ends in a consonant.

　　　(d)　<u>V</u> (C) V (C) V (C)]_N: stress the antepenultimate vowel if this is followed by two short vowels, with or without intervening single consonants, regardless of whether or not the noun ends in a consonant.

It is possible to collapse these conditions under a single linear stress-assignment rule, the detailed formalisms of which need not concern us here.[21]

The statements in (14) can be simplified if the recurring condition 'regardless of whether or not the noun ends in a consonant' is replaced by the declaration, already appealed to in relation to verb stress, that final consonants are extra-metrical. However, the linear account remains inadequate for various reasons. Not the least of these is that it fails to capture the intrinsic connection that exists between the length of a vowel and some of the consonants in the string. For example, it fails to identify the equivalence of conditions (14b) and (14c), in which, for the purposes of attracting stress, a long vowel 'counts the same as' a short vowel bracketed with a following consonant.

The linear account is essentially a collection of circumlocutions referring to conditions that can be much more straightforwardly formulated in terms of constituent quantity. As a preliminary formulation in these terms, all we have to say is that stress in English nouns falls on the rightmost heavy syllable and otherwise on the antepenult. (By default, it will fall on the penult in words consisting of two light syllables, as in ⟨cíty⟩.)

We have already seen how we can express the quantitative equivalence of long vowels and certain VC sequences in terms of an identical two-point structure on the skeletal tier. But not all VC sequences count as heavy; the important point is that the C in a heavy sequence must be bracketed with the preceding V. So we need to impose some type of constituency on the skeletal tier. In ⟨veránda⟩ (15a), for example, the bracketing of *n* in the same syllable as the preceding vowel means that the stressed syllable contains the same number of timing points as that in, say, ⟨aróma⟩ (15b):

(15)　(a)　[x　x]　[x　x　x]　[x　x]
　　　　　　 |　 |　 |　 |　 |　 |　 |
　　　　　　 v　 ə　 r　 æ　 n　 d　 ə

　　　(b)　[x]　　 [x　x　x]　[x　x]
　　　　　　 |　　　 |　 |　 |　 |　 |
　　　　　　 ə　　　 r　 o　 w　 m　 ə

How many timing slots does a syllable have to have before it qualifies as heavy? And do all slots in a syllable contribute to its weight? The stressed syllables in (15) both contain three timing points. But comparison of these forms with, say, ⟨payóla⟩ reveals that a consonant does not necessarily have to be present in the initial portion of a syllable in order for the syllable to count as heavy:

(16)   [x   x   x] [x   x] [x   x]
           | | | | | | |
           p   e   y   o   w   l   ə

To calculate weight, it seems, we only need to take into account the vowel and whatever follows.

Light syllables are those in which only one slot is occupied by the vowel and no other material follows. The final syllables in (15) and (16) are of this type and thus fail to attract stress. Allowing for extra-metricality, we find the same final light pattern in a form such as ⟨horízon⟩:

(17)   [x   x] [x   x   x] [x   x]   ⟨x⟩ₑₘ
           | | | | | | | |
           h   ə   r   a   y   z   ə   n

The fact that weight is measured without regard to whatever precedes the vowel within the syllable is confirmed when we increase the number of syllable-initial consonants beyond one. The second syllable of, for example, ⟨Katrína⟩ is no heavier than the stressed syllables of ⟨aróma⟩ or ⟨payóla⟩, even though it begins with two consonants. Take a form such as ⟨álgebra⟩, syllabified as in (18a).

(18)   (a) [x   x] [x   x] [x   x   x]
              | | | | | | |
              æ   l   ǰ   ə   b   r   ə

        (b) [x] [x   x   x] [x   x]
              | | | | | |
              æ   f   r   ə   k   ə

The final syllable of ⟨algebra⟩ has three skeletal slots, as many as the heavy syllables in (15). However, it counts as light, as is evident from the fact that it fails to attract stress. Instead, the word is stressed like those in (13d), i.e. on the antepenult, in accordance with condition (14d). For a similar reason, ⟨Africa⟩ (18b) also bears antepenultimate stress; in this case, it is the second syllable of the word that contains CCV but still counts as light.

Thus, in establishing the weight of a syllable, we only count material appearing in a span which runs from the left edge of the vowel to the right edge of the syllable. In the data we have looked at so far, if this span contains two timing points, the syllable is heavy; if it contains one, the syllable is light. Quantity facts such as these have been taken as evidence supporting the existence of two sub-syllabic constituents: the **rhyme**, containing those positions which determine weight, and the **onset**, containing those positions which precede the rhyme and are irrelevant to the determination of weight.[22] When we say that stress assignment is more adequately characterized in syllabic than in linear-segmental terms, we are thus using the notion of syllable in a very loose sense. The quantity facts support the onset–rhyme dichotomy but are silent on the question of whether it is necessary to recognize the syllable as an autonomous constituent. When we speak of syllable weight, we are thus really referring to rhyme weight.

2.2.3 The 'syllable'

Throughout this book, we will have many opportunities to examine diverse phonological phenomena in English which are clearly sensitive to constituent structure. None of them, it turns out, needs make reference to an independent node directly corresponding to the syllable, at least as this notion is usually understood in the western tradition of versification. Whether this means that such a constituent has no place in Universal Grammar whatsoever is another matter and depends naturally on whether motivating evidence is to be found in languages other than English.[23] All that need be said at this point is that, for our present purposes, we can manage quite happily without a syllable node.[24] We will have occasion to return to the issue of its theoretical status later in this chapter as well as in chapter 4.

The term **syllable** is in any event potentially misleading in phonological discourse, since, in spite of what is commonly believed, the notion has no pre-theoretical standing. One reason we should be wary of employing the notion is that its status as a metalinguistic term in literate societies derives almost exclusively from conventions governing written language and versification. And these conventions vary, often quite widely, according to different orthographic traditions. The term can be formally taught as a means of labelling some aspect of phonological reality, but it is by no means always obvious exactly what that reality is. In alphabetic traditions, calculating the number of syllables in a word typically involves identifying the number of peaks of perceptual prominence, each typically associated with a vowel. In some other traditions, by contrast, any VC sequence is deemed to straddle a syllable boundary, even when the C in question is not followed by an audible vocalic peak.[25] In a CVCV word, the counts by both methods will converge on two: CV.CV (where the full stop indicates a syllable boundary). However, a CVC word will be rated as monosyllabic by the first method (CVC.) but as disyllabic by the second (CV.C.).

Moreover, even within one and the same alphabetic tradition, there can be disagreements over the location of syllable boundaries in polysyllabic words (as the notoriously variable conventions regarding the placement of line-breaks in the printing of long words testify).[26] As the discussion in this chapter unfolds, it will become clear that constituent nodes in the phonological hierarchy can be labelled without reference to the syllable. Nevertheless, I will occasionally employ the term in an informal sense where its use is unlikely to give rise to ambiguity.

Having established the onset (O) and the rhyme (R) as independent nodes in the phonological hierarchy, our next task is to determine their internal structure. The weight of a rhyme is straightforwardly indicated by the number of positions it contains. Employing a tree-structure representation of constituency, as in syntax, we can establish the weight of a rhyme on the basis of whether or not it branches. In the following forms, the medial rhymes are branching and thus heavy (hence stress-attracting), while the initial and final rhymes are non-branching and thus light.

(19)

```
O  R        O   R         O  R          R        O   R         O  R
|  |        |  / \        |  |          |        |  / \        |  |
x  x        x  x  x       x  x          x        x  x  x       x  x
|  |        |  |  |       |  |          |        |  |  |       |  |
v  ə        r  æ  n       d  ə          ə        r  o  w       m  ə
```

We have now established the outlines of a rudimentary hierarchical representation in which skeletal positions form the terminal nodes of onset and rhymal constituents.

A number of questions arise in connection with this mode of representation, three of which will come up for discussion in this chapter. What constraints are there on the number of skeletal positions that can occur within a constituent? What constraints are there on the type of segments that can occupy these positions? And is there any evidence to suggest that these constituents have any internal hierarchical organization? The last question relates primarily to the rhyme, since it is sometimes assumed that this constituent is itself composed of two sub-constituents: a nucleus (usually but not always containing a vowel) and a coda (containing post-vocalic consonants). Informally speaking, this implies the following structure:[27]

(20)
```
            Rhyme
            /   \
      Nucleus   Coda
```

The question which we will return to below is whether either the nucleus or the coda or both need to be recognized as independent nodes in constituent structure.

2.3.4 Phonotactics

So far, the main motivation we have seen for the skeletal tier has to do with its function as a means of coding phonological quantity. If this were its sole function, there would be good grounds for confining it to rhymes, given the non-participation of onsets in the determination of the quantity relations examined up to now. However, we have clear evidence that skeletal positions have at least one other important role to play in phonological representations: in so far as they form the terminal nodes of syllabic constituents, they help define the level at which **phonotactic** relations are established. Phonotactic constraints place restrictions on the ability of particular segment-types to stand next to one another. And there is sound evidence that onsets are subject to these restrictions no less than rhymes.

As briefly illustrated in 1.2.2, it is a fundamental property of phonological systems that systematic gaps exist in the distribution of different segment-types at different points in phonological strings. These phonotactic lacunae can be viewed as reflecting the reduced capacity of particular positions in constituent structure to support a full range of melodic contrasts. What we typically find is that such positions occur next to other positions which enjoy a fuller contrastive potential. The skewed distributional patterns thus involve adjacent segments, where adjacency is established on the basis of the constituent contexts occupied by skeletal positions.

Phonotactic asymmetries of this sort do not occur randomly across phonological strings; rather they are systematically restricted to certain contexts – call them **phonotactic domains** – which are defined in terms of constituent structure. Three domains which are most often cited as displaying phonotactic constraints involve adjacent positions in the following contexts:

(21)   **Phonotactic domains**

   (a)   within an onset (e.g. *pl* in ⟨play⟩);
   (b)   within the nuclear portion of the rhyme (e.g. *ow* in ⟨go⟩); and
   (c)   within a cluster composed of a coda followed by an onset (e.g. *nt* in ⟨winter⟩).

We will examine each of these contexts in some detail below. By way of a preliminary illustration of the distributional patterns involved, consider the following facts.

Within a two-position onset or nucleus, the distribution of segments in each slot is tied up with that of its sister slot. The example of ⟨play⟩ in (21a) illustrates the classic branching-onset pattern in which the first position is filled by an obstruent and the second by a liquid or glide; hence grammatical *pl-*, *kr-*, *tw-* and the like (as in ⟨play, crow, twelve⟩) but ungrammatical **km-*, **ps-*, **bt-*, etc. (In fact, as we will see later, this is probably the **only** type of branching onset permitted universally. This, in spite of appearances to the contrary, such as the initial cluster of a form like ⟨splay⟩.) On the other hand, when two positions are separated by an onset–rhyme boundary, we typically find that they are phonotactically independent of one another.[28] A single onset position in English displays a near-maximal inventory of consonantal contrasts, disregarding to a large extent the nature of the vowel that occurs in the following rhyme. This independence provides further justification for the onset–rhyme split.

Within a branching nucleus (21b), the distributional possibilities in the left-hand position are much greater than in its sister. The right-hand slot can either be filled by an off-glide, specifically *y*, *w* or *ə* (as in *ey*, *aw*, *iə*); or, as in the case of a long monophthong, it must be identical to its sister on the left. By contrast, the vocalic content of the left-hand slot is in principle unrestricted (although the particular set of contrasts varies from dialect to dialect).

Some of the phonotactic patterns evident in the cross-constituent sequence of a coda-onset cluster (21c) are the reverse of those found within branching onsets. Thus, while obstruent-liquid makes for a well-formed onset, liquid-obstruent belongs to the set of well-formed coda-onset clusters. Compare onset *kl*, *fl*, *tr* in, say, ⟨clay, flay, tree⟩ with coda-onset *lk*, *lf*, *rt* in, say, ⟨falcon, dolphin, quarter⟩. (The *rt* sequence is of course only found in rhotic dialects, those which allow constricted *r* to appear before consonants. More on this in chapter 5.) Other coda-onset clusters are of course possible, including nasal-obstruent (as in ⟨winter⟩), fricative-plosive (⟨mister⟩) and dual oral stops (⟨chapter⟩). In forms of the shape represented by ⟨winter⟩, it is the onset *t* that partially determines the identity of the coda *n* to its left. This particular example illustrates one of the systematic phonotactic constraints that operate intramorphemically in this context: a coda nasal must be homorganic with a following onset obstruent. Hence the grammaticality of forms such as ⟨pamper, winter, a[ŋ]chor⟩ and the ungrammaticality of clusters such as *-ŋp- and *-mk-. Another example involves the impossibility of *t* appearing in the coda position of such clusters. Compare ill-formed *-tp-, *-tk- with well-formed -pt-, -kt- (as in ⟨doctor, chapter⟩).[29]

Our initial motivation for recognizing the skeletal and constituent levels of representation was based exclusively on quantitative considerations. The foregoing brief preview of English phonotactics introduces an independent source of additional supporting evidence. In tandem, these two representational levels define the conditions of adjacency under which phonotactic constraints operate. That is, restrictions on the ability of different melodic units to occur next to one another are stated in terms of the skeletal positions to which the units are attached and the place occupied by these positions in constituent structure. However, unlike quantitative relations, those involving phonotactics are not specific to the rhyme; rather they are defined both within and between onsets and rhymes. This observation indicates the need for a level of representation that is common to both types of constituent. The skeletal tier, already independently motivated by quantitative facts, fits this bill.[30]

When we think more about the coda-onset phonotactics just mentioned, apparent counterexamples might spring to mind. At first sight, the embargo on the occurrence of *t* in codas, for instance, would seem to have been lifted in a form such as ⟨catcall⟩. It is significant, however, that the *t*C sequence in this and similar examples contains an intervening word-level morpheme boundary. The phonological shape of such forms testifies to their word-level structure, even if the morphology in question ceases to be synchronically active. This is particularly true of proper names, as in the pronunciation of ⟨Aitken⟩ with -*tk*-. The variant *eykən* shows the effects of phonological restructuring, in line with what would be expected of a morphologically underived form (cf. ⟨bacon⟩). For reasons touched on in 1.4 and to be expanded on presently, a pair of consonants flanking a word-level morpheme boundary are not truly adjacent and thus cannot be reckoned to reveal systematic phonotactic interactions.

The general issue at stake here is this: defining adjacency in terms of the constituent status of skeletal positions presupposes a determination of the relevant morpho-syntactic domains within which this constituency is established. In other words, we have to take into account the relation between segment strings in syllabic constituents on the one hand and segment strings in morphemes, words, phrases or sentences on the other. In the case of English and many other languages, it is not usual to take the sentence or phrase as the relevant domain within which the basic set of possible constituents is established. Thus, a word-final consonant would not generally be considered to form a constituent with a following word-initial consonant. This fact is reflected in the lack of any systematic phonotactic dependency between the two positions. The sequence *s-θ* in ⟨Tess thinks⟩, for example, does not manifest any systematic phonotactic interaction; rather it is the accidental result of the juxtaposition of two morphemes.

Below the phrase level, it is often assumed that the word domain has a privileged position in the establishment of phonological constituency. According to this view, the set of possible syllabic constituents in a given language can be determined by simply inspecting word structure. In particular, it is frequently taken for granted that well-formed onsets and rhymes can be identified on the basis of segment sequences at word edges. That is, the set of well-formed onsets supposedly coincides with the set of word-initial consonant sequences, and the set of well-formed rhymes with the set of word-final sequences consisting of the rightmost vowel and any following consonants.[31]

From a general theoretical point of view, the claim that syllable structure is equivalent to word structure, if correct, actually constitutes a very good argument for not recognizing syllable structure as an integral part of phonological representations at all. If, for example, phonotactic conditions stated at the syllable level simply duplicated those stated at the word level, it would follow that one of the levels is superfluous. Since there is independent morpho-syntactic motivation for word structure, it is clear which level could be dispensed with. This is essentially the position adopted in SPE, where all phonotactic constraints are formulated in terms of morpheme-structure conditions. But one of the main arguments leading to the rehabilitation of the syllable in generative phonology has been precisely that phonotactic constraints cannot be adequately expressed without reference to syllable structure as an independent dimension of phonological representation.

There is a further, this time empirical problem with the position that syllable structure can be directly read off word structure. This concerns the observation that there exist systematic asymmetries between the distribution of segmental sequences at the edges of words and within words. In particular, as we will see in the next couple of sections, the set of word-internal segmental sequences is much smaller than that found at word edges. This discrepancy partly reflects the fact that not all segment sequences which are possible in morphologically complex words are also possible in single morphemes. Because of the central role played by suffixation in English, the mismatch is especially evident word-finally. For example, the word ⟨six-th-s⟩ contains the right-edge sequence -*ksθs*, with one morpheme boundary intervening between the first *s* and the *θ*, and another between *θ* and the second *s*. If this sequence is assumed to constitute a coda, we have to explain why codas of this shape never occur morpheme-internally. The question then is whether the cross- morpheme sequence *sθ* in ⟨sixth⟩ provides any more or less evidence of systematic phonotactic interaction than the same cross-morpheme sequence in ⟨Tess thinks⟩. As we will see presently, there is good reason to conclude that we are dealing with arbitrarily juxtaposed segments in the former case no less than in the latter. One consequence of this conclusion is that segments in a word-internal sequence cannot automatically be considered adjacent in terms of constituent structure if they are split by a morpheme boundary. Moreover, as we will see, the strings that constitute the difference between word-edge and word-medial sets of sequences display patterned behaviour which has to be accounted for in some way or another.

There can be two responses to the distributional discrepancy between morpheme-level and word-level segment sequences. One alternative is to continue with the basic assumption that syllabic structure can be directly read off word structure, in which case the over-generation of syllable types in morpheme-internal contexts somehow has to be staunched. The other is to determine the set of possible constituent structures purely on the basis of morpheme-internal sequences and then, if necessary, make special provision for the distributional peculiarities of word-edge strings. In the next two sections, I will demonstrate some of the problems inherent in the first approach and rehearse some of the main arguments that have convinced many phonologists of the correctness of the second.

Let us explore the phonotactic discrepancy between intra- and cross-morphemic sequences in more detail. In order to do so, we need to take into account the distinction between root-level and word-level morphology referred to in 1.4. As noted there, from the viewpoint of phonological structure, root-derived forms are non-analytic in the sense that they are indistinguishable from morphologically simplex forms. On the other hand, forms derived at the word level are analytic in the sense that their phonological shape more often than not advertises their morphological complexity. This distinction is particularly striking in the realm of phonotactics. As illustrated in the examples in (22) (some repeated from the last chapter), word-level forms frequently contain segment sequences which are either marginal or impossible in underived and root-level forms but which coincide with cross-word sequences found at the sentence level.

(22)		Compound	Phrase/sentence level
	p-m	lap marker	stop me
	v-t	dove tail	live to
	θ-b	moth ball	path belongs
		Word-suffix	Phrase/sentence level
	t-h	parenthood	parent who

b-n	drabness	drab neighbourhood
v-l	lively	live lynx

In the context of the present discussion, the immediate relevance of the distinction between analytic and non-analytic forms is that it helps delimit the morpho-syntactic domain within which the set of well-formed phonological constituents is appropriately identified. We are proceeding on the assumption, remember, that the existence of phonotactic dependencies between neighbouring segments provides evidence of adjacency in constituent structure. The distributional independence of segments occurring either side of an analytic morpheme boundary suggests that word-level derived forms fall outside the domain within which the basic set of well-formed constituents is established, at least in English.[32] The major systematic phonotactic constraints of English operate within non-analytic domains; and it is for this reason that the following discussion of phonological constituents is restricted in the first instance to underived and root-level forms. It will still of course be necessary to say something about how segment sequences occurring at word-level boundaries are integrated into phonological structure. Later, however, I will argue that this integration does not involve constituents which straddle analytic domains. In other words, two segments separated by a word-level boundary are never syllabified within the same constituent.

A factor to bear in mind when establishing the relevant data over which phonotactic restrictions are defined is that the analyticity or otherwise of a form does not necessarily remain stable over time. For example, as a result of one well-known type of historical change, a compound can become reanalysed as a morphologically simplex form. This is usually accompanied by a phonological restructuring whereby the form loses its original analyticity, a development that is not always reflected in the spelling. Examples include ⟨bosun⟩ (from ⟨boatswain⟩), ⟨gospel⟩ (from Old English ⟨gōd⟩ 'good' plus ⟨spell⟩ 'message') and *fɒrəd* ⟨forehead⟩. Historically, these words contained the cross-morpheme sequences *t-s*, *d-s* and *r-h* (the last still evident in the variant *fɔːrhɛd*) which never occur intra-morphemically. Now, however, they exhibit the same kind of non-analytic structure as we find in forms such as ⟨basin⟩, ⟨rascal⟩ and ⟨torrid⟩.

On the other hand, as noted briefly above, some forms continue to bear witness to historically analytic structure, even though they no longer participate in productive morphological alternations. This is particularly true of many proper names. Originally compound names such as ⟨Sopwith, Babcock, Nazeby⟩ contain sequences (*p-w, b-k, z-b*) which do not otherwise occur morpheme-internally and are identical to those encountered in productive compounds, cf. ⟨tapeworm, lab, coat, rose border⟩. Proper names themselves are sometimes subject to historical restructuring, as illustrated by the word ⟨Aitken⟩ already mentioned. To take another example, the former compound ⟨Greenwich⟩, when pronounced *grɛnɪǰ* or *grɛnɪč*, displays the same kind of non-analyticity as ⟨manage⟩. Since forms which continue to put their historical analyticity on phonological view fail to exhibit the systematic phonotactic restrictions encountered in non-derived forms, it is necessary to exclude them from the data set on which the following discussion of intra-constituent clusters draws.

A pertinent question to ask at this point is whether sound sequences missing from particular morpheme-internal contexts reflect synchronically active phonological constraints or are merely accidental lacunae in the vocabulary transmitted from earlier stages in the history of English. To put it in terms introduced in 1.3.4, do these gaps constitute **core** facts of the language that we should attempt to derive from general and possibly universal principles? Or are they unsystematic facts that belong to the **periphery** of the grammar? The oft-cited pair *bnɪk* and *blɪk* illustrates the point at issue here.³³

Lexical gaps such as *blɪk* can be shown to fall into the peripheral category. This particular form is grammatical, even if unattested (at least in standard English). Its non-occurrence cannot be put down to systematic restrictions on any of the sound sequences it contains. The initial *bl* cluster, for example, shows up as a well-formed branching onset in a host of attested lexical items, including ⟨blow, blot, black⟩. Nor is there any bar on *lɪ* or *blɪ* sequences (cf. ⟨limp, blink⟩). The same goes for *ɪk* (cf. ⟨trick, click⟩).

The form *bnɪk*, on the other hand, must be judged ungrammatical. The complete lack of any words in English beginning with *bn* suggests that this cluster is not a possible onset in the language. Moreover, this absence is evidently related to a more general ban on plosive-nasal onset clusters. That this is a systematic property of the grammar, in need of principled explanation, is confirmed by the fact that precisely the same constraint is found in numerous other languages, including many with little or no historical affiliation with English.

There are various pieces of external evidence which bolster the conclusion that lexical gaps of the *bnɪk* type, unlike those of the *blɪk* type, are not simply accidental residues bequeathed by earlier stages of language history. For example, the phonotactic constraints associated with the former type vigorously assert themselves when new vocabulary items enter the language, as foreign borrowings, neologisms, acronyms, product brand names, or whatever. They also figure prominently in characteristically English second-language errors. The absence of word-initial plosive-nasal sequences in English, for example, means that the German borrowing ⟨gneiss⟩ (pronounced *gnays* in the donor language) has been adopted as *nays*. For the same reason, English learners of German frequently render initial *gn-* and *kn-* sequences as *n-*, or else insert an intervening vowel, as in *kəniː* (German *kniː* 'knee'). Note that errors of this type cannot be put down to some vague notion of articulatory difficulty. English-speakers have no problem getting their tongues round plosive-nasal sequences in, for example, cross-word contexts, as in ⟨big noise, pick no⟩. The source of such errors is phonological and has to do with the deep-seated nature of phonotactic constraints operating in particular constituent contexts.

The situation is quite different with accidental gaps such as *blɪk*. It is quite possible to imagine *blɪk* as a neologism in English. It would make a perfectly good product brand name (unlike *bnɪk*, for example). And English learners have no problem pronouncing this form in German (where it means 'glance').

All of the phonotactic patterns briefly surveyed in this section and to be discussed in much more detail in the following sections can be shown to be non-accidental in the sense just described. That is, they fall within the domain of core grammar and as such call for principled explanation.

2.4 Onsets, rhymes, nuclei

2.4.1 *Some traditional assumptions*

A traditional specification of the set of possible syllabic constituents in English usually runs something like this:[34]

(23) (a) The onset can contain between zero and three positions, illustrated in the word-initial portions of ⟨eye, pie, pry, spry⟩.
      (b) The coda part of the rhyme contains between zero and four positions, illustrated in the word-final portions of ⟨see (∅), sick (-*k*), six (-*ks*), sixth (-*ksθ*), sixths (-*ksθs*)⟩.
      (c) The nuclear part of the rhyme contains at least one and at most two positions, illustrated by the short–long vowel contrast in ⟨bid⟩ versus ⟨bead⟩.

Conclusions (23a) and (23b) are based on the assumption that the set of possible onsets and codas is established on the basis of clusters occurring at word edges. In (23c), the setting of a lower limit of one position on the nucleus reflects the obligatory presence of this constituent within a syllable.

Taken together, the statements in (23) define a well-formedness template for the English syllable which we might formalize as follows:

(24) $[x_0^3]_{onset} [x_1^2]_{Nucleus} [x_1^4]_{Coda}$

Of course a template of this sort only establishes the gross limits on the number of positions that can occur in each constituent. It says nothing about additional restrictions that exist on the co-occurrence of different segment-types within each position.

Having established the onset and coda portions of the template (24) on the basis of word-initial and word-final consonant sequences, we run into the problem already alluded to: we find that the maximal inventory of possible syllable types defined by the template is massively reduced when we turn our attention to word-internal contexts. Moreover, the potential for individual onset and coda positions to support phonological contrasts decreases spectacularly as we move to the periphery of the onset and the coda. In other words, we have a serious case of over-generation: the template defines a set of possible syllable-types which is significantly larger than the set that is actually attested. The immediate response to this problem might be to try patching up the template by supplementing it with conditions which eliminate a subset of the syllables it allows to be generated. We can illustrate the issues that are at stake here by first examining the onset condition in (23a).

2.4.2 *Onsets*

In this section, we will review the evidence which suggests that English onsets maximally contain not three positions, as claimed in (23a), but two.

Single-position onsets in English display virtually the entire gamut of consonant contrasts in the language, while in two-position onsets we find a reduced set of distinctions involving the obstruent–glide/liquid restriction already mentioned. However, it is a well-known fact about English (and many other languages) that, in the first position of a word-initial three-consonant cluster, the distinctive possibilities reduce to one. Only a voiceless coronal fricative can occur in this context – in English, *s*. If word-initial structure is equated with onset structure, as implied in (23a), we would have to formulate some kind of co-occurrence constraint limiting the first position in a three-slot onset to *s*. However, there are at least two sorts of evidence which indicate that this solution is unsound. One involves the syllabification of *s* in word-medial clusters, the other its phonotactic interactions with following consonants. Both point to the conclusion that *s* in initial clusters is not integrated into onsets in the way that other consonants are.

In order to discuss the syllabification of *s* in medial clusters, it is necessary to say something about the syllabification of word-internal consonants in general. There is a consensus among phonologists that the universally unmarked pattern in VCV sequences is for the inter-vocalic consonant to be syllabified in the onset of the second syllable rather than in the coda of the first. So ⟨city⟩, for example, would be syllabified as *sɪ.ti*. This principle is sometimes referred to as **Onset Maximization:**[35]

(25)   **Onset Maximization**

Syllable-initial segments are maximized to the extent consistent with the syllable structure conditions of the language in question.

(The universality of this principle is compromised in some frameworks by allowing V.CV to undergo resyllabification to VC.V under certain circumstances, a point we will return to in chapter 4.) Onset maximization also forces VCCV sequences to be syllabified as V.CCV, if the two-consonant sequence constitutes a well-formed onset, as in *pɛ.trəl* ⟨petrol⟩. Otherwise, an inter-vocalic cluster of two consonants will be syllabified as VC.CV, i.e. with the first consonant in the coda of the syllable on the left and the second in the onset of the one on the right, as in ⟨plen.ty⟩.

If *s* in initial clusters occurs in an onset, we might expect this syllabification to carry over into medial clusters. That is, on the basis of onset maximization, medial V*s*CV sequences should be consistently syllabified as V.*s*CV, as in *mɪ.stər* ⟨mister⟩. There is at least some evidence in English that this expectation is unfounded. There are certain stress facts, for example, which seem to suggest a V*s*.CV syllabification. This pattern is evident in, say, ⟨Aláska, Nebráska, aspidístra⟩, where the penultimate rhymes are heavy, as demonstrated by the fact that they attract stress. This indicates that *s* in these forms is syllabified not in the onset of the final syllable but rather in the coda of the penult, the same pattern as that found in, for example, ⟨magénta, propagánda, Esmerálda⟩. It has to be acknowledged that not all words containing medial *s*C clusters display this kind of stress pattern. We find antepenultimate rather than penultimate stress in, for example, ⟨índustry, órchestra⟩. Nevertheless, the inconsistency of stress placement in words with pre-consonantal *s* shows that the existence of medial *s*C onsets can certainly not be taken for granted.

In certain other languages with medial *s*C clusters, the relevant syllabification evidence is quite unambiguous: *s* in this context clearly occupies a coda. In standard Italian, for example, stressed vowels are long in open syllables but short in closed. Hence forms such as *viːta* 'life' (CV.CV) versus *vinta* 'defeated (fem.)' (CVC.CV).[36] If *s*C constituted an onset, a form such as *vista* 'sight' would be expected to contain a long vowel (**viː.sta*), on the pattern of *viːta*. However, the fact that *vista* lines up with *vinta* in having a short vowel confirms that V*s*CV is syllabified as V*s*.CV

There are two responses we could have to the English and Italian facts just outlined. The weaker position would be to assume that *s* in medial clusters is free to vacillate between coda and onset. Later in the chapter, I will present arguments for favouring the stronger view that medial *s*C clusters universally conform to the *s*.C pattern. If this position is correct, then the fluctuating stress patterns evident in forms such as ⟨aspidístra⟩ and ⟨índustry⟩ must be attributed to the unsystematic lexical selectivity which, quite independently of syllabification, afflicts the English stress system as a whole.

If we persist in the belief that *s* in word-initial clusters is syllabified in onset position, we now have to come up with an explanation for why it should mysteriously migrate to the coda in medial clusters. But, even if we confine our attention to initial clusters, we find additional distributional evidence against *s*C onsets. If *s* in word-initial clusters does indeed occur in the same constituent as a following consonant, we might expect the same sort of co-occurrence restrictions to be evident in this context as in other complex onsets. On the face of it, the fact that there is a phonotactic dependency here at all (the constraint on the first of an initial three-consonant cluster being *s*) does seem to be symptomatic of just this kind of situation. However, the other distributional properties of *s* in this context suggest that we should be wary of drawing any such conclusion. In order to assess this evidence, we now need to examine in more detail the nature of the rather severe restrictions that are placed on the co-occurrence of segment-types within syllabic constituents.

The main dimension that has traditionally been cited as being implicated in both intra- and inter-constituent phonotactic constraints is **sonority**.[37] This is a scalar property attributed to segments which, very broadly speaking, manifests itself perceptually as differences in loudness. (Acoustically, this correlates with differences in the output of energy and in the extent to which this is concentrated in particular frequency bands.) In articulatory terms, this corresponds roughly to the degree of aperture in the vocal tract. Segments arrange themselves on a hierarchy ranging from least to most sonorous, the latter being characterized by maximization of energy output and articulatory aperture. The outlines of this hierarchy are generally assumed to be universal:[38]

(26) **Sonority hierarchy**

Increasing sonority
- Low vowels
- Glides/high vowels
- Liquids
- Nasals
- Fricatives
- Plosives

The role of sonority in restricting the co-occurrence of different segment-types in syllabic structure has two aspects. One involves the principle of **sonority sequencing**:[39]

(27) **Sonority sequencing**

An optimal syllable consists of a sonority peak, corresponding to the nucleus, optionally flanked by segments which decrease in sonority the further they occur from the nucleus.

Viewed from left to right, segment-sequences within an onset thus have an upward sonority slope, while those in rhymes have a downward slope. The other aspect involves the observation that languages impose a **minimum sonority distance** on neighbouring segments, which can be calculated by reference to the ranks occupied by individual segment-types on the hierarchy.[40] Setting aside the issue of *s*C clusters for a moment, we observe in English a general requirement that segments within an onset should be separated by at least one sonority rank; hence the illegitimacy of onsets such as * *ks-*, *tp-*, *ml-*.

Sonority on its own is insufficient to derive all the characteristic cluster restrictions that recur across different languages. For example, it cannot account for the bar on plosive-nasal and *tl/dl* onset clusters evident in English. This raises the issue of whether the whole collection of cluster constraints is derivable from some more fundamental representational property of which sonority is but one reflection. This is a matter we will take up in chapter 4. For the time being, we can simply employ the sonority hierarchy as a notational device for describing phonotactic constraints.

A related question is whether restrictions imposed by sonority or its representational source have universal force. At first sight, they would appear not to, at least if available language descriptions are taken at face value. For example, the literature is replete with examples of supposed onset clusters which flagrantly contravene sonority sequencing constraints. Well-known cases include the multiple word-initial consonant sequences of a language such as Polish. In *lgnõt^y* 'adhere', *ls^ynit^y* 'shine' and *mdlet^y* 'faint', for example, we find three-consonant clusters in which the sonority profile falls and then rises again before the following vowel. One response has been to deny the universality of the sonority hierarchy and seek refuge in the notion that it does no more than express preferences which can be overridden on a language-specific basis.[41] This of course immediately robs the hierarchy of whatever explanatory force it might have had. At worst, it leaves us with little more than a redescription of the very distributional facts the hierarchy was designed to account for in the first place.

The alternative view to be taken here is that the restrictions underlying sonority effects are universally imposed. It then has to be demonstrated that any alleged counterexamples have been inaccurately described. For instance, in the case of supposed onset clusters which clash with the sonority sequencing generalization, it has to be shown that they are not onsets at all but represent other constituent configurations. Onset treatments of this type can indeed be exposed as misanalyses founded on the misconception that any word-initial consonant sequence automatically qualifies as a well-formed onset.[42] As we will now see, this is precisely the point that can be made in respect of initial *s*C clusters.

When we compare the distribution of *s* in initial two-consonant clusters with that of other segments appearing in this position (all of them obstruents), we find some significant differences, some of which can be expressed in terms of sonority relations. The differences are set out below:[43]

(28)	C_1 \ C_2	l	r	w	p	t	k	m	n
(a)	p	+	+	−	−	−	−	−	−
	t	−	+	+	−	−	−	−	−
	k	+	+	+	−	−	−	−	−
	b	+	+	−	−	−	−	−	−
	d	−	+	+	−	−	−	−	−
	g	+	+	+	−	−	−	−	−
	f	+	+	−	−	−	−	−	−
	θ	−	+	+	−	−	−	−	−
(b)	s	+	−	+	+	+	+	+	+

Omitted from this array are co-occurrence possibilities which are of marginal status, such as *vr-* (⟨vroom⟩) and *sf-* (⟨sphere⟩). I have also omitted *y* from C_2, because I want to devote more attention to it a little later. *sr* is unattested in all but a few dialects; elsewhere the corresponding cluster is *ʃr* (as in ⟨shrimp, shrink⟩).[44]

There is one obvious similarity between the distributions displayed in (28a) and (28b). In both series, C_2 can be occupied by a liquid or glide. The clearest difference between the two distributional patterns is that *s* can co-occur with a larger set of segments than other C_1 consonants.

The two main co-occurrence restrictions operating in (28a) can be considered characteristic of intra-onset phonotactics. One is a bar on homorganic clusters with *l* and *w* (hence inadmissible * *tl-*, * *dl-*, * *θl-*, * *pw-*, * *bw-*). The other is a restriction on C_2 being occupied only by a liquid or glide, a pattern that is expressible in terms of minimum sonority distance. Note that, whenever an obstruent and liquid occur in an order which is the reverse of that in (28a), the sonority sequencing principle will debar them from being syllabified within an onset. Thus *lt*, for example, is an impossible onset; on the other hand, it constitutes a well-formed coda-onset sequence, as in ⟨shel.ter⟩.

Neither of these restrictions holds of (28b). The homorganic *sl-* sequence is admissible (as in ⟨sling⟩). And after *s* C_2 can be not only a liquid or glide, as in (28a), but also a nasal or oral non-continuant. This means that, were initial *sC* clusters to be treated as onsets, they would constitute the sole exception to the otherwise general principles of sonority sequencing and minimum sonority distance. Note that *sC* represents a downward sonority slope, in contradistinction to the uniformly upward patterns evident in (28a). And, again unlike the pattern in (28a), the segments in an *s*-plus-plosive cluster occupy adjacent positions on the sonority hierarchy.

The clusters in (28b) are not without their own phonotactic restrictions. However, these cannot be considered exclusively diagnostic of onset constituency, since they operate in other environments as well. The single factor which has the most far-reaching effect of constricting the contrastive possibilities in C_2 in (28b) is voicing assimilation between *s* and a following plosive. This results in a suspension of the *p–b*, *t–d* and *k–g* distinctions, each of which is neutralized under a voiceless unaspirated stop in this context. In so far as this process provides any evidence bearing on the constituency of adjacent segments, it actually favours the interpretation that they are not sisters. One of the other contexts in which it occurs is across constituent boundaries, specifically between a coda consonant and a following onset consonant. This is not only true of *s*-plus-obstruent clusters, where the obstruent is always voiceless; we get, for example, ⟨aspic,master, basket⟩ but no forms containing * *-sb-*, * *-sd-*, * *-sg-*.[45] But it is also true of other obstruent clusters; we can have, for example, ⟨hefty, chapter, factor⟩ but no forms with * *-fd-*, * *-pd-*, * *-kd-*. Voicing assimilation also operates in word-final clusters, both with *s* (as in ⟨clasp, test, ask⟩ (* *-sb*, * *-sd*, * *-sg*)), and with other obstruent sequences (as in ⟨aft, apt, act⟩ (* *-fd*, * *-pd*, * *-kd*)). We have yet to discuss the syllabification of the latter context; but, whatever else it might be, it certainly does not involve *sC* onsets. So the absence of the *b–p*, *d–t*, *g–k* contrasts from C_2 in (28b) cannot be attributed to a phonotactic restriction that is exclusive to onsets.

We can summarize the phonotactic possibilities in initial *sC* clusters as follows. They fail to conform to the principles of sonority sequencing and distance which otherwise constrain onset clusters. Moreover, the set of consonants appearing after initial *s* is equal to the set of consonants appearing in a simplex onset minus those that are ruled out by a voicing assimilation process that can be shown to operate independently of onset contexts. In short, the C_2 position in *s*C clusters enjoys a degree of distributional freedom which is not at all in keeping with the assumption that the two positions are onset sisters on a par with those in (28a).

The relative autonomy of *s* from a following consonant is further underlined when we extend our investigation to three-consonant clusters:

(29) C_1 C_2 C_3
      s   {p, t, k}   {l, r, w}

The distribution here can be derived by combining the restrictions associated with two-consonant clusters in (28a) and (28b).[46] That is, the set of combinatorial possibilities involving C_2 and C_3 in (29) is equal to the set of C_1-C_2 possibilities in (28a) minus those that are ruled out by the constraints operating in (28b). Generally speaking, the C_2-C_3 part of an initial three-term cluster thus looks just like a two-term obstruent-liquid/glide cluster. The only phonotactic dependency involving the initial *s* concerns the exclusion of *s*C sequences by the voicing assimilation process which, we have seen, cannot be considered diagnostic of onset constituency. Forms with initial *sdr- or *sbl-, say, are ruled out for the same reason that forms with the same sequences in medial V*s*.CCV strings are.

Staying with initial three-segment clusters, let us turn to one last piece of distributional evidence which further calls into question the onset syllabification of initial pre-consonantal *s*. In doing so, we will discover additional support for the onset–rhyme split. The evidence concerns the constituent status of *y* in clusters, which I excluded from (28).

Let us start by considering the significance of using the *y* transcription to represent a high front non-round vocalic segment. On purely phonetic grounds, this means that the sound is related to and possibly identical to that usually transcribed as *i* or *ɪ*. The reason for having distinct symbols here is a phonological rather than a phonetic one. The distinction is designed to reflect the different positions that a high front vocoid (vowel or glide) can occupy in syllabic structure. The symbol *i* usually indicates sole occupancy of a nucleus, while *y* is usually reserved for the off-glide portion of a nucleus (as in *dey* ⟨day⟩) or for onset position (as in *yet* ⟨yet⟩). The same relation holds of the symbols *u* and *w*; *w* is to *u* as *y* is to *i*. Taking the symbol I to stand for a melodic unit which is high, front and non-round, we can represent the transcriptional difference between onset *y* and nuclear (rhymal) *i* purely in terms of constituent structure:[47]

(30)   (a)   '*y*'   (b)   '*i*'

             O   R
             | |
             x   x
             | |
             I   I

Exploiting the representational distinction in (30), we can now examine some additional evidence in support of the onset–rhyme split. So far, we have considered evidence involving syllable quantity and the statement of phonotactic constraints. This time, the evidence relates to the role of syllable structure in conditioning phonological processes. We will look at two such processes which operate in many (but by no means all) dialects of English. One is responsible for the alternation between ⟨a⟩ and ⟨an⟩ in the indefinite article, the other for the alternation between ə and *i* in ⟨the⟩.

The conditions under which the alternations occur are identical:

(31)   a/an   th[ə/i]
      (a)   an apple   th[i] apple
            an arrival   th[i] arrival
            an eel   th[i] eel
      (b)   a pear   th[ə] pear
            a nut   th[ə] nut
            a lord   th[ə] lord
      (c)   a yacht   th[ə] yacht
            a willow   th[ə] willow

As an informal statement of the conditions governing these alternations, we might say that ⟨an⟩ and ⟨th[i]⟩ are selected when a vowel follows but ⟨a⟩ and ⟨th[ə]⟩ when a consonant follows. This is only accurate if we understand the notions **vowel** and **consonant** in syllabic terms. The phonetic identity of the segment following the article is irrelevant, as can be seen when we compare (31a) with (31c). In both sets, the noun begins with an vocalic segment (i.e. one produced without consonantal constriction), but they behave differently with respect to the alternation. The crucial determining factor is whether or not the article is followed by an onset that is filled by a segment of some sort. If it is, the alternants ⟨a⟩ and ⟨the[ə]⟩ are selected, irrespective of whether the sound occupying the onset is consonantal, as in (31b), or vocalic, as in (31c). The ⟨an⟩ and ⟨th[i]⟩ alternants are only selected if an immediately following vocalic sound occurs in a rhyme, as in (31a). The difference between the filled and empty onset conditions is illustrated below:

(32)

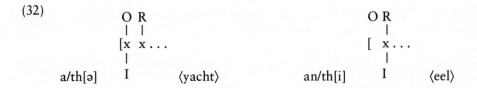

The representational difference here suggests an analysis under which the *n* of ⟨a(n)⟩ only appears when it is able to attach itself to a following onset not already occupied by some other segment. We will not pursue this possibility here, but in chapter 5 we will see how just this sort of analysis can be developed for another consonant–zero alternation.

We are now in a position to determine the syllabification of *y* in C*y*V sequences. Historically, *y* did not feature in complex onsets at all. It occurred in nuclei as part of the diphthong *yuː* (from earlier *iw*, a reflex that still survives in some dialects). In this position it was free to co-occur with virtually any onset consonant (including sonorants). This is exactly what we would expect, given the general paucity of phonotactic dependencies between an onset and a following rhyme. However, the signs are that the glide has since been reanalysed into onset position. The arguments supporting this conclusion are brought out by an analysis of the various reflexes of historical *yuː* given in exercise 2 at the end of this chapter. For the time being, let me simply mention the piece of supporting evidence that is most relevant to the present discussion: C*y* sequences are now subject to the same sort of co-occurrence restrictions as are characteristic of C-plus-sonorant clusters in onsets. In some dialects, *y* in this environment has either disappeared under certain conditions or coalesced with a preceding coronal to produce palato-alveolar reflexes of historical alveolars. For example, dialects vary according to whether a *y* appears in all, some or none of the following forms: ⟨tune, due, lieu, new, sue, enthusiasm⟩). Hence variants such as *tyuːn–tuːn–čuːn* ⟨tune⟩, *dyuːn–duːn–juːn* ⟨dune⟩ and *ɪsyu–ɪʃu* ⟨issue⟩. The effect of such changes has been to introduce constraints on the co-occurrence of *y* with a preceding coronal.[48]

The most conservative dialects, those in which post-consonantal *y* retains a relatively wide distribution, provide striking confirmation of the conclusion that *s* in word-initial clusters is not integrated into the onset.[49] In conservative standard dialects most closely associated with the south of England, *y* potentially occurs after any coronal. (The only proviso is that this is true of *r* only if an unstressed vowel follows. Hence ⟨vir[y]ulent⟩ but *ruːd* ⟨rude⟩ (*ryuːd).) Any suggestion that this phonotactic independence might reflect a continuation of the historical nuclear status of *y* in *yuː* is contradicted by the fact that the occurrence of the sound is dependent on the relative complexity of a preceding cluster. As seen in (33), the glide is free to occur after a lone consonant. This is true whether the consonant is non-coronal (33a) or coronal (T) (33b), including *l* (33c). However, it cannot appear after a lateral when this forms part of a two-consonant cluster (33d). (The missing historical palatal in forms such as ⟨blue⟩ is still to be heard in dialects which retain the earlier *iw* reflex.)

(33)	(a)	C*yu*	(b)	T*yu*	(c)	*lyu*	(d)	C*lu* (*C*lyu*)
		cute		tune		lieu		blue
		pewter		dune		lewd		clue
		beauty		new		lucid		plumage
		music		suit		luminous		glue

The pattern in (33d) is consistent with the assumption that English onsets can have a maximum of two positions. In (33a, b, c), *y* appears in a two-slot onset, as depicted in (34a).

(34) (a)

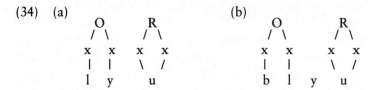

The failure of *y* to appear in (33d) can be attributed to the fact that both positions in the onset are already occupied. The blocking of the glide's historical migration into the onset is illustrated in (34b).

We now have a way of testing the alleged onset status of *s* in initial *sC* clusters. If *sC* is an onset, it should behave just like the CC onsets in (33d) in never being followed by *y*. The forms in (35) show this prediction to be false.

(35) *sCyu*   *slyu*
      stew   slew
      skew   sluice
      spew

These forms show that C*y* is a well-formed onset cluster in the relevant dialects, irrespective of whether it is preceded by *s*. (Initial *sCCy* clusters (e.g. *splyu-*) are excluded for the same reason as the non-occurring CC*y* clusters in (33d).) If we are to maintain the explanation that *y* is excluded from two-position onsets because these are already saturated (as in (33d)), we are forced to conclude that the initial *sC* sequences in (35) do not count as onsets.

We have just reviewed various pieces of evidence bearing on the issue of how *s* is syllabified in initial clusters. All point to the same negative conclusion: as shown in (36), *s* does not belong to the onset occupied by the following consonant.

(36)

```
 ?   O   N
 |   |  / \
 x   x  x  x
 |   |  |  |
 s   t  e  y      ⟨stay⟩
```

So what exactly is the syllabic status of *s* in this context, not only in English but also in other languages with similar initial clusters? One proposal is that *s* in initial consonant sequences is directly adjoined to some higher node in phonological structure (the syllable or the word, for example).[50]

According to another proposal, *s* in this context occurs in a coda preceded by an unrealized nucleus.[51] It is not easy to come by convincing evidence from English that supports this analysis. Striking confirmation, however, comes from Romance languages. The difference between, for example, Italian ⟨stadio⟩ and Spanish ⟨estadio⟩ 'stadium', it has been argued, resides in whether or not the nucleus preceding *s* is phonetically realized; in Spanish it is, in Italian it is not. Nevertheless, the presence of the initial 'silent' nucleus in Italian is indicated by the fact that words with initial *s*C clusters behave exactly like vowel-initial words with respect to certain alternations. For example, the general pattern for consonant-initial words is to select the ⟨i⟩ form of the masculine plural definite article (e.g. ⟨i doni⟩ 'the gifts'). However, *s*C-initial words line up with vowel-initial words in selecting the alternant ⟨gli⟩ (e.g. ⟨gli alberi⟩ 'the trees', ⟨gli stadi⟩ 'the stadiums'). That this selection is conditioned by the special constituent status of *s* in clusters rather than by its phonetic quality is confirmed by the fact that words with a single onset *s* take the regular consonant-initial alternant (e.g. ⟨i signori⟩ 'the gentlemen'). (Parallel alternations involving the same conditioning factors affect such forms as ⟨il/l(o)⟩ (masculine singular definite article) and ⟨dei/degli⟩ (masculine plural indefinite article).)

We will not pursue the question of which of these alternatives is the most satisfactory. However, we will return to the issue of how the distributional peculiarities at word edges should be treated, when we move on to discuss the structure of rhymes in the next section.

In the meantime, it is worth emphasizing one important implication of the recognition that *s* is not integrated into initial onset clusters. We now reject the claim made in (23a) that English onsets can contain up to three positions. Instead, we must assume that they can contain no more than two slots. The same conclusion has been reached in regard to other languages. In fact, it is now widely assumed that the imposition of a two-position limit on onsets is universal, although a book devoted to English is not the place to review the relevant evidence. The next question to be asked is whether this limit is peculiar to onsets or is imposed on all syllabic constituents.

2.4.3 Rhymes

Up to now, I have been referring informally to two sub-portions of the rhyme, depicted in (20) – the nucleus and the coda. In this section, we will consider whether or not these represent independent nodes in constituent structure. Let us start by examining the status of the nucleus.

Earlier we saw that, for the purposes of calculating quantity, a rhyme counts as heavy as long as it contains two positions, irrespective of whether these are occupied by a long vowel or by a short vowel followed by a coda consonant. This equivalence seems to suggest a unitary treatment in which both types of sequence occur in a rhymal constituent lacking an independent nuclear node:

(37)

```
      R          R          R
    /   \      /   \      /   \
   x     x    x     x    x     x
   |     |     \   /     |     |
   v     v       v       v     c
```

(The symbols v and c stand for melodic units typically containing vocalic and consonantal material respectively.) However, there are certain distributional considerations which indicate that this conclusion is incorrect.

Consider the following facts which show that the distributional relations involving VV rhymes are of a different order to those involving VC rhymes. The coda
of a VC rhyme is subject to phonotactic restrictions imposed by a following onset
consonant. One example is the homorganic dependency that a coda nasal exhibits
in relation to a following obstruent, as illustrated in ⟨ta[m]per, wi[n]ter, a[ŋ]chor⟩.
No such interactions are observed between a V or VV rhyme and a following
onset; virtually the whole gamut of vowel qualities is able to manifest itself in the
first nucleus of a V(V).CV sequence, regardless of the nature of the onset consonant.

On the other hand, there are very severe constraints on the co-occurrence of
melody units within a vocalic rhyme, whereas there is little or no phonotactic
dependency between the positions of a VC rhyme. True, there are restrictions on
the **length** of the vowel before a coda consonant, involving the phenomenon of
closed-syllable shortening (on which more in 2.4.4) which excludes long vowels
from this context. But there is no restriction on the type of vocalic melody unit
that can occur before a coda consonant.[52] This is in sharp contrast to the situation
in a V_1V_2 rhyme, where the identity of the melody unit in V_2 is heavily constrained. Specifically, it is limited to one of the following off-glides: *y*, *w* and *ə*.
Thus, we can have two-position diphthongs such as *ey, ay, ow, aw, iə* but not, say,
*ia, *uo, *ue.[53] This is not to deny that vocalic sequences which might be
transcribed in terms such as *ia/ya, uo/wo, ue/we* do not occur. (Bear in mind the
equivalence of *i* and *y* and of *u* and *w* remarked on earlier.) However, when they
do, they can be shown to form part of structures which are different from the
heavy-rhyme type we are discussing here. They can represent one of the following
alternatives: an onset-nucleus sequence, or a sequence of two independent nuclei,
or a short diphthong (i.e. a contour segment in which two vocalic melody units
are associated to a single skeletal point).[54]

The defective distributional property of the right-hand position of a vocalic
rhyme is strongly reminiscent of the situation that obtains in onsets. The vocalic integrity that is indicated by this asymmetry has been taken as evidence for
the existence of a nuclear constituent within the rhyme. Thus it appears necessary
to recognize two types of bi-positional rhyme, one containing a branching nucleus, the other a single nuclear position:

(38) (a)

(b)

Given the structures in (38), the weight of a rhyme is still identifiable on the basis
of the number of skeletal points it contains. Now, however, we cannot define a
heavy rhyme as one which directly branches. We have to specify that it dominates

two positions, regardless of whether this involves indirect domination of both positions, as in (38a), or immediate domination of the right-hand position and indirect domination (via N) of the nuclear position, as in (38b).

We have yet to consider the possibility that rhymes may contain more than two positions. A number of questions arise in this connection. What is the maximum number of positions that can occur in a nucleus? Is there a limit to the number of positions that can occur in the post-nuclear portion of the rhyme? If there is, is this limit independent of the number of positions in the nucleus? Is there any evidence that the post-nuclear rhymal portion contains an independent coda constituent?

The least controversial of these issues concerns the nucleus. There is general agreement among phonologists that nuclei are universally restricted to two positions. Not all languages have branching nuclei, just as not all languages have branching onsets. The difference between branching and non-branching nuclei is the formal expression of a contrast between long and short vowels, and not all languages have such a distinction. Claims have occasionally been made that some systems display a three-way vowel-length contrast, which would imply the possibility of ternary-branching nuclei. However, reported cases of so-called overlong vowels can be shown to involve other structures, for example a sequence of two or more nuclei, or the occurrence of a long vowel under word stress.[55]

Given the maximally binary branching structure of onsets and nuclei, we might reasonably ask whether rhymes pattern the same way.[56] If this is the case, and setting aside for the moment the possibility of there being an autonomous coda constituent, we expect the four logically possible types of rhyme depicted in (39).

(39)

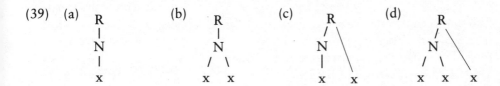

So far we have seen evidence for the light structure in (39a) and the heavy structures in (39b) and (39c). The pattern in (39d), for which we have not yet seen any evidence, presents the maximal structure allowed for under binary branching. Note that, although the rhyme contains three positions, neither the rhymal nor the nuclear node branches more than twice. In the next section we will see that it is necessary to recognize such 'super-heavy' rhymes, although they only occur under very specific conditions.

On the face of it, the statement in (23b), which allows for the occurrence of up to four positions in the English coda, suggests not only that the coda exists as an additional independent constituent but also that it is not subject to the same binarity restriction as the other constituents. If this is correct, it greatly increases the number of possible rhyme-types defined by the theory. The following, for example, would have to be considered grammatical in English:

(40)

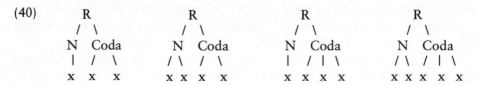

However, we will now examine a considerable amount of evidence which indicates that the assumption in (23b) is simply incorrect.

2.4.4 *'Codas'*

This section surveys the main structural and distributional properties of the rhyme in English. The primary purpose at this stage is simply to determine what the relevant facts are rather than to suggest explanations for why the rhyme takes the shape it does. The facts fall into two broad categories. On the one hand, there are those which help establish the gross typological outlines of the rhyme in English, relating specifically to the number of positions the constituent can contain.

On the other hand, there are facts which relate to the distributional characteristics of particular positions within the rhyme. Some of the distributional findings are quite robust. We will see, for example, that the ability of the coda position to support consonantal contrasts is much more tightly constrained than that of certain other positions. Other distributional facts may seem at first sight somewhat arcane. For example, where a coda *l* occurs in a super-heavy rhyme, a following onset can only be occupied by a coronal consonant. Hence grammatical ⟨shoulder, cauldron⟩ versus ungrammatical *⟨owlbər⟩, *⟨ɔːlgrən⟩, or the like. Some of the apparently more esoteric distributional patterns to be reviewed here continue to elude satisfactory explanation. In such cases, it has to be conceded, currently available formalizations of the relevant facts amount to little more than carefully devised stipulations.

Later in this section, we will discuss the syllabification of English word-final clusters, traditionally considered to exhibit the full range of possible rhyme structures in a language. First, however, let us consider the range of possible sequences that occur before a morpheme-internal onset consonant or onset cluster.[57]

As illustrated by the first syllables of the following forms, the four systematically occurring medial rhyme-types in English are as follows:

(41) (a) V.   (b) VV.   (c) VC.   (d) VVC.
          city   Peter   factor   shoulder
          ladder   putrid   chapter   angel
          petrol   booty   kestrel   chamber
          baton   capon   biscuit   council

Forms with internal rhymes show either an open syllable, as in (41a) and (41b), or a syllable closed by a single coda consonant, as in (41c) and (41d). Both types occur with a contrast between short and long nuclei: (41a,c) versus (41b,d). In forms with a super-heavy VVC rhyme (41d), the phonotactic latitude accorded the coda position is somewhat more restricted than that observed in (41c). To gain an idea of the inequality of the distributional possibilities, we now need to take a more detailed look at the phonotactics of coda-onset clusters briefly touched on in the last section.

The distributional profile of internal coda-onset clusters is subject to an extension of the sonority sequencing generalization given in (27):[58]

(42) **Sonority sequencing II**

In an optimal coda-onset cluster, the first consonant is no less sonorous than the second.

Typical coda-onset clusters show a falling sonority slope (viewed from left to right). In this respect, this pattern is the reverse of that found between the two positions of an onset cluster (although the precise distributional details of the two contexts are by no means mirror-images). Coda-onset clusters of this type include those consisting of a sonorant (liquid or nasal) followed by an obstruent, as in ⟨filter, dolphin, winter, fancy⟩. In a large number of languages with codas, this is in fact the only permissible pattern. Fricative-plosive clusters also display the falling shape, as in ⟨mister, biscuit⟩. The formulation in (42) also allows for consonants of equal sonority to occur in the coda-onset context, as in ⟨chapter, factor⟩.

Apparent counterexamples to (42) spring readily to mind, such as the obstruent-sonorant sequences in, for example, ⟨atlas, cutlass, athlete, kidney, atmosphere⟩. As with the sonority sequencing clause in (27), such evidence has confirmed some phonologists in the belief that the relations expressed in the sonority hierarchy are merely preferences rather than absolute universals. Once again, however, we should be wary of reaching too hasty a conclusion on this matter. Interpreting such cases as genuine counterexamples is based on the assumption that any internal consonant sequence not forming a branching onset automatically qualifies as a coda-onset sequence. This position is rarely if ever explicitly defended, and in chapter 4 I will argue that it is unfounded. Such obstruent-sonorant sequences, it can be shown, constitute bogus clusters; that is, the consonants in question are not truly adjacent and as such are not subject to the kind of systematic phonotactic restrictions that are evident in authentic coda-onset clusters. To anticipate the discussion, the position to be defended in chapter 4 is that the *θl* of, say, ⟨athlete⟩ is split by a nuclear position (which is audible in some dialects). That is, the alleged cluster is similar to the *θl* of, say, ⟨cath(o)lic⟩, where the intervening nucleus is optionally expressed. If this line of reasoning is sound, it follows that whatever representational principle it is that underlies the generalization in (42) can be maintained as a universal.

In true coda-onset clusters, the identity of the second consonant partially determines the identity of the first. This results in a number of distributional asymmetries, two of which we have already seen as being characteristic of this context. First, coda nasals cannot support a place contrast; they must be homorganic with the onset consonant. Second, the coda cannot be occupied by a coronal plosive (bearing in mind the comment just made on words such as ⟨kidney, cutlass⟩). A coda plosive of any kind is in fact only possible after a short vowel, and this is but one of a number of phonotactic restrictions which set VVC rhymes apart from VC rhymes. Thus although we can have, say, ⟨chapter, doctor⟩ with a short vowel, there are no occurrences of underived or root-level forms such as, say, *eyptər* or *owktər*. A further constraint is that, in a VC.CV sequence, a coda obstruent lacks a distinctive voice value, taking on instead the voice specification of the following obstruent; in the overwhelming number of cases such clusters are voiceless.[59]

Subject to these restrictions, the coda position after a short nucleus can be occupied by an oral stop (43a), a fricative (43b), a nasal (43c), or *l* (43d):

(43)	(a)	chapter	(b)	blister	(c)	pamper	(d)	shelter
		factor		whisker		winter		balcony
		doctor		whisper		anchor		children
				after		timber		dolphin
				wisdom		finger		
						fancy		

(An additional constraint restricts coda fricatives to *s*, *z* and *f*.) Forms containing historical *r* before an internal onset consonant (as in ⟨quarter, party, farthing⟩) line up with the VV. pattern in (41b). This is more obvious in the case of non-rhotic dialects, in which the *r* in question has been vocalized; the first rhyme of a form such as *paːti* ⟨party⟩ (originally *r*-ful) displays the same branching-nucleus structure as that in, say, *faːðə* ⟨father⟩ (in which the first rhyme is historically *r*-less). In rhotic dialects, the retained *r* in this context can be shown to occupy the second position of the branching nucleus. (More on this in chapter 5.) This means that, in these dialects too, forms such as ⟨party, quarter⟩ pattern with ⟨father, capon, booty⟩.

Compare the distributional array in (43) with that encountered in VVC rhymes. There are two basic patterns here: the coda is filled either by a fricative (as in ⟨oyster⟩) or by a sonorant (as in ⟨council⟩). As noted above, there is a bar on super-heavy rhymes containing a plosive coda. Many super-heavy sequences result from formerly short vowels having undergone various historical lengthenings, which have affected individual dialects to differing extents. In the following description, it will be necessary to distinguish those super-heavy forms which are firmly established throughout English from those with a more restricted geographical distribution.

The general pattern evident in sonorant-coda VVC rhymes is illustrated below:

(44) (a) launder   (b) shoulder
           saunter   cauldron
           ancient   boulder
           council   poultry
           danger

One observation we can make about forms of this type is that the onset following the super-heavy rhyme is almost invariably occupied by a coronal. Exceptions to this generalization are few and far between: ⟨chamber, cambric⟩, for example.[60] (To these can be added ⟨example, sample⟩ in those dialects with lengthened *aː* or *æː* in these forms.) Second, the consonant sequences in question are all of the **partial-geminate** type – homorganic sonorant-obstruent clusters. It is usually assumed that the place value of any kind of geminate consonant is distinctively specified in the onset and spreads into the preceding coda position.[61] This is illustrated in the following representation of ⟨dainty⟩ (where the italicized *N* stands for a nasal stop which acquires its place specification from the following oral stop):

(45) ⟨dainty⟩

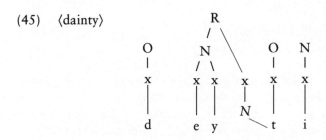

Only one of two fricatives can occur in the coda of a super-heavy rhyme: *s* or *f*. VV*f* rhymes are only found in dialects which show lengthened reflexes of historically short vowels (most usually only *æ*) in this context. Examples from southern English and derivative dialects include ⟨after, laughter, rafter⟩ with *aː*, *æː*, or some similar long vowel. A further restriction is that the following onset in such cases can only be occupied by *t*, something that is also true of coda *f* after a short nucleus (as in ⟨hefty⟩). Forms with a VV*s* rhyme are more widespread. Besides examples such as those in (46a), which occur in most if not all dialects, we also find cases such as those in (46b), but only in dialects that show the historical vowel-lengthening just described.

(46) (a) easter   (b) bastard
           oyster   caster
           pastry   basket
           boisterous   exasperate

Unlike in the majority of forms with sonorant-coda VVC rhymes, the onset following a VV*s* rhyme is not restricted to a coronal, as forms such as ⟨basket, exasperate⟩ with possible *aː/æː* indicate.

Let us now turn our attention to the constituent structure of word-final consonants and consonant clusters, traditionally assigned to codas. There are several
respects in which these sequences differ significantly from internal codas. Let us
briefly note two which will be discussed in more detail below.

First, unlike internal closed rhymes, a lone final consonant, irrespective of its
melodic content, tolerates a short–long contrast in a preceding nucleus:

(47)   VC]   lid, run, back, top, step, foot
       VVC]   slide, spoon, rake, soap, steep, boot

Since the supposed coda in a final (V)VC] sequence is not followed by an onset
within the same domain, we must consider it to be distinctively specified for all
melodic content, including the place dimension. This immediately sets it apart
from an internal coda, which, as we have seen, is subject to a variety of restrictions on the melody units it can contain.

A second noteworthy fact about word endings is that they display consonant
clusters which cannot occur within an internal rhyme. Some two-consonant
examples:

(48)   (a)   fact, apt, list, bend, help, find, old
       (b)   rungs, tipped, summed, likes, dames

It is the assumption that such clusters are exhaustively syllabified in the rhyme
that underlies the traditional claim in (23c) that the English coda can contain up
to four positions. Recall from our earlier discussion that the distributional discrepancy between medial and final clusters is bound up with the morphological
structure of the latter. Note that some 'over-weight' sequences, those illustrated
in (48b), involve an analytic morpheme boundary. As we have already established, the distributional independence of segments occurring either side of such
a boundary indicates that word-level derived forms fall outside the domain within
which the major systematic phonotactic constraints of English operate.

This point is particularly clear in the case of word-level derived forms where the
second of two morphemes begins with a consonant or consonant cluster followed
by a nucleus. This configuration obtains in compounds and suffixed forms with
⟨-hood, -ness, -ly⟩, etc. In such cases, it is uncontroversial to assume that the
morpheme-initial consonant occupies its own onset, rather than being syllabified
in the same constituent as the final segment of the preceding morpheme, e.g.
⟨spot.light, hat.rack, bad.ly, late.ness⟩. Assigning such trans-morphemic sequences to separate constituents is consistent with the phonotactic independence that
they display in relation to one another.

Rather less straightforward are consonant-only suffixes, in particular the *t–d*
and *s–z* alternants of ⟨-ed, -s⟩ illustrated in (48b). Apart from the voicing interaction which is responsible for the alternations, these suffixes exhibit the same
sort of phonotactic independence from the preceding stem-final segment as
analytic morphemes with vocalic content. The simplest interpretation of this

relative independence is to assume that ⟨-ed⟩ and ⟨-s⟩ are no more qualified to be syllabified in the same constituent as a preceding stem-final segment than other word-level suffixes are. Rather, a consonant-only suffix occurs in a separate constituent. (Exactly what that constituent is a question we will take up in 4.6.1.) However, the traditional view, which underlies the statement in (23c), has been that a final consonant of this type occupies a coda position incorporated in the same syllabic structure as the stem. This ignores the fact that such consonants fail to conform to otherwise general phonotactic constraints which are established independently of cross-morphemic contexts.[62]

As soon as we confine our attention to the domain in which systematic phonotactic constraints operate, i.e. to forms containing no analytic morphological structure, the distributional possibilities in word-final environments decrease considerably from those allowed for in (23c). The full set of sequence-types appearing in the final stressed portions of forms containing no analytic boundary is as follows:

(49)   2-position sequence
    (a) VV   day, so, see, pie
    (b) VC   pat, tip, den, gull
    3-position sequence
    (c) VVC   late, light, town, feat
    (d) VCC   fist, fact, desk, gulp
    4-position sequence
    (e) VVCC   paste, paint, rind
    (f) VCCC   text

(The absence of final stressed light V is due to an independent constraint operating in all Germanic languages, whereby a stressed nucleus in this position is required to branch. More on this in chapter 5.)

As an immediate consequence of excluding forms containing analytic morphological structure, the upward limit on final consonant clusters shrinks from the four positions allowed for in (23) to three. Four-term clusters invariably involve word-level suffixation, e.g. ⟨text-s, sixth-s⟩. As a further consequence of this narrowing of focus, we may observe that the number of final consonants is in part dependent on the quantity of the preceding nucleus. For example, three-consonant clusters only occur after a short nucleus, which means that a VVCCC sequence can never form part of a non-analytic domain. A sequence of this shape always indicates the presence of word-level suffixation, as in ⟨point-s, pounce-d⟩. As our investigation proceeds, it will become clear that the interdependence of nuclear quantity and the length of a following consonant cluster is actually more far-reaching than this. Although two-consonant sequences following a long nucleus do occur (as in (49e)), their distributional potential is considerably curtailed. By far the most favoured maximal final sequences are VVC (49c) and VCC (49d). In other words, the preferred maximal sequence preceding a final consonant is a heavy VX rhyme (where X represents either a nuclear or a coda position).

We have come across the configuration of a heavy rhyme followed by a final consonant before, but under different circumstances. Recall the extra-metrical status of final consonants in stress assignment; in verbs, for example, we saw how a heavy VV or VC rhyme preceding a final extra-metrical consonant attracts stress. The parallel between the stress and syllabification facts, which at first blush may seem rather odd, turns out under close inspection to be anything but coincidental.

The clusters which on the face of it present the most convincing evidence in favour of an independent coda constituent are the two- and three-consonant sequences in (49d, e, f). However, we will now consider evidence which indicates that, of all the clusters shown in (49), only (49a) is exhaustively syllabified in a rhyme. The absolute final consonant position illustrated in (49b) through (49f) can be shown to exhibit certain distributional peculiarities which are at odds with the notion that it forms part of a coda. We will start by considering how this point relates to the three-position sequences in (49c) and (49d).

If the word-final consonant of a V(V)C or VCC cluster were syllabified in coda position, it would be reasonable to expect it to display the same kind of distributional characteristics as morpheme-internal coda consonants. In fact, it does not. If anything, it behaves just like a morpheme-internal onset. One rather obvious respect in which the final consonant differs from an internal coda consonant is that the former is not constrained by the phonotactic dependency that the latter displays in relation to a following onset. For example, a nasal in an internal coda is dependent on the following onset consonant for its place specification. A word-final nasal, on the other hand, has its own distinctive place value (even though in the case of a coronal nasal this is optionally overridden by the place value of a following word-initial consonant, as in ⟨te[n → m] past⟩). Another distributional difference is that *t* can occur word-finally but not in an internal coda. In terms of distributional potential, the final position of a V(V)C or VCC sequence is in most respects identical to an internal onset; in both positions, we find a more or less full range of consonantal contrasts.

An even more striking parallel between final consonants and internal onsets relates to the manner in which both positions interact with the quantitative characteristics of a preceding nucleus. As illustrated in (47), it is a quite general characteristic of single word-final consonant positions that they are able to support a short–long contrast in a preceding nucleus; compare (49b) with (49c). In this respect, consonants in this position are identical to the internal onset consonants illustrated in (41a) and (41b). Moreover, a word-final consonant is able to support a preceding VC cluster in exactly the same way that an internal onset can; compare (49d) with (41c).

The failure of consonants in absolute word-final position to demonstrate coda-like behaviour has led many phonologists to the conclusion that they are not integrated into the preceding rhyme. Exactly what the syllabic status of such consonants is a matter of debate. One proposal is that final consonants are 'extra-

syllabic'.[63] That is, at least until some stage of derivation, they remain unsyllabi-fied. As it stands, the notion of extra-syllabicity contravenes a general principle of grammar whereby each unit in a representation is legitimized by virtue of belonging to some higher node in the linguistic hierarchy. (This is the notion of **licensing** on which much more in chapter 4.) It follows that the extra-syllabicity of a position can only be contingent; at some point in a derivation the position must become integrated into the phonological hierarchy in order for it to be phonetically expressed.[64] This integration, it has been proposed, involves attach-ing the extra-syllabic position to the coda of the preceding syllable. The result is a mismatch between the set of possible coda types defined as well-formed in lexical representations and a larger set legitimized in derived representations. (In chapter 4, we will assess the desirability of permitting a discrepancy of this type.)

The notion of extra-syllabicity obviously parallels that of extra-metricality. Each notion is motivated by an independent array of facts, relating to syllabifica-tion in the first instance and to stress assignment in the second. But, at least as far as the facts we have reviewed are concerned, the effect is the same – the separation of a word-final post-nuclear position from a preceding rhyme. This commonality has led to the two notions being subsumed under a more general dimension known as **extra-prosodicity.**[65]

However, there is at least one reason for rejecting the extra-syllabicity analysis: it makes wrong predictions about the phonotactics of final CC clusters. As depicted in the following VCC] structure, the independence of an extra-syllabic consonant (indicated by $\langle x \rangle_{es}$) from a preceding coda implies that the two posi-tions should be phonotactically independent:

(50)

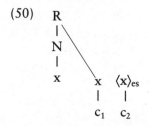

This is incorrect. There are very strict distributional dependencies operating in this context. And significantly they are more or less identical to those holding of internal VC.CV sequences. Compare the main distributional patterns that are evident in the two contexts:

(51)   Medial -C.C- and final -CC] clusters

Medial	Final		Medial	Final
	Stop-stop			**Sonorant-stop**
chapter	apt		pamper	damp
vector	sect		winter	flint
			filter	guilt
			wrinkle	rink
			scalpel	scalp
Stop-fricative			**Sonorant-fricative**	
mister	mist		cancer	manse
after	raft		dolphin	golf
whisper	wisp			
whisker	brisk			

The only distributional difference between the two contexts involves an independent development which bars the domain-final occurrence of *mb* and, in some dialects, *ŋg*. (See exercise 1 at the end of this chapter.) Thus we find medial *mb* in, say, ⟨clamber⟩ but not in, say, ⟨climb⟩ where the ⟨b⟩ corresponding to historical *b* is now silent.

We might try to formulate the phonotactic restrictions on the final clusters illustrated in (51) in terms of an interaction between an extra-syllabic position and a preceding coda. This would amount to treating extra-syllabicity as an independent constituent node. But distributional statements couched in these terms would simply duplicate statements relating to internal coda-onset clusters. The simplest solution is to assume that the distributional parallel reflects parallel constituent structures. In other words, the second C of a final -CC] cluster occupies an onset position in the same way as the second C of an internal -C.C- cluster. This means that a form such as ⟨mist⟩ is syllabified as *mis.t*, with the final *t* occurring as the onset of a 'degenerate syllable'.[66] Degeneracy here refers to the absence of an audible nucleus.

The immediate advantage of recognizing domain-final onsets is that it allows us to unify the statement of phonotactic restrictions on medial -C.C- and final -C.C] clusters. Both of these involve coda-onset interactions, as illustrated in the following representations of ⟨mister⟩ and ⟨mist⟩:[67]

(52)   (a)   (b)

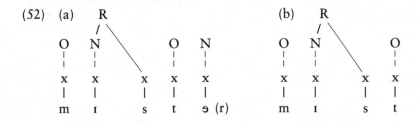

The representation in (52b) contains what might be termed a 'stray' onset – one that is not followed by a nucleus. However, as the discussion proceeds, it will become clear that an onset of this type requires support from a following silent nucleus.

Assigning the second position of a final -CC] cluster to an onset raises the question of whether this analysis should be extended to single final consonants, i.e. those occurring in -VC] and -VVC] sequences. Answering this question in the affirmative brings with it a number of advantages. First, we are able to explain why a single final consonant position enjoys a degree of distributional freedom that is similar or identical to that of an internal onset but is quite unlike the more restricted pattern associated with internal codas. Second, as we will now see, we are in a better position to account for the quantitative characteristics of final sequences.

The notion of degenerate syllable allows us to assign constituent structure to the four consonant-final sequences illustrated in (49b) through (49e) without adding to the set of rhyme-types given in (39). That is, we can dispense with the coda as an independent node without compromising the position that constituents are maximally binary branching. The set of rhyme-types preceding a final onset consonant is thus identical to the set encountered morpheme-internally. The difference between -VC] and -VVC] is now shown to be identical to that between medial -V.C- and -VV.C, illustrated in (41a,b). As shown in the following representations of ⟨am⟩ and ⟨aim⟩, the difference consists in a contrast between light and heavy rhymes preceding an onset:

(53)   (a)

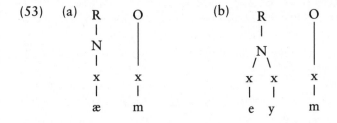

Note that, by replacing the notion of extra-syllabicity by the notion of degenerate syllable, we may also dispense with extra-metricality as an independent diacritic. As we saw in our brief survey of quantity-sensitivity in stress assignment (2.2.3), a final consonant in English (and indeed other languages) fails to contribute to the weight of a preceding rhyme. We now have additional reasons, quite independent of stress, for concluding that this consonant is not part of the preceding rhyme. The extra-metrical behaviour of this consonant is captured if we make the assumption that the degenerate syllable in which it occurs is not projected onto the level at which metrical relations are computed. As illustrated in (54), this means that a final consonant is ignored for the purposes of stress assignment. In (54a), the final *t* of ⟨lamént⟩ occurs in the onset of a degenerate syllable; the preceding rhyme *en*, being heavy, attracts stress.

(54)   (a)   R   (b)
                                                     |＼
              O   N   O   N   O   N   O   N   O
              | | | | ＼ | | | | |
              x   x   x   x   x   x   x   x   x   x
              | | | | | | | | | |
              l   ə   m   ɛ   m   t   ɛ   d   i   t

In ⟨édit⟩ (54b), on the other hand, the rhyme preceding the final onset *t* is light (occupied by the short vowel spelt ⟨i⟩) and thus fails to attract stress.

That is not say that final degenerate syllables are invariably invisible to metrical computation. In languages such as English, they happen to be. But in other languages they play a full role in stress assignment. In Spanish, for example, stress tends to fall on the penultimate syllable of a vowel-final word: ⟨sabána, pistóla, perdída⟩. However, it falls on the last vowel if the word ends in a consonant (unless the consonant represents a suffix): ⟨civíl, mercéd, altár⟩.[68] This can be captured as a unitary penultimate pattern if we assume that, in languages of this type, final degenerate syllables are projected metrically.[69] This supports the conclusion that a word-final onset is followed by a silent nucleus, which, in Spanish at least, is counted for stress purposes. (We will explore the notion of silent nuclei in a good deal more detail in chapter 4.) Thus a consonant-final form such as ⟨civíl⟩ (with a final silent nucleus) can be said to bear penultimate stress in the same way as ⟨sabána⟩ (with a final audible nucleus).

Turning now to the four-position final sequences illustrated in (49e) and (49f), we may note two quite different patterns. There is a very limited number of forms containing a plosive-*s* cluster, in apparent contravention of the sonority sequencing principle. Included in this class are ⟨text, coax, traipse⟩, which we will return to below. In the vast majority of cases, however, a final four-position sequence consists of a long nucleus followed either by a coronal partial geminate (as in ⟨paint⟩) or a fricative plus plosive (as in ⟨paste⟩). In other words, the configuration in question is pretty much identical to that encountered in medial VVC.C sequences of the type we find in, say, ⟨council, oyster⟩. The similarities between the medial and final contexts in this regard can be seen by comparing the partial-geminate forms in the two contexts (some of the medial examples repeated from (44) and (46)).

(55)

	Final	Medial
(a) VVnt	saint, mount, pint	fountain
(b) VVnd	rind, sound	flounder
(c) VVns	pounce, ounce	council
(d) VVnʒ	range, scrounge	angel
(e) VVlt	revolt, colt	poultry
(f) VVld	child, cold, field	shoulder

(56)

	Final	Medial
(a) VVst	paste, boast, boost	pastry
(b) (V)VsC	cast, clasp, cask	basket

The final partial-geminate forms are entirely restricted to coronals after VV. That is, there are no examples equivalent to the handful of labial partial geminates found medially after VV (⟨chamber, cambric⟩). We do not expect to find final VV*mb* forms in any event, in view of the independently attested bar on final *mb* clusters already alluded to. But the preference for coronality in post-VV partial geminates is rigidly enforced in final position. There are no forms of the shape *-u:mp* or *-eyŋk*.[70] (⟨Oink⟩ must be considered marginal.) As with the medial cases, coronality is also clearly favoured in final fricative-plosive clusters after VV (VV*s*C in (56)). VV*st* forms such as those in (56a) are the best established (although in some dialects final *t* has been lost in this context). Long-vowel forms such as those in (56b) are only found in dialects affected by the lengthening of historically short vowels already described. The effects of the latter development are most widespread in the case of historical *æ*, where we find lengthening not only before *st* but also before *sp* and *sk*, as the examples ⟨clasp, cask⟩ illustrate. But the change has extended to other vowels in various dialects, so that the VV*s*C class can include forms such as ⟨frost, cost⟩ (historically short *o*) and ⟨nest, desk⟩ (historically short *e*).

The final VVCC forms submit to exactly the same analysis as that proposed earlier for the medial VVC.C cases. That is, we have a super-heavy rhyme followed by an onset (in this case, the onset of a final degenerate syllable). The coronal place value of the partial geminate in, say, ⟨paint⟩ is distinctively specified in the onset *t* and spreads into the preceding nasal, just as in ⟨dainty⟩ (45).

The facts we have discussed so far in this survey of the English rhyme can be summarized as follows. As far as its gross typological outlines are concerned, we may note that all four of the structures depicted in (39) are attested. There is no evidence to support any of the branching-coda structures illustrated in (40). In other words, the coda portion of the rhymes contains at most one position. Moreover, these are restricted to contexts where they are followed by an onset. That is, there are good grounds for rejecting the traditional belief in the existence of word-final codas; a word-final consonant occurs instead in the onset of a degenerate syllable.

On the distributional side, the ability of the coda to support consonantal contrasts is severely curtailed, more so in the case of VVC rhymes than in VC. The restrictions on super-heavy rhymes can be summarized as follows:[71]

(57)   English super-heavy rhymes:

    (a)   The coda position is restricted to a sonorant or fricative.

    (b)   A coda sonorant is unable to support a distinctive place contrast.

    (c)   In the case of (b), the favoured place category determined by the following onset consonant is coronal.

Each of these stipulations refers to the nature of the melodic units that are permitted to occur in particular syllabic positions. We cannot say much more about them until we have had a chance to examine the internal make-up of segments in more detail in the next chapter. All we need note at this stage is that the constraints on the qualitative (place and manner) content of the coda reflect the general phonotactic dependency that exists between this position and the following onset in both heavy and super-heavy rhymes. Clause (57a) reflects the general applicability of Sonority Sequencing II (42) to all coda-onset contexts. Clauses (57b) and (57c) describe the preferred partial coronal geminate pattern found in coda-onset clusters after a branching nucleus.

It remains true, however, that nothing akin to the qualitative dependency between a coda and a following onset is to be observed between the coda and a preceding nucleus. That is, the quality of a coda consonant is largely independent of that of the preceding nucleus.[72] As noted in 2.4.3, this is one of the main motivations for recognizing an autonomous nuclear constituent in the first place. There is a quantitative relation between the nucleus and coda – the phenomenon of closed-syllable shortening mentioned in 1.4.2 and to be discussed in more detail immediately below. But the qualitative independence of the two sorts of position is demonstrated by the fact that, irrespective of the nature of the coda consonant, we find full sub-systems of short and long vowels in closed heavy and super-heavy rhymes respectively. The full set of six short stressed vowels (the system associated with southern English and derivative dialects) is illustrated in the closed heavy rhymes of, for example, ⟨filter, shelter, alp, halt, gulp, pulpit⟩.[73] The potential for the complete set of long vowels to occur in super-heavy rhymes is exemplified by ⟨east, paste, boast, boost, joust, heist, moist⟩ (to which we can add ⟨past⟩ in dialects with lengthened *a:* or *æ:*).

In short, the curtailed distributional potential of the coda is evidently due to a combination of two factors – the quality of the consonant in the following onset and the quantity of the preceding nucleus. In chapter 4, we will consider how these dependencies might be derived from general conditions governing the well-formedness of rhymes. For the present, we may further explore the interacting effects of these two factors by taking a closer look at **closed-syllable shortening**. This, recall, manifests itself in root-level alternations between long and short vowels in forms such as the following:[74]

(58)		(i)	(ii)
(a)	receive	receptive
	perceive	perception
	describe	descriptive
	reduce	reduction
	scribe	scripture
(b)	retain	retentive
	intervene	intervention
	five	fifty
	wise	wisdom

Note how the rightmost long vowel of the morphologically simple roots in column (58i) alternates with a short vowel in the internal closed rhymes of the suffixed forms in column (58ii). In accordance with the position argued for in 1.8, we may assume that the root-suffixed forms have non-analytic structure. That is, they are lexically listed forms which are not phonologically derived from the corresponding unsuffixed forms. Viewed in these terms, closed-syllable shortening is a purely static distributional regularity. The term **closed-rhyme shortness** is thus perhaps more appropriate. (The alternations exemplify several other root-specific phenomena, Vowel Shift and adjustments to the voice and manner properties of the root-final consonant, which are not directly relevant to the point at hand. Again on the basis of the arguments in 1.4.3, we may regard these as lexical matters.)

The forms in (58b), unlike those in (58a), contain partial geminates or coda fricatives. In these cases, the closed-rhyme shortness effect cannot be considered an automatic response to local conditions in the representation. This is because shortened forms of this shape co-exist with otherwise similarly structured forms such as ⟨dainty⟩ (see (44)) and ⟨easter⟩ (see (46)) which nevertheless display an unshortened super-heavy pattern. In contrast, the shortness effect in column (ii) of (58a) is an automatic consequence of the fact that the forms contain other than partial geminates or coda fricatives. That is, the conditions in (57) rule out forms with super-heavy rhymes such as *-ayp.t-, *u:k.t- and the like.

Were we to continue labouring under the misapprehension that a final consonant occupies a coda, we would be at a loss to explain why closed-rhyme shortness affects, say, ⟨receptive⟩ but not ⟨receive⟩. After all, the relevant nucleus, according to the coda view, supposedly occurs in a closed rhyme in both forms. On the other hand, by invoking the notion of final degenerate syllable, we are able to account for the immunity to closed-rhyme shortness displayed by ⟨receive⟩ and similar forms such as those in column (i) of (58a). In these cases, the final consonant occupies an onset, with the result that the preceding rhyme is open and its nucleus free to branch:

(59)

```
                            R
                            |
        O   N   O       R       O
        |   |   |      / \      |
        x   x   x     x   x     x
        |   |   |      \ /      |
        r   ɨ   s       i       v
```

Compare this with ⟨receptive⟩, where the root-final *p*, occurring word-medially, occupies a coda. Were the first nucleus of ⟨receptive⟩ to preserve the length it has in ⟨receive⟩, the result would be a medial super-heavy rhyme – something like *risi:ptiv. But the occurrence of the labial stop in the coda falls foul of the condition in (57a), with the result that such a form would be ungram- matical:[75]

(60)   *

```
                          R
                         / \
        O   N   O      N       \       O   N   O
        |   |   |     / \       \      |   |   |
        x   x   x    x   x       x     x   x   x
        |   |   |     \ /        |     |   |   |
        r   ɨ   s      i         p     t   ɨ   v
```

In the correct form *risɛptiv*, the vowel in the medial rhyme closed by *p* is short, resulting in a heavy rhyme, in which configuration the coda consonant is no longer subject to the conditions in (57):

(61)

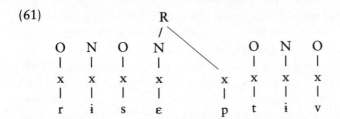

This outcome follows as an automatic consequence of the requirement that a super-heavy rhyme must satisfy the conditions in (57). Otherwise an upward limit of two positions is automatically imposed on the rhyme, thus producing the closed-rhyme shortness effect.

Closed-rhyme shortness is not confined to medial rhymes in English. As the following root-level alternations show, the same pattern also occurs in final -VCC] clusters:

(62) (a) keep   kept
         deep   depth
         wide   width
         leap   leapt
         sleep   slept
     (b) deal   dealt
         heal   health
         wide   width
         clean   cleanse
         leave   left
         thief   theft

As with the medial cases illustrated in (58), we cannot assume that shortness is automatic in forms such as those in (62b), since they contain partial geminates or a coda fricative (cf. the forms with super-heavy rhymes shown in (55)). In (62a), however, shortness is a direct consequence of condition (57a). Compare ⟨weep⟩, containing a root-final onset consonant preceded by a long nucleus, with ⟨wept⟩, in which the root-final consonant occupies a coda:

(63) (a)   (b)

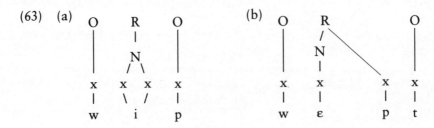

Under condition (57a), the coda *p* renders ill-formed the super-heavy rhyme that would result from the retention of the long nucleus; hence the short vowel in ⟨wept⟩.

In accordance with their root-level status, each of the alternants of the type shown in (62) constitutes a single phonological domain. This is reflected in the different syllabic affiliations of the root-final *p* in (63): it occupies a domain-final onset in ⟨weep⟩ (63a) but a domain-internal coda in ⟨wept⟩ (63b). Compare this with the form ⟨seeped⟩, which contains the regular word-level suffix ⟨-ed⟩.[76] Here we are dealing with two independent phonological domains, viz. [si:p] *t*]. That is, the *p* of ⟨seep⟩ remains domain-final irrespective of whether the form is inflected with a word-level suffix or not. This means that the consonant occurs consistently in the onset of a degenerate syllable, with the result that the preceding nucleus is free to branch in both ⟨seep⟩ and ⟨seeped⟩. (The syllabic affiliation of the word-level suffix consonant in such forms is something we take up in chapter 4.)

2.4.5 'Appendices'

The last set of word-final sequences to be discussed are those containing clusters of plosive followed by *s*, exemplified in (49f). The number of forms displaying this pattern after a long nucleus (or nucleus plus *r*) is extremely small: (64a) exhausts the set of apparently genuine examples. Rather more frequent are instances of this cluster following a short nucleus (64b). The occurrence of the same sequence followed by another consonant is limited to the -V*kst* string found in ⟨next, text⟩ and derivative forms of the latter (64c).

(64)   (a)   coax, hoax, traipse, corpse
         (b)   lapse, box, tax, eclipse
         (c)   next, text, context, pretext

The sonority profile of these C*s* clusters poses a problem for the view that the two consonants are adjacent in constituent structure. This is true regardless of whether adjacency is understood as co-occupancy of a coda, as under a traditional analysis, or as occurrence in a coda-onset cluster, as per the analysis developed in this chapter. In both instances, we have a contravention of the otherwise general principle of sonority sequencing: the final consonant is more sonorous than the one preceding it, not less as the principle would predict if they were co-constituents or formed a coda-onset cluster.

In recognition of the peculiar status of final *s* in consonant clusters, some phonologists have assigned it to an extra-syllabic margin or **appendix**.[77] It has been proposed that this position is directly integrated into the phonological hierarchy at word level, bypassing, as it were, intermediate levels of constituent structure such as the rhyme.[78] Whatever the precise status of this site might be, we should be careful to distinguish it from the position occupied by other consonants in final clusters. This slot, as we have noted, systematically behaves like an onset and, in English at least, is not subject to any major constraints on the type of melodic unit that can occupy it. This is in stark contrast to the defective distribution of the appendix. The exclusion of all but *s* from this site is puzzling, but it does at least contain a number of parallels with restrictions operating in certain other contexts. Let us briefly note two of these. It is a matter for future research to determine whether and how these parallels are to be accounted for in a unified way.

First, the appearance of *s* in domain-edge consonant clusters, in contravention of the otherwise general principle of sonority sequencing, is of course not restricted to word-final contexts. We have already discussed the similarly anomalous position it enjoys in word-initial clusters (see 2.4.2).

Second, in forms containing analytic morphological structure, over-weight segment strings can result from the juxtaposition of morphemes at word level. This means that underived forms terminating in *s* are phonologically indistinguishable from derived forms to which the *s* alternant of ⟨-s⟩ is attached. Compare the underived forms in (65a) with the suffixed forms in (65b).[79]

(65) (a) fix   (b) sticks
          box   locks
          lapse   laps
          hoax   folks
          traipse   apes

This relation between the appendix and word-level morphology provides one of the arguments for the claim that the appendix is integrated into the phonological hierarchy at the level of the word, rather than within a constituent such as the rhyme. Indeed many of the words in (64) derive historically from forms in which the appendix was clearly not adjacent to the preceding consonant, either because the terminal segment was an independent word-level suffix, or because the final two consonants were separated by a vowel which has since been syncopated. For example, ⟨coax⟩ is historically related to the plural form of an obsolete noun ⟨coke⟩ 'fool', ⟨hoax⟩ to ⟨hocus⟩, ⟨corpse⟩ to ⟨corpus⟩, and ⟨next⟩ to the superlative of a cognate of ⟨near⟩.[80]

2.4.6 The rhyme: summary

Summing up the evidence reviewed in the last two sections, we can say that a binary limit is imposed on the branching structure of English rhymes. As with onsets and nuclei, this conclusion is consistent with findings reported for other languages. We take this ability to branch as a reflection of the autonomous status of onsets, rhymes and nuclei as nodes in the phonological hierarchy. This conclusion removes any motivation for recognizing the coda as a constituent node in its own right. In other words, the term **coda** is no more than an informal label for a post-nuclear rhymal position, and this is the usage I will adopt throughout the rest of this book. In sum, only the four types of rhyme shown in (39) and repeated in (66) are possible.

(66) (a) light   (b) heavy   (c) heavy   (d) super-heavy

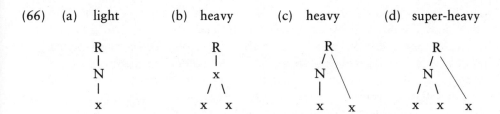

A light rhyme (66a) is composed of a single nuclear position. Of the two heavy types, one contains two nuclear positions (66b), the other a single nuclear position followed by a position directly dominated by the rhymal node (66c). The super-heavy type (66d), whose occurrence is constrained by the conditions in (57), consists of two nuclear slots followed by a single position directly dominated by the rhyme.

2.5 Syllabification

One question we have only briefly touched on is how strings of skeletal positions come to be associated with constituent structure. In this connection, we might ask whether constituent structure is already present in lexical representation or is constructed by some sort of syllabification algorithm. The very possibility of postulating general principles which regulate constituency, such as onset maximization and sonority sequencing, testifies to the fact that this aspect of representation is predictable in at least some respects.

The predictability of constituent structure has led some phonologists to assume that it is absent from underlying representations and is built by algorithm.[81] The latter incorporates universal principles of syllabification supplemented by language-specific constraints on the co-occurrence of different segment-types in different syllabic contexts (expressed, for example, in terms of minimum sonority distance). The algorithm typically begins by locating nuclei, in recognition of the pivotal status enjoyed by these constituents as obligatory heads of onset–rhyme pairs. In subsequently assigning non-nuclear positions to onsets and rhymes, the algorithm implements onset maximization by giving precedence to the former.

Under an alternative view, lexical representations redundantly contain syllable structure. Syllabification principles are then interpreted not as derivational processes but rather as well-formedness conditions on the structure of lexical representations.[82] According to one version of this approach, universal principles and language-particular phonotactic constraints together define for each language a set of syllable structure **templates**. The constituent structure of a given representation is then deemed well formed if it can be parsed in accordance with the templates.

Whichever of these views of syllabification is adopted, this much is clear: constituent structure must be established before forms are submitted to derivation. This conclusion is based on the observation that many types of phonological process are conditioned by aspects of constituency. In other words, constituent structure must either be present lexically, as assumed under the template approach, or be constructed 'first thing' before phonological processes proper come into operation. This point means that any pair of templatic and algorithmic accounts that incorporate the same general principles and language-specific constraints are probably no more than notational variants.

2.6 Summary

In this chapter, we have examined some of the evidence which indicates that segment strings are organized into constituents. The evidence involves the statement of (a) phonotactic dependencies; (b) suprasegmental patterns; and (c) the conditions under which certain types of phonological process occur. We have considered further arguments which lend support to the views that (a) there are only three constituent nodes, namely onset, nucleus and rhyme; and (b) a binary limit is uniformly imposed on the branching structure of constituents. Outsize segment clusters, which at first sight seem to contradict these conclusions, can be shown to dissolve into smaller sub-sequences, some of which are peculiar to word edges.

It would be extraordinary if the convergent behaviour of all three constituents with respect to the binarity of branching structure were purely accidental. In chapter 4, we will go on to consider whether this property might be derivable from some more general principle of grammar.

Another important issue is whether there is something in the nature of different sound-types that influences their ability to occur in particular constituent positions. To answer this question, we need to subject melodic units to an internal inspection – the task of the next chapter.

Exercises

1 English nasals

In 1.4.2, we briefly looked at the distribution of ŋ in English. Now we have the opportunity to undertake a more detailed analysis which also takes account of a related set of phenomena involving the other nasals.

The data The data below illustrate the realization of nasals and nasal-plus-plosive clusters in Scots and two types of English. The three systems are: the general southern pattern found in many parts of the English-speaking world (A); a pattern typically associated with the north and Midlands of England (B); and Scots (C).

Each of the data rows illustrates a particular combination of phonological and morphological environments. Where two or more nasals or nasal clusters appear in a word, the emboldened character instantiates the context illustrated by the row.

The task Provide a comparative phonological account of the three systems, and discuss the general theoretical issues that your analysis raises.

Questions relating specifically to this set of data include the following.

(a) What is the phonological distribution of *m, n* and *ŋ* in each of the systems?
(b) What role does constituent structure play in conditioning the distribution?
(c) What role does morphological structure play in conditioning the distribution?
(d) In regard to (b), what is the significance of the vowel-length facts outlined in IV?
(e) Is the velar nasal lexically distinctive?
(f) How should we treat the alternation between *g* and zero that is evident after *ŋ* in one of the systems?
(g) If your own system does not tally exactly with any of those represented here, construct your own data column, and work out precisely in what respects it differs from the others.

I CORONAL

	A	B	C	
1	n	n	n	need, nail, note
2	nd	nd	n	hand, send, wand
3	n	n	n	man, ten, sun
4	nt	nt	nt	rant, sent, flint
5	nd	nd	n	handle, bundle, thunder, cinder
6	n	n	n	funnel, money, spanner
7	nd	nd	n	sending, sender
8	nd	nd	n	kinder, blander

II LABIAL

	A	B	C	
1	m	m	m	more, met, mail
2	m	m	m	lamb, thumb, limb, dumb
3	m	m	m	sum, rim, ram
4	mp	mp	mp	pump, lamp, limp
5	mb	mb	m	thimble, tremble, number

6	m	m	m	plumber, lambing
7	m	m	m	dumber
8	m	m	m	summer, pumice

III VELAR

	A	B	C	
1	*	*	*	*Foot-initial position (* ŋiː, * bəŋét)*
2	ŋ	ŋg	ŋ	sing, sang, sung, strong, long, hang, hung, string
3	ŋk	ŋk	ŋk	sink, sank, sunk, thank, monk
4	ŋg	ŋg	ŋ	finger, bangle, single, hunger, linger, anger
5	ŋg	ŋg	ŋ	England, angry, hungry
6	ŋk	ŋk	ŋk	donkey, monkey, rankle, wrinkle
7	ŋ	ŋg	ŋ	banger, banging, singer, hanger, songster, stringer, longing
8	ŋg	ŋg	ŋ	longer, stronger

IV VOWEL LENGTH BEFORE NASALS

In all three systems, the contrast between long and short vowels holds before word-final *n* and *m*:

Systems A, B and C

Short	**Long**		**Short**	**Long**
fin	fine		dim	time
pen	vain		rum	plume
sun	moon		ram	same

Before word-final *ŋ(g)*, Systems A and B only ever show short vowels: e.g. ⟨sing, hang, lung⟩ but ** seyŋ(g)*, ** lawŋ(g)*, ** tiːŋ*. System C, on the other hand, maintains the short–long contrast in this context:

System C

Short	**Long**	
sung	*reːŋ*	('reign)
hang	*leːŋ*	('long')
sing	*kiːŋ*	('king')

2 Palatal glides in English

As briefly noted in 2.4.2, dialects of English vary according to whether or not they show a palatal glide in certain pre-vocalic environments. For example, ⟨new⟩ is pronounced as *nyuː* in some dialects, as *nuː* in others, and as *niw* in still others. In this exercise, we investigate the distribution of *y* in more detail.

The data Five different types of dialect are represented in the data below. System A is the standard pattern most closely associated with the south of England; B is widely represented in North America and parts of southern England; C includes most Scottish and Irish varieties; D is characteristic of vernacular usage in East Anglia; E is found in rural south Wales.[83]

The data illustrate the incidence of the palatal approximant (glide or vowel) in syllable-initial sequences consisting of one or two consonants followed by a long high back vowel. Each set of words illustrates a particular configuration of phonological conditions relating primarily to stress and the preceding consonantal context. Each of the five realizations given in each data-row records whether or not a palatal appears in that particular context and, where appropriate, identifies the preceding consonant. In several cases, a consonant-plus-*y* cluster in some dialects corresponds to a single palatalized reflex in others: *ty–č, dy–ǰ, hy–ç, sy–ʃ* (see data-rows 27, 29, 31, 36–9).

The task

(a) What is the contrastive potential of the palatal approximant in each of the systems?
(b) State the distribution of the palatal approximant in each of the systems, focusing on both segmental and stress conditions.
(c) Account for the palatalized consonants that appear in two of the systems.
(d) What issues arise in determining whether a pre-vocalic palatal approximant occurs in the onset or the nucleus?
(e) It is quite possible that you are familiar with a *y*-system that is not exactly like any of those represented here. In that case, using the word list provided, collect as much relevant data as you can, and reconsider the four questions above.

System

	A	B	C	D	E	
1	yuː	yuː	yuː	yuː	yuː	you, ewe, youth
2	myuː	myuː	myuː	muː	miw	music, mule, mew
3	muː	muː	muː	muː	muː	moon, moot
4	byuː	byuː	byuː	buː	biw	beautiful, bureau, abuse
5	buː	buː	buː	buː	buː	boon, booze
6	vyuː	vyuː	vyuː	vuː	viw	view, revue
7	vuː	vuː	vuː	vuː	vuː	voodoo
8	fyuː	fyuː	fyuː	fuː	fiw	few, futile, future
9	fuː	fuː	fuː	fuː	fuː	fool
10	pyuː	pyuː	pyuː	puː	piw	pew, pewter, spew

11	puː	puː	puː	puː	puː	pool, spoon
12	kyuː	kyuː	kyuː	kuː	kiw	cute, queue, cure
13	kuː	kuː	kuː	kuː	kuː	cool, coot
14	nyuː	nuː	nyuː	nuː	niw	new, continuity
15	nuː	nuː	nuː	nuː	nuː	noose, noon
16	lyuː	luː	luː	luː	liw	lewd, lieu
17	luː	luː	luː	luː	luː	loom, loose
18	ruː	ruː	ruː	ruː	riw	ruse, rue
19	ruː	ruː	ruː	ruː	ruː	Ruth, root
20	syuː	suː	suː	suː	siw	assume, pursuit
21	suː	suː	suː	suː	siw	suicide, suit, sue
22	suː	suː	suː	suː	suː	soon, soothe
23	zyuː	zuː	zuː	zuː	ziw	presume, Zeus
24	zuː	zuː	zuː	zuː	zuː	zoom, zoo
25	θyuː	θuː	θuː	θuː	θiw	enthuse
26	θuː	θuː	θuː	θuː	θuː	thuja
27	tyuː	tuː	čuː	tuː	tiw	Tuesday, perpetuity
28	tuː	tuː	tuː	tuː	tuː	too, tool
29	dyuː	duː	ǰuː	duː	diw	dew, duty, during
30	duː	duː	duː	duː	duː	doom, do
31	hyuː	yuː	çuː	uː	hiw	huge, Hugh
32	huː	huː	huː	uː	huː	who, hoot
33	nyuː	nyuː	nyuː	nuː	niw	continue, annual
34	lyuː	lyuː	lyuː	luː	liw	value, volume
35	ryuː	ryuː	rə	ruː	rə	erudite, virulent
36	syuː	ʃuː	ʃuː	suː	ʃiw	issue, tissue
37	tyuː	čuː	čuː	tuː	čiw	virtue, perpetual
38	dyuː	ǰuː	ǰuː	duː	diw	residual, incredulous
39	dyuː	duː	ǰuː	duː	diw	residue
40	pruː	pruː	pruː	pruː	priw	prude, prune
41	pruː	pruː	pruː	pruː	pruː	proof
42	pluː	pluː	pluː	pluː	pliw	pleurisy
43	pluː	pluː	pluː	pluː	pluː	plume
44	bluː	bluː	bluː	bluː	bliw	blew
45	bluː	bluː	bluː	bluː	bluː	blue
46	bruː	bruː	bruː	bruː	briw	bruise, brewed
47	bruː	bruː	bruː	bruː	bruː	brood
48	truː	truː	truː	truː	triw	truant
49	truː	truː	truː	truː	truː	troop, true
50	druː	druː	druː	druː	driw	drew

51	druː	druː	druː	druː	druː	droop
52	kruː	kruː	kruː	kruː	kriw	crew
53	kruː	kruː	kruː	kruː	kruː	croon
54	kluː	kluː	kluː	kluː	kliw	clue, include
55	gruː	gruː	gruː	gruː	griw	grew
56	gruː	gruː	gruː	gruː	gruː	groom
57	fruː	fruː	fruː	fruː	friw	fruit, frugal
58	fluː	fluː	fluː	fluː	fliw	flew
59	fluː	fluː	fluː	fluː	fluː	flu
60	θruː	θruː	θruː	θruː	θriw	threw
61	θruː	θruː	θruː	θruː	θruː	through

3 Melody

3.1 Introduction

A major goal of phonological theory is to provide a model of the set of possible
processes to which sounds may be subject. One aspect of this task is to specify
where processes occur; this was a theme which we touched on in the last chapter
and which we will return to in the next. Another aspect concerns **what** can happen
to a sound, the topic to be discussed in this chapter. Clearly, the answer to this
question depends to a large extent on what we take to be the set of primitive
operations in phonological processing. It also crucially depends on what we
consider the internal composition of a sound to be and how this influences its
susceptibility to processing.

3.2 The primes of melodic representation

3.2.1 Sounds are componential

So far in this book, units on the melody tier have appeared as phonemic-
alphabetic symbols attached to slots in the skeletal tier. This is not supposed to
imply that melody units are indissoluble entities. Rather, the symbols are no more
than convenient shorthand for phonological expressions, each of which is decomposable into smaller components. In this chapter, we will consider how these
components can be identified and how they are organized within melodic expressions. Responses to the more specific questions raised by these issues range from
those on which there is near-universal agreement among phonologists to those
which continue to be the subject of lively debate. Let us begin by staking out the
common ground.

First, as just indicated, segments are decomposable into components which
constitute the primes of melodic representation. These are most widely known as
features, although they are also referred to by such terms as **elements, gestures**
and **particles.**[1] One of the most convincing pieces of evidence in favour of this
view is that sounds pattern into non-random sets, known as **natural classes**, with
respect to their participation in phonological processes. The unified behaviour of

a given natural class is explicable if it is assumed that the members of that class share a particular property. The number of overlapping natural classes to which a particular sound belongs thus provides an indication of the number of distinct properties of which it is composed.

Second, the set of primes is universal and comparatively small. According to the literature, the going rate is somewhere between eight and twenty, although there have been attempts to reduce components to combinations of even more fundamental atoms.[2] The set of primes is initially established on the basis of phonological evidence, relating primarily to the participation of sounds in processes and their organization into systems. From this evidence emerge patterns which recur with such massive regularity across different languages that it is difficult to avoid the conclusion that melodic substance, no less than other aspects of linguistic organization, is rooted in a genetic endowment that is common to all humans. It is a matter of ongoing research to determine exactly how much of this substance should be attributed to universals of physiology, reflecting constraints imposed by vocal and auditory anatomy, and how much to general cognitive or specifically linguistic universals. What is beyond dispute amongst those committed to this programme is that melodic primes have relatively stable interpretations in articulation, the acoustic signal and audition. This remains true even if the mapping between primes and their phonetic exponents is not always direct.

Of course, it is always possible to profess a lack of interest in the phonetic and psychological dimensions of melodic content, in which case primes are treated as purely abstract mathematical constructs whose only function is to classify phonological contrasts in particular systems.[3] However, the impact that Platonist views such as this have had on the recent development of phonological theory (and linguistic theory in general) has been minimal.

Third, phonological substance consists of two quite different types of information, each of which requires its own independent mode of representation. As we saw in the last chapter, relational aspects of a representation, involving such details as quantity, syllabicity and stress, are encoded in terms of skeletal and constituent structure. On the other hand, the strictly componential aspect of a segment's representation, comprising those attributes that have a comparatively stable phonetic interpretation, is deployed on a separate plane devoted to melodic content.

So much for the issues on which there is broad agreement within the phonological community. Beyond this point, opinions differ to varying extents. Let us now consider some of the more significant moot points.

3.2.2 *Privativeness vs. equipollence*

Each melodic prime defines a bifurcation of segments.[4] One source of disagreement is the question of whether the two classes produced by a given bifurcation are of equal status. To make the matter more concrete, take a pair of segments that are minimally distinct; that is, they are identical in all respects save in relation to a single prime. In such a situation, does one segment possess the prime in question while the other lacks it? If so, we are dealing with what is known as a **privative opposition**. Or is it a question of both segments possessing the prime and differing in terms of the value they assign to it? If this is the case, there is a further question regarding the range of values that the prime may assume. According to one view, there are two values (usually expressed in terms of plus versus minus); that is, primes define **equipollent** oppositions. According to another view, the coefficient associated with a prime varies along a scale of three or more values. The scalar mode, if recognized at all, is usually assumed to be confined to the level of phonetic implementation and to be inappropriate for expressing the bifurcations into natural classes that characterize phonological distinctions. The issue thus boils down to the question of whether phonological oppositions are privative or equipollent.

The tradition that at least some oppositions are privative goes back to the Prague School linguists (to whom we owe the terms **privative** and **equipollent**) and has continued in various theoretical guises up to the present day.[5] By contrast, the position adopted in SPE is that distinctions are uniformly expressed in terms of equipollent features. More recent incarnations of feature theory, however, have shifted in the direction of privativeness.[6]

The distinction between the equipollent and privative formats is not a trivial one. They differ quite clearly in terms of their empirical content. Consider again the case of a minimal distinction, in which a single prime divides sounds into two classes. Equipollence implies that the classes should behave symmetrically. That is, as the term indicates, the two poles of the opposition are predicted to stand an equal chance of being accessed by phonological processes involving that particular prime. Coupled to a rule-based treatment of processes, this arrangement greatly multiplies the number of possible processes defined by the theory.[7] Take for instance a situation in which a two-valued feature such as [±round] is deemed to be active in vowel harmony. Equipollence generates at least two types of system: one in which [+round] is active and another in which [−round] is active. Indeed it generates a third system, one in which both values are active. Unfortunately, this tripartite prediction fails to correspond to the observation that one value of each two-valued feature is universally preferred. (In the case of [±round], it is the plus value.)

Early recognition of the asymmetries that are to be observed in the phonological behaviour of features helped spur the development of the theory of markedness, touched on in 1.3.2.[8] In any given opposition, one of the terms is unmarked in the sense that it is universally preferred. This preference manifests itself in various ways: for example, the unmarked term is more widely distributed throughout the phonological systems of the world's languages; the presence in a given system of the marked term implies the presence of the unmarked one, but not vice versa; and in systems possessing both terms, it is the unmarked one that appears first during the course of child language acquisition. According to the SPE interpretation of this notion, Universal Grammar contains statements to the effect that certain feature specifications are unmarked. The fewer the marked values that a rule incorporates, the more highly valued it is adjudged to be.

In a recent descendant of this theory, segments in lexical representation are **underspecified,** in the sense that they contain only a subset of the feature values they display in phonetic representation.[9] The default case is for unmarked feature values to be left blank underlyingly and to be filled in by **redundancy rules,** some or all of which are universal. However, in one version of this theory, individual languages are free to select either the marked or the unmarked value as being lexically distinctive for a particular feature.[10] The potential for overriding universal markedness conventions in this way means that the set of possible processes defined by the theory remains comparatively large. What markedness statements and underspecification tell us is that the possibilities are unequal. The generative capacity of the model further snowballs as a result of allowing redundancy rules to be ordered in various ways in relation to rules which characterize phonological processes.

The set of markedness conventions constitutes an independent look-up table against which the values of individual features are gauged. A more radical alternative is to build markedness relations directly into phonological representations. This notion can be implemented quite straightforwardly within a framework in which phonological oppositions are uniformly privative. Privativeness implies an asymmetry in the phonological behaviour of a pair of segment classes that are distinguished by the presence versus absence of a particular prime. Only the class possessing the prime can participate in a process involving that prime. There can be no complementary process involving the class which lacks the prime in question. This conclusion is based on the premise that phonological processes can only access what is present in a representation.

This arrangement has the potential for greatly reducing the set of possible processes defined by the theory.[11] Take for example the case of labial harmony just alluded to. Let us assume for the sake of argument that the equipollent feature [±round] corresponds to a single privative prime [round], which is present in round vowels and absent from non-round vowels. While the equipollent feature predicts the three harmony patterns mentioned above, the privative prime predicts only one system, namely one in which [round] is active. Within a strictly privative framework, there is no way of expressing a complementary system in which 'absence-of-[round]' is harmonically active. Any attempt to introduce a negation operator (such as ~[round], 'not-[round]') immediately reclassifies the framework as equipollent.[12]

All other things being equal (in particular, assuming an equal number of primes), a privative model of phonological oppositions is more constrained than one based on equipollence. A priori, this would lead us to favour the former over the latter – provided of course that the privative model can be shown to be observationally adequate. Potential counterevidence to the more restrictive model comes in the form of any equipollent analysis which incorporates a rule containing a feature value for which there is no direct privative equivalent. And it has to be acknowledged that such accounts are myriad, given the almost unchallenged ascendancy that the equipollent view enjoyed during a period which included the publication of SPE. In some cases, such examples can be straightforwardly reanalysed in terms of the opposite feature value. In other words, they turn out not to constitute counterevidence at all but rather reflect one of the recurring problems that is symptomatic of over-generation – the possibility of analysing a single phenomenon in more than one way. Nevertheless, there no doubt exists a corpus of more robust equipollent accounts that need to be reassessed on a case-by-case basis.

3.2.3 Phonetic interpretation

The position adopted with respect to privativeness versus equipollence has an indirect bearing on another important representational question: does each prime enjoy independent phonetic interpretability?[13] In the case of orthodox features, the answer is no. Although each feature is taken to have its own stable phonetic signature, this cannot actually manifest itself unless it is harnessed to those of other features. For example, a [+high] segment cannot be concretely realized as such unless it also includes a slate of feature specifications (some distinctive, others redundant) such as [–back], [–round] and [–consonantal], in which case it surfaces as a palatal approximant. In combination with other specifications, [+high] can show up in, say, *u*, *k*, *x* or *ç*. This arrangement, when coupled to the underspecification view briefly outlined above, has the consequence that segments are not fully interpretable until all redundant features are filled in.

In SPE, all lexically blank specifications were filled in immediately prior to the entry of forms into phonological derivation. One objection to this proposal is that it results in redundant feature values being carried through derivation even though, in most cases, they fail to participate actively in phonological processes and do no more than clutter up the formulation of rules. Take for example a language in which the feature [round] is non-contrastive; all front vowels are non-round and all non-low back vowels are round. Say the language has a rule which fronts *u* to *i*. Fronting is represented as [+back] → [–back], which on its own yields **ü*. So there has to be an additional 'clean-up' rule which adjusts [round] from plus to minus (to give **ü* → *i*) even though this feature is redundant.[14]

In response to this objection, more recent versions of feature theory allow for redundant values to be underlyingly unspecified and to remain suppressed until later stages of derivation. The redundancy rules which fill in missing values are interspersed among the phonological rules proper. The result is that segments are not phonetically interpretable until the final stage of derivation, the level sometimes known as **systematic phonetic representation**.[15]

Three remarks about the implications of the underspecification approach are in order here. First, allowing redundancy rules to be intercalated among phonological rules, it has been claimed, is justified on the grounds that the same feature value can be shown to be active at different stages of derivation in different grammars. However, as already noted, the multiplicity of possible rule orderings that this arrangement permits grossly inflates the expressive power of the theory.

Second, one of the original motives behind the postulation of redundancy-free lexical representations seems to have been the assumption that long-term memory constraints compel speakers to confine storage to idiosyncratic information and to maximize the rule-based computation of predictable information.[16] The psycholinguistic validity of this idea has never been seriously defended. In fact, the notion implies a model of lexical access which is not particularly plausible. Economizing on the amount of phonological information contained in lexical representations would incur a significant computational cost to the speaker or hearer: it would greatly add to the amount of work that has to be done when forms are retrieved from the lexicon.[17] Before the underspecified form of a lexical entry could be submitted to articulation or recognition, it would first have to be unpacked by having its missing feature values filled in.

Third, underlying this arrangement is the assumption that the main *raison d'être* of the phonological component is to convert abstract underlying representations into ever more concrete phonetic ones. The mismatch between the underlying and systematic phonetic levels has sometimes been justified on the grounds that they allegedly perform quite different roles: the former serves the function of memory and lexical storage, while the latter supposedly serves as input to articulation and perception. According to one interpretation of this notion, the derivation of phonetic forms occurs 'on line' – that is, as the speaker is articulating or the listener decoding a particular utterance.[18] This view places the phonological component outside the domain of generative grammar proper, at least if we understand this in the usual sense of a model of internalized linguistic knowledge which exists independently of its performance. It is not simply a matter of the systematic phonetic level constituting a buffer between internalized phonological competence and its articulatory or perceptual externalization. Under this view, the phonological component as a whole is designed to carry out the essentially extra-grammatical task of assembling phonetic forms for production or reception on particular occasions.

Compare this performance-centred view with one in which phonology remains wholly rooted in the domain of linguistic competence. To be consistent with the latter notion, phonological derivation should do no more than capture generalizations governing alternations and distributional regularities. This task can be performed quite independently of any provision that needs to be made for articulation and perception. Conceived of in this way, derivation is strictly generative in the sense that it does no more than define a set of well-formed phonological representations. Processes map phonological objects onto other phonological objects, rather than onto phonetic ones.

So where does phonetic interpretation fit into this scheme? If processes map like onto like, it follows that one phonological representation should be no more or less interpretable than another. As a result, an initial representation cannot be considered any less phonetically interpretable or 'concrete' than a final representation. Such an arrangement is of course incompatible with the notion that non-final representations are underspecified and thus not directly interpretable. What is evidently called for is a conception of melodic form according to which segments are phonetically interpretable at all levels of derivation. This might seem to imply a return to the SPE notion of full feature specification throughout derivation – and a reprise of the problem whereby superfluous feature values make unwelcome appearances in the statement of phonological processes. However, we are only forced into that corner, if we persist in a long-held belief of feature theory – that the smallest phonological unit capable of independent phonetic interpretation is the segment. A corollary of this view is the idea that subsegmental status deprives each feature of the ability to be interpretable without support from other features occurring within the same segment.

This is in fact not a necessary conclusion at all. It is perfectly possible to conceive of a phonological prime as being 'small' enough to fit inside a segment and yet 'big' enough to enjoy stand-alone phonetic interpretability. For example, one such prime that is widely assumed in privative approaches is independently manifested as *a*. Another is interpreted as *i*. The ability of each of these primes to be made phonetically manifest is not contingent on its being combined with other primes. That is, *a* and *i* may be viewed in some sense as 'primitive' segments; each is composed of a single prime and is thus the direct phonetic embodiment of that particular prime.[19] Nevertheless, primes of this type can be combined to form compound or non-primitive segments. Amalgamating *a*'s and *i*'s primes, as we will see in the next section, yields *e*. Conceived of in these terms, primes are appropriately labelled **elements**.[20] The analogy with physical matter is apt, in view of the ability of each element both to exist independently and to enter into compounds with other elements.

This view of melodic form has the desired consequence that segments are phonetically interpretable at any level of derivation. Within a framework such as this, there is nothing resembling feature underspecification and thus nothing akin to blank-filling operations of the type that can be ordered in relation to phonological processes. Since phonological representations uniformly adhere to the principle of full phonetic interpretability, there is no motivation for recognizing an autonomous level of systematic phonetic representation. Any phonological representation at any level of derivation can be directly submitted to articulatory or perceptual interpretation. Derivation is thus not an operation by means of which abstract phonological objects are transformed into increasingly concrete physical objects. Rather it is a strictly generative function which defines the grammaticality of phonological strings.

The representational model just sketched is the one to be expanded on in the remainder of this chapter. It takes the following stances on the issues raised in the foregoing discussion. Melodic expressions are decomposable into a relatively small set of elements, which are uniformly privative and have stable and independent phonetic exponence. This type of approach is restrictive in the following respects. Relative to an equipollent framework which posits the same number of primes, privativeness narrows the set of segment classes that are potentially active in phonological processing. The principle of full phonetic interpretability excludes the multiple orderings that are possible in a model in which segments are only partially specified and in which redundancy rules are interpolated among phonological processes.

A continuing research task is to demonstrate that the observed facts of phonological systems can be accommodated within this more constrained model. The
methodological orientation is the minimalist one outlined in 1.3.2: start with an
available model which generates a relatively small set of possibilities, and identify
as research problems those areas where it apparently under-generates. This is in
preference to an orientation which starts with an over-generating model and
supplements it with constraints (such as markedness conventions) designed to
filter out or disfavour possibilities that fail to be confirmed by observation.

3.3 Elements for vowels

3.3.1 A, I, U

In different privative approaches, there is broad agreement on three elements
which are considered to play a pivotal role in the representation of vowels. The
independent phonetic exponents of these elements are the three 'corner' vowels *a*,
i and *u*.[21] I will adopt one established practice of symbolizing these elements as **A**,
I and **U** respectively:

(1)   Element   Independent interpretation
          A   a
          I   i
          U   u

Any given vowel is composed either of a single element (a simplex expression) or
of a **fusion** of two or more elements (a compound).[22] For example, fusing **A** with
I results in *e*; fusing **A** with **U** yields *o*. Informally, we may think of the addition
of **A** as creating a more open version of a vowel defined by either **I** or **U**. Or: **A**, **I**
and **U** represent primary colours which, when mixed, yield such secondary
colours as *e* and *o*.

The combinatorial possibilities of the elements **A**, **I** and **U**, occurring either
singly or in two-element compounds, yield the six melodic expressions shown in
(2) (*ü* is a close front round vowel).

(2)   Simplex   Compound
          a   [**A**]   e   [**A, I**]
          i   [**I**]   o   [**A, U**]
          u   [**U**]   ü   [**U, I**]

The sound defined by the three-element compound [**A, I, U**] may be thought of as
a rounded version of *e*; in other words, it is *ø*. It will be necessary to refine the
notion of fusion and to recognize further elements, in order to derive other
dimensions of vocalic contrast, including nasality and tenseness (the latter involved in the representation of distinctions such as *i*/ɪ, *u*/ʊ, *e*/ɛ and *o*/ɔ).

Let us examine some of the main phonological arguments that support the postulation of **A, I** and **U**. One important source of evidence used in determining the set of melodic primitives is the behaviour of sounds when they are subject to phonological processing. The reasoning is that, when it moves, a sound reveals its stripes. In order to be in a position to interpret evidence of this sort, we need to have a clear idea of the set of possible processes to which a sound is potentially subject. One of the most significant developments in modern phonological theory, discussed in 1.3, is a move away from the open-ended model of phonological processing that is inherent in orthodox rewrite rules. In its place has evolved a more restrictive theory in which all processes are reduced as far as possible to two fundamental operations, which may be characterized as **composition** and **decomposition**.[23] Composition processes result in the fusion of melodic material. Decomposition involves **fission**, the operation by which the fusion of elements within an expression is undone. Fission may or may not be accompanied by the suppression of all or part of the melodic material that is lexically specified in a particular position. This view of phonological activity can be further constrained by insisting that processes of composition must have a local cause. That is, they involve melodic material lodged in one position being fused with melodic material lodged in a neighbouring position.

Limiting all phonological activity to these two basic operations has the potential for excluding a significant class of non-occurring process-types that are readily expressible in terms of traditional rewrite rules. For example, it forbids in principle the random substitution of one piece of melodic material by another, something that can easily be accommodated in the input and output portions of a rewrite rule. Rather, the introduction of any melodic material into a position must have some local source; that is, it must propagate from an adjacent position. (In 3.3.5 we will consider a very limited class of cases in which, at least on the basis of our present understanding, it seems necessary to relax this principle.)

This view of phonological processing becomes even more restrictive when coupled to a uniformly privative model of phonological distinctions. The two lines of thinking come together to place a strict limit on the number of processes a sound can undergo. In particular, the set of decomposition processes to which a sound is susceptible is logically limited by the number of elements of which it is composed. Moreover, as we observe a sound breaking up under fission, we are privy to aspects of its melodic identity that might otherwise have remained concealed. Conceiving of phonological processes in these terms helps us identify what the individual elements are.

Various types of process provide insights into the fusion of elements within vocalic compound expressions, including raising, lowering, diphthongization, monophthongization and coalescence. These constitute a sizeable portion of the recurrent processes that affect vowels and can be straightforwardly characterized in terms of operations involving the elements **A, I** and **U**. Many of the examples of such processes to be reviewed below involve historical changes which in some form or another have left their mark on Modern English. Not all of these, however, remain active as processes in the present-day language. That is, although the input and output stages of a change may co-exist in the same lexicon as etymologically related reflexes, this is no guarantee that they continue to be derivationally linked through some phonological process. For reasons outlined in 1.4.3, this is particularly true of the procession of historical raisings and diphthongizations, collectively known as the Great Vowel Shift, which have affected long nuclei.[24]

Nevertheless, though now phonologically extinct, the individual stages of this particular series are observed to have active counterparts in other languages. Moreover, as we will see, some of the changes are now in the of act of being reprised in English (although affecting a fresh slate of word classes), with successive developments showing up as different phonological variants in different present-day dialects.

Coalescence involves the mutual assimilation of pairs of adjacent sounds. A recurrent pattern in vowel coalescence produces *e* and *o* from the sequences *a-i* and *a-u* respectively. This can be seen in Zulu, for instance, where the attachment of the proclitic *na-* ('and, with') to a vowel-initial noun yields alternations such as *na-inkosi* → *nenkosi* ('and the chief') and *na-umuntu* → *nomuntu* ('and the person').

A similar effect manifests itself in the type of historical monophthongization by which the Early Modern English diphthongs *ay*, and *aw*, developed into ɛː and ɔː respectively.[25] I will adopt the practice of identifying the class of words containing a particular vowel sound by means of a representative head-word, printed in capitals. In this example, as shown in (3), the relevant word classes are BAIT and CAUGHT. The extent of these classes in Early Modern English can be roughly determined on the basis of their spelling. Words in the original BAIT set are generally spelt with ⟨ai⟩ or ⟨ay⟩, for example ⟨bait, maid, day, stay⟩. The spelling of CAUGHT-class words includes ⟨au, aw, augh, ough, all⟩, as in ⟨taut, trawl, caught, bought, call⟩.

(3) Earlier > later English
     ay > ɛː   BAIT
     aw > ɔː   CAUGHT

The type of process illustrated in (3) is straightforwardly expressible as the compacting of sequentially ordered elements into a single melodic expression. The first portion of the diphthongs *ay* and *aw* consists of a skeletal position occupied by **A**; the second portion consists of a position occupied by an off-glide represented by **I** (= *y*) or **U** (= *w*). As depicted in (4), the fusion of these elements results in a long mid-monophthong – that is, a single vocalic expression attached to two positions:

(4) (a)   ay > ɛː   (b)   aw > ɔː

Later in its history, the front monophthongal outcome of the process shown in (4a) underwent merger with *e:* (the latter occurring in the MATE class, including words such as ⟨make, fate, same, tale⟩). This vowel and its back congener *o:* (BOAT, as in ⟨boat, home, go, road⟩) then became subject to a series of diphthongization changes, the results of which show up as different reflexes in different present-day dialects. The principal developments are the following:

(5)   e: >   ey   >   ay   BAIT = MATE
      o: >   ow   >   aw   BOAT

The original mid monophthongal reflexes are retained in some dialects spoken in Scotland, Ireland and parts of England (principally the North and the West). The most widespread subsequent development has been diphthongization to *ey* and *ow*. In the southeast of England, this process has proceeded as far as *ay* and *aw*, the former also showing up in the southern hemisphere.[26]

Representationally speaking, the diphthongizations in (5), examples of which could be furnished from any number of languages, are simply the converse of the monophthongization processes shown in (4). They can be directly expressed in terms of fission, the linear unpacking of a previously fused structure. As shown in (6a), diphthongization of *e:* to *ay* takes the form of a fission of the elements **A** and **I**. The lone association of **I** to the second position of the nucleus defines the palatal off-glide of the diphthong.

(6)   (a)   e: > ay   (b)   o: > aw

                N   N   N   N
               / \   / \   / \   / \
              x x   >   x x   x x   >   x x
               \ / | \ / |
              ⎡I⎤   [I]   ⎡U⎤   [U]
              ⎣A⎦   ⎣A⎦

                          [A]   [A]

As shown in (6b), the development of *o:* to *aw* is expressed in parallel fashion.

3.3.3 Autosegmental representations

The task of representing the intermediate developments in (5), *e:* to *ey* and *o:* to *ow*, raises an important question about the organization of elements within melodic expressions. Up to now, I have been depicting compound expressions as matrices of elements with no internal structure. As briefly discussed in 1.3.2, this is essentially the format assumed in SPE-style linear representations. It is now acknowledged, however, that this mode of representation is inappropriate, since it fails to give expression to an important characteristic of primes – a propensity to behave independently of one another under phonological processing. In the western phonological tradition, the formal implementation of this insight dates back at least to the 1940s.[27] Its adoption within generative phonology began in the 1970s, since when it has become widely accepted that primes are arrayed on separate tiers, rather than being lumped together in unordered bundles. Within this arrangement, each prime is capable of behaving as an autonomous segment; hence the term **autosegmental** used to describe this aspect of non-linearity.[28]

In the last chapter, we examined evidence supporting the dissection of phonological representations into skeletal and melodic planes. The autosegmental insight is that the melodic plane itself is split into a series of sub-tiers, each of which is occupied by a particular prime. For the time being, we may assume that association lines, which synchronize material on the melodic and skeletal levels, supply a direct link between each prime and a position. In this 'bottle-brush' mode of representation, a melodic expression comprises a three-dimensional configuration of associations to particular elements:[29]

(7)

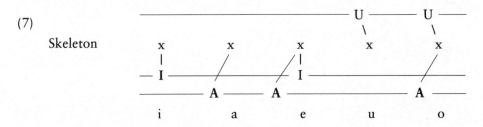

Employed in this way, the function of association lines is to indicate that a particular element is co-indexed with a particular skeletal point. The slope of the lines in (7) simply reflects the constraints of representing a three-dimensional object on a two-dimensional page. It is not meant to imply a relation of precedence between elements that are co-registered with the same skeletal slot. (The representation of contour segments calls for certain notational refinements, to be introduced later. As discussed in 2.2.3, contour segments such as affricates consist of two sequentially ordered expressions of opposing quality attached to the same point.)

For space-saving reasons and wherever expository considerations permit, fully articulated autosegmental representations such as those in (7) can be compressed as in (8).

(8)   Skeleton

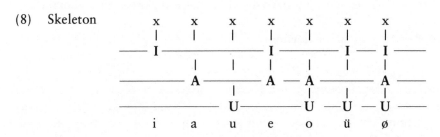

The vertical-line graphics here are not intended to imply a relation of dominance or dependency between elements. In other words, the association of each element to a position is direct and is not mediated through some other element. (Nevertheless, as we will see shortly, there is evidence to support the recognition of dependency relations within melodic expressions. It will be necessary to introduce some additional notational conventions to distinguish such relations from the co-indexing that is indicated in (7).[30])

Some languages, such as French and German, exploit the full range of vocalic contrasts generated by the free co-occurrence of **A**, **I** and **U** in (8). Others fail to do so; most dialects of modern English, for example, lack front round vowels. The exclusion of particular melodic combinations can be accounted for by assuming that systems have the option of conflating two or more autosegmental tiers.[31] Conflation of the **I** and **U** tiers, for example, prevents the fusion of these elements and results in the following five-way set of contrasts:

(9)

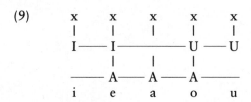

The independent behaviour of elements, which supports the autosegmental mode of representation, can manifest itself in one of two ways: either an element can delete without affecting the integrity of elements on other tiers; or it can propagate from one segment to another without dragging other elements along with it. These process-types can be directly expressed in terms of composition and decomposition, effected by means of two formal operations referred to in 2.2.2: line deletion (delinking) and line insertion (spreading). The relevant evidence is of the same order as that adduced to motivate the split between the skeletal and melodic levels. Just as a whole melodic expression can spread without setting off changes in the skeleton, so can an individual element spread independently of other elements. By the same token, quantity stability, the phenomenon whereby a skeletal position can ride out the delinking of a complete melodic expression, is matched by element stability. That is, an element on one tier can be suppressed, while those on other tiers remain unscathed.

The latter operation can be illustrated by the diphthongizations *eː > ey* and *oː > ow* exemplified in (5). The process involves the partial breaking-up of the two-element compounds representing the mid monophthongs. In the case of *eː > ey*, shown in (10a), the elements **A** and **I** remain fused in the first position of the nucleus; however, the link between **A** and the second slot becomes severed, without affecting the double association of **I**. In the second position, the lone association to **I** defines the palatal off-glide.

(10) (a) eː > ey   (b) oː > ow

```
      N           N                    N           N
     / \         / \                  / \         / \
    x   x   >   x   x                 x   x   >   x   x
     \ /        |                      \ /        |
      A         A /                      A         A /
      |         | /                      |         | /
      I         I /                      I         I /
```

As shown in (10b), diphthongization of oː to ow can be treated in like fashion.

This example illustrates how the link between an element and a position can be independently removed without implicating links involving other elements in the same expression. In this particular case, the delinking element, **A**, retains one of its associations and thus remains phonetically interpretable. The same autonomy of elements is demonstrated in cases where delinking results in the total suppression of an element while other elements remain intact. Certain vowel-raising processes in English illustrate this point.

The relatively recent changes shown in (5) can be viewed as continuations of an ongoing tendency towards vowel shifting in English. Each of the individual stages in this overall development provides evidence in support of **A, I** and **U** as the pivotal elements of vocalic structure. One stage saw mid front and back monophthongs raising in tandem:

(11)   Earlier > later English
        eː   > iː   MEET (⟨green, feet, feel, . . .⟩)
        oː   > uː   BOOT (⟨soon, loop, lose, . . .⟩)

The original mid quality of these vowels is retained in root-level alternants with short nuclei (which remained unaffected by the Great Vowel Shift); compare, for example, ⟨keep–kept, serene–serenity, lose–lost, goose–gosling⟩. Viewed in terms of its elemental effects, mid-vowel raising is a reduction process. That is, it involves the suppression of part of the melodic content of a sound (in this case **A**):

(12) eː > ˙iː   oː > uː

```
      N           N                    N           N
     / \         / \                  / \         / \
    x   x   >   x   x                 x   x   >   x   x
     \ /         \ /                   \ /         \ /
      A          |                      A          |
      |          |                      |          |
      I          I                      U          U
```

Logically we should expect another type of reduction process to affect mid vowels, one involving the loss of **I** or **U**. In this case, decomposition results in lowering to **a**, the manifestation of the remaining **A** element. An example from the history of English is the lowering and unrounding of Early Modern short ɔ to *a* (e.g. in ⟨pot, top, lock, solid⟩), the effects of which show up in some present-day dialects.[32]

The cases of diphthongization and raising represented in (10) and (12) exemplify one type of evidence supporting the autosegmental mode of representation – the ability of processes to target melodic expressions in such a way that they selectively take out particular elements without disturbing others. As mentioned above, the other main source of supporting evidence comes from the observation that part of an expression can display mobility under processing while the rest remains inert. We will see numerous examples of this phenomenon in the following pages. A rather simple example will give some preliminary idea of what is involved.

In many types of English, the direct juxtaposition of vowels across a word boundary tends to lead to the creation of an intervening segment, typically a glide or a glottal stop, as in ⟨two [w] of, two [ʔ] of⟩. The excrescent segment can be viewed as a hiatus-breaker which fills the otherwise vacant onset between the two nuclei. The glide realizations, *w* and *y*, only occur after a certain class of vowels, namely *iː, uː*, (see (13a)) and, depending on the dialect, either up-gliding diphthongs (i.e. those ending in *y* or *w*) or the monophthongs *eː, oː* (see (13b)).

(13) (a) *iːV → iːyV*   three [y] and
           uːV → uːwV   two [w] of
      (b) *eyV → eyyV, eːV → eːyV* day [y] of
           owV → owwV, oːV → oːwV go [w] and
      (c) **Shah [y] of, *Shah [w] of*

The backness of the glide is evidently determined by the nature of the preceding vowel – front *y* after a front vowel, back *w* after back. Moreover, the conditioning vowel must have some element of palatality or labiality in it, which explains why neither glide appears after a low non-round vowel (see (13c)). (Some dialects show so-called 'intrusive' *r* in the latter context, as in ⟨Shah [r] of⟩, but that is another topic for another time (chapter 5).)

The hiatus glide can be straightforwardly explained as the spreading of an element from the first nucleus into the vacant onset. Assuming that a skeletal slot is automatically created in the onset to accommodate the incoming element, we can see in (14a) that it is I in a vowel such as *iː* that gives rise to *y*.

(14) (a) *iːV → iːyV*   (b) *uːV → uːwV*

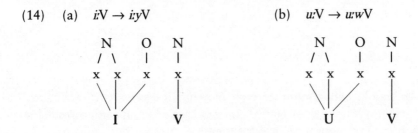

By the same token, as shown in (14b), it is U in a vowel such as *u:* that yields *w* (V indicates some vocalic expression).

In dialects with up-gliding diphthongs, the excrescent glide is simply the continuation of the I or U that is the lone occupant of the second position of the nucleus. What is significant from the viewpoint of the present discussion is that exactly the same process is operative in dialects which have long mid monophthongs (*e:* and *o:*) in place of up-gliding diphthongs (*ey* and *ow*). This means that I and U can spread independently of the element A, with which they are fused in the triggering nucleus:

(15) (a) *e:V → e:yV* (b) *o:V → o:wV*

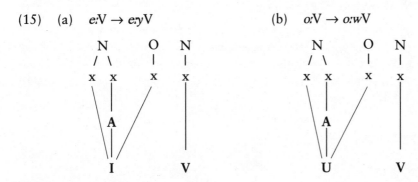

In this independent spreading behaviour we find further evidence in support of the autosegmental mode of representation.

3.3.3 *Dependency relations between elements*

Most approaches to melodic structure which incorporate the primitives A, I and U subscribe to the notion that fusion involves some kind of asymmetric relation between the elements of a compound. This is understood as a means of expressing the notion that the phonetic manifestation of a compound reflects the preponderance of one element over another. The most widely established implementation of this idea has been to designate one element in a compound as the **head** of that expression and any other elements that may be present as **dependents**.[33] In a simplex expression, the lone element is the head.

Take for example two A–I compounds, one headed by I, the other by A. Informally, we can think of the I-headed expression as an open version of an essentially palatal vowel; the A-headed expression meanwhile can be considered a palatalized version of an essentially open vowel. Let us assume that these asymmetric fusions define the vowels *e* and *æ* respectively (head element underlined):[34]

(16) (a) e (b) æ

$$
\begin{array}{ccc}
\text{x} & \qquad & \text{x} \\
| & & | \\
\underline{I} & & I \\
| & & | \\
A & & \underline{A}
\end{array}
$$

By the same token, the asymmetric fusion of **A** and **U** defines the vowels *o* and *ɒ* respectively:

(17) (a) o   (b) ɒ

       x   x
       | |
       U̲   U
       | |
       A   A̲

The fusion asymmetries illustrated in (16) and (17) provide a straightforward means of representing widely attested processes of raising and lowering involving low and mid vowels. One example involves the portion of the English Great Vowel Shift which produced the inputs to the changes shown in (5). Early Modern English *eː* and *oː* are the raised reflexes of Middle English *æː* and *ɒː* respectively:

(18) Earlier > later English
      æː   > eː   MATE = BAIT
      ɒː   > oː   BOAT

In terms of their elementary make-up, the inputs and outputs of each of these raisings are **isomers**.[35] That is, the elements of which they are composed are identical but are arranged in different ways: **A** is a head in both *æː* and *ɒː* but a dependent in both *eː* and *oː*. In other words, the raising of low vowels involves neither the loss nor the addition of elements; it consists rather in a switch in the headedness of a melodic expression:

(19) (a) æː > eː   (b) ɒː > oː

      x   x   x   x
      | | | |
      I   I̲   U   U̲
      | | | |
      A̲   A   A̲   A

Lowering of mid vowels presents the inverse operation, in which **A** in a compound switches from dependent to head status. This can be illustrated by one of the stages in the recent history of originally short *ɔ* briefly mentioned above. (The representational difference between *ɔ* and *o* is something to be taken up later.) This vowel displays three main dialect reflexes in present-day English, each of which recapitulates a stage in its diachronic development:

(20) ɔ > ɒ > a   POT (⟨top, lock, solid, . . . ⟩)

The sequence of events involves the following representational changes, one of which (21b) takes the form of an isomeric alteration:

(21) (a) ɔ   (b) ɒ (lowering)   (c) a (unrounding)

      x   x   x
      | | |
     U   U |
     ‾| | |
     A   **A**   A

In what follows, I will only indicate headedness where it is directly relevant to the point at hand.

3.3.4 *Elements and sound patterns*

At this point, it is in order to say something more about the phonetic interpretation of elements and element fusion.[36] One question is whether the phonetic specification of elements should be couched in terms of the articulatory mechanisms of the speaker, or the acoustic signal, or the auditory perception of the hearer. In view of the assumption that a grammar, as a model of linguistic competence, is neutral as between speakers and hearers, it might reasonably be expected that each element should be definable with reference to all three domains. From a purely procedural viewpoint, however, it would seem to make sense to begin with the acoustic dimension, since this is the communicative experience that is shared by speaker and hearer. This stance was explicitly adopted by Roman Jakobson in early distinctive-feature theory but was largely abandoned in generative phonology by the time of SPE.[37] Since the 1960s, the primacy of articulatory-based definitions has gone largely unchallenged in feature theory. The assumption made in much of this work, usually implicitly, is that the articulatory specifications of features can be mapped (not necessarily directly) onto acoustic and auditory specifications.[38]

It is certainly possible to provide articulatory definitions of **A**, **I** and **U**. This can be done by referring to the two major resonating cavities, the oral and the pharyngeal, which are involved in the production of *a, i* and *u*, the independent manifestations of the elements in question. The lowering and retraction of the tongue body that produce *a* result in an expansion of the oral tube and a constriction of the pharyngeal tube. In *i*, the oral cavity is constricted and the pharyngeal cavity expanded. The production of *u* involves a trade-off between expansion of both the oral and pharyngeal tubes.

Nevertheless, we should not lose sight of the fact that phonological primes are not in themselves articulatory events. Rather, like all aspects of phonological representation, they are cognitive categories which serve the grammatical function of helping to code lexical contrasts. From a Jakobsonian viewpoint, the phonetic interpretation of these categories involves in the first instance a mapping onto the acoustic signal. Speech production and perception are then to be considered parasitic on this mapping relation.

Applied to the model of melodic content being outlined in this chapter, this view implies that elements should be thought of as internally represented objects which map onto sound patterns. **Sound** is being used here in its literal sense to refer to the acoustic signal, rather than in the loose metaphorical sense frequently encountered in articulatory definitions of segments. That is, elements constitute pattern templates by reference to which speakers orchestrate and monitor articulatory output and listeners decode auditory input. In speech production, the speaker marshals whatever articulatory resources are available or necessary to create signal mappings of particular elements. In speech perception, the listener seeks to detect sound patterns which can be matched to particular elements.

Viewed in these terms, the phonetic effects of element fusion consist primarily in the amalgamation of sound patterns. The articulatory results of the operation are then specified by identifying whatever vocal-tract gestures are required for achieving particular targets represented by composite sound patterns.

One of the arguments in favour of this view relates to the indirectness of the link between the acoustic identity of a sound and the articulatory mechanisms by which it is produced. For example, it is not always possible to establish a direct correlation between the acoustic characteristics of a vowel and traditional articulatory labels referring to tongue position, such as [high], [low] or [back]. Features such as these are usually defined in terms of the point of maximum tongue constriction relative to the palate. But this factor on its own does not provide an invariant specification of the supralaryngeal vocal-tract configurations that generate the acoustic profiles of different vowels. It is by manipulating the overall shape and size of the supralaryngeal airway that the speaker targets particular sound patterns (as any good ventriloquist will confirm). In vowel production, determining factors other than tongue contour involve adjustments to total vocal-tract length, including the height of the larynx, the size of lip aperture, and the relative protrusion or retraction of the lips. Most vowels can be generated by means of many different articulatory configurations. A given token of a vowel sound classified as [low], for example, may indeed be produced with a lower tongue position than a vowel classified as [high]; but another token of the same sound may actually be achieved with a **higher** tongue position than a [high] vowel.[39]

This is perhaps not the place to provide detailed specifications of the signal mappings of elements or of the acoustic consequences of fusion. Interested readers can pursue the matter in the appendix to this chapter (3.8).

3.3.5 *The neutral element*

The sound patterns associated with *a*, *i* and *u* are inherently large and distinct. This is a reflection of the fact that these vowels, the universally limiting articulations of the vowel triangle, represent extreme departures from a neutral position of the vocal tract. The supralaryngeal vocal-tract configuration associated with the neutral position approximates that of a uniform tube and generates a schwa-like auditory effect. The resonating characteristics of this configuration are such that it lacks the bold sound patterns found in *a, i* and *u*. Most researchers within the A–I–U tradition accord this neutral quality some special status, either by treating it as a segment devoid of any active elementary content or by taking it to be the independent manifestation of a fourth element, which I will symbolize here as @.[40]

Building on the colour metaphor, the element @ can be thought of as a blank canvas to which the bold strokes represented by **A, I** and **U** can be applied. From the perspective of production, this metaphor reflects the point just made that **A, I** and **U** are realized by means of articulatory manoeuvres that perturb the vocal tract from its neutral state. From an acoustic point of view, the amorphous signal presence of @ constitutes a base-line on which the well-defined sound patterns associated with **A, I** and **U** are superimposed.

Schwa-like vowels can occur in stressed nuclei; they are to be found, for example, among the various reflexes of the vowel in CUT (⟨cut, blood, sun⟩, etc.) and, in non-rhotic dialects at least, of that in THIRD (⟨third, shirt, burn⟩, etc.). However, realizations of this sort are particularly prevalent in contexts favouring vowel reduction. This is the phenomenon whereby prosodically recessive nuclear positions display a considerably smaller set of vocalic contrasts than are found in other positions. Positions of this type manifest recessiveness in one of a number of ways: they may bear weak stress, for example; or they may occur within a harmonic span in which their melodic identity is partially or wholly determined by a neighbouring vowel; or their presence in a representation may be solely motivated by syllabification constraints. In such contexts, many languages display only one vocalic reflex, its quality varying from system to system. In Spanish, for instance, it is *e*, in Japanese *i*, and in Telugu (Dravidian, southern India) *u*.[41] Reflexes of this type can be thought of as default vowels which show up spontaneously when no other quality is to hand. Although the elementary composition of such vowels is not lexically distinctive, it cannot be attributed to spreading from a neighbouring position. Cases of this type thus appear to call for a relaxation of the requirement that all phonological processes have a local cause. The appearance of a default element may be viewed as reflecting a language-specific quality that is latently omnipresent in representations.

Of the various vocalic reflexes that appear in recessive nuclei, by far the most common are those of schwa-like quality. Frequently, the curtailment of distinctive potential in such contexts involves the neutralization of peripheral vowel qualities under a centralized reflex. In English, a stress-sensitive version of this phenomenon shows up in root-level alternations between full and reduced vowels in forms such as ⟨phótograph⟩ *fowtəgræf*–⟨photógraphy⟩ *fətɒgrəfi*. Indeed in some languages, a schwa-like reflex is the only vowel to occur in prosodically weak contexts. Because of this behaviour, schwa is widely acknowledged to be the reduction vowel *par excellence*. That is, it is the default reflex that surfaces when other vocalic material is absent or suppressed.

As a means of transcribing reduction reflexes, the symbol ə is used to cover a relatively wide range of qualities, some of which are not even central. (For example, employed in the transcription of French, the symbol stands for a vowel of mid front round quality, as in *prəmye* 'first'.) Even amongst non-peripheral reduction reflexes, there can be considerable variation in the quality of vowels symbolized as ə. Rather than being symptomatic of sloppy transcriptional practice, this fluctuation can be put down to the fact that the distinctive potential associated with the non-palatal non-low region of the traditional vowel diagram is not as great as its relatively large area might suggest. Variability between systems with respect to the favoured reduction vowel can be taken to reflect differences in the fixing of the base line on which other resonance components are superimposed. From a speech production viewpoint, this variability is sometimes characterized in terms of different articulatory or vocal settings.[42]

The range of values attested in the non-peripheral region can be identified by reference to the neutral quality represented by the element @. Other centralised categories that are potentially distinct from this baseline can then be thought of as displaced versions of the neutral quality, expressed as the fusion of @ with some other element. For example, the relatively open ɐ value of the vowel transcribed as ə for some types of English and other languages (Catalan, for instance) can be represented as a compound of @ and A. In some dialects of English, this relatively open quality is distinct from a closer non-peripheral vowel, as illustrated by the contrast between the second nucleus of ⟨Rosas⟩ (with ə) and that of ⟨roses⟩ (with ɨ). This suggests a distinction between [A, @] and [@].

Let us take a closer look at the English alternations between full and reduced vowels in forms such as ⟨photograph–photography⟩. The full vowels occur in nuclei bearing primary or secondary word stress, while reduced reflexes show up in alternants in which the nucleus is unstressed. These alternations are all of the root-level type, which means that, following the line of reasoning outlined in 1.4.3, vowel reduction in this case takes the form of a static distributional regularity. That is, words such as ⟨photographic⟩ and ⟨photography⟩ are not phonologically derived from ⟨photograph⟩.

There are two main types of vowel-reduction system in English, illustrated by the emboldened characters in (22). In one, System A in (22), schwa occurs as the sole weak reflex; in the other, System B, an additional weak reflex, ɨ, is attested.

(22) (a) Reduced vowel = ə (Systems A and B)

ɒ	product–production, photography–photograph
ow	photograph–photography
æ	photograph–photography

      (b) Reduced vowel = ə (System A), ɪ (System B)

iː	demon–demonic
ay	horizon–horizontal
ɛ	telepathic–telepathy

Note that the contrast between reduced ɪ and ə in System B retains one aspect of the distinctions holding of full vowels: the weak reflex is ə unless the corresponding full vowel is front or ends in a front glide. In element terms, the latter pattern implies that the only element supported by the weak nucleus in question is I, a proper subset of the expressions defining various types of front vowel in the corresponding stressed nuclei. Failure to sustain other than I in a weak context may be seen as a distributional analogue of dynamic processes of melodic decomposition such as we have already seen at work in various forms of vowel shifting.

Extending the decomposition account to cases involving weakening to schwa would have the desirable consequence of providing us with a unified treatment of vowel reduction. It is not immediately clear, however, whether such an extension is possible. The problem is that the reduction of a full vowel to ə apparently involves substitution of one set of elements by another. Alternations between, for example, ɒ and ə or between ɛ and ə would be characterized as follows:

(23) (a) ɒ   – ə   (b) ɛ   – ə
           [A, U]   [@]   [A, I]   [@]

On the face of it, the expression defining ə is not a proper subset of the expressions defining full vowels. The operation of element substitution that this implies runs counter to the principle that the class of possible phonological processes is restricted to operations of delinking or spreading.

However, viewing reduction to schwa in terms of substitution reflects a misconception about the behaviour of @ under fusion. A solution to the apparent problem in this case lies in the recognition that @ fails to display the sort of active resonance properties that characterize the other elements discussed so far.

The notion that @ is without an active resonance component can be captured by assuming that the only circumstances under which its autonomous phonetic signature will be made manifest are when it occurs as the head of an expression. It will fail to contribute anything to an expression in which it occurs as a dependent. This silence is consistent with the assumption that @ is latently present as a dependent in all vocalic expressions and has the potential to become audible only when other elements in a compound are suppressed for some reason. In other words, rather than occupying its own melodic tier, @ should be viewed as being resident at any intersection of a tier and a skeletal position that is not already filled by some other element.[43] This means that the expressions corresponding to *a*, *i* and *u* are most accurately represented as in (24).

(24) (a) a   (b) i   (c) u

           x   x   x
           | | |
           A   @   @
           | | |
           @   I   U

The @-headed isomers of these expressions define various non-peripheral qualities, including the relatively open ɐ vowel already discussed:

(25)   (a)   ɐ   (b)   ɪ   (c)   ʊ

        x   x   x

        | | |

        A   @   @

        | | |

        @   I   U

The representation of lax vowels such as *ɪ* and *u* as @-headed compounds is a matter to be considered in more detail in the next section.[44]

The idea that @ defines the baseline on which other resonances are superimposed is thus implemented by assuming that it is omnipresent in vocalic expressions but fails to manifest itself wherever it is overridden by the presence of another element. Viewed in these terms, reduction to a centralised vocalic reflex does not involve the random substitution of one set of elements by @. Rather it consists in the promotion of a latently present @ to the status of head of an expression. Under such circumstances, other elements are either totally suppressed (through delinking/deletion) or demoted to dependent status. As depicted in (26a), the first operation derives reduction to some schwa-like reflex; the second, illustrated in (26b), derives reduction to one of the other centralized reflexes given in (25).

(26)   (a)   i   >   ə   (b)   i   >   ɪ

        N   N   N   N

        | | | |

        x   >   x   x   >   x

        | | | |

        I   @   I   I

        | | | |

        @   @   @   @

I will henceforth follow the practice of recording the presence of @ in an expression only when it occurs as a head.

One of the advantages of viewing centralization in these terms is that it unifies the representation of the process with that of certain processes of raising and lowering which, although not involving reduction to non-peripheral reflexes, nevertheless occur under the same prosodically weak conditions. A widespread phenomenon in the world's languages is a tendency for mid vowels to be banished from prosodically recessive nuclear positions. In metrical systems, recessiveness refers to positions of weak stress; in harmony systems, it refers to nuclei whose harmonic identity is determined by an adjacent dominant position. Under such conditions, it is common to find neutralization of vocalic contrasts in favour of either non-peripheral reflexes or the 'corner' vowels *a, i, u* or some mixture of both. In Bulgarian, for example, the stressed five-vowel system (*i, e, a, o, u*) contracts to three vowels under weak stress: *a* undergoes centralization to *ɐ*, while *i–e* and *u–o* are neutralized under *i* and *u* respectively.[45] In Catalan, a stressed seven-term system (*i, e, ɛ, a, ɔ, o, u*) gives way to three terms under weak stress: the *a–ɛ–e* contrast is neutralized under *ɐ*, *ɔ–o–u* under *u*, and *i* remains as *i*.[46] In vowel-height harmony systems, such as occur for example in Central Bantu languages and certain Romance dialects, mid vowels are barred from appearing in harmonically recessive positions unless sanctioned by the presence of a mid vowel in the harmonically dominant position.[47]

The fact that the processes just mentioned, raising or lowering of mid vowels and centralization, all occur in the same general context indicates that we are dealing with a single phenomenon. Although this commonality has long been recognized, it has not always been clear how it should be captured formally. In terms of element structure, however, the processes in question are uniformly expressible as decomposition (with or without a concomitant switch in the headedness of the expression). As illustrated in (27), all involve the total or partial suppression of melodic material.

(27) (a) Raising   (b) Lowering   (c) Centralization

        o   >   u   o   >   a   o   >   ə

        N   N   N   N   N   N
        | | | | | |
        x > x   x > x   x > x
        | | |
        A   A   A   A
        | | |
        U   U   U   U   @

In (27a) the structure on the left (o) has head A and operator U; decomposition yields u. In (27b) lowering yields a with head A. In (27c) centralization yields ə with operator @.

3.3.6 English vowel systems

This is an appropriate point at which to exemplify the combinatorial possibilities of the elements introduced so far by providing a specification of the vocalic contrasts utilized in English. The size and shape of the maximal inventory of distinctions appearing in stressed nuclei varies from dialect to dialect. For illustrative purposes, however, it will be sufficient to focus on those patterns that are widely reported in the literature.

The classic descriptions of English vocalic phonology typically begin by noting a fundamental typological property that the language shares with its West Germanic cousins such as German and Dutch – a bifurcation of the inventory into sets of vowels referred to variously as long versus short or tense versus lax.[48] (The tense–lax dimension, it is now widely recognized, can be subsumed under the distinction between advanced tongue root (ATR) and non-ATR vowels.[49]) The differential phonological behaviour that reflects the long–short dichotomy manifests itself in a number of ways. In English, for example, phenomena involving only vowels from the long set include an ability to attract stress and an ability to occur in word-final stressed open syllables.

It is usually acknowledged that, at least as far as the West Germanic family of languages is concerned, long tends to correlate with tense and short with lax. However, there has not always been agreement on the question of which of the two dimensions is the more basic in English. In SPE, it is assumed that length is derivative of tenseness. According to an older tradition, length is the fundamental distinctive property, which is not necessarily uniformly correlated with tenseness.[50] The latter view has re-established itself in more recent generative theory.[51] This is partly a reflection of a desire to restrict the conditioning of metrical processes to aspects of prosodic structure. As discussed in 2.3.2, the quantity-sensitivity of stress assignment is expressed by granting metrical processes access to the arboreal structure internal to rhymes. By representing the contrast between long and short vowels as a difference between branching and non-branching nuclei, we derive the result that heavy nuclei pattern with closed rhymes in terms of their ability to attract stress. To grant metrical processes access to melodic material, including whatever component is involved in the expression of tenseness, is to open the way for the generation of unattested systems in which stress assignment is sensitive to such dimensions as vowel height, backness or roundness.

Once length is acknowledged to be the fundamental dichotomizing property of the English vowel system, the question of how tenseness/ATR should be represented takes on a good deal less significance than when considered in relation to many other languages. English shows little evidence of phonological activity involving the ATR dimension; it certainly has nothing equivalent to the vigorous ATR harmony systems found in many other languages (particularly well represented in West Africa).

There have been two approaches to the characterization of ATR in privative frameworks. One is to recognize an independent ATR element.[52] The more widely adopted solution, is to derive the contrast between ATR and non-ATR vowels by means of different combinations of the established **A, I** or **U** elements.[53] According to the specific implementation of this proposal briefly illustrated in the last section, lax/non-ATR vowels are represented as neutral-headed versions of their tense/ATR counterparts. This provides us with contrasts such as those depicted in (28) – long tense *i:* versus short lax *ɪ* (28a) and tense diphthongal *ey* versus short lax *ɛ* (28b).

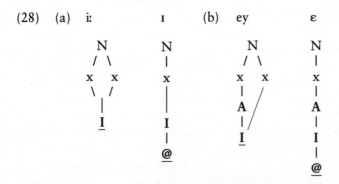

The full set of neutral-headed compound vowels generated by the theory is seven. One of these is [**A, @**], the open *ɐ* described in 3.3.5. The other six define the lax counterparts of the peripheral non-low vowels that are generated by the remaining possible combinations of **A**, **I** and **U**:

(29) (a) [I, @] ɪ [U, @] ʊ
           [A, I, @] ɛ [A, U, @] ɔ
      (b) [I, U, @] ü
           [A, I, U, @] œ

Lax vowels in English are typically drawn from the subset in (29a), although the precise selection varies from dialect to dialect. Standard German is an example of a language which displays the full range of contrasts in (29).

The most familiar subsystem of short stressed vowels in English is the six-term pattern that is historically associated with the south of England and is now widely established across the English-speaking world.[54]

Typical realizations of the six-way contrast, observed in the nuclei of BIT, BET, BAT, POT, CUT and PUT, include a subset of the neutral-headed expressions in (29), supplemented by a selection headed by **A**:

(30) (a) BIT ɪ   [I, @]
      (b) BET ɛ   [A, I, @]
      (c) BAT æ   [I, A]
      (d) PUT ʊ   [U, @]
      (e) POT ɒ   [U, A]   a   [A]
      (f) CUT ʌ   [@]   ɐ   [A, @]

Well established realizational variants of two of the vowels are shown in (30e) and (30f). (The *a* reflex in POT occurs in parts of the United States, Ireland and England, the *ɒ* reflex in Canada, the southern hemisphere, and other parts of England and the USA. The more open *ɐ* variant of the CUT nucleus is usual in southeastern England and the southern hemisphere.[55])

Consideration of the long sub-system of vowels returns us to a discussion of the Great Vowel Shift and some of the more recent diphthongizations mentioned earlier in the chapter. With the element @, we are now in a position to fill in a number of representational details involving vocalic developments not yet touched on. The historical raising of originally mid *eː* and *oː* in MEET and BOOT shown in (11) might have been expected to threaten merger with originally high *iː* and *uː* in BITE and SHOUT. That this did not happen was due to the fact that the latter were deflected out of the path of the raising monophthongs through diphthongization, first to *əy* and *əw* (reflexes retained in some present-day dialects), and subsequently to *ay* and *aw*.[56]

In a recapitulation of the initial stage of this process, some present-day dialects in England show the effects of a more recent diphthongization of the MEET and BOOT vowels to *əy* and *əw*. Representationally, this 'breaking' of an original monophthong involves a dissociation of either the element I (in MEET) or U (BOOT) from the left-hand position of the branching nucleus. As shown in (31b) and (31d), this allows latent @ to manifest itself in the vacated slot:

(31) (a) iː   (b) əy   (c) uː   (d) əw

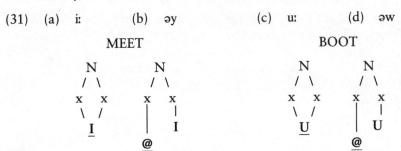

A similar proposal accounts for one of the developments to have affected the vowels of the MATE and BOAT classes. Historical *æː* and *ɒː* in these classes were first raised to *eː* and *oː*, reflexes which survive to this day in some conservative dialects. As shown in (5), these vowels have been subject to subsequent diphthongization, first to *ey* and *ow* and more recently in some dialects to *ay* and *aw*. Another diphthongization, not yet mentioned in connection with these vowel classes, has resulted in the breaking of *eː* and *oː* to *iə* and *uə*. Dialects showing these reflexes include some spoken in the northeast of England, parts of Ireland and the Caribbean. Representationally, this development has involved the suppression of **A** (producing raising) accompanied by a severing of the link between the remaining element (**I** in MATE, **U** in BOAT) from the second nuclear position. As in the reflexes represented in (32d) and (32h), this has resulted in the surfacing of latent **@**, giving rise in this case to a ə in-glide. The full range of MATE and BOAT reflexes just discussed can now be summarized as follows:

(32) MATE

(a) eː   (b) ey   (c) ay   (d) iə

BOAT

(e) oː   (f) ow   (g) aw   (h) uə

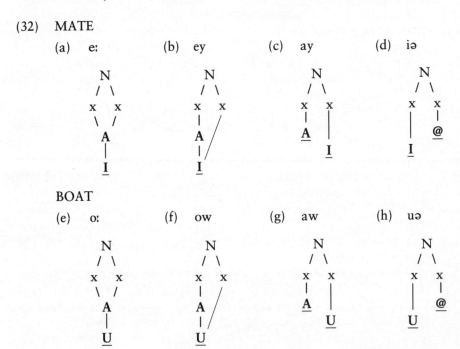

The vowels *iə* and *uə* are examples of in-gliding diphthongs (those ending in schwa) which have developed spontaneously from original monophthongs. In chapter 5, we will discuss the representation of another class of in-gliding vowels, those that result from the presence of following historical *r*, as in *fiə(r)* ⟨fear⟩. The remaining up-gliding diphthongs in the system (i.e. those ending in *y* or *w*) are those found in the word classes BITE, SHOUT and TOY:

(33) (a) ay BITE   (b) aw SHOUT   (c) ɔy TOY

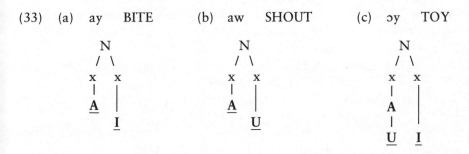

Finally, there are two long-vowel classes, CAUGHT and CALM, the status of which differs quite dramatically from dialect to dialect, in terms not only of their realization but also of their distribution across the lexicon. Both classes participate in various patterns of contextual or total merger with each other as well as with other classes. The merger patterns include CAUGHT–CALM, CAUGHT–POT, CALM–BAT, although there are some dialects in which either one or both of the classes in question remain distinct.[57] Typical realizations are shown in (34).

(34) (a) ɔː CAUGHT   (b) aː CALM   (c) ɒː CAUGHT/CALM

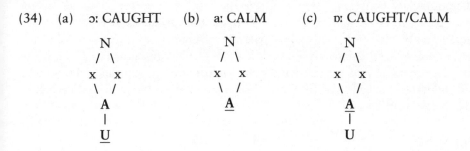

The vowels in (34) clearly fall into the long sub-system, as demonstrated by their ability to occur in final stressed open syllables, as in ⟨paw, law⟩ (CAUGHT) and ⟨ma, bra⟩ (CALM). In some dialects, the classes have fallen together with classes containing vocalized reflexes of historical *r*, so that the nuclei of CAUGHT and COURT, for example, are identical, as are also the nuclei of CALM and FARM. (More on this in chapter 5.)

3.4 Elements for consonants

3.4.1 *'Place'*

The melodic composition of consonants is frequently described in terms of the traditional articulatory dimensions of place, manner and voice. While this arrangement might suffice for presentation purposes, the distinction between place and manner will turn out to be somewhat blurred when viewed from an element-based perspective. I will postpone discussion of the laryngeal elements until 3.6. Until then, it is possible to abstract away from this dimension as we focus on the other two aspects of consonantal representation.

As regards the place dimension, one question that can be posed right away is whether the elements used to represent vowels can and should be extended to expressions attached to non-nuclear positions. In SPE, the cavity characteristics of vowels and consonants are represented by means of separate sets of features, a view that is still held in some current frameworks. However, the majority position nowadays, based primarily on evidence involving assimilatory interactions between adjacent consonants and vowels, is that identical or overlapping sets of components are appropriate for both types of sounds (the so-called 'one-mouth' principle).[58] The widespread palatalization of a consonant in the vicinity of a front vowel, for example, can be straight forwardly expressed as the spreading of a single palatal component from a vowel to a consonant.

As far as the elements introduced up to now are concerned, we have already seen (2.4.2) how the onset glides *y* and *w* are simply instances of the elements **I** and **U** occurring outside nuclei. The participation of these sounds in certain assimilatory processes justifies the decision to deploy the same elements in nuclear and non-nuclear contexts. One such process is the palatalization phenomenon just referred to. As it affects coronal plosives, this produces one of two main results – an alveolar with a secondary palatal articulation (as in Russian and Irish t^y/d^y), or a displaced palato-alveolar affricate. As briefly discussed in 1.1, it is the latter development that occurs widely in English. In collocations containing a word-final alveolar followed by y, recall, it is quite usual in connected speech to find palatal assimilation:

(35)   t → č   d → ǰ   s → ʃ   z → ʒ
        bet you   did you   kiss you   buzz you
        hit you   would you   bless you   faze you

This assimilatory behaviour appears quite natural if it is assumed that the element **I** representing the palatal glide spreads into the preceding position occupied by the coronal. This indicates that the distinction between a plain and a palatalized consonant consists in the presence of **I** in the latter but not in the former. In the case of t^y/d^y, palatalization can be assumed to result in a contour segment. As noted in 2.2.3, these are segments containing two separate melodic expressions attached to a single skeletal point. In this particular instance, the structure is one in which the incoming I fails to fuse with the other elements in the position affected by spreading. With the palato-alveolar series, I does fuse with other elements in the segment. In this case, it is necessary to account for the additional sibilance that accompanies affrication. We will return to this issue once we have had the opportunity to consider the manner dimension of consonantal contrasts in more detail.

As an example of assimilation involving U in an onset, we may note the historical change whereby original æ in many dialects became rounded and retracted to ɒ following *w*, as in ⟨want, wad, swan, quality⟩. The original front vowel is retained in all contexts in some conservative dialects (in Scotland and Ireland, for example) as well as in all dialects in forms containing following velars, which blocked the change (as in ⟨wax, wag, twang⟩).[59] The rounding is straightforwardly expressed as the spreading of U from the onset glide into the following nucleus. The conflation of the I and U tiers, responsible for the absence of front rounded vowels in English, means that the I in æ is usurped by the incoming U. Spreading of U produces rounding, while suppression of I produces retraction. This is depicted in (36) (where *I* indicates the delinking of I).

(36)

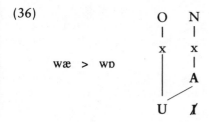

wæ > wɒ

The spreading of I to create palato-alveolars constitutes one piece of evidence favouring the extension of the resonance elements to sounds which, unlike glides and vowels, are produced with consonantal constriction. It is a natural step to conclude that the element U inheres in labial consonants and A in uvular and pharyngeal consonants (which, like *a*, are produced by lowering and retracting the tongue body). Since @ independently defines a sound which is articulated as dorsal (produced with the tongue body), non-palatal, non-labial and non-open, it can be taken to specify velarity in consonants. By employing the four main resonance elements reviewed so far, we thus identify all the major cavity dimensions of consonants save one, coronality, which evidently requires an independent element.

3.4.2 Lenition: doing things to a t

In seeking to determine the additional elements needed to define coronality as well as the stricture characteristics of consonants, we can turn to the same sort of evidence as that adduced for the resonance elements introduced so far. That is, by observing the behaviour of consonants under phonological processing, we can hope to gain an idea of how they are made up. The consonantal equivalent of the vocalic fission processes that produce diphthongization and vowel reduction generally goes under the name **lenition** or weakening. The class of processes falling under this rubric includes vocalization (weakening to a glide or liquid, as in $p \rightarrow w$), spirantization (the development of a plosive into a fricative, as in $t \rightarrow s$) and debuccalization (loss of supralaryngeal gesture, as in $s \rightarrow h$).

The term **lenition** makes implicit appeal to the notion of relative segmental strength. Unless interrupted for some reason, consonantal weakening processes typically pass through a series of stages which ultimately culminate in segment deletion.[60] The weakest sounds are those that constitute the penultimate stage of this progression; that is, they represent the last vestige of a segment before it disappears altogether. The strongest sounds are those occurring at the other end of the scale.[61] In articulatory terms, lenition manifests itself as an opening of consonantal stricture. So for example, close approximation of the articulators marks a fricative gesture out as weaker than the complete closure of a stop and as stronger than the open approximation associated with a glide.

As they affect oral consonants, opening processes follow one of three trajectories:[62]

(37) Opening trajectories

    (a) Spirantization   >   'aspiration'   >   deletion
          plosive > fricative   >   h   > $\emptyset$

    (b) Glottalling   >   deletion
          plosive > ? > $\emptyset$

    (c) Vocalization   >   deletion
          non-continuant > resonant   > $\emptyset$

The notion of trajectory here refers in the first instance to the historical development of sound changes. It is not meant to imply that every lenition process inexorably leads towards elision. As noted above, progression through the various stages on a particular path may be arrested at some point. The synchronic relevance of this observation is that two or more stages on a particular trajectory may be retained within the same grammar as stable alternants or distributional variants. English provides numerous examples which illustrate this state of affairs. A good place to start a review of this evidence is with *t*, which in recent times has proved to be one of the most unstable consonants in the language. Examining the fate of this sound under lenition teaches us a good deal about the internal composition of consonants in general.

At various times and in various dialects, English *t* has found itself on all three of the weakening trajectories shown in (37). The phonological contexts in which it has been susceptible to lenition can be identified informally as word-final and inter-vocalic within a foot:

(38) Word-final: ⟨pet, bit, late, boat, . . .⟩
      Foot-internal: ⟨pity, photograph, Peter, . . .⟩

In particular cases, *t* has been targeted by lenition in either or both of these contexts. An important question concerns why it should be this particular combination of conditions that favours *t*-lenition rather than any other. This is an issue that we will devote a good deal of attention to in the next chapter. What is relevant for our present purposes is the set of processes to which *t* has been subject in these environments.

   One of the opening processes to have affected *t* in one or both of the contexts in (38) is glottalling (37b), a phenomenon that is particularly prevalent in Scotland and England. This takes the form of debuccalization, the loss of the coronal gesture, with the residual reflex being realized with glottal stricture, as in ⟨bi[ʔ]⟩, ⟨pi[ʔ]y⟩.[63]

   Another development has resulted in tapping or flapping – vocalization to tap *ɾ* (37c), a process that has also affected *d* (as in ⟨ready⟩). Tapping is firmly established in most of North America, as well as in Australia, Ireland and parts of England. Tapping (in English at least) generally occurs in pre-vocalic contexts; that is, it takes place both foot-internally and word-finally before a vowel. However, as illustrated in (39), word-finally before a consonant or pause, tapping dialects show an unreleased and sometimes pre-glottalized reflex of *t* (indicated here by *t˥*).

(39) Foot-internal   Word-final
                          Before V   Before C or pause
      pi[ɾ]y   fi[ɾ] us   fi[t˥] me

   Yet another weakening process to have affected *t* is spirantization, a phenomenon that is most firmly established in Ireland and the Merseyside area of England. The fricative reflex, illustrated in (40a), can be of the 'slit' type, in which case it remains distinct from the grooved manifestation typical of original *s*.

(40) (a) gɛs   ⟨get⟩   lɛsə   ⟨letter⟩
      (b) æh   ⟨at⟩   nɒh   ⟨not⟩
           dæh   ⟨that⟩   bʊh   ⟨but⟩

Nevertheless, the potential for merger here is sometimes realized, with the result that, for some speakers at least, ⟨letter⟩ can be identical to ⟨lesser⟩. As the forms in (40b) show, spirantization has given way to debuccalization to *h* in function words which typically bear weak stress.

   Summarizing, we may note that lenited *t* in modern English can show up as one of the following reflexes: glottal stop, tap, unreleased coronal stop, coronal fricative, or *h*. One of the advantages of a framework in which melodic expressions are composed of privative, independently interpretable elements is that the processes responsible for these reflexes, and indeed lenition processes in general, receive a uniform representation. Specifically, every weakening process can be characterized as the suppression of some aspect of the elementary content of a segment.[64] According to this approach, lenition along each of the trajectories in (37) involves a progressive decrease in the melodic complexity of a segment, where complexity is straightforwardly gauged by the number of elements of which a segment is composed. Thus each trajectory corresponds to a scale of complexity, where the strongest segment-types are the most complex and the weakest the least complex. It then makes sense to suppose that the weakest segments, those occupying a stage immediately prior to deletion, contain only one element. From the perspective of a framework in which elements are held to be independently interpretable, this observation is highly significant: pre-deletion stages in lenition chains allow us actually to 'hear' individual elements.

The full set of 'primitive' segments which show up as pre-deletion targets in lenition is as follows:

(41)	Pre-deletion target	Element
Glottalling	?	?
'Aspiration'	h	h
Vocalization	ɾ	R
	y	I
	w	U
	ɣ	@

(ɣ symbolizes a velar approximant.) Given the line of argumentation being pursued here, each of these sounds should be the autonomous phonetic instantiation of a particular element. And indeed, three of them are independently motivated as the manifestation of resonance elements already introduced, namely w = U, y = I and ɣ = @. (ɣ indicates the non-nuclear counterpart of *i*, in the same way that *w*, say, corresponds to *u*.) The lenition facts suggest the need to recognize three additional elements, independently realized as ɾ, ? and h and labelled in (41) as R, ? and h respectively.[65]

3.4.3 *'Manner'*

The element ? may be thought of as a **stop** or an **edge** pattern which maps onto the acoustic signal as an abrupt decrease in overall amplitude.[66] In articulatory terms, this effect is achieved by a non-continuant gesture of the type that characterizes oral and nasal stops and laterals. In isolation, the element is interpreted as a glottal stop, since this is the only articulatory means of achieving an amplitude drop without introducing resonance characteristics into the signal. That is, **glottal** is not a defining property of ? but is simply an articulatory by-product of the speaker targeting an edge elemental pattern. In compound expressions, the location of the constriction necessary for producing ? is determined by one of the other constituent elements. For example, the articulatory execution of a compound expression containing U and ? calls for a sustained vocal-tract closure at the lips, resulting in a labial non-continuant. Stops with other places of articulation are formed by the fusion of ? with I (palatal), @ (velar), A (uvular), or R (coronal).

The signal mapping of the element R is the set of resonance transitions associated with **coronal** gesture. When not harnessed to any other component, the transition is rapid; in articulatory terms, this means that the independent interpretation of R is a coronal tap.

The elemental pattern of h may be defined as **noise**, which maps onto the speech signal as aperiodic energy. The articulatory targeting of this effect involves a narrowed stricture which produces turbulent airflow. This element contributes a noise component to the class of obstruent consonants (not to sonorants, which are characterized by periodicity). This property, in as far as it is deemed phonologically significant, is usually only associated with fricatives and affricates. Aperiodic energy, in the form of a noise burst, also characterizes the release phase of genuine plosives (as opposed to unreleased stops). However, this effect has generally not been considered distinctive for this class of segments within orthodox feature frameworks. Nevertheless, as we will now see, the lenition evidence suggests that a noise component is indeed part of the phonological identity of plosives.

The element h in isolation is produced as a glottal fricative. As with ?, the absence of any supralaryngeal gesture here simply reflects the fact that the element lacks its own resonance property. In a compound expression, a place-defining element will indicate the location of the noise-producing gesture. Thus, fricatives with supralaryngeal resonance are formed by combining h with, for example, R (s), with U (f), or with @ (x).

Pursuing the notion of lenition as progressive decomplexification, let us consider the various stages on the opening trajectory in (37a). If *h* is the least complex segment, the plosive input must be the most complex and oral fricatives of intermediate complexity. It is reasonable to assume that an oral fricative differs from *h* by one degree of complexity: the former contains a place-defining element that is absent from the latter. By the same token, the internal structure of a plosive includes whatever material is present in a homorganic fricative but is more complex than the latter by virtue of the presence of an additional element, the stop property represented by ?.[67] This line of reasoning leads us to conclude that h inheres in all released obstruents, both plosives and fricatives.

We are now in a position to show how consonantal lenition can be directly represented as the suppression of melodic material. Continuing to abstract away from the laryngeal dimension, we may represent movement along opening trajectory (37a) as a progressive loss of elementary content, illustrated here for coronal place:

(42) (a)   (b)   (c)   (d)
      t   >   s   >   h   >   ∅

      x   x   x   (x)
      | | |
      h   h   h
      | |
      R   R
      |
      ?

Plosive *t* in (42a) is defined as a coronal (contributed by **R**) stop (?) accompanied by noise release (**h**). Loss of closure yields a coronal fricative (42b). Further loss of the supralaryngeal component contributed by **R** leaves an expression containing **h**, which on its own defines a glottal fricative (42c). Loss of the remaining element results in elision of the melodic expression, which may or may not be accompanied by loss of the position to which it was attached (42d). Similar decompositions can be assumed for other place types.

The three-way place contrast among plosives found in English and most other languages can now be represented as follows:

(43) Plosives

      (a) Labial   (b) Coronal   (c) Velar

           x   x   x
           | | |
           h   h   h
           | | |
           U   R   @
           | | |
           ?   ?   ?

We might ask what type of sound it is that lacks **h** but includes ? fused with a place-defining element. Such a compound naturally defines a non-continuant without noise release. Three categories of segment fit this bill: unreleased oral stops ('applosives'), laterals, and nasal stops. To complete the representation of the last of these, we need an additional element which will be introduced presently.

As shown in (39), an unreleased oral stop is one of the reflexes of *t* that shows up in dialects which otherwise have tap *r*. We now see how the process that gives rise to this reflex, the loss of audible release, is straightforwardly represented as the suppression of **h**. The treatment of this process as melodic reduction is supported by the fact that it recurs in what are generally regarded as lenition-favouring environments. In many languages, all place-types are affected by loss of noise release in such contexts (for example, in word-final position in Korean and Thai).

The three main reflexes of *t* that show up in tapping dialects of English are represented in (44a, b, c). Loss of **h** from plosive *t* (44a) results in an unreleased stop (44b).[68] Suppression of both **h** and ? leaves a lone **R** element, which independently manifests the tap reflex (44c).

(44) (a)   (b)   (c)   (d)
       t   t⁻   ɾ   ʔ

       x   x   x   x
       | | | |
       h | | |
       | | | |
       R   R   R |
       | | |
       ʔ   ʔ   ʔ

Suppression of all elements save ʔ yields a stop devoid of supralaryngeal content and noise release; in other words, it results in ʔ, the independent realization of ʔ in (44d).[69]

There is every reason to suppose that ʔ also inheres in another subclass of noiseless non-continuants, namely laterals. One reason for reaching this conclusion is that laterals can be observed to pattern with coronal plosives in certain processes. Evidence of a phonological connection happens not to be particularly easy to come by in English. One example is the dialect-specific process mentioned in 2.4.4 whereby historically short æ (in ⟨man, pass⟩, etc.) is tensed before certain consonants. In a subset of the dialects in question, *l* can be seen to line up with oral coronal stops in inhibiting tensing; æ is tense before *n* and *s* (as in ⟨man, pass⟩) but remains lax not only before *t* and *d* (⟨bat, bad⟩) but also before *l* (⟨pal⟩).[70] In many languages (well represented among the Bantu family of African languages, for example), *l* alternates with *d* or *t* in certain contexts; in some cases, the two types of sound are in complementary distribution. In Sesotho, for instance, the pattern shows up in alternations such as the following: *bal-a* 'read, count', *bad-ile* 'have read, have counted'; *lat-a* 'fetch', *n-tat-a* 'fetch me'.

It has been proposed that, within an element-based approach, the phonological relation between coronal stops and laterals can be captured by means of isomeric representations.[71] In particular, both types of coronal non-continuant contain **R** and ʔ; the former can be taken as the head of expressions defining stops, the latter as the head of those defining laterals. This asymmetry is consistent with the observation that the extent of coronal stricture is different in the two types of consonant. The preponderance of **R** in *t/d* is reflected in the fact that the coronal closure is tight, including both medial and lateral occlusion. In *l*, on the other hand, coronality is limited to medial closure.

Representation of the third class of noiseless non-continuants, nasal stops, requires recognition of a nasality element, which may be labelled **N**.[72] This manifests itself in the signal as low-frequency broad-band 'murmur', an effect that is achieved through lowering of the velum. The same element can be assumed to inhere in nasalized vowels. The autonomy of **N** is reflected in its participation in assimilatory processes, such as long-distance nasal harmony and the more localized nasalization of vowels in the vicinity of nasal stops.[73]

The isomeric relation between expressions corresponding to laterals and oral stops raises the more general issue of the headedness of consonantal representations. Take first the relation between a resonance element and ʔ occurring within the same expression. We have already seen how an R-headed expression can be taken to define a coronal stop, while ?-headedness characterizes *l*. In the case of labial non-continuants, the phonetic manifestation of a segment can be expected to vary in the following way, according to whether or not U enjoys head status. As a head, U is free to assert the full elemental pattern it displays in isolation, typically achieved by labial-velar articulation. In conjuction with ?, this configuration thus provides us with a representation of doubly articulated labial-velar stops (*kp, gb*) such as occur in many languages, perhaps the best known of which are spoken in West Africa. When U occurs as a dependent, the full effect of its elemental pattern is attenuated; in this case, fusion with a head ? defines a bilabial stop.[74] Velar stops, represented in (43c), are necessarily @-headed. This follows from the assumption that this element is unable to contribute to the phonetic interpretation of an expression unless it occurs as a head.

The head-dependent relation also provides a means of representing the difference between strident and non-strident fricatives and affricates. h-headed expressions can be expected to display greater stridency or 'noisiness' than those in which h occurs as a dependent. The contrast between strident *s* and non-strident *θ* can thus be expressed as in (45a) and (45b).

(45) (a)   (b)   (c)   (d)   (e)   (f)

     s   θ   f   ʍ   ʃ   x

    x   x   x   x   x   x
    | | | | | |
    h   h   h   h   h   h
    | | | | | |
    R   R   U   U   R   @
                                 |
                                 I

The distinction between strident *f* (45c) and non-strident ʍ (45d) involves the same kind of relation. The voiceless labial-velar fricative ʍ occurs in some dialects of English (chiefly spoken in Scotland, Ireland and parts of the United States), where it contrasts with *w* in pairs such as ⟨which–witch, why–Y, what–watt⟩. As with labial-velar stops, the double articulation of ʍ reflects its U-headedness.

Other fricatives relevant to English are shown in (45e) and (45f). As indicated by the assimilation process illustrated in (35), a palato-alveolar fricative or affricate should be considered a palatalized version of a plain alveolar. In element terms, this means that ʃ includes the h and R elements contained in *s*, supplemented by the palatal element I. Palatalization, evident in a phrase such as ⟨miss you⟩, can thus be expressed as the spreading of I from the position occupied by the initial glide of ⟨you⟩ into the position occupied by the fricative of ⟨miss⟩.[75]

The representation in (45f) defines the velar fricative that occurs as a distinctive lexical category in some Scottish and Irish dialects (where, for example, the *x* at the end of ⟨lough⟩ contrasts with the *k* of ⟨lock⟩). It also appears as the spirantized reflex of *k* in those dialects that display forms such as those in (40b).

3.5 Melodic geometry

As mentioned at the outset of the chapter, one of the motivations for recognizing the dissolubility of segments into smaller primes is the observation that they pattern into natural classes on the basis of shared phonological behaviour and certain phonetic commonalities. A given natural class is captured by identifying the common phonetic property with a particular prime. The unified phonological behaviour of the class is then accounted for by assuming that it is the shared prime that is being targeted by processes.

In order to tighten this notion further, we need to exclude the possibility of capturing unnatural (that is, non-occurring) classes. Achievement of this goal clearly depends to a great extent on successfully identifying the appropriate set of elements. But this is only part of the story. Even with an appropriate set of elements, there still exists a danger of capturing unnatural classes, if phonological processes are allowed simultaneously to manipulate random conjunctions of two or more elements. To prevent this, we might make appeal to the following principle:[76]

(46)   Each phonological process can access only one unit in a representation.

However, (46) turns out to be too restrictive, at least when allied to the bottle-brush mode of autosegmental representation we have been working with up to now. The view that elements are directly linked to the skeletal tier implies that each element is individually accessible to phonological processing, independently of all other elements. This much is in accord with the empirical record. The problem is that there exists a set of processes which do indeed display a tendency to access more than one element simultaneously. In other words, elements no less that segments pattern into natural classes. The number of element classes involved is relatively small, and, like segment classes, they are identifiable on the basis of certain phonetic commonalities.

One of the most frequently recurring element classes is one that can informally be specified in terms of resonance characteristics or place of articulation.[77] We have in fact alluded to this grouping at several points over the last couple of chapters. An example of a phonological phenomenon that makes exclusive reference to the place dimension is the set of conditions governing the melodic content of the coda of an English super-heavy rhyme (see 2.4.4). One condition, recall, prevents a sonorant in this position from bearing a distinct specification for place of articulation. In element terms, this means that A, U, I, @ and R form a class that is lexically barred from this context. Related to this is the general homorganicity of nasal-obstruent clusters, as in ⟨pa[m]per, wi[n]ter, a[ŋ]chor⟩, expressible as the spreading of a place-defining element from the obstruent on to the nasal.

It may seem a rather obvious point to make, but adopting a fully autosegmental view of phonological representation should not cause us to lose sight of the original insight that melodic expressions can and often do behave as units. In other words, certain processes can access all elements in a melodic expression simultaneously. These are processes which either spread or suppress a segment in its entirety.[78] Note that the integrity of a melodic expression cannot be defined by reference to the skeletal point to which it is attached. The fundamental motivation for the split between the skeletal and melodic dimensions militates against such a move. There is plenty of evidence to indicate that entire melodic expressions must be allowed to spread or delink quite independently of the skeletal tier. And there are many cases where the total suppression of melodic material evidently occurs without a concomitant loss of a position; witness the phenomenon of compensatory lengthening discussed in 2.2.2. The latter process also exemplifies the potential for whole melodic expressions to spread into vacant slots.

Another subset of elements that can function as a class are those that code laryngeal information, to be discussed in the next section. The relevant contrasts associated with this dimension, including tone in vowels and phonation-type in consonants, are frequently accessed as a group and quite independently of other dimensions.

On the other hand, there exist many logically possible combinations of elements which simply never show such group behaviour. Take for example the non-occurring three-element subset composed of **A**, **h** and **R**. Together these define a class that includes non-high vowels, coronals, fricatives and plosives. No attested process operates on all of these segment-types simultaneously. Other examples of unattested three-element classes, selected more or less at random, include: **?, I, N; h, N, U, @, A, ?**.

The challenge then is somehow to be able to pinpoint the small number of recurring element classes without also capturing the large number of non-occurring classes that an abandonment of the principle in (46) would imply. In autosegmental theory, the response has been to modify the bottle-brush model of representations. In its place has evolved a hierarchical model in which the functional unity of particular groups of primes is expressed by having them gathered under **class nodes**, which mediate between primes and the skeleton. The result is a geometric model of the sort schematized in (47), where the non-terminal nodes indicated by upper-case characters represent class nodes, while the terminal nodes in lower-case represent primes (features or elements, depending on the framework).[79]

(47)

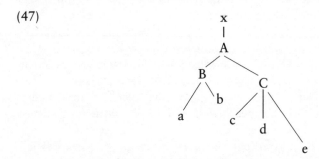

As before, elements are arrayed on separate tiers, and association lines indicate co-indexing with the skeletal tier. Thus, unlike the trees of syntactic theory, the geometric model does not imply that terminal elements are ordered in sequence (except in a special case to be discussed presently). The hierarchical arrangement is, however, similar to a syntactic tree in defining relations of dominance between mother and daughter nodes; in (47), a class node dominates terminal elements, either immediately (as in the case of B and C) or indirectly via an intervening class node (as in the case of A).

Applied to the geometric model, the principle in (46) allows each phonological process to target either a single terminal node or a single class node. The functional unity of groups of elements is captured by assuming that a process targeting a class node automatically affects any nodes it dominates. For example, delinking a class node results in the delinking of its daughters, whether these be class nodes themselves or terminal elements.

The class nodes for which there is the firmest empirical support involve the recurrent groupings mentioned above. As shown in the geometric fragment in (48), elements defining resonance or place-of-articulation properties are gathered under a PLACE node, while laryngeal elements are dominated by a LARYNGEAL node. These class nodes are grouped under a ROOT node, the matrix which defines the integrity of the melodic expression.[80]

(48)

$$
\begin{array}{c}
\text{x} \\
| \\
\text{ROOT} \bullet \\
\text{LARYNGEAL} \bullet \quad \diagdown \\
\quad \bullet \text{ PLACE}
\end{array}
$$

More controversial is the question of whether the phonological behaviour of primes defining degree and manner of stricture warrants representation under an independent class node. Even amongst phonologists who assume there is evidence to support such a view, there is considerable disagreement about where such a node should be located in the geometric model and about whether this dimension is itself subdivided into further class nodes.[81] Here we may follow one well established view on this matter, namely that the number of class nodes should not be multiplied beyond that which is minimally necessary to account for the uncontroversial evidence. The implication of this position is that the 'manner' elements N, h and ? should be directly and independently attached to the ROOT node.[82]

The geometric arrangement of the elements discussed up to now is thus as follows:[83]

(49)

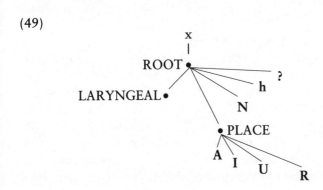

The functioning of the ROOT and PLACE nodes can be illustrated by comparing the representation of full and partial geminates. Complete identity between the melodic contents of adjacent positions is represented as the sharing of a single ROOT node. A full geminate consonant, such as the *tt* shown in (50), consists in the association of ROOT to two positions. Sharing ROOT implies sharing all the class and terminal nodes it dominates. (The LARYNGEAL node can be omitted for the time being, pending further discussion in the next section.)

(50)

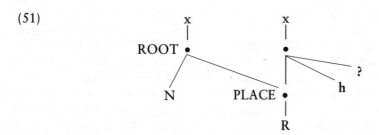

(The directionality of the spreading indicated here is something to be taken up in the next chapter.) A partial geminate such as *nt*, on the other hand, implies the presence of independent ROOT nodes, one dominating ? and **N** (in the case of the nasal stop), the other ? and **h** (in *t*). As shown in (51), the homorganicity of the cluster is represented as the sharing of the PLACE node together with the element it dominates, R.

(51)

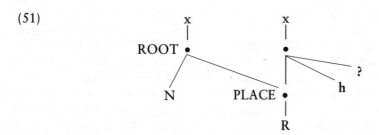

In this case, the shared place element happens to be **R**; in other cases, it can be, say, **U** (as in *mp*) or **@** (as in *ŋk*). The point is that the general homorganicity of nasal-plosive clusters is captured by referring to PLACE, rather than to individual elements separately.

The mechanism of PLACE sharing can be extended to the representation of homorganicity in certain types of contour segment, including affricates. By treating such sounds as occurrences of two melodic expressions attached to a single skeletal point, recall, we are able to capture the fact that they count as single segments for the purposes of phonological weight but as two segments when viewed in terms of their melodic make-up. Implicit in the notion of contour structure is the idea that elements can co-exist in a position without necessarily being fused. In the case of affricates, this suggests a configuration in which a single position is associated to two ROOT nodes, one dominating ? the other **h**.[84] The homorganicity of the closure and release phases is represented as the sharing of PLACE. In the case of *č/ǰ* (in ⟨chew, jaw⟩), this implies the following representation, in which the fusion of **R** and **I** defines palato-alveolar place:

(52)

Note that, unlike the geometric representations considered above, the one in (52) contains two nodes on a single tier, that of the ROOT node. This can be taken to indicate sequential ordering, which allows us to capture the two-phase nature of contour segments. The stop-closure phase of the affricate is characterized in the first ROOT node containing **ʔ**; the fricative-release phase corresponds to the second ROOT node dominating **h**. The separateness of the two ROOT nodes indicates a lack of fusion between **ʔ** and **h**. On the other hand, each is independently fused with the PLACE elements **R** and **I**.

Besides the lexically distinctive affricates *č* and *ǰ*, some dialects of English also display alveolar *ts* and *dz*, which result from the affrication of *t* and *d* respectively. Hence forms such as ⟨pi[ts]y⟩, ⟨[ts]en⟩, ⟨[dz]ip⟩.[85] In some cases, this process is evidently a precursor of spirantization on the opening trajectory in (37a). A typical sequence of events in this case is thus something like *t > ts > s*. (Parallel developments affecting other places of articulation have produced chains such as *p > pf > f* and *k > kx > x* in other languages and at other times in the history of English.[86]) The structure of affricates other than *č* differs from that in (52) only with respect to the elemental content of the PLACE node: for *ts* the relevant element is **R**, for *pf* **U**, and for *kx* **@**.

The process of affrication consists in the fission of a plosive's single ROOT node into two. In the case of the alveolar series, the resulting contour segment is identical to the palato-alveolar in (52), save for the fact that it lacks the palatal element **I**. Viewed in these terms, the process does not involve element loss, unlike other lenition processes. Nevertheless it does qualify as decomposition in the sense that, like other opening processes, it results in a reduction in the degree of fusion contained in a position.

The affricate-contour structure also figures in an assimilatory phenomenon which affects nasal-fricative clusters. Nasal stops by definition contain not only the nasal element but also, as indicated in (51), the stop element **ʔ**. The full representation of, say, *m* thus includes **N**, **ʔ** and **U**. The behaviour of **ʔ** in nasal consonants serves to illustrate a class of processes usually referred to as **fortition** or strengthening. It is worth emphasizing that fortition is not simply the inverse of lenition. The latter is a much more generalized phenomenon than the former, in that it affects a wider range of contexts and segment-types. In terms of its melodic effects, fortition involves the transformation of a continuant sound into a stop, as in *f > p* or *w > p*. In other words, it is a 'closing' process, taking the form of movement in the opposite direction to that expressed in portions of the opening trajectories in (37a) and (37c). Representationally, all such processes consist in the addition of ʔ to a melodic expression.

Some historical cases of strengthening are apparently spontaneous, in the sense that the emergence of a stop component cannot be attributed to spreading from a neighbouring position. Compare, for example, Latin *y* in *mayor* with its geminate affricate development in Italian *majjore*. Indeed many such spontaneous fortitions go hand in hand with gemination, something that is in all likelihood related to the propensity of such sounds to display what is known as **inalterability**.[87] That is, they typically resist lenition processes which affect their non-geminate counter-parts. There is evidently some general pressure on geminate consonants to appear in the guise of stops, although precisely what its representational motivation is remains somewhat unclear.

The majority of strengthening processes, particularly those that are synchronically active, can be shown to have a local cause. The usual site is one where the target sound is adjacent to some kind of a non-continuant consonant. A classic example is found in many Bantu languages, in which a stem-initial fricative, for example, hardens into a homorganic stop when a nasal prefix is attached. Compare the Sesotho root *-fa* ('give') with the derived form *m-po* ('gift'). The fact that such processes have a local stop trigger indicates that strengthening of this type is simply a sub-case of assimilation. In element terms, the compositional nature of fortition is expressed as the spreading of ʔ from one position to another. In the Sesotho example, the elements U and h, which together define the root-initial *f*, are fused with the ʔ spreading from the prefix nasal stop; the resulting three-element compound defines a labial plosive.

In English, fortition is evident in the widespread excrescence of an oral stop within nasal-fricative and lateral-fricative clusters. This process manifests itself in some dialects as the appearance of a *t* between *n* or *l* and *s* in forms such as ⟨prince, else⟩. The interval of voiceless occlusion is shorter than that which characterizes a lexically present *t* in forms such as ⟨prints, belts⟩.[88] This may be taken as evidence that the excrescence does not involve epenthesis of a skeletal point. Rather it should be seen as the strengthening of the fricative to a homorganic affricate. Viewed in these terms, excrescent *t* arises through ʔ spreading from the preceding non-continuant lateral or nasal into the position occupied by the fricative. There ʔ fuses with R but not with h. This implies a contour structure with one ROOT node containing the fusion of R and ʔ (defining the excrescent *t*) and another containing the fusion of R and h.[89] The process is illustrated in the following representation of *ns > nᵗs*:

(53) (a) ns   (b) nᵗs

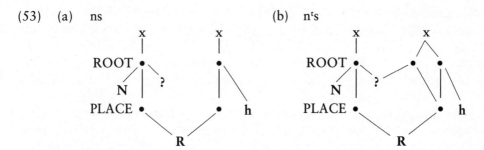

In the following pages, I will continue with the practice of using the truncated representational format illustrated in (8) and only spell out geometric details where the exposition so requires.

3.6 Laryngeal elements

We may now consider the melodic content of the LARYNGEAL node in (48). A range of different vocal-fold settings is available for executing contrasts in phonation-type (traditionally referred to in such terms as **voiced** versus **voiceless**) and pitch. The representation of laryngeal contrasts raises a number of issues, some of which continue to be subject to debate. One point is generally agreed on: the labels **voiced** and **voiceless** are inadequate for exhaustively classifying the phonetic and phonological aspects of this dimension. Their usefulness is limited to the informal identification of the two-way laryngeal distinction amongst consonants that typifies many phonological systems. However, this description obscures the fact that the phonetic manifestation of such a contrast is by no means constant across languages.

Two of the most widespread patterns of realization are exemplified by English and French. In the context of a word-initial CV sequence, the main exponent of laryngeal contrasts amongst plosives is **voice onset time**, the interval between the release of oral closure and the onset of vocal-fold vibration in the vowel.[90] In a truly voiced plosive, vibration commences prior to release and continues into the articulation of the following vowel. A voiceless aspirated plosive (sometimes referred to as **fortis**) is produced if there exists a time-lag between closure release and the onset of voicing. Where closure release and the onset of voicing coincide, the result is a 'neutral' voiceless unaspirated plosive. In French and many other languages, the contrast in this position between, say, the sounds symbolized as *b* and *p* is realized by means of the first and last of these types. That is, *b* is fully voiced, and *p* is voiceless unaspirated. In most dialects of English, on the other hand, the corresponding distinction alphabetized in the same manner is manifested as voiceless unaspirated *b* versus voiceless aspirated *p*.[91] This mismatch underlines the potentially misleading nature of the gross terms **voiced** and **voiceless,** to say nothing of the potential transcriptional confusion inherent in the use of symbols such as *p* and *b*. In the initial CV context, the allegedly 'voiced' *b/d/g* series in English is in fact not phonetically voiced at all and is to all intents and purposes identical to the neutral *p/t/k* series of French. In most systems of transcription, the selection of symbols such as *p* and *b* is thus guided by contrastive considerations rather than by any attempt to represent the physical properties of the sounds in question.

Some languages, such as Thai, utilize all three of the voice-onset categories just mentioned for consonantal contrasts. Other languages make use of other phonation types.[92] Various proposals exist for providing a more accurate characterization of the laryngeal dimension than the simple voiced–voiceless bifurcation allows. According to one approach, which has been widely adopted in current phonological theory, the relevant categories are defined in terms of vocal-fold tension and the degree of glottal aperture.[93] A detailed exposition of the phonetic correlates of this classification would take us well beyond the brief of this book. Besides, much of the relevant phonological evidence comes from languages other than English. For our present purposes, it will suffice to mention two categories within this system which play a role in the consonantal contrasts discussed in the previous paragraph. These are **slack vocal cords** and **stiff vocal cords**, each of which we may take to correspond to a particular element.

The slack element inheres in truly voiced obstruents, while the class of fortis obstruents (including voiceless aspirated plosives) contains the stiff element. Neutral obstruents can be assumed to possess neither of these elements. The signal characteristics of slack and stiff are respectively lowered and raised fundamental frequency. This observation has led to the suggestion that these same two categories are also involved in the specification of pitch contrasts in vowels, especially as employed in tone systems. There is some phonological evidence to support such a connection. For example, certain processes indicate a correlation between full voicing in a consonant and low tone in a neighbouring vowel, as well as between aspiration and high tone.[94] It is for this reason that the slack element is sometimes symbolized as L and the stiff element as H. According to this view, a mid-toned vowel in a three-tone system is equivalent to a neutral consonant in lacking an active laryngeal element.[95] Nevertheless, the unification of tonal and consonant-phonation categories remains controversial.[96] Since lexical tone contrasts play no role in English, this is not an issue we need dwell on here.

What is relevant, however, is to determine which segment-types in English bear which laryngeal elements. In traditional feature-based treatments of laryngeal contrasts in the language, it is usual to specify the distinction in terms of [voice]. Aspiration is deemed to be non-contrastive and is assigned to [-voice] plosives by rule.[97] An element-based approach is quite different. The lexical representation of fortis obstruents contains the element H. Aspiration is the particular interpretation this element receives when it is present in an expression defining a fortis plosive. On the other hand, obstruents in the neutral series, transcribed as *b*, *d*, *g*, *ǰ*, *v*, *ð*, *z*, *ʒ*, lack a laryngeal element. The two types represent the maximal set of English contrasts found in certain onset contexts, including in the initial CV site. In other contexts, however, the contrast is suspended in favour of the neutral series. This is true, for example, of an onset preceded by a fricative. In the CC clusters of, say, ⟨stay, mister, after⟩, the plosive is unaspirated (hence neutral) in most dialects of English. In systems displaying tapping, the neutralized reflex of *t/d* (as in ⟨fitter–bidder⟩) also lacks a laryngeal element.

Fully voiced obstruents of the type that occur in French contain the element L, contrasting in this case with neutral. The manner in which the laryngeal specification of the plosive series in French differs from English is illustrated in (54).

(54)

	Element	English	French
Voiced	L	—	bo 'beautiful'
Neutral	—	⟨bay⟩	po 'skin'
Voiceless aspirated	H	⟨pay⟩	—

Thai differs from French and English in displaying all three of the categories in (54). Free combination of elements in fact predicts a fourth category, one in which L and H are fused. This can be taken to represent the so-called 'voiced aspirate' or breathy-voice class of consonants. Gujarati is an example of a language which exploits all four possibilities. The following forms illustrate the Thai and Gujarati plosive systems:[98]

(55)

	Element	Thai	Gujarati
Voiced	L	bàa 'shoulder'	baɾ 'twelve'
Neutral	—	pàa 'forest'	pɔɾ 'last year'
Voiceless aspirated	H	phàa 'split'	phɔdz 'army'
Breathy	L, H	—	bhaɾ 'burden'

The default condition for sonorants (both vowels and consonantal resonants) is to be produced with vocal-cord vibration, a property that gives them their characteristic periodicity in the signal. This attribute cannot on its own be taken as evidence that sonorants contain the element L. The reason for this is that voicing in sonorants has a very low phonological profile when compared to true voicing in obstruents. The latter property systematically participates in a range of phonological processes which rarely if ever affect sonorants. For example, the classic process of final devoicing, such as occurs in any number of languages including German, Russian, Catalan and Old English, only ever affects obstruents. Voicing assimilation between segments (some cases of which we will consider presently) almost always affects obstruents to the exclusion of sonorants. And in some cases, sonorants are transparent to a laryngeal category spreading between flanking obstruents.[99] This behaviour has led to the recognition of two types of voicing: the **spontaneous** type that characterizes sonorants and the non-spontaneous or **active** type associated with obstruents.[100] It is the active type that is predominantly, and in many cases exclusively, involved in phonological processing. A consequence of this view is that the representation of phonation categories in terms of laryngeal elements is either restricted to obstruents or only allowed for in sonorants under special circumstances.

This conclusion leads us to rethink certain processes which previously have been treated in terms of laryngeal assimilation involving sonorants. A well-known example from English concerns the inter-vocalic tapping of *t* discussed in the previous section. This has sometimes been analysed as a voicing process; specifically, the voicing of the surrounding vowels is supposedly assimilated by the target consonant.[101] There is little doubt that the tap can be phonetically voiced, a fact we might try to account for by saying that vowels contain a phonation category which they are free to pass on to an adjacent consonant. If correct, such an analysis would contradict the claim that sonorants do not bear an active laryngeal element. However, an alternative analysis is available which is consistent with the latter view. According to the account of tapping outlined in the preceding section, the process primarily affects the manner rather than the laryngeal aspect of the consonant, taking the form of a suppression of the elements **?** and **h**. Viewed in this way, the phonetic voicing of the tap reflex is no more than a secondary effect, reflecting the fact that the residual element (**R**) is independently realized as a spontaneously voiced sonorant.

For a similar reason, it is necessary to rethink the traditional analysis of the durational difference displayed by English vowels before different classes of consonant.[102] Very broadly speaking, a vowel is relatively longer before a neutral obstruent or a sonorant than it is before a fortis obstruent. In the past, this has been treated as a case of lengthening before a 'voiced' consonant. The allegedly unified nature of the 'voiced' class is difficult to sustain in the face of the evidence just reviewed: neither sonorants nor the relevant sub-class of obstruents can be said to possess a phonologically active laryngeal component. This means that the durational phenomenon should rather be thought of as a type of shortening, conditioned by a following fortis obstruent. (The opportunity of examining just such a proposal is provided in exercise 1.I of chapter 4.) In terms of the account being offered here, the class of conditioning sounds in this case is identified by the presence of **H**.

A number of assimilatory phenomena in English illustrate the autonomous nature of laryngeal elements. One, which we will examine in detail in the next chapter, involves a distributional restriction whereby obstruents in coda-onset sequences must agree with respect to their laryngeal identity, as in the medial clusters of forms such as ⟨mister, chapter, factor⟩. Another concerns the dynamic voice alternation affecting the suffixes ⟨-s⟩ and ⟨-ed⟩, touched on in 1.4.2. These have three alternants each, conditioned by the nature of the final segment of the stem to which they are attached: *z, s, əz* and *d, t, əd* respectively. The vocalic reflexes, evident in forms such as ⟨dishes⟩ and ⟨fitted⟩, occur whenever the stem ends in a consonant which shares certain place and/or manner characteristics with the consonant of the suffix; specifically, *əz* occurs after a sibilant and *əd* after *t* or *d*. We will postpone discussion of this aspect of the alternation until the next chapter.

As shown in (56), the appearance of the other alternants of ⟨-s⟩ and ⟨-ed⟩ is dependent on the laryngeal property of the stem-final segment:

(56) ⟨-s⟩   ⟨-ed⟩

 (a) -*s*   -*t*

   cats   packed

   tops   stopped

   safes   doffed

 (b) -*z*   -*d*

   dogs   logged

   robs   robbed

   pods   dodged

 (c) -*z*   -*d*

   days   stayed

   goes   bowed

   sons   sunned

   calls   called

There are good grounds for taking *z* and *d* to be the lexical forms of ⟨-(e)s⟩ and ⟨-ed⟩, since these are the shapes they assume when, as in (56c), they occur next to sonorants.[103] If we are right in assuming that sonorants lack an active voicing component which could be passed on to an adjacent segment, then it follows that the laryngeal value of the suffix consonants in this context must reflect their lexical identity. In terms of their melodic make-up, *z* and *d* in English share with other neutral obstruents a lack of a laryngeal element. The alternants in (56a) thus result from assimilation to a preceding fortis obstruent. The process consists in the rightward spreading of H from a stem-final position occupied by a fortis obstruent to the position occupied by the suffix consonant. This is illustrated in the following relevant fragment of a representation containing *t-z-* > *ts*:

(57)

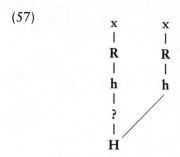

 The fortis–neutral contrast among obstruents appears to be by far the best established pattern in English. Nevertheless, there are some dialects which have a fully voiced series corresponding to the otherwise general neutral set (in ⟨bin, din, gun⟩, etc.). As in French, these contrast not with voiceless aspirates but with neutral (in ⟨pin, tin, kin⟩, etc.). (One area where this pattern is attested is the northeast of England.) The indication that the first series is truly voiced, and thus contains the element L, is confirmed by the observation that a subset of the dialects in question displays a voicing assimilation process not found in other dialects. This is a word-edge anticipatory phenomenon, in which fully voiced obstruents pass on their laryngeal identity to a preceding obstruent:[104]

(58)   top gun   to[b g]un
       football   foo[d b]all
       pitch black   pi[ǰ b]lack
       backbone   ba[g b]one

In this instance, it is the element L that spreads leftwards, a process that is widespread in other languages (including Polish and Russian).

3.7 Conclusion

In this chapter we have reviewed some of the evidence supporting the existence of sub-segmental primes. The bulk of this evidence derives from the behaviour of segments under phonological processing. The representational model that has emerged is one in which the set of processes to which a sound is susceptible is circumscribed, on the one hand, by the number and nature of the elements it contains and, on the other, by the requirement that all processing be expressible in terms of the fundamental operations of composition and decomposition.

In order to constrain our model of phonological processing still further, we could require of every process that it have a local cause. Leaving aside the special case of spontaneously appearing elements (such as appear in certain examples of fortition and vowel epenthesis), we can see how compositional processes begin to satisfy this criterion. The mechanism of autosegmental spreading, by which an element from one position becomes fused with an element in a neighbouring position, establishes a intimate bond between a process and its triggering context.

Two further questions connected to the local-cause requirement remain to be answered, however. First, what determines whether two positions are adjacent and thus form a domain within which spreading can take place? Second, it may not seem immediately obvious how decompositional processes can have a local cause. What is the nature of the relation between process and context in such cases, and what is it about this relation that triggers delinking? These are issues to be taken up in the next chapter.

3.8 Appendix: specification of elements

3.8.0

Elements are cognitive categories which serve the grammatical function of coding lexical contrasts.[105] They are mapped in the first instance onto the acoustic signal. This mapping relation guides the manner in which elements are input to production and perception. That is, elements constitute internalized templates by reference to which listeners decode auditory input and speakers orchestrate and monitor their articulations.

The purpose of this appendix is (a) to specify the internalized elemental patterns which, according to one set of proposals, represent the elements introduced in this chapter; and (b) to suggest how these patterns are mapped onto the acoustic signal.

3.8.1 *Resonance elements*

We may think of each pattern associated with a resonance element such as **A, I** and **U** as being displayed in a frame mimicking a spectral slice, in which the vertical axis corresponds to intensity and the horizontal axis to frequency. The

(a)

(b)

(c)

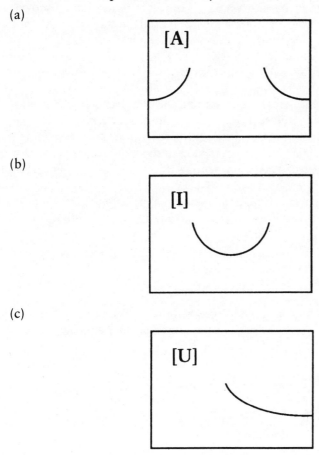

Figure 1 Elemental patterns: (a) **A (mAss)**, (b) **I (dIp)**, (c) **U (rUmp)**
Note: The contours are schematic spectral envelopes, plotted in frames which map onto acoustic spectral slices (vertical axis: amplitude; horizontal axis: frequency).
Source: Harris and Lindsey in press

latter coincides with what may be termed the **sonorant frequency zone**, corresponding to the frequency band within which the perceptually significant resonant characteristics of vowels are concentrated. Roughly speaking, this region covers the range between 0 kHz and 3 kHz, in which the first three formants are located. Within this zone, the convergence of two formants produces prominent peaks of energy (spectral peaks) corresponding to various vowel qualities. It is these peaks that match the peak–valley profiles of individual elemental patterns.

The elemental patterns of **A, I** and **U**, shown in figure 1, are plotted in frames of the type just described. Figure 1a shows what can be termed a **mAss** pattern for **A**. This shows energy minima at the top and bottom of the frame; i.e. there is a mass of relatively higher energy in the middle of the frame. The precise outline of the energy mass is not a crucial part of the definition of this pattern and is thus left blank in the diagram. Figure 1b depicts a **dIp** pattern for **I**, with energy lower in the middle of the frame than on either side. The **rUmp** pattern of **U**, shown in figure 1c, is characterized by energy of a higher amplitude in the lower part of the frame (its exact outlines not criterial) than in the upper part.

The following summaries of each element provide (a) an informal label by which it can be identified; and (b) a specification of its signal mapping.

A   (a) **mAss**; (b) a spectral peak (representing the convergence of Formants 1 and 2) located in the middle of the sonorant frequency zone.

I   (a) **dIp**; (b) low first formant coupled with a spectral peak (representing the convergence of Formants 2 and 3) at the top of the sonorant frequency zone.

U   (a) **rUmp**; (b) a spectral peak (representing the convergence of Formants 1 and 2) at the bottom of the sonorant frequency zone.

@   (a) **neutral**; (b) dispersed formant structure, i.e. no salient spectral peak.

R   (a) **'coronal'**; (b) the set of formant transitions associated with coronals.

3.8.2 *'Manner' elements*

h   (a) **noise**; (b) aperiodic energy.
?   (a) **stop**; (b) abrupt and sustained decrease in overall amplitude.
N   (a) **nasal**; (b) broad resonant peak at lower end of the frequency range.

3.8.3 *Laryngeal elements*

L   (a) **'slack'**; (b) low fundamental frequency.
H   (a) **'stiff'**; (b) high fundamental frequency.

3.8.4 *Element fusion*

The effects of element compounding are derived by overlaying one elemental pattern on another. Figure 2 illustrates two complex profiles which result from the pair-wise combination of patterns displayed in figure 1. The profile of *e* in

(a)

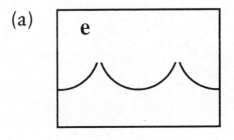

(b)

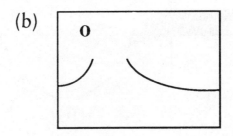

Figure 2 Compounded elemental patterns: (a) **A** and **I** (*e*); (b) **A** and **U** (*o*)
Source: Harris and Lindsey in press

figure 2a might be viewed as 'dIp within a mAss'. That is, it is an amalgam of two patterns: (a) energy higher in the middle of the frame than at top or bottom, indicating the presence of **A**; and (b) energy lower in the middle than on either side, indicating the presence of **I**. In the case of *o*, depicted in figure 2b, we can again identify two patterns: (a) energy higher in the middle of the frame than at top or bottom, i.e. **A**, and (b) no energy above the middle, i.e. **U**. Both of these compound patterns map rather directly onto the spectral envelopes of *e* and *o*.

Figure 3 shows patterns resulting from various combinations of ʔ, h and U, displayed in stylized spectrographic frames (in which the horizontal axis mimics time, the vertical axis frequency, and darkness intensity). Fusion of all three elements defines a labial plosive (figure 3a). Different lenition reflexes are defined by the suppression of particular elemental patterns: spirantization (figure 3b), debuccalization to *h* (figure 3c), debuccalization to ʔ (figure 3d), and vocalization (figure 3e).

Exercises

1 Scots vowel systems

The data The data below show the subsystems of vowels found in final open stressed syllables in five Scots dialects.[106] Each row of words (listed in English as

(a) labial plosive

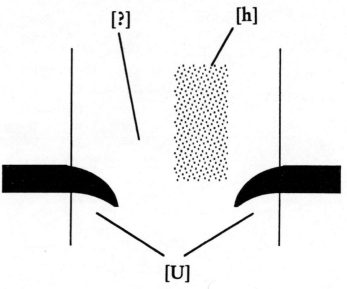

(b) labial fricative

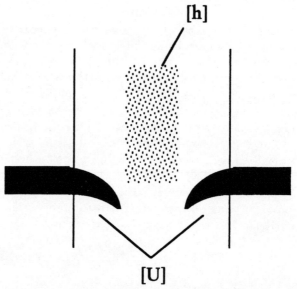

Figure 3 Stylized spectrograms showing various combinations of the elements ʔ (**stop**), **h** (**noise**) and **U** (**rUmp**): (a) labial plosive, (b) labial fricative, (c) glottal fricative, (d) glottal stop, (e) labial approximant.
Source: Harris and Lindsey in press

(c) glottal fricative

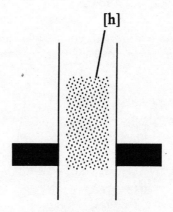

(d) glottal stop

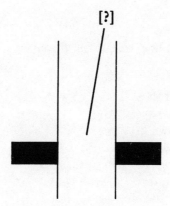

(e) labial approximant

Figure 3 contd.

opposed to Scots spelling) gives a very rough guide to the lexical incidence of each vowel.

The task For each different vowel, provide a representation which includes details of its nuclear structure and melodic content.

FETLAR, SHETLAND

iː	die, eye, give, knee, tree
eː	clay, have, no, say, toe
aː	fall, gnaw, two, snow, who, wall
oː	low, below, row
uː	cow, full, how, through
yuː	dew, new, spew
øː	do, she, shoe
ɛy	pay, stay, weigh, aye
æy	fry, kye ('cattle'), ay
ɒy	boy, joy, toy
əw	ewe, grow, hoe, roll, knoll, through

KEISS, CAITHNESS

iː	die, eye, give, key, tree
eː	clay, day, do, no, toe, too
aː	away, fall, gnaw, two, wall, who
oː	below, low, row
üː	cow, full, how, now, pull, shoe
yüː	new, spew, stew
ɛy	aye, hay, pay, stay, weigh, why
æy	ay, die, fry, way, whey
oy	joy, toy
ɛü	dew, ewe, grow, knoll, roll, through

NEW LUCE, WIGTOWNSHIRE

iː	die, eye, tree, give
ɪ	do, flea, have, no, shoe
eː	day, say
ɒː	away, fall, gnaw, law, two, who
oː	below, low
uː	cow, full, how, now, pull, through
yuː	dew, new, spew

εy   aye, clay, hay, pay, stay, way, whey
ɒy   fry, kye, why
ɔy   joy, toy, buoy
əw   ewe, grow, hoe, knoll, roll

BALLYWALTER, CO. DOWN (IRELAND)

iː   die, eye, give, knee, tree
eː   no, Tay
εː   clay, day, do, have, tea, toe, show, say
aː   gnaw, fall, law, snow, wall
ɔː   two, who, away
oː   below, low
üː   through, too, zoo
yüː   dew, new, spew, stew
εy   aye, clay, hay, pay, weigh, why
æy   fry, kye
ɒy   ay, boy, joy, toy
øw   cow, ewe, full, grow, knoll, roll

GRETNA GREEN, DUMFRIESSHIRE

ey   die, eye, key, knee, tree, aye, clay, hay, whey
ɪː   flea, give, no, pay, she, toe, two, who
eː   day, say, stay, way
aː   fall, gnaw, law, snow
oː   below, low
əuː   cow, full, how, now, through, you
iw   blue, dew, new, spew
øː   do, shoe, too
εy   ay, weigh
ay   fry, kye, why
oy   buoy, joy, toy
uy   boy
əw   ewe, grow, hoe, knoll, roll

2 *Yorkshire assimilation*

The data The set of laryngeal contrasts in Yorkshire English is the same as that found in most other dialects. However, for many Yorkshire speakers, the forms ⟨bag pack⟩ and ⟨back pack⟩ are homophones.[107] The process responsible for this merger is more fully illustrated in the data below.

The task What is the representation of the process? What element(s) does it target? What does it reveal about the representation of laryngeal contrasts in different classes of sounds?

1	Bob goes	Bo[b g]oes
	Bob came	Bo[p k]ame
2	rub out	ru[b] out
	rub shoulders	ru[p ʃ]oulders
3	told Viv	tol[d v]iv
	told Fred	tol[t f]red
4	dread it	drea[d] it
	dreadful	drea[tf]ul
5	bad boy	ba[d b]oy
	bad time	ba[t t]ime
6	judge ruled	ju[ǰ] ruled
	judge took	ju[č t]ook
7	bridge the	bri[ǰð]e
	bridge party	bri[č p]arty
8	big nose	bi[g] nose
	big thumb	bi[k θ]umb
9	rag and	ra[g] and
	rag trade	ra[k t]rade
10	love Davy	lo[v] Davy
	love Pat	lo[f p]at
11	smooth over	smoo[ð] over
	smooth top	smoo[θ t]op
12	rose garden	ro[z] garden
	rose petal	ro[s p]etal
13	ribbed back	ri[bd b]ack
	ribbed pattern	ri[pt] pattern
14	forged more	for[ǰd] more
	forged cheque	for[čt č]eque
15	rigged local	ri[gd] local
	rigged sample	ri[kt s]ample
16	loved Zoe	lo[vd z]oe
	loved Fiona	lo[ft f]iona
17	squeezed Joe	squee[zd ǰ]oe
	squeezed past	squee[st p]ast

3 More Merseyside consonants

The data The following data expand on the description of Merseyside English given in 3.4.2. (Symbols: Φ = voiceless bilabial fricative; β = neutral bilabial fricative; γ = neutral velar fricative.)

The task Suggest representations which account for the consonantal realizations shown in the bracketed portions of the words.

1	people	peop[ɸ]le	pepper	pe[ɸ]er
2	later	la[s]er	matter	ma[s]er
3	joker	jo[x]er	packet	pa[x]et
4	Robbie	Ro[β]ie	rabbit	ra[β]it
5	ready	rea[z]y	Maddy	ma[z]i
6	baggy	ba[ɣ]y	boggle	bo[ɣ]le

4 Nasals in African American English

The data In some varieties of African American English, nasal sounds participate in the processes illustrated in the data below.[108]

The task Provide representations which (i) distinguish the vowels in columns (a, b) from those in column (c); and (ii) capture the alternations evident in columns (a) and (b).

(a) Before pause		(b) Before vowel	(c) Non-nasal
1	hĩ͂ə ⟨him⟩	⟨h[ĩ͂əm] and⟩	bɪəd ⟨bid⟩
2	wĩ͂ə ⟨win⟩	⟨w[ĩ͂ən] a⟩	
3	kĩ͂ə ⟨king⟩	⟨k[ĩ͂əŋ] of⟩	
4	sæ͂ə͂ ⟨Sam⟩	⟨s[æ͂ə͂m] and⟩	sæəd ⟨sad⟩
5	pæ͂ə͂ ⟨pan⟩	⟨p[æ͂ə͂n] of⟩	
6	hæ͂ə͂ ⟨hang⟩	⟨h[æ͂ə͂ŋ] a⟩	
7	tã͂ə͂ ⟨time⟩	⟨t[ã͂ə͂m] of⟩	haəd ⟨hide⟩
8	sã͂ə͂ ⟨sign⟩	⟨s[ã͂ə͂n] of⟩	

4 Licensing

4.1 Introduction

This chapter develops some of the notions of phonological constituent structure introduced in chapter 2. There we reviewed arguments in favour of the view that syllabic constituents (onsets, rhymes and nuclei) are maximally binary branching. Here we will examine a range of facts which support the conclusion that the relation between positions within a constituent is asymmetric. A uniform pattern of left-headedness can be shown to manifest itself in all constituents; that is, the left-hand position is dominant in relation to its recessive sister on the right. We will go on to consider the question of headedness as it relates to other domains, including those formed by coda-onset clusters and those involving relations between nuclei, for example at the level of the word.

A major concern of the chapter is to establish that the properties of binarity and headedness in phonological constituent structure are derivable from more fundamental principles of grammar. One such principle, that of licensing, integrates the various parts of a representation by requiring that each unit be bound in some way to some other unit. In order to be phonetically interpretable, a melodic expression, for example, must be associated to a skeletal position; a position itself must belong to a syllabic constituent; and each constituent must also be incorporated into some larger domain, such as the word.

Licensing defines the circumstances under which a pair of positions can be considered adjacent. In so doing, it establishes the necessary conditions of locality that must prevail in order for phonological processes involving an interaction between the two positions to occur. In this respect, licensing provides an answer to the question of where phonological processes take place.

I will also attempt to demonstrate how the theory of phonological licensing can begin to answer the more fundamental question of **why** phonological processes occur where they do. This involves making appeal to a principle which imposes severe constraints on the relation between the melodic content of a skeletal position and the niche occupied by the position in the constituent hierarchy. By way of illustrating this relation, I will devote the second part of the chapter to a detailed analysis of the contextual conditions that regulate the various processes of *t*-lenition in English introduced in 3.4.2.

4.2 The phonological hierarchy

4.2.1 *Headedness*

Terms such as **onset** and **nucleus** refer to **categories** of syllabic structure. **Head,** on the other hand, is not a categorial term but rather refers to a phonological function or **relation,** specifically one that is contracted between positions.

The headedness of a branching constituent can be determined in the first instance on the basis of the phonotactic possibilities associated with each position.[1] In a metrically prominent context (for example, in the dominant syllable of a word), a non-branching constituent typically displays a maximal or near-maximal set of contrasts. In a branching constituent, on the other hand, the distributional possibilities diminish, but in an unequal fashion. At least in the case of onsets and nuclei, it is clear that the position on the left enjoys a greater degree of distributional freedom than its sister. As we saw in 2.4.2, in a branching onset, occupation of the right-hand position is restricted to a liquid or a glide, while the position on the left can be filled by any of a range of plosives or voiceless fricatives. In a branching nucleus, the right-hand slot can only be distinctively specified as a glide, whereas the melodic specification of the position on the left potentially covers a full range of vocalic contrasts (see 2.4.3). Let us assume that this asymmetric division of phonotactic potential is symptomatic of a headed relation and further that the greater degree of distributional freedom is invested in the dominant member of a constituent. On this basis, we may conclude that onsets and nuclei are left-headed.

This distributional argument does not extend directly to branching rhymes. The incidence of melodic contrasts in a coda is indeed constrained, but not by the nuclear position on its left; instead, it is dependent on the onset appearing to its right. Under the assumption just outlined, this fact establishes the coda as a recessive position, but it fails to signal any kind of relation between the positions of a branching rhyme. Nevertheless, phenomena such as closed-rhyme shortness and rhymal weight indicate that some kind of link exists between these positions, although it does not immediately suggest a pattern of headedness. However, there is at least one observation we can make which does point to an asymmetry in this context: a nuclear position is obligatorily present in a rhyme, whereas the coda is only optionally so. This is reflected in an implicational universal according to which no language possesses branching rhymes to the exclusion of non-branching rhymes. On the assumption that obligatoriness indicates dominance and that optionality indicates recessiveness, we may conclude that rhymes are left-headed.

4.2.2 *Constituent parameters*

Research into a wide range of languages of quite diverse genetic affiliation indicates that the properties of left-headedness and maximal binarity are universally characteristic of phonological constituents. The full set of possible constitu-ent structures is thus as set out in (1). From now on, it will be useful to adopt the convention of representing constituent heads by means of a vertical line.

(1)   Non-branching   Branching

   Onsets   O   O
                      | I\
                      x   x x

   Nuclei   N   N
                      | I\
                      x   x x

   Rhymes   R   R
                      | | \
                      N   N   \
                      I\   I\   \
                   x (x)   x (x) x

Languages vary with respect to whether they possess one or more type of branching constituent. English happens to be a language in which all three constituents may branch. Onsets in some languages, however, can only be non-branching (Arabic, for example). Rhymes in some languages, a subset of so-called 'open-syllable' (i.e. coda-less) systems, can only be non-branching (Zulu, for instance). Nuclei in some languages can only be non-branching (Yoruba, for example), with the result that they lack vowel-length distinctions. We can charac-terize these cross-linguistic differences in terms of three parameters which deter-mine the structure of each constituent:

(2)   **Constituent structure parameters**

	Branching constituent	[OFF]	ON
(a)	Onset	Arabic	English
(b)	Nucleus	Yoruba	English
(c)	Rhyme	Zulu	English

Whether these parametric settings can be assumed to hold throughout derivation is a matter we take up later in 4.6.4.

Implicit in (2) are two implicational universals. According to one, the legitimi-zation of branching structure in a particular constituent (corresponding to an ON setting on one of the parameters) implies that the language in question also possesses the non-branching variant; the reverse implication does not hold. This establishes the OFF setting as the unmarked value (indicated in (2) by the square bracketing), an observation that is confirmed by a range of other facts. For example, exclusively non-branching structures enjoy a much wider distribution throughout the world's languages and are the first to be acquired by native speakers of languages displaying one or more of the ON options.[2] Second, for some reason that is at present not clearly understood, a positive setting on (2a) depends on (2c) also being positive. That is, no language possesses branching onsets without also possessing branching rhymes.[3]

4.2.3 *The prosodic hierarchy*

For some time, it has been recognized that the asymmetric nature of intra-constituent relations shows certain parallels with that of relations holding between units in suprasegmental structure. These similarities are particularly clear in the case of the metrical relations involved in stress assignment. Indeed it is now usual to view the skeletal and constituent dimensions as being integrated into a hierarchy of prosodic levels which includes the **foot**, the **phonological word**, the **phonological phrase**, and perhaps even larger domains. Together the various domains make up the **prosodic hierarchy**:[4]

(3) **Prosodic hierarchy**
      Phonological phrase
      Phonological word
      Foot
      Syllabic constituent
      Skeletal position

A foot, recall, is a rhythmic unit consisting of one or more syllables – more technically, rhymes. In the event of a foot containing two or more rhymes, one is dominant. English is one of a large class of languages inhabited by that most exotic of beasts, the left-headed foot. This is revealed in the location of primary and secondary word-stress. A word such as ⟨Cinderélla⟩ contains two feet: ⟨Cìnde-⟩ and ⟨-rélla⟩. The word ⟨cíty⟩ contains one.

There have been various proposals for capturing the parallelism of relations at different levels of the prosodic hierarchy. One approach has been to represent all relational aspects of phonological structure in terms of metrical tree structures in which each branch is labelled as dominant/strong or recessive/weak.[5] A related mode of representation is the metrical grid, in one version of which units at different levels of the prosodic hierarchy are gathered into bracketed constituents, with one unit in each constituent being designated as the constituent head.[6] According to related proposals, asymmetries within the prosodic hierarchy are characterized in terms of relations of dependency or government (on which more presently).[7]

The representation of constituent structure in terms of trees or bracketing has a clear precedent in syntax. We can pursue this parallel further by examining some of the structural and relational properties of the prosodic hierarchy. Focusing initially on the lower reaches of the hierarchy, let us consider a number of generalizations that can be made about constituent heads and the positions that can follow them.

4.2.4 *Projection*

There is a sense in which a constituent category can be said to reflect certain properties of its head position. For the time being, we can think of this relation in terms of the notion of sonority. (As mentioned in 2.4.2, this is merely an informal label for a more fundamental property that is directly coded in melodic structure, a point to be expanded in 4.4.5.) Typically, the nucleus is the locus of relatively more sonorous or 'V-like' melodic material, while the onset is the locus of relatively less sonorous, more 'C-like' material. However, within each of these constituents, the burden of maintaining this distinction is not equally shared. In both instances, it is the head position which optimizes the sonority profile of its constituent. A recessive position, in contrast, contains material which compromises the profile. For example, the right-hand slot of a branching onset can contain a V-like glide.

The notion we would like to be able to capture here is that a head position is somehow a better representative of its constituent than is its sister. Suppose we provisionally assign the category V to the head position of a nucleus. Then the category of the nuclear node itself should match V. In phrase-structure terminology, the nucleus can be referred to as V' (V-bar).[8] To make the analogy with syntax even more explicit: V' (the nucleus) is a **projection** of V (its head position), in much the same way that a verb phrase is a projection of its head verb. By the same token, if an onset head position is C, then the onset category is C'.

Generalizing across both the onset and nucleus domains, we may use the category variable X to stand for any constituent head position and Y for an optionally present sister position. X and Y are terminal nodes of the prosodic hierarchy. The onset and nuclear nodes are then **immediate projections** of X:

(4)   (a)   X'   (b)   N   (c)   O
              | \ | \ | \
              X Y x_1 x_2 x_1 x_2

As for the rhyme, it is properly considered a projection of the nucleus. That is, the term **rhyme** does not refer to an independent constituent category; it is rather an informal label for the second projection (X" or X-double-bar) of a nuclear head position:

(5)
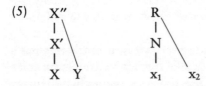

Some additional syntactic terminology will be useful for referring to particular relations that hold between different nodes in the hierarchy. X is the **immediate**

head of X′ and the **ultimate head** of the overall rhymal constituent X″. Under X′, Y is the **complement** of X. Thus the x_2 positions in (4b) and (4c) are respectively nuclear and onset complements (in much the same way that a noun phrase is the complement of a head verb within an X′ verb phrase). Under X″ in (5), Y (the 'coda') is an **adjunct** of X. (The nearest syntactic analogue is a configuration in which an adverbial or prepositional phrase is said to be the adjunct of a verb within an X″ verb phrase.) The term **rhymal adjunct** is thus technically more accurate than **coda** (which, as we saw in 2.4.4, has no categorial status).

There is evidence, to be reviewed below, that the prosodic hierarchy extends 'upwards' beyond the level of the rhyme.[9] In English, the head of a bi-rhymal foot, for example, is the rhyme on the left (as in ⟨cíty⟩). Feet in their turn enter into headed relations at the level of the phonological word. Of the two feet that make up the example ⟨Cínderélla⟩, mentioned above, it is the one on the right (⟨-rélla⟩) that is dominant, as revealed in the fact that its prominent rhyme bears the primary word stress. These prominence relations at different levels of the prosodic hierarchy are illustrated in (6), where we follow the precedent of representing headship by means of a vertical line.

(6)

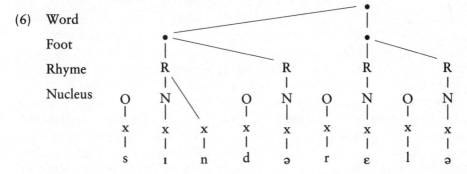

Here we see that the foot and the phonological word contain projections of nuclear positions. Thus nuclear heads have the potential to be projected through successive levels of the prosodic hierarchy. The ultimate head of the whole word in (6) is the nuclear position containing the vowel ε.

Beyond the word, nuclear heads project first to the phonological phrase and ultimately to the intonational phrase. Prominence relations at these levels manifest themselves in phrasal stress and sentence accent. Very broadly speaking, within a two-word phrase in English, the ultimate head is the dominant nucleus of the word on the right, as in ⟨prètty bónnet⟩.

The representation in (6) illustrates one important respect in which the phonological implementation of X-bar principles differs from that in syntax. The prosodic hierarchy lacks the recursive property of syntactic phrase structure whereby a constituent of one category can be embedded within a constituent of a different category. A noun phrase, for example, can be embedded within a verb phrase; but a nucleus, for example, cannot be embedded within an onset. The absence of recursion lies behind the 'spinal' configuration of head projections in the prosodic hierarchy. That is, the ultimate head of a phonological representation is defined by a straight line which runs through all prosodic levels and which contains nothing but projections of a single nuclear position.

4.3   Phonological licensing

4.3.1   *Prosodic and autosegmental licensing*

In this section, we address the question of whether the left-headed and maximally binary-branching properties of phonological constituents are derivable from grammatical principles which govern constituent structure in general. We begin by considering one such principle, that of **licensing**, as originally developed in syntactic theory.

One requirement of sentence well-formedness is that each unit in a representation must be integrated into the phrase-structure hierarchy in order for it to be semantically interpretable. For this integration to be achieved, the presence of each node in sentence structure has to be sanctioned or licensed by the presence of some other node. Licensing thus defines a binary asymmetric relation between units in the grammatical hierarchy. For example, within a verb phrase, a noun phrase complement is licensed by the verb that is its head. The only unit in a given structure that is exempt from the licensing requirement is the ultimate head of the whole sentence (in technical terms, the matrix node of a root sentence).

It is now usual to assume that licensing extends 'downwards' into the phonology, where it controls the phonetic interpretability of units in a representation. The phonological application of the principle can be viewed as an attempt to formalize the traditional idea that all sounds in a string have to be gathered into syllable structure. That is, it is not possible to have 'stray' sounds which are syllabically unaffiliated.[10]

Expanding this notion to the entire prosodic hierarchy results in the requirement that each unit within a representation must belong to some higher-order unit – a skeletal position to a syllabic constituent, a constituent to a foot, a foot to a word, and so on up the hierarchy. To put it somewhat differently: the presence of each unit within a phonological representation must be sanctioned by some other unit. Licensing is the mechanism by which this authorization is granted.

Within the phrase-structure and prosodic hierarchies, it is assumed that a position is licensed by its head. Thus within a branching onset or nucleus, for example, the head position licenses its complement. At the foot and word levels, one nuclear position is licensed by another. We can go further and view licensing as also regulating the relation between melodic and prosodic structure. Specifically, a melodic expression is licensed through association with a skeletal point.

Licensing, then, can be thought of as the mortar that binds together all components of the phonological hierarchy, both prosodic and melodic. Purely as a matter of convenience, we can label licensing relations differently according to the levels of the phonological hierarchy at which they hold. Under **prosodic licensing**, each unit in the prosodic hierarchy is required to belong to some higher-order structure.[11] **Autosegmental licensing** regulates the attachment of melodic material to skeletal slots.[12] These terms simply refer to different facets of the same fundamental mechanism, rather than to two independent mechanisms.

Any unit in the phonological hierarchy which fails to be sanctioned by phonological licensing is phonetically uninterpretable. This situation arises, for example, in cases where a melodic expression becomes detached from its skeletal slot. Our discussion of compensatory lengthening in 2.2.2 implicitly invoked the autosegmental dimension of licensing; recall that, once the velar fricative of a form such as *nixt* ⟨night⟩ becomes dissociated from its position, it is no longer phonetically expressed. Some versions of prosodic theory allow for circumstances under which certain constituents or skeletal points fail to get integrated into the phonological hierarchy; under the prosodic aspect of licensing, such stray material is then assumed to be erased at some point in derivation.[13]

Each level of the phonological hierarchy defines a **licensing domain**. At the autosegmental level, this takes the form of a skeletal point together with its associated melodic material. A prosodic licensing domain corresponds to a particular level of projection in the prosodic hierarchy. Reflecting the asymmetry of licensing relations, the presence of any non-head within a given prosodic domain is sanctioned by the presence of the head of that domain. Within the domain of a branching nucleus, for example, the **directionality** of the licensing asymmetry is necessarily head-initial, reflecting the fact that constituents are uniformly left-headed.[14] In this configuration, the left-hand position licenses its sister by virtue of being the head of that domain and thus being projected up to the next (nuclear) level of structure.

With this notion of domain, we may define phonological licensing as follows: within a domain, all phonological units must be licensed save one, the head of that domain.[15] The unlicensed head of a domain is itself licensed at some higher level of projection.

To illustrate this last point, let us train our sights on a fragment of the network of licensing relations holding in the representation of ⟨Cinderella⟩ in (6). A subset of the relations contracted specifically by the first nucleus are shown in (7), where the arrows indicate the directionality of licensing. In order to focus on the licensing aspect of the representation, I characterize syllabic constituency here by means of labelled bracketing rather than arboreally.

(7)

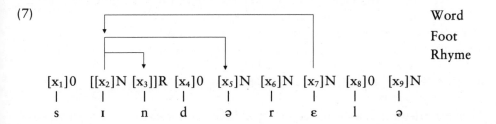

Word
Foot
Rhyme

$[x_1]0 \quad [[x_2]N \; [x_3]]R \; [x_4]0 \quad [x_5]N \quad [x_6]N \quad [x_7]N \quad [x_8]0 \quad [x_9]N$

s   ɪ   n   d   ə   r   ɛ   l   ə

The nuclear position x_2 in (7) autosegmentally licenses the melodic expression defining *ı*. By virtue of being the head of its rhyme, the same position prosodically licenses the coda position x_3 on the rhyme projection.[16] And by virtue of being the head of its foot, it licenses the nuclear position x_5 on the foot projection. On the word projection, x_2 is itself licensed by x_7, the nuclear head of the second foot.

There thus exists a chain of licensing extending from the lowest to the highest level of phonological structure. From this it follows that only one unit within the phonological hierarchy may remain unlicensed. This is the ultimate head of a representation – the head of the highest-level domain in phonological structure, which in this respect is thus equivalent to the root node of a matrix sentence in syntax.[17]

Consideration of the representation in (7) reveals that directionality is one of the fundamental notions in terms of which licensing is defined. It also demonstrates that the direction of licensing varies according to the level of the prosodic hierarchy at which it operates.

The other fundamental property of licensing is that it is subject to the condition of **locality**.[18] That is, a licensor must be adjacent to its licensee. This observation is obviously true of a branching constituent, in which the relation between the two positions is local on the skeletal tier. But the extension of this principle to all levels of the prosodic hierarchy is perhaps not so immediately obvious, in view of the fact that one or more skeletal positions may intervene between a licensed position and its licensor. Turning again to (7), we may note for example that, although the nuclear positions x_2 and x_5 enter into a licensing relation at the foot level, they are separated by two other positions (one a coda, the other an onset).

The key to understanding the uniformly local nature of licensing lies in the insight that adjacency is defined in terms of the particular level at which two positions are projected. Licensing between sister positions within a constituent involves locality at the level of the skeletal tier, a relation sometimes known as **strict locality** or **string-adjacency**.[19] On the other hand the licensing relation between nuclear projections within a foot involves locality at the foot level; this remains true even though the skeletal positions dominated by these nodes are not necessarily string-adjacent.

Summarising the discussion to this point, we may define the Phonological Licensing Principle as follows:[20]

(8)   **Phonological Licensing**

    (a) Within a domain, all phonological units must be licensed save one, the head of that domain.

    (b) Licensing relations are local and directional.

4.3.2 *Constituent and projection licensing*

As noted briefly above, the directionality of licensing appears to vary from one level of the prosodic hierarchy to another.[21] In view of the universal left-headedness of onsets, nuclei and rhymes, we may conclude that licensing at this level proceeds from left to right:

(9) **Constituent licensing**
Within constituents, licensing relations are head-initial.

Licensing between the projections of nuclear heads at higher levels of the prosodic hierarchy – **projection licensing** for short – is evidently not fixed in this way. Here directionality, revealed in a range of phenomena including stress, harmony, vowel reduction and syncope (on which more in 4.6.2), varies from one language to another. As illustrated in (6) and (7), English is one of those languages in which relations on the foot projection are left-headed. That is, the strong–weak stress pattern that characterizes this domain involves a configuration in which a dominant nucleus licenses a recessive nucleus to its right. In other languages, the opposite directionality obtains.

The same cross-linguistic variability is in evidence at the word level. Word-stress, for example, displays left-dominance in some languages (such as Hungarian) but right-dominance in others (French, for example). Indeed it is quite usual for the same language to display opposite directional patterns at different metrical levels. Thus in English, while feet are left-headed, the main pattern at the word level (to generalize grossly) is one of right-headedness, as illustrated in (7).[22] That is to say, where a word contains two or more feet, it is the rightmost one (more particularly its dominant rhyme) which is typically prominent. (Of course, this pattern cannot manifest itself in a word containing only one foot. The left-dominant pattern of, say, ⟨cíty⟩ is a foot-level matter.)

These choices in suprasegmental directionality, it is now generally assumed, are determined by parameter:[23]

(10) **Projection licensing**
Between the projections of nuclear heads, licensing relations are parametrically head-initial or head-final.

4.3.3 *Inter-constituent licensing*

We have yet to consider whether licensing relations are also observed to hold between string-adjacent positions occurring in different constituents. The sort of sequence at stake here is illustrated by the *nt* of ⟨winter⟩. We should start by considering which of the possible two-position **inter-constituent** sequences involving each syllabic category are actually attested. In view of the left-headedness of constituents, the second position in every case will be a (nuclear or onset) head. In surveying the relevant facts, we should also bear in mind that string-adjacency implies occurrence within the same morpho-syntactic domain. The fact that some of the possibilities turn out to be systematically excluded calls for some kind of principled explanation.

(11) lists the set of logically possible sequences in which the first position occurs within an onset. The rightmost column either records an example of an attested type (with the relevant sequence emboldened) or asterisks an ungrammatical type.

(11)		First position	Second position	
	(a)	Onset	Nucleus	
		head	head	⟨tip⟩
		complement	head	⟨trip⟩
	(b)	Onset	Onset	
		head	head	*
		complement	head	*

As (11a) shows, an onset position is free to precede a nucleus. Moreover, as we know from the discussion in 2.3.4, no systematic phonotactic dependencies are to be observed in this context, one of the considerations that led us to recognize the split between these two categories in the first place. In the absence if any obvious compelling evidence to the contrary, there seems to be no support for the existence of string-adjacent clusters of positions occurring in independent onsets, the pattern in (11b).

As shown in (12), all permutations of sequences in which a nuclear or rhymal position is followed by an onset are attested:

(12)	First position	Second position	
	Nucleus/rhyme	Onset	
	(a) Nuclear head	head	⟨lizard⟩
	(b) Nuclear complement	head	leyzi ⟨lazy⟩
	(c) Rhymal adjunct	head	⟨winter⟩

The independence of the onset and nucleus categories is further evidenced by the lack of systematic distributional dependencies in (12a) or (12b). That is, an onset consonant is free to follow either a non-branching nucleus (12a) or a branching one (12b).

By contrast, the coda-onset type of sequence in (12c) constitutes a context where phonotactic interactions are very much in evidence (illustrated by the homorganicity of the nasal-plosive cluster in ⟨winter⟩). It was this observation that prompted us to set up the distinction between the nucleus and rhyme in 2.4.3. In terms of its ability to influence the distributional potential of a preceding position, an onset can evidently penetrate a branching rhyme but not a nucleus. In the next chapter, we will see further independent support for the nucleus-rhyme distinction.

As (13a) and (13b) show, two–nucleus sequences are also possible in English.

(13)	First position	Second position	
	Nucleus/rhyme	Nucleus	
	(a) Nuclear head	head	⟨various⟩

(b)	Nuclear complement	head	⟨variety⟩
(c)	Rhymal adjunct	head	*

The distribution of the two patterns in (13a, b) is to some extent skewed by a tendency for the first nucleus to be lengthened or tensed in this context. That is, the pattern in (13a) gives way to that in (13b), although the strength of this tendency varies from dialect to dialect.[24] There is apparently something quite special about string-adjacent nuclei, since there is strong pressure on them to be collapsed. This raises the question of whether positions in this context can be said to enter into any kind of licensing relation with one another. We must postpone consideration of this matter (until 4.7.4), pending discussion of a number of additional points germane to the issue.

(13c) defines a sequence in which a coda is immediately followed by a nucleus. The syllabification it implies (VC.V, as in ⟨pit.y⟩) violates the otherwise quite robust principle of onset maximization. As we saw in 2.4.2, one of the effects of this principle is to ensure that the C of a VCV sequence is universally syllabified in onset position. As we will see in 4.6.3 and 4.7.3, there is little or no independent support for analyses which allow for deviations from this basic pattern.

Of the various types of inter-constituent sequence just described, two are worthy of immediate attention. One, the coda-onset cluster, involves an attested pattern in which systematic phonotactic restrictions are in evidence. The other involves two patterns for which we have no independent evidence and which we would wish to exclude on general theoretical grounds, namely a coda-nucleus sequence and a cluster of two onsets.

The existence of a distributional interaction between a coda and a following onset indicates that a headed licensing relation holds in this context. In this case, the direction of the phonotactic dependency is the opposite of that holding within constituents; it is the right-hand position which enjoys a greater degree of distributional freedom than that on the left.

The right-to-left directionality that is indicated by this asymmetry, it can be argued, extends to another of the inter-constituent sequences just reviewed. It is traditionally assumed that every onset must be supported by a following nucleus. This implies that a nucleus licenses a preceding onset, rather than vice versa. Although onset-nucleus sequences are not subject to anything like the same degree of phonotactic restrictiveness as coda-onset sequences, the directionality implicit in this assumption is further bolstered by the observation that onset heads, unlike their nuclear counterparts, are not projected to higher levels of the prosodic hierarchy.

We conclude therefore that licensing relations in the inter-constituent domains depicted in (15) universally proceed from right to left:

(14)   **Inter-constituent licensing**
       Between constituents, licensing relations are head-final.

(15)   (a) 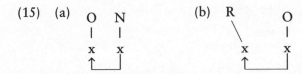   (b)

The inter-constituent licensing relation in (15a) is perhaps the nearest we have come to some traditional notions of the syllable. As we have seen, however, there is little or no motivation for recognizing the syllable as an independent node in phonological structure.[25] Instead, it is has been proposed that segment strings are organized into iterated constituent pairs consisting of an onset followed by a nuclear projection.[26]

Since the question of whether or not constituents may branch is subject to parametric variation (as shown in (2)), constituent licensing will manifest itself to differing degrees in different grammars. Licensing relations within a particular constituent will naturally only be evident in a language if the branching parameter is set at ON for that constituent. In contrast, there are grounds for assuming that the inter-constituent licensing relation shown in (15a) is obligatorily present in all languages, while that in (15b) is obligatorily present in all languages with branching rhymes. In other words, every onset must be licensed by a nucleus, and every coda must be licensed by an onset. Let us formulate these constraints in terms of the following universal principles:[27]

(16)   (a) **Onset Licensing**
        An onset head position must be licensed by a nuclear position.
        (b) **Coda Licensing**
        A rhymal adjunct position must be licensed by an onset position.

Given the head-final directionality of inter-constituent licensing, the licensing position in both cases of (16) will necessarily occur to the right.

By means of Onset Licensing we exclude clusters of two onsets. In the absence of an intervening nucleus, the first onset would remain unlicensed.

By means of Coda Licensing we derive the onset maximization effect mentioned above. From the perspective of licensing, the exclusion of VC.V syllabification follows from the requirement that a coda be licensed by a following onset. A syllabification such as * pɪt.i ⟨pity⟩ is ill-formed in terms of (16b), since the coda *t* is unlicensed.[28]

4.3.4 *Final consonants revisited*

Consider now the bearing that Coda Licensing has on the syllabification of consonants appearing at the end of an analytic domain.[29] In 2.4.4, we considered a number of arguments supporting the view that, rather than occurring in coda position as assumed insome traditions, such consonants actually occupy the onset of what we termed a degenerate syllable. Here is a brief recap of the main evidence. (a) In failing to induce closed-rhyme shortness, final consonants behave quantitatively like word-internal onsets rather than like internal codas. (b) The final consonant position enjoys more or less the same degree of distributional freedom as an internal onset. (c) The systematic phonotactic dependencies observable within final two-consonant clusters are more or less identical to those operating in internal coda-onset clusters. In addition to this empirical evidence, we now see that the syllabification of a final consonant in coda position must in any case be rejected on theory-internal grounds; it is automatically ruled out by the Coda Licensing principle. The following representation of ⟨pit⟩, in which the *t* appears in a coda, is ill formed for the same reason that a syllabification such as *pɪt.i* is: in both cases, there is no following onset to license the coda.

(17)

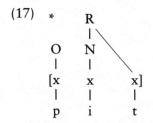

The main arguments for syllabifying domain-final consonants in onset position make appeal to quantitative and distributional considerations which are independent of any particular theory of phonological constituent structure. Having made the decision to recognize the onset status of such consonants, we then reach the following conclusion which may at first sight seem rather surprising but which we are driven to by considerations that are internal to the theory of licensing: a domain-final onset consonant is not strictly speaking final at all but is followed by a nucleus of some kind. This conclusion is a direct consequence of the Onset Licensing principle (16a). In other words, a final 'degenerate syllable' is not degenerate in the sense of lacking a nucleus; it does possess a nucleus, albeit one that is inaudible.[30] According to this view, a form such as ⟨pit⟩ contains two onsets, each of which is licensed by a following nucleus, the second of which is not phonetically expressed:

(18)
```
      O   N   O   N
      |   |   |   |
     [x   x   x   x]
      |   |   |
      p   i   t
```

The notion that 'empty' positions exist in phonology suggests a parallel with empty categories in syntax, a matter we will pursue below. Actually, the term **empty** turns out to somewhat infelicitous. As we will see presently, there are certain specific circumstances under which such positions do receive phonetic interpretation.

In fact, there is yet another reason for rejecting the assumption that final consonants are syllabified in coda position: it makes false predictions about the major types of syllabic systems attested in the world's languages. According to the final-coda view, the typology is exhaustively characterized in terms of a straightforward bifurcation into open-syllable 'CV' systems versus closed-syllable 'CVC' systems. Inherent in this classification is the notion that internal codas and final consonants have exactly the same status. The facts, however, contradict this taxonomy. The internal-coda and final-consonant dimensions are actually independent of one another, as a result of which there are four rather than two major types of syllabic system. Two of the attested types do indeed correspond to the predictions of the final-coda view. Some languages, such as Zulu, lack both internal codas and final consonants; that is, word-final polysyllabic sequences can only be of the shape . . . VCV]. Others, such as English, potentially have consonants in both contexts (. . . V(C)CV(C)]). However, the two other types are not allowed for under the simple CV-versus-CVC taxonomy. A third type of system (Italian and Telugu are examples) has internal codas but no final consonants (. . . V(C)CV]). In the fourth type, we find final consonants but no internal codas (. . . VCV(C)]), as in Luo (a Western Nilotic language spoken in northern Kenya).

The four-way classification of syllabic systems is derivable from the intersection of two independent parameters. The presence versus absence of (internal) codas results from a setting on parameter (2c), which determines whether or not rhymes may branch. We can characterize the presence versus absence of final consonants in terms of a parameter which determines whether or not final empty nuclei are sanctioned in the language:

(19) **Final-empty-nucleus parameter**
      Final empty nucleus licensed?   [OFF]/ON

In a system which selects a positive setting on this parameter, a final empty nucleus is able to license a preceding onset, which is occupied by the rightmost consonant in the word. In a system in which final empty nuclei are not sanctioned, the rightmost onset consonant of the word will always be followed by a phonetically realized nucleus. (20) summarizes the four language types defined by the intersection of this parameter with the branching-rhyme parameter:[31]

(20)

		Branching rhyme	
		[OFF]	ON
Licensing of final empty nucleus	[OFF]	VCV] Zulu	V(C)CV] Telugu
	ON	VCV(C)] Luo	V(C)CV(C)] English

The unmarked setting on the final-empty-nucleus parameter can be taken as OFF. This is consistent with implicational patterns such as the following: the existence of final VC] sequences in a language implies the existence of V] but not

vice versa; languages which sanction final consonants are outnumbered by those
that do not; and in languages permitting both V] and VC] the former is acquired
before the latter.

4.3.5 *Deriving binary branching*

Together, the principles of constituent and inter-constituent licensing derive the
set of constituent structures shown in (1). Any other shape of constituent is
automatically ruled out on the grounds that it will contravene licensing require-
ments. Take for example the following representations of a ternary-branching
nucleus:[32]

(21) (a)   (b)

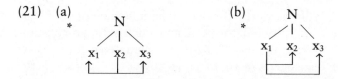

The structure in (21a), in which the licensing position is flanked by two licensees,
is ill-formed because, although locality is respected (both licensed positions are
adjacent to the licensor), the strict directionality of constituent licensing is con-
travened: position x_2 licenses simultaneously from right to left and from left to
right. (21b) is ill-formed because, although strict left-to-right directionality is
respected, locality is not: x_3 is not adjacent to the licensing position x_1. In this
way, we derive one of the quantitative effects that are observable at this level of
structure – a binary limit on vowel-length contrasts (short versus long).

Under constituent licensing, we expect three-position super-heavy rhymes to be
ruled out for the same reason that ternary-branching nuclei are:

(22)

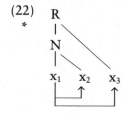

In this instance, locality is not respected: the rhymal adjunct position x_3, not being
adjacent to the constituent head x_1, remains unlicensed.

Nevertheless, as we saw in 2.4.4, super-heavy rhymes do occur (as in ⟨paint,
bold, moist⟩). The well-formedness of a three-position rhyme, however, depends
on the additional support of inter-constituent licensing. To see this, compare the
licensing properties of the coda in heavy and super-heavy rhymes. In both cases,
the position in question must be followed by an onset under Coda Licensing
(16b). This is illustrated in the following representations, which correspond to the

emboldened portions of forms such as ⟨fact, fist, chapter, winter⟩ (23a) and ⟨paint, wild, mountain, shoulder⟩ (23b):[33]

(23)   (a)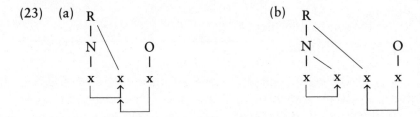

   (b)

The rhymal adjunct of a heavy rhyme (23a) is doubly licensed: once by the preceding nuclear position (constituent licensing) and again by the following onset position (inter-constituent licensing). The coda of a super-heavy rhyme (23b) is, however, only singly licensed, specifically by the following onset. In the latter case, it is the complement position of the branching nucleus that is constituent-licensed. A language for which the branching-rhyme parameter in (2c) is set at ON but which, unlike English, lacks super-heavy rhymes is subject to the constraint that codas must be doubly licensed.

A rhyme containing any more than one coda consonant is ill-formed for the reason that it would feature at least one position that is not sanctioned by either constituent or inter-constituent licensing. In the following four-term rhyme, for example, position x_3 remains unlicensed:

(24)

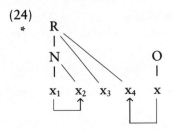

4.3.6 *Spreading and autosegmental licensing*

Under the autosegmental aspect of the Phonological Licensing Principle, we have seen, the phonetic interpretation of an element is contingent on its being attached to a skeletal position. The appearance or non-appearance of a given element α at particular locations within a representation hinges on whether or not α is granted an autosegmental licence. The overall melodic complexion of a representation will thus be shaped to a large extent by local responses to a fundamental choice facing individual positions – to license α or not to license α. In the following sections, we will try to identify the general constraints that influence or force decisions on this matter. The immediate concern of this section, however, is ·to explore the significance that this conception of melody-to-prosody association has for our understanding of the operations of spreading/composition and delinking/decomposition.

Delinking may be thought of as a specific response to conditions under which an element's autosegmental licence is revoked or withheld. Viewed in this way, the dynamic connotation that attaches to the notion of severing the association between a melodic expression and a position is not particularly fortunate. The operation of withdrawing an element's autosegmental licence can indeed be involved in dynamic alternations. There are plenty of cases where an element occupying a particular position is phonetically interpreted in one set of contexts but suppressed in another. Think, for example, of one of the first processes discussed in this book, one in which a domain-final *t* or *d* is realized before a vowel but not before a consonant (as in ⟨send it⟩ versus ⟨send Tom⟩; see 1.1). This phenomenon is straightforwardly represented as the delinking of an entire melodic expression in the second context.

Nevertheless, there are also plenty of cases in which the withholding of autosegmental licensing is not manifested in any dynamic way but is restricted instead to purely static distributional regularities. When we say, for example, that a laryngeal element cannot be distinctively associated to a coda position, we are not claiming that such an element is lexically present and then actively delinked in this context. What we are assuming rather is that the element is permanently denied independent access to this position.

However, it would be wrong to conclude from this that two autonomous formal operations are required for the sorts of phenomena just described. This is confirmed by cases in which what is evidently one and the same phonological process displays both dynamic and static effects, a point already made in 1.2.2. For example, the process whereby a domain-final *n* loses its coronality and takes on the place property of a following consonant (as in ⟨te[n → m] past⟩) can be viewed as a dynamic analogue of the static homorganicity exhibited by morpheme-internal nasal-plus-consonant clusters. As pointed out in 1.2.2, one way of conceptualizing this situation is to think of place-delinking as operating dynamically in one context and vacuously in the other.[34]

This all suggests that the fundamental mechanism at work in all such cases is the denial of autosegmental licensing under particular conditions. The active severance of an association line and the failure of a particular element ever to appear in a particular context are thus superficially different implementations of this one basic mechanism.

A similar point can be made in relation to spreading. The term has connotations of dynamic activity, but in the case of many phenomena the device must be assumed to work in a static fashion. The place-sharing of partial geminates in the coda-onset context just mentioned is but one example. One consequence of Coda Licensing is that codas never constitute sites of dynamic alternation activity. Since a coda is necessarily followed by an onset within the same non-analytic domain, it never has the opportunity to participate in an alternation by coming to stand next to the initial segment of some other morpheme. Any generalizations that can be made about the phonological behaviour of codas are thus only ever purely distributional.

Up to now, we have been following the convention of using line graphics to represent the linking of a single melodic expression to more than one skeletal position. In fact, I have been using two rather different variants of this notation (α here stands for some melodic expression):

(25)   (a) x_1 x_2 (b) x_1 x_2
               \ / | /
                α   α

In (25a), α is 'unplaced' with respect to positions x_1 and x_2.[35] (25b), on the other hand, implies an asymmetry in the association: α is distinctively located in x_1, whence it spreads into x_2. I have been employing (25a) simply as a matter of convenience (particularly in the last chapter), in order to direct attention towards the notion of element-sharing itself, while ignoring any specific asymmetries that might be involved.

In fact, all the evidence indicates that a notation incorporating the assumption that spreading is directional is to be preferred. This is perhaps most obvious in the case of dynamic alternations, illustrated by the very first case of spreading we examined, the compensatory lengthening of the vowel in *nixt* → *ni:t* (see 2.2.2). Here there is a clear sense in which the source of the vocalic material which fills the shoes of the disappearing velar fricative is located in the skeletal slot to the left. The extension of directionality to static cases of melody-sharing is motivated by the headed nature of relations between adjacent positions. The inequality with which distributional possibilities are divided between adjacent positions in certain contexts can be explained if we assume that all or part of the phonetic interpreta-tion of a licensed position is determined by the melodic content of its licensor. This implies that the relevant melodic content is distinctively lodged in the licensing position, even though its phonetic manifestation is smeared over both positions.

Oblique-line graphics of the type in (25b) are simply a way of making the directionality of spreading notationally explicit. This is further illustrated in the following coda-onset representation of the partial geminate *-mb-*:

(26)

In (26), the element U is distinctively attached to the licensing onset position, while the licensed coda is unspecified for a place element. Or to put it somewhat differently, U is autosegmentally licensed by the onset position, whereas the coda fails to license an independent place element. Note that the spreading indicated by the oblique line does not result in a copy of U being inserted into the coda; nor does it result in the same U being moved from one part the representation to another. Spreading is not a derivational device which bestows on the coda an autosegmental licensing ability it lacks in lexical representation. What the operation does is help indicate the distinctive locus of U as well as demarcate the domain over which the element is phonetically interpreted.

Understood in these terms, spreading is a purely **interpretive** matter, as opposed to a **representational** one. That is, it triggers no changes in the structure or content of a representation. It simply specifies how part of a representation is to be phonetically interpreted. A technical definition of the operation might thus run as follows:

(27)   **Spreading**
A licensed position is identified with its licensor with respect to the phonetic interpretation of some element that is distinctively lodged in the latter.

We have yet to consider the precise conditions under which autosegmental licensing can be granted or refused. As we will see in the next section, the conception of spreading in (27) will turn out to have a significant bearing on how we approach this question.

4.4 Licensing and melodic complexity

4.4.1 *Government*

In this section, we will see how an apparently disparate range of phonological phenomena can be derived by means of a single principle which defines an intimate connection between licensing and melodic structure. The principal phenomena to be treated in this way are the following: consonantal weakening, vowel reduction and syncope, and sonority relations as reflected in the phonotactic dependencies that manifest themselves within and between constituents. All of these can be related to a fundamental asymmetry in the ability of different types of melodic expression to occupy particular positions of licensing. Concretely, some sounds make better licensors than others.

Let us begin by taking stock of the criteria by which the directionality of licensing within different domains is established. One criterion has to do with whether or not the presence of a position is mandatory within a given domain. It is partly on the basis of the assumption that obligatoriness indicates headship that a nucleus is identified as the licensor of an optionally present onset (to its left) or rhymal adjunct (to its right). By the same criterion, Coda Licensing (16b) establishes the obligatorily present onset as the head of a coda-onset domain. A second criterion concerns quantitative interactions within the rhyme: as observed in the phenomenon of closed-rhyme shortness, the presence of a branching nucleus greatly curtails the availability of a rhymal adjunct position. Third, the head of certain licensing domains can be established by reference to the greater degree of distributional latitude it enjoys relative to its licensee. It is on the last of these criteria that we focus our attention in this section.

The first point to note is that the pivotal role played by the nuclear head in licensing networks appears to insulate it from distributional dependencies with surrounding onset and coda positions. It is as if its obligatory presence as a licensing anchor accords it the privilege of selecting melodic material independently of whatever material is contained in these other positions. Hence the lack of any systematic phonotactic interaction between a nuclear position and a following rhymal adjunct. In fact, this distributional independence is one of the main motivations for recognizing an autonomous nuclear constituent in the first place. By the same token, onset-nucleus sequences display little or no phonotactic interplay.

Given this proviso about the special status of nuclear positions, we may observe various types of distributional asymmetries at all levels of phonological licensing. However, it is in the following three domains, identified in 2.3.4, that quite particular phonotactic restrictions are universally in force:

(28)   **Phonotactic domains:**
    (a)   within a branching onset;
    (b)   within a branching nucleus;
    (c)   between a coda and a following onset.

In each of these contexts, the licensed position displays a seriously depleted set of distributional options. This indicates that the licensing relations involved are of a quite specific type. We may refer to this restrictive sub-case of licensing as **government**.[36] That is, each of the following licensing domains corresponds to a domain of government:

(29)   Governing domains

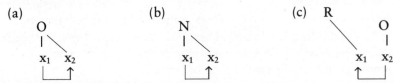

In the sub-cases of constituent licensing in (29a) and (29b), a constituent head governs its complement. In the sub-case of inter-constituent licensing in (29c), an onset head governs a preceding rhymal adjunct.

What formally unifies the three governed positions in (29) is that they are what might be termed **persistent non-heads**; that is, they never enjoy head status at any level of projection. This immediately sets them apart from all other positions, which, although they may be non-heads at some level of projection, are nevertheless guaranteed headship at some lower level. This is true of nuclear heads, which have the potential to function as such throughout the prosodic hierarchy. It also applies to onset heads, whose headship extends to both constituent and inter-constituent domains. To put it somewhat differently, we can say that

(30)   Heads are ungoverned.

(30) is a necessary but not sufficient condition for factoring out the set of domains in (29). The following configurations also contain non-head positions, but they must be excluded as possible domains of government:

(31)   (a)   Rhymal domain

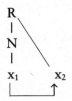

Non-domains

(b)   (c)

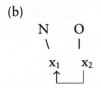

(31a) constitutes a licensing domain, as demonstrated by such phenomena as closed-rhyme shortness and rhymal weight. It does not, however, constitute a governing domain, as demonstrated by the phonotactic independence of the nucleus and the coda. Evidently, the notion of immediate projection is crucial to the definition of government. Specifically, within a branching constituent, the governor must be the immediate head of its governee. Thus the complement x_2 positions in (29a) and (29b) are governed, by virtue of the fact that the onset and nucleus categories are immediate projections of their x_1 heads. The adjunct x_2 position in (31a), on the other hand, is not governed within its constituent, since the rhymal node is not an immediate projection of its head x_1.

Neither (31b) nor (31c) constitutes a licensing domain; and, since government is a sub-case of licensing, this rules them out as governing domains. However, it is instructive to consider why this should be so, since the notion of immediate projection can again be shown to be implicated. As noted briefly above, for the purposes of imposing phonotactic restrictions on a preceding position, an onset-head position can evidently penetrate a rhyme at the level of the adjunct, as in (29c), but not at the level of the nuclear complement, as in

(31b). In syntactic terms, the nucleus behaves as an 'island', insulated from potential governing relations emanating from outside the constituent. This effect can be interpreted as a specific response to a general grammatical constraint, the **Minimality Condition**. According to one clause of the Condition, a position A is prevented from governing a position B, if the immediate projection of B's head excludes A.[37] This means, among other things, that an external position cannot 'reach inside' a nucleus to govern a position within the constituent, as in (31b). The same principle blocks a nuclear head from governing inside an onset, as in (31c).

The coda-onset domain (29c) is exempt from this constraint. That is, an onset head is able to govern inside a rhyme, since the latter does not itself constitute a governing domain.

The idea to be developed in the following sections is that the asymmetries that are observable in the phonotactic domains listed in (28) reflect inequalities in the ability of different types of melodic expression to occur in particular positions of government. The specific proposal is that the capacity of a sound to occupy a particular position is determined by the **complexity** of its elemental make-up. Complexity is gauged by the degree of fusion embodied in a melodic expression. For most purposes, this boils down to a straightforward calculation of the number of elements of which the sound is composed. For example, the two-element compound [U, h] (defining *f*) is more complex than the simplex expression [h] (defining *h*). The basic idea is that, within the domains specified in (29), the melodic expression occupying the governing position must be at least as complex as the expression occupying the governee. This principle may be formulated as follows:[38]

(32)   **Complexity Condition**
Let α and β be melodic expressions occupying the positions A and B respectively. Then, if A governs B, β is no more complex than α.

4.4.2 *Complexity relations within onsets*

The bottom line drawn by (32) is that the complexity differential between a governor and a governee can be zero. Otherwise, a more stringent requirement holds, whereby the governor must be more complex than the governee. We will now see that the more stringent condition controls the relation between a head position and its complement within an onset constituent. Since the directionality of constituent licensing is head-initial, this means that the well-formedness of a branching onset depends on there being a downward complexity slope between the two positions (viewed from left to right). This pattern manifests itself in well-formed branching onsets which, as we saw in 2.4.2, consist of an obstruent followed by a liquid or glide.[39] As illustrated in (33), the element profile of this type of sequence is uniformly downward.

(33)

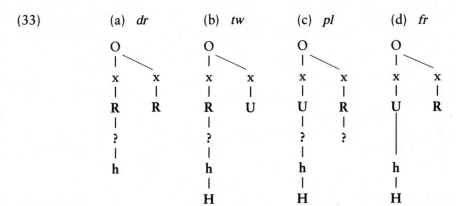

(a) *dr* (b) *tw* (c) *pl* (d) *fr*

Compare the well-formedness of these structures with the malformedness of the following, two of which (34a, b) display an upward complexity profile and one (34c) a level pattern.

(34) (a) *rd* (b) *st* (c) *sm*

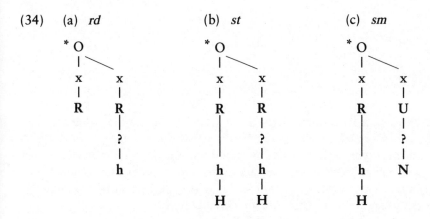

As a comparison of (33) and (34) shows, the complexity of an onset complement is restricted to one element (glides and *r*) or maximally two (*l*). In some languages, a maximum of one element is tolerated in this position. (Witness, for example, the historical reduction of *l* in this position to a simplex segment in some Romance languages: *r* (**R**) in Portuguese and *y* (**I**) in Italian, cf. French ⟨plat⟩, Portuguese ⟨prato⟩, Italian ⟨piatto⟩ 'dish'.)

The Complexity Condition goes a long way towards deriving the sonority effects that are observable within branching onsets. Other phonotactic restrictions operating in this context are attributable to an independent constraint on the amount of melodic material that the head and complement of an onset can have in common. Complete identity, for example, appears to be universally ruled out. That is, there are no known languages possessing onset geminates. The upward limit on the number of elements that can be shared between the two positions appears to be one. Thus, while *tr*/*dr* are well-formed onsets (one element in common, **R**), the following are malformed: *tl*/*dl* and *tn*/*dn* (all with two elements in common, **R** and **?**).[40] Note that *st* clusters are doubly ruled out as onsets (see (34b)) – once for having an upward complexity gradient, and again for sharing more than one element.

4.4.3 *Complexity relations within nuclei*

When we turn our attention to branching nuclei, we find at least one similarity with the complexity profile of onsets: the number of elements that can be contained in the complement position is severely restricted, in this case to one. The latter can be **I**, **U** or **@**, each of which characterizes an off-glide, as illustrated in diphthongs such as *ey*, *ow*, *iə*. With this configuration, a branching nucleus displays either a level or a downward complexity profile:

(35)   (a) *aw*   (b) *iə*   (c) *ow*   (d) *ey*

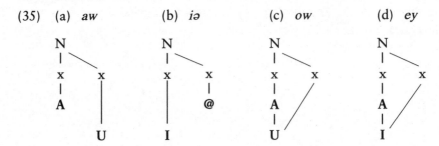

The toleration of a level complexity differential is not the only characteristic that distinguishes branching nuclei from onsets. The existence of long mono-phthongs indicates that, unlike in onsets, gemination is possible in nuclei. As we saw in 3.5, true geminates are represented as the simultaneous association of one melodic expression to two skeletal points. It is widely accepted that this arrange-ment reflects the operation of the following convention:[41]

(36)   **Obligatory Contour Principle (OCP)**
        At the melodic level, adjacent identical units are disfavoured.

The term **principle** here may not be entirely felicitous, at least if we take it to imply universal inviolability. The OCP was initially designed to account for certain tonal regularities but has subsequently been extended to a range of other phenomena, including some in which its effects are evidently not enforced in all languages. Although it is thus more appropriate to think of the OCP as embodying a strong tendency in natural language rather than a rigid principle, the name has stuck.[42]

Under the OCP, apparently consecutive identical segments are represented as a single melodic expression attached to two skeletal points. There has been some debate about the precise workings of the OCP and the domain within which it is operative. It is generally agreed that minimally the convention acts as a static condition on the well-formedness of morphemes as they appear in the lexicon. According to this aspect of the OCP, any intra-morphemic geminate cannot constitute a sequence of independent melodic expressions (as in (37a)); instead it can only be represented as the simultaneous association of a single expression to two skeletal positions (as in (37b)).

(37) (a) * x   x   (b)   x   x
           | | \   /
           α   α   α

A further assumption regarding the operation of the OCP is that it remains active during derivation. In this guise, it intervenes in a language-particular manner to block processes which would violate it or to set off processes which repair such violations. In the latter function, the convention triggers the coalescence of identical melodic expressions which accidentally become juxtaposed as a result of morphological concatenation. This affects so-called 'fake' (i.e. non-lexical) geminates, such as the *nn* in ⟨un-nerved⟩.

In all instances, true gemination involves a relation of licensing between two positions. In the case of nuclear geminates, the relation is one of constituent licensing. As indicated in 4.3.6, the melodic content of a geminate can be assumed to be lexically specified in the licensing position and spreads automatically into the licensee. Given the left-headedness of constituents, this means that spreading within a nucleus is from left to right. Thus in the representation of a long monophthong such as

(38) *aː*

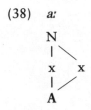

the governed position is empty. Its phonetic interpretation depends on its being identified with the melodic material that is lexically specified in its governor. Interpreted in this way, long monophthongs, and indeed all geminates, display a complexity slope between governor and governee.

A well-formed branching nucleus then is one which displays either a downward or a level complexity profile. The following upward patterns are ruled out by the Complexity Condition:[43]

(39) (a) *ae*   (b) *io*   (c) *uo*

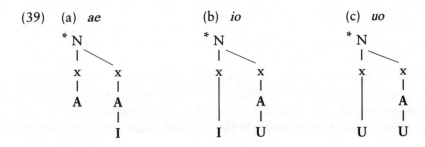

(Recall from the discussion in 2.4.3 how vocalic sequences transcribed in terms such as *ae, io, uo* are analysed in terms other than branching nuclei, for example as sequences of independent nuclei or as contour structures attached to a single nuclear point.)

4.4.4 *The melodic content of codas*

The amount of melodic material that a coda position can sustain is tightly constrained, an effect that is due to the governance of this position by a following onset. That is, the Complexity Condition can also be observed to operate within the inter-constituent domain shown in (29c). Here a complexity gradient appears to be universally in force, in this case an upward incline (viewed from left to right) in line with the right-headedness of licensing at this level.

The most stringent enforcement of the Complexity Condition in the inter-constituent context is observable in so-called 'Prince' languages, i.e. those languages in which coda-onset sequences are restricted to full or partial geminates.[44] As indicated above, the distinctive source of melodic material in a geminate is the licensing position. The melodic identification of the licensee with the licensor consists in the spreading of the entire melodic expression (under the ROOT node). The relevant geometric detail is supplied in the illustration in (40). As in the case of a long monophthong, the governed position of a full geminate consonant has zero complexity:

(40)   *tt*

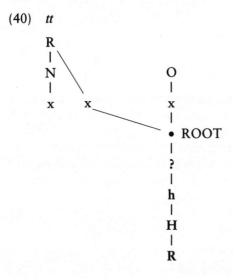

In the case of nasal-obstruent partial geminates, illustrated in (26), the coda must be assumed to license the nasal element (otherwise *mb*, say, would be indistinguishable from *bb*). We must also conclude that ? is distinctively specified in the coda rather than having its source in the licensing onset. This conclusion is supported by the fact that the occlusive property of a nasal stop manifests itself irrespective of whether it is followed by a plosive (which also contains ?) or a fricative (which lacks it). That is, although the stop property of a nasal could conceivably be attributed to spreading of ? from a following plosive, this analysis cannot be extended to nasal-fricative clusters. In fact, as we saw in 3.5, a nasal can pass its occlusion on to a following fricative to create an affricate of the type seen in *prɪnʦ* ⟨prince⟩.

On the other hand, the place-defining element in a homorganic cluster is specified in the onset and spreads (under the PLACE node) into the coda. This observation, together with the observation that the noise element and, if present, a laryngeal element are also lodged in the onset, confirms the existence of an upward complexity slope in partial geminates. The pattern is illustrated in the following representation of -*nt*- (41):

(41) *nt*

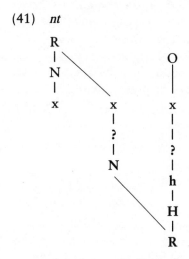

The Complexity Condition can also be observed to operate in non-Prince languages, i.e. those that permit obstruent clusters which are not necessarily homorganic. In such sequences, we must conclude that a place-defining element is distinctively present in the coda, since obstruents in this position contrast with respect to this dimension in languages of this type. In English, we have a contrast between *s* and *f* before *t* (for example, ⟨castor⟩ versus ⟨after⟩), as well as between *p* and *k* before *t* (⟨chapter⟩ versus ⟨factor⟩).[45] In fricative-stop clusters, the onset position contains at least one more element than the coda, namely ?. A characteristic of oral stop clusters is that only the second sound is released, an effect that can be interpreted as an optimization of the complexity differential between the two positions. The governing onset position contains an element, **h** (contributing noise release), which is absent from the governed coda position. Abstracting away from the laryngeal dimension for the moment, we can see from the following structures how an upward complexity gradient is maintained in obstruent clusters:[46]

(42) (a) *ft*   (b) *pt*

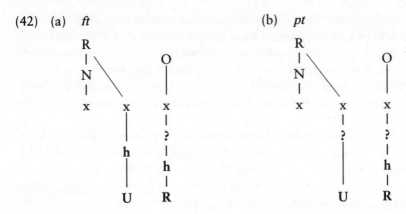

Another phonotactic restriction on coda obstruents can be viewed as a complexity effect – the absence of a distinctive laryngeal property. We noted in 2.4.2 that coda-onset clusters of obstruents uniformly agree with respect to voice. As with geminates, this state of affairs reflects the distinctive specification in the governor of melodic material that spreads into the governee. In fact, it has been proposed by some researchers that lexically specified laryngeal elements are uniformly excluded from all governed positions and are universally present in all obstruents occupying governing positions.[47]

4.4.5 Deriving sonority

To sum up the discussion so far: the Complexity Condition accounts for the phonotactic relations that obtain within the contexts identified in (28) and formalized in terms of government in (29). In chapter 2, these distributional patterns were informally described in terms of sonority. In some approaches, this notion is accorded theoretical status and is embodied in the principle of sonority sequencing (discussed in 2.4.2), which regulates the co-occurrence of different segment types within the same set of contexts.

One respect in which the complexity proposal is similar to the sonority approach is in the presentation of a fixed range of choices which determine phonotactic differences among languages. Under the sonority account, what varies is the minimal sonority distance a language imposes on pairs of segments in each syllabic context. Roughly speaking, this corresponds to variability in the steepness of the complexity gradient between adjacent positions, where the direction of the slope is determined by the direction of licensing.

In other respects, however, the sonority and complexity approaches are not at all similar. Rather than being an intrinsic property of segments that can be directly read off representations, sonority is calculated by reference to an external look-up table, the sonority hierarchy, which translates the feature make-up of a segment into a rank on the hierarchy. According to the complexity proposal, sonority has no theoretical status. Instead, it is no more than an informal label for an effect which derives from a more fundamental property, namely melodic complexity. And this property, being directly coded in melodic structure, can be determined without reference to any independent hierarchy. In this respect, the complexity approach is simpler than the sonority account. But not only that – the empirical domain it covers is much larger. The complexity dimension can also be shown to be involved in consonantal weakening and vowel reduction, processes which do not readily submit to interpretation in terms of sonority.

In spirantization, for example, suppression of ʔ results in a reduction in the melodic complexity of the lenited segment. Viewed in this way, lenition is simply the dynamic counterpart of the static distributional patterns that are traditionally described in terms of sonority. What is perhaps not so obvious, however, is how the licensing aspect of the complexity approach can be made to account for the contexts in which consonantal lenition typically applies. One of the classic lenition sites is word-final position, where, according to the licensing principles discussed in this chapter, the target consonant occupies an onset followed by an empty nucleus. Although this context does not directly coincide with any of the licensing domains described so far, the reduction in melodic complexity that occurs here can be shown to be indirectly sensitive to licensing. We will return to this issue later in the chapter.

4.4.6 *Complexity relations between nuclei*

The contexts in which phonological interactions between positions are observable are not limited to those listed in (28). A whole range of both distributional and dynamic phenomena can also be witnessed at higher levels of the phonological hierarchy. Processes which reflect close interactions between nuclear projections include stress-conditioned vowel reduction, vowel syncope, vowel harmony and tonal alternations. As we saw in 3.3.5, vowel reduction results in a contraction of the melodic contrasts capable of appearing in positions of weak stress. In the case of vowel syncope (to be discussed in detail later in 4.6), the melodic content of a nucleus is completely suppressed under a specific set of conditions, one of which involves the nucleus occurring within the same licensing domain as a neighbouring nucleus. In the case of harmony, one nucleus determines one or more of the quality characteristics of other nuclei within the same domain (usually the word). The parametric variability to which the directionality of projection licensing is subject is no less evident in harmony than in stress systems. In some harmony systems, for example, the harmonic category propagates from the left edge of a harmonic span, whereas in others it propagates from the right. In spite of their superficially disparate nature, all of these phenomena share a pattern in which a nuclear licensor enjoys a greater degree of distributional leeway than its nuclear licensee.

In terms of their melodic effects, each of these phenomena displays a particular type of complexity interaction between nuclei at some level of projection. Vowel reduction in a metrically weak nucleus consists in the suppression of one or more of the elements it contains. In height harmony systems of the type discussed in 3.3.5, the absence of mid vowels from certain harmonically recessive nuclei consists in the suppression of **A**. What these processes have in common is a diminution in the melodic complexity of a licensed position in relation to its licensor. Vowel syncope manifests the same phenomenon but in a more extreme guise, resulting in the complexity of a licensed position being reduced to zero. In keeping with the cross-linguistic variability that characterizes other phenomena triggered by nuclear licensing, complexity differentials between positions are not strictly enforced at higher levels of the prosodic hierarchy. Not all languages exhibit vowel reduction, height harmony or syncope, just as not all languages have, say, stress feet.

4.5 Principles and parameters of phonological structure

Reviewing the discussion to this point, let us now summarize the principles and parameters which control the prosodic and melodic construction of phonological representations. Together with the Complexity Condition, the Phonological Licensing principle, in its various incarnations at different levels of the phonological hierarchy, defines the most important design properties of the phonological structure of natural language.

The main effects of the Phonological Licensing principle are: (a) to make the phonetic interpretability of representational units dependent on their integration into the phonological hierarchy; (b) to impose a binary limit on the branching structure of constituents; and (c) to define the conditions of locality under which phonological processes operate. The Complexity Condition controls the association of different types of melodic expression to particular positions in phonological strings and in this way derives the effects of sonority sequencing.

The scope for cross-linguistic variability in the design of phonological structure is circumscribed by a number of parameters, including the following:

(43)　(a)　Branching constituent
　　　　　　Onset　　　　　　　　　　　　　[OFF]/ON
　　　　　　Nucleus　　　　　　　　　　　　[OFF]/ON
　　　　　　Rhyme　　　　　　　　　　　　　[OFF]/ON
　　　(b)　Licensing of final empty nucleus　[OFF]/ON
　　　(c)　Direction of projection licensing　→/←
　　　(d)　Complexity gradients within governing domains

Settings on the constituent parameters (43a) determine whether or not a particular language displays such properties as distinctive vowel length or closed syllables. (43b) controls the sanctioning or otherwise of word-final consonants. The setting on (43c) establishes the difference between, for example, left-dominant and right-dominant stress patterns. Different values on (43d) determine such factors as the sonority distances between sounds in adjacent positions.

For each language, the universal principles of Phonological Licensing and the Complexity Condition, supplemented by particular settings on the parameters in (43), define a set of well-formed prosodic templates and a set of well-formed melodic association patterns. The grammaticality of a phonological representation is dependent on its being parsable in terms that satisfy these prosodic templates and melodic patterns.[48]

It is now time to examine in more detail the issues raised by the postulation of the type of position referred to in parameter (43b) – the empty nucleus.

4.6 Empty positions

4.6.1 Domain-final empty nuclei

So far, the only argument I have advanced in favour of the recognition of empty nuclei is a theory-internal one. As we have seen, there is sizeable body of independent evidence supporting the view that word-final consonants occur in onset position. The principle of Onset Licensing (16a) then leads us to conclude that this position must be sanctioned by the presence of a following nucleus, even if this apparently has no phonetic expression. Among the questions raised by this analysis are the following. Is there any additional, independent support for empty positions? Is the occurrence of empty nuclei restricted to the right edge of words? If not, what constraints are there on their appearance in other contexts? Are empty nuclei truly empty in the sense of being completely and consistently devoid of all phonetic content? Do empty positions have any analogues elsewhere in phonology or indeed in grammar in general?

On the last of these questions, the precedent of recognizing empty positions in phonology was originally set not for nuclei but for onsets. One of the first analyses to incorporate the notion of an empty onset position was proposed to handle the phenomenon of *h-aspiré* in French.[49] Vowel-initial words in French pattern into two sets according to whether or not they trigger certain phonological processes, one of which involves the suppression of the vowel of the singular definite article *lə* (masculine) or *la* (feminine). In words such as *ami* ('friend'), the vowel of the article fails to appear: *lami* ('the friend'). The vowel-zero alternation is usually treated in terms of a process which deletes the first of two adjacent nuclei: *lə ami* → *l ami*. In *h-aspiré* words, however, the vowel of the article is retained, as in *lə ariko* ('the bean'). Forms of the latter kind, it has been proposed, begin with an empty onset position which separates the nucleus of the article from the first nucleus of the noun and thus shields the former from deletion. (As the term *h-aspiré* suggests, the empty position is the present-day reflex of what historically was an onset occupied by *h*. The *h* has long since been lost, although its original presence is still recorded as ⟨h⟩ in French orthography.[50]) A little later, we will consider the question of whether the notion of empty onsets and nuclei in phonology has anything at all in common with empty categories in syntax.

Turning to another of the questions raised above, let us now consider a number of arguments in support of the view that so-called 'empty' nuclei are not entirely without melodic content. Rather they have latent content which manifests itself phonetically under certain specific circumstances. This is a suitable point at which to return to the suffixes ⟨-(e)s⟩ and ⟨-ed⟩, since the manner in which they alternate sheds light on this issue.

Of the three alternants displayed by each of these suffixes, we have already seen in 3.6 how two, *z–s* and *d–t* can be accounted for in terms of voice assimilation. Let us now focus on the third alternant, the one found in forms such as those in (44) containing a vocalic reflex before the suffix consonant. (In (44), the vowel in question is represented in one of its most widespread guises, namely ə. Other attested reflexes include *ɪ*.)

(44)   ⟨-s⟩   ⟨-ed⟩
       -əz   -əd

       kisses   voted
       houses   faded
       bushes
       catches
       judges

The vocalic reflex occurs whenever the stem ends in a consonant which shares certain place and/or manner characteristics with the consonant of the suffix: əz occurs after a sibilant and əd after *t* or *d*. The presence of the vowel is usually interpreted as breaking up a potential sequence of identical or similar consonants. Traditionally, this effect has been treated in terms of a rule of vowel epenthesis – in non-linear terms, the insertion of a nuclear position. Underlying this analysis is the now-discredited assumption that the stem-final consonant occupies a coda. Once epenthesis has applied, the stem-final consonant undergoes **re-syllabification**; that is, it is moved out of its original coda position and into the onset of the newly created syllable. For ⟨voted⟩, this yields the following derivation: *vowt.(d)* → *vowt.əd* (epenthesis) → *vow.təd* (resyllabification).[51] This particular movement operation is representative of a whole class of resyllabification transformations which have been proposed in the literature. We will have cause to question their validity in due course.

Suppose, on the other hand, we take the vocalic reflex of ⟨-(e)s⟩ and ⟨-ed⟩ to be part of the stem domain rather than the suffix. We then have no need to invoke resyllabification if, as depicted in the representation of ⟨voted⟩ in (45), we assume that the vowel is the phonetic expression of a latently present neutral element (@) in the stem-final 'empty' nucleus.[52] (Here and elsewhere, I will only indicate the presence of those elements that are directly relevant to the point at hand. The remaining melodic content of a representation can be abbreviated by means of phonemic symbols in inverted commas.)

(45)
```
      O   N         O   N   O   N
      |   | \       |   |   |   |
      [[x  x  x      x  x]  x  x]        ⟨voted⟩
      |   |  |       |   |   |
      'v   o  w'      |   @   |
                     R       R
                     |       |
                     ?       ?
                     |       |
                     h       h
                     |
                     H
```

The idea that @ is latently present in an 'empty' nucleus is in accord with the assumption made in 3.3.5 that it inheres in every intersection between a skeletal position and an autosegmental tier that is not filled by some other element. It is consistent with this view to consider an 'empty' nucleus as comprising intersections which contain nothing but @. In a system in which a nuclear position of this type is parametrically sanctioned domain-finally, this melodic material remains autosegmentally unlicensed and thus phonetically unexpressed. (The absolute final nucleus in (45), the one following the *d* of the suffix, thus also contains latent @, although in this context it is not made phonetically manifest.) However, should special circumstances arise under which the melodic content of the nucleus is phonetically interpreted, it should have the schwa-like quality that independently manifests @. In this case, the special circumstances evidently involve a ban on consecutive identical elements of a particular type, those shared by the sibilants or by the coronal plosives in (45). This constraint can be viewed as an instantiation of the OCP (36).[53]

The claim that a final 'empty' nucleus is latently realizable as the neutral element raises the question of how this is to be distinguished from a final nucleus which is consistently realized as schwa. In what way are the representations of, for example, ⟨dine⟩ and ⟨Dinah⟩ distinct? In the case of some dialects to be discussed in the next chapter, there are grounds for assuming that there is no genuine contrast here at all, since stable schwa is absent from this context. These are the systems that display so-called 'intrusive' *r*; pre-vocalically, a form such as ⟨Dinah⟩ shows final *r* and is thus indistinguishable from ⟨diner⟩ (so that ⟨Dinah[r] is⟩, for example, is identical to ⟨diner is⟩). As we will see, such forms can uniformly be assumed to end in a lexical *r* which fails to materialize pre-consonantally. This means that all apparently schwa-final forms are in fact *r*-final in these systems.

Nevertheless, those dialects which lack intrusive *r* and thus contrast ⟨Dinah⟩ and ⟨diner⟩ do have final stable schwa in words of the first type. The manner in which this vowel is distinguished from a final empty nucleus in a form such as ⟨dine⟩, I will assume, has to do with whether the melodic content of the position in question is headed or not. Specifically, when the melodic content of an 'empty' position is not autosegmentally licensed, it has no element as its head. As shown in (46), this is in contradistinction to a non-empty nucleus corresponding to stable schwa, in which the relevant position autosegmentally licenses a headed melodic expression.

(46)   'Empty' nucleus   Schwa

     N   N
     | |
     x   x
                             |
     @   <u>@</u>

4. 6. 2 *Vowel syncope*

Focusing now on another of the issues raised by empty nuclei, let us consider whether they are restricted to domain-final contexts. A recurring theme in chapter 2 and the present chapter has been the claim that the existence of systematic interactions (phonotactic or quantitative, for example) between two positions can be taken as evidence that they are adjacent in phonological structure. Conversely, the absence of any such interdependence between two superficially abutting segments indicates lack of adjacency. As we saw in 2.3.4, cross-word contexts are one of the sites where no systematic distributional interactions are evident in English, in this case since they involve arbitrary juxtapositions of segments created by lexical insertion. Under the licensing account developed above, the lack of phonological adjacency between two consonants appearing in this configuration is reflected in the fact that they are separated by the empty nuclear position which appears on the right edge of the first word. This is illustrated in a string such as ⟨ . . . kid lay . . . ⟩ [[kɪdØ] [ley]] (where Ø indicates the presence of an empty nucleus), in which no phonotactic dependency exists between the *d* and *l*. The same point can be made with respect to word-internal segment sequences separated by an analytic morpheme boundary, as in ⟨bad-ly⟩ [[*bædØ*]*li*].

It might be objected that the lack of distributional interactions in such contexts can be explained purely in terms of morpho-syntactic domains, without recourse to empty nuclei. Indeed, it might be tempting to assume that all cases of phonological non-adjacency between superficially contiguous consonants are due to the intervention of an analytic morpheme boundary. This assumption, however, turns out to be wrong. The world's languages abound with examples where superficially abutting but phonologically non-adjacent consonants co-occur within the same morpheme. The cases in question involve contexts in which a pair of consonants flank a site displaying an alternation between the presence and absence of a vowel. In linear rule-based frameworks, the decision to treat alternations of this type in terms of vowel insertion (epenthesis) or deletion (syncope) hinges on the predictability or otherwise of the alternating vowel. The insertion analysis is only available if both the quality and the incidence of the vowel are predictable. (The incidence is predictable as long as there are no forms containing the epenthesis context which systematically fail to show the vowel.) If either of these conditions is not satisfied, the alternating vowel is represented lexically and then deleted by rule.

An example of a language in which the incidence but not the quality of the syncopating vowel is predictable is Tonkawa, an Amerindian language of Texas.[54] The syncope site is the second nucleus in the word (counting from the left). Thus the second vowel of a stem such as *picena* 'cut' is suppressed in *picna-noʔ* 's/he is cutting'. When a prefix containing a vowel is attached to the stem, however, the second stem-vowel is no longer second in the word, and it is the first stem-vowel that is suppressed, as in *we-pcena-noʔ* 's/he is cutting them'.

Various forms of syncope occur in English, although these are typically optional rather than obligatory as in Tonkawa. One type, which is subject to regional and stylistic variation, is reflected in the suppression of the parenthesized vowel in words such as ⟨ref(e)rence, choc(o)late⟩. The optionality of the process is reflected in the fact that it is favoured in casual speech styles and is more likely to affect high-frequency words than rarer words.[55] The syncope site in this case is located in the second of three nuclei in a strong-weak-weak metrical configuration. That is, as shown in the representation of ⟨sep(a)rate⟩ (adjective) in (47), syncope occurs in the post-tonic nucleus of a left-dominant foot which forms the left branch of what is sometimes termed a **super-foot**.[56]

(47)

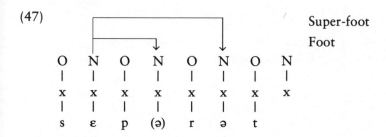

Super-foot

Foot

The sensitivity of syncope to the presence of a following weak nucleus is demonstrated by the fact that the process fails if the post-tonic nucleus is followed by a secondary-stressed nucleus occurring in an independent foot. Thus, while syncope is possible in the adjective *sɛp(ə)rət* ⟨séparate⟩, it is ungrammatical in the differently stressed verb *sɛpəreyt* ⟨séparàte⟩ (*sɛpreyt*).

In most dialects, the suppressible vowel appearing in the syncope context is some kind of schwa. The process thus presents the converse case of syncope to that found in Tonkawa, one in which the quality of the alternating vowel is predictable *(ə)* but not its incidence. Compare, for example, the *f(ə)r* string of ⟨ref(e)rence⟩, in which an optional schwa intervenes, with *fr* in ⟨Africa⟩, which never contains schwa. This unpredictability renders an epenthesis solution impossible; a rule inserting schwa in ⟨ref'rence⟩ would also erroneously insert it in ⟨Africa⟩, yielding *⟨Af[ə]rica⟩. The obvious alternative is to assume that, in lexical representation, a vowel intervenes between the *f* and *r* of ⟨reference⟩ (but not of ⟨Africa⟩) which is then suppressed by syncope. (In some dialects, the identity of the alternating vowel is unpredictable, since there is a contrast in this context between *ə* (as in ⟨ref([ə])rence⟩) and *ɪ* (as in ⟨def([ɪ])nite⟩).[57])

4.6.3 Resyllabification?

The linear treatment of syncope as vowel deletion converts into non-linear format in one of two ways: either (a) delete the nuclear position together with its melodic content; or (b) delete the vocalic melody while leaving the nuclear position intact. The consequences of these two approaches are quite different. The first requires the mechanism of resyllabification to repair the damage inflicted on constituent structure by the obliteration of a nuclear position. When applied to ⟨sep(a)rate⟩, the latter operation casts the preceding onset consonant adrift, as illustrated in (48).

(48) (a)   (b)   Syncope

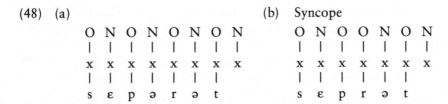

Two resyllabification strategies are potentially available for reintegrating the stray onset consonant of (48b) into constituent structure: it can join either the preceding rhyme (49a) or the following onset (49b).

(49) (a)   (b)

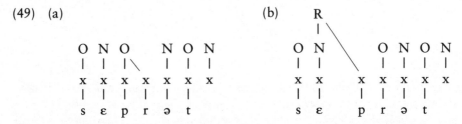

In this particular instance, appeal might be made to sonority sequencing and onset maximization; together, these would favour (49a) over (49b) on the grounds that *pr* exists independently of the syncope contexts as a well-formed onset in English.[58] However, this account cannot be extended to all cases of this type of syncope, since, as we will now see, many of the consonant strings resulting from the process do not coincide with the set of grammatical onsets.

The type of English syncope under discussion is sensitive to the identity of the consonant immediately following the syncope site. In the overwhelming majority of cases, the process affects forms in which this segment is a resonant. Thus we find syncope in words such as ⟨op(e)ra, especi(a)lly, pers(o)nal⟩ but not in the likes of ⟨bracketing, gossiping, menacing⟩. For most forms which display unsyncopated and fully syncopated variants, there exists an intermediate variant containing a syllabic reflex of the consonant in question: for example, ⟨op[r̩]a, especi[l̩]y, pers[n̩]al⟩. The triggering of syncope by a following resonant is thus related to the fact that these are the only consonants in English that can enjoy syllabic status. (This is a characteristic they exhibit in other contexts as well; cf. forms such as ⟨bottle, button⟩ with final syllabic *l* and *n* respectively and, in rhotic dialects, ⟨ladder⟩ with syllabic *r.*) In forms in which the consonants flanking the syncope-prone nucleus are both coronal resonants, it is frequently difficult to distinguish the syllabic from the fully syncopated variant (presumably because of the potentially continuous sonorant gesture involved).[59] Nevertheless, there are dialects in which syncope appears to be disfavoured in this context, to some extent after *n* (as in ⟨finally, general⟩) but more particularly where the consonant on the left is a liquid (as in ⟨felony, salary, quarrelling, irony⟩). As with the vocalic ⟨-(e)s, -ed⟩ reflexes discussed above, this pattern evidently constitutes another case where the suppression of vocalic material is blocked by the OCP, if the process would result in sequences of identical or similar melodic expressions.

By way of a more extensive illustration of the consonantal conditioning of this type of syncope, compare the forms in (50a, b), in which the syncopated variant is readily attested in many dialects, with those in (50c), in which it is either marginally possible or downright impossible (indicated by ?/*):[60]

(50) (a) sep(a)rate   (b) mis(e)ry   des(o)late
           temp(e)rature   ev(e)ry   especi(a)lly
           elab(o)rate   surg(e)ry   fin(a)lly
           fact(o)ry   cent(u)ry   fam(i)ly
           bound(a)ry   nurs(e)ry   ped(a)lling
           lic(o)rice   cam(e)ra   jav(e)lin
           choc(o)late   treas(u)ry   gen(e)ral
           myst(e)ry   pris(o)ner   marg(i)nal
           ref(e)rence   dec(i)mal   comp(a)ny
           quand(a)ry   def(i)nite   pers(o)nal
           awf(u)lly   op(e)ner   nati(o)nal

      (c) ?/*
           rock(e)ting   ball(o)ting
           mon(i)tor   opac(i)ty
           goss(i)ping   men(a)cing

Note that the difference between (50a, b) and (50c) cannot be explained by saying that syncope only occurs between consonants that can potentially form a branching onset. True, the grammatical forms in (50a) demonstrate syncopated consonant strings which superficially correspond to onset clusters that are attested independently of the syncope site, including *pr, br, tr, dr, kr, kl, fr, θr*. Moreover, many of the ungrammatical sequences that would result from syncope in (50c) correspond to independently established coda-onset clusters rather than onsets, (*kt, lt, nt, st, sp, ns*, for example). This result is, however, fortuitous in view of the fact that the largest set of forms, those in (50b), contains syncope-derived strings which fail to correspond either to onset or to coda-onset clusters that are independently identifiable outside the syncope site. These include *zr, mr, čr, jr, zr, vl, ml, ʃl, pn, fn, zn, jr, ʃn*.

How then does a resyllabification account deal with the forms in (50b)? Since the resyllabification of the syncopated strings in such forms is not responsive to pre-existing phonotactic constraints, it will have to be guided by some other set of factors. One possibility would be to assume that the sonority sequencing principle continues to operate after syncope but with a relaxation in the severity with which the requirement on minimum sonority distance is enforced. In this way, strings such as *ml, fn, pn*, for example, could be made to pass muster as onsets.

Another tack would be to assume that sonority sequencing switches off at some point in derivation, in which case any syncope-generated string that does not correspond to a pre-existing onset (those shown in (50b)) could be parsed as a novel coda-onset sequence. The problem then is how to derive the novel clusters while preventing the creation of the very clusters that correspond to otherwise well-formed coda-onset clusters, those illustrated in (50c). A further problem with this alternative is that, in some of the syncopating forms, the rhyme of the tonic syllable is already occupied by a coda consonant (the *m* in ⟨comp(a)ny⟩ for instance). In such cases, resyllabification of a post-syncope consonant into the preceding rhyme would result in a two-consonant coda, something for which there is absolutely no independent evidence, as we saw in 2.4.4.

Whichever of these two alternative solutions is preferred, one result remains the same: two sets of phonotactic conditions are deemed to obtain in the grammar, a more restrictive pre-syncope set, and a less restrictive post-syncope set.

At this point, it is reasonable to ask what justification there is for transformations which modify constituent structures established in lexical representation. If we follow the lead of much of the phonological literature in taking the validity of resyllabification for granted, then we are wedded to the notion that the constraints which hold over lexical structures can be overturned during the course of derivation. We should be very wary of taking such a step, since some of the constraints at stake involve extremely robust cross-linguistic generalizations. Any concession to the idea that they might be revoked during derivation represents a retreat from the strongest possible interpretation of this fact, namely that they are universal.

For example, one widely invoked constituent transformation to be considered below detaches a consonant from its original onset position and moves it into a preceding coda, as for instance in ⟨ci.ty⟩ → ⟨cit.y⟩.[61] This resyllabification can only be achieved at the expense of overriding the Coda Licensing principle, in order to undo the onset maximization effect which lies behind the initial syllabification ⟨ci.ty⟩.

One empirical result of adopting resyllabification is a significant increase in the set of possible grammars defined by phonological theory. This proliferation stems not just from the prediction that some grammars may take up the resyllabification option while others may not but also from the possibility that the nature of the structural and phonotactic mismatch between underlying and resyllabified representations varies from system to system. Moreover, acceptance of the notion that such discrepancies may exist between different levels of derivation allows for the possibility that later levels may actually enforce **more** stringent constraints on constituency than earlier levels. In practice, analyses which invoke the notion almost invariably conform to the pattern in which constraints are **less** restrictive at later stages of derivation.[62] This observed asymmetry is only derivable by means of some additional mechanism. One such proposal is the **Strong Domain Hypothesis,** according to which all rules (including those which formalize syllable-structure constraints) are available from the outset of derivation and may be switched off at some later point; however, once switched off, they cannot be subsequently reactivated.[63]

Before considering the empirical consequences of resyllabification in any more detail, we should remind ourselves that the device forms part of a research hypothesis that has to be justified not just in relation to the data it is designed to account for but also in relation to any competing analyses that happen to be available. In the first instance, it should be weighed up against the null hypothesis – in this case the assumption that nothing happens to constituent structure during the course of a phonological derivation. Under the latter view, constraints on syllable structure remain stable throughout derivation. As with any research hypothesis, we should only accept the resyllabification model once it has been shown consistently to out-perform and not just match a model based on the null hypothesis.

At various points in the remainder of this chapter, we will consider whether the position that constituent structure is immutable can be maintained in the face of evidence involving a number of process-types for which resyllabification analyses have been proposed. At least as far as the syncope facts are concerned, the resyllabification account can be shown to come out second best.

4.6.4 *Preserving prosodic structure*

Inherent in the resyllabification account of syncope is a distributional paradox that can be summed up as follows. According to phonotactic constraints that can be identified independently of the syncope context, one type of cluster supposedly generated by syncope submits to reanalysis as a branching onset. On the other hand, there is another type which resists resyllabification into a either a branching onset or a coda-onset sequence without forcing a relaxation of the same constraints. In other words, consonants flanking the syncope site are not subject to the stringent phonotactic constraints that independently can be shown to operate within intra- and inter-constituent domains. All that can be said about the melodic aspect of the syncope conditions is that the right-hand consonant must be a resonant.

A conclusion that may reasonably be drawn from these observations is that consonants bordering a syncope site are bogus clusters, since there are no systematic phonotactic dependencies between them. The lack of true adjacency that is suggested by this independence obviously stems from the fact that the consonants are separated by a vowel in lexical representation. But what reason is there to suspect that this lack of adjacency is not retained even when the vowel is syncopated? The simplest hypothesis that is consistent with this observation is that syncope has no effect on constituent structure. That is, consonants flanking a vowel-syncope site continue to occupy independent onset positions after the process has occurred.[64]

This view is expressible in the second of the non-linear approaches to syncope alluded to briefly above. Under this account, it is only the vocalic melody of a syncopating vowel that is suppressed. The constituent structure is meanwhile preserved intact, as shown in the following representations of ⟨def(i)nite⟩:

(51)   Syncope

```
O  N  O  N  O  N  O  N        O  N  O  N  O  N  O  N
|  |  |  |  |  |  |  |         |  |  |  |  |  |  |  |
x  x  x  x  x  x  x  x         x  x  x  x  x  x  x  x
|  |  |  |  |  |  |            |  |  |        |  |  |
d  ε  f  ə  n  ə  t            d  ε  f        n  ə  t
```

What remains after syncope is an empty nucleus. The non-adjacency of *f* and *n*, reflected in their abiding distributional independence, is accounted for by the fact that they continue to be separated by a nuclear position even after the latter has lost its melodic content. The same type of analysis can be extended to all cases of syncope.

To facilitate assessment of the proposal that constituent structure remains stable throughout derivation, let us consider how the view might be formally expressed in terms of phonological licensing. Resyllabification transformations have the effect of altering licensing relations established at the level of lexical repres-entation. These modifications can be viewed in terms of their impact not only on the structure of individual forms but also on the set of licensing conditions that hold of lexical representations in general. For example, from the first perspective, the deletion of the nuclear position shown in (48) results in a destruction of the relation of projection licensing which that position contracts with the preceding nuclear head. The resyllabification of the resulting stray position into a following onset, shown in (49a), creates a new relation of constituent licensing. Resyllabifi-cation into a coda, shown in (49b), creates a new relation of inter-constituent licensing. Viewed in terms of their effect on the set of constituent structures defined by the prosodic licensing conditions operating in English, neither of these transformations results in the creation of novel structures not encountered else-where in lexical representation. This happens to be true of these particular cases; in 4.7.3 we will discuss a couple of analyses in which resyllabification does involve overriding pre-existing prosodic constraints.

Nevertheless, the transformations shown in (49) do introduce one type of innovation: they generate melodic associations which fail to conform to the autosegmental licensing conditions holding at the lexical level. Many of the

clusters supposedly arising from the resyllabification of the syncopated forms in
(50b) fail to respect the Complexity Condition, which we have seen to be strictly
enforced in lexical representations. Take for example the alleged coda-onset
sequence resulting from the restructuring of ⟨cam(e)ra⟩:

(52) (a)   (b)

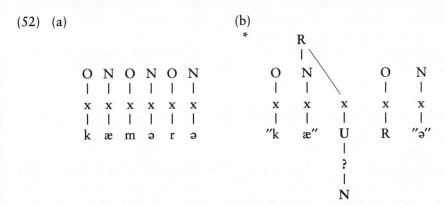

In (52b), the downward complexity slope observable within the inter-constituent
domain formed by the coda, occupied by *m*, and the following onset, occupied by
r, constitutes a flagrant contravention of the Complexity Condition. The assumption inherent in resyllabification analyses is thus that licensing conditions, including those relating to melodic complexity, can be overridden during the course of
derivation.

The contrary view that phonological structure remains immutable throughout
derivation amounts to the claim that licensing relations at derived levels of
representation consistently match those established in lexical representation. In
some respects, this parallels the situation in syntax and at LF, where the major
properties of any level of representation are independently carried over from the
lexicon. According to this requirement (known as the **Projection Principle**), for
example, the lexically specified argument structure of a verb (which determines
such properties as whether or not it takes a direct object) is respected identically
at all levels of derivation.[65] The effect of this constraint is that syntactic movement
operations are **structure-preserving**; that is, they cannot alter the categorial status
of a syntactic position whose presence is required in underlying structure. For
example, a position projected as an noun phrase underlyingly cannot be turned
into a verb phrase position during derivation.

Extending the Structure Preservation Principle into the phonological domain
has the following consequences for prosodic and autosegmental structure. If
Phonological Licensing requires the presence of a skeletal position in lexical
representation, it will also require its presence at derived levels of representation.
One implication of this is that certain skeletal positions projected as particular
constituent categories in lexical representation cannot be assigned to other categories during derivation. For example, under Coda Licensing, a coda position
requires the presence of a following licensing onset position. In lexical repres-

entation, the syllabification of a VCV sequence is thus universally established as V.CV. A transformation which reassigned the onset position to the coda of the preceding rhyme, as proposed in a number of analyses to be discussed below, would fail to be structure-preserving, since it would create a structure lacking the position required to prosodically license the coda. At the autosegmental level, structure preservation requires that the Complexity Condition be observed in both lexical and derived representation.

The phonological instantiation of the structure preservation principle may be stated as follows:[66]

(53)   **Structure Preservation Principle**
Licensing conditions holding of lexical representations also hold of
derived representations.

The principle prevents phonological processes in a language from augmenting the set of prosodic templates and patterns of melodic association defined at the lexical level by universal principles and specific parametric settings.

Phonological frameworks which permit resyllabifying transformations require structure preservation to be shut off at some point in derivation.[67] That is, creating novel structures through resyllabification implies overriding particular licensing conditions that hold at lexical representation. Conceptually, this view is out of tune with current assumptions in syntax. The alternative position adopted here is that phonological processes preserve prosodic structure throughout derivation. This view, I will try to show, can be maintained in the face of evidence involving processes for which resyllabification analyses have been proposed. We will consider a number of well-known examples of such accounts later in this chapter.

As suggested by the analysis of syncope illustrated in (51), one of the keys to maintaining the stability view of prosodic structure lies in the concept of empty phonological categories. One of the points illustrated by this particular account is that empty nuclei are not restricted to the domain-final context where their function is to license a preceding onset. The empty nuclei for which we have just seen evidence occur stem-internally.

If an internal empty position really is in some sense the same object as a parametrically licensed final empty position, we should expect the two of them to function identically for at least some phonological purposes. This expectation is in fact borne out. In one case to be discussed in 4.7.8, internal and final empty nuclei constitute a unified context before which *t*-lenition operates in various dialects of English. In the Tonkawa case briefly mentioned above, we find that the two positions behave identically with respect to syncope. Recall that the second vowel of a word is suppressed in this language, as revealed in the alternation evident in forms such as *picna-noʔ* versus *we-pcena-noʔ*. Now consider verb forms which contain a consonant-final prefix such as *nes-* (causative). In line with licensing principles, the domain-final consonant in the prefix occupies an onset position followed by an empty nucleus. As illustrated in (54), the latter position constitutes the second nucleus of a prefixed verb form and thus coincides with the syncope site.

(54)
```
O   N   O   N   O   N   O   N   O   N ...
|   |   |   |   |   |   |   |   |   |
[[x  x   x   x  [x   x   x   x   x   x ...
|   |   |       |   |   |   |   |   |
n   e   s       p   i   c   e   n   a ...
```

The prediction is that syncope in this case should operate vacuously in the context of the second nucleus and thus should not affect the first nucleus of the stem itself. This is exactly what we find: *nes-picena-no?* as opposed to **nes-pcena-no?*.

4.6.5 Proper Government

Inherent in the acceptance of morpheme-internal empty nuclei is the danger that the concept might be abused through unconstrained deployment in phonological analyses. We might now ask whether there is any principled restriction on the occurrence of empty categories in phonology. The key to this question lies in an observation that can be made with respect to both the Tonkawa and English syncope cases: a vowel can only be suppressed if it is adjacent to a vowel which is itself not suppressed. This characteristic in fact extends to the vast majority of examples of the process reported in the literature. It is particularly striking in languages displaying an alternating succession of syncopated and non-syncopated vowels that is iterated across the word domain.[68]

The adjacency requirement suggests that the target and trigger vowels involved in syncope enter into a relation of licensing at some level of nuclear projection. This has led to the proposal of a constraint on the occurrence of empty nuclei which is formulated as a more restrictive case of projection licensing known as **Proper Government**.[69] To be empty, a nucleus must either be parametrically sanctioned domain-finally (according to the parameter in (19)) or be properly governed by another nucleus. In the latter instance, Proper Government requires that the licensing nucleus must itself not be empty. In all reported cases, the proper governor stands to the right of its proper governee.

By way of illustration, consider the following representation of ⟨fam(i)ly⟩ (in which the arrow indicates Proper Government):

(55)
```
                    ┌──────────┐
              N₁      N₂     ↓  N₁
         O   |   O   |   O   |
         |   |   |   |   |   |
         x   x   x   x   x   x
         |   |   |       |   |
         f   æ   m       l   i
```

The nuclear position N_2 is empty, by virtue of its being properly governed by N_3. The fact that vowel syncope is obligatory in some languages, not present in others and optional in others (as in English) indicates that Proper Government is not strictly enforced in all systems.

Vowel–zero alternations in English are also evident in certain root-derived forms, although whether this phenomenon belongs to the general ⟨fam(i)ly⟩ type is questionable. According to one resyllabification account, the lexical representation of roots involved in alternations such as ⟨simple–simplicity, metre–metric⟩ and ⟨couple–couplet⟩ contains a CC cluster which is broken up by an epenthetic vowel in word-final context. Hence $k \Lambda pl \rightarrow k \Lambda p \partial l$ versus ⟨cou[pl]-et⟩.[70] Under this analysis, a form such as ⟨couplet⟩ contains the same foot structure as the syncopated variants of the forms in (50). Note, however, that the allegedly epenthetic vowel is obligatorily absent from root-derived forms; hence the impossibility of *⟨coup[ə]let, met[ə]ric⟩, etc. Forms of this type are thus phonologically indistinguishable from forms such as ⟨poplar, petrol, patron⟩ which have no final CVC] alternants. (Poplar trees no more popple than patrons pater.) For the reasons given in 1.4.3, I assume that root-level alternants such as ⟨simplicity, couplet, metric⟩ are simply listed in the lexicon.

On the other hand, word-level alternations can display exactly the same optional syncope pattern as that illustrated in (50): hence ⟨puzz([ə])l-ing, batt(e)r-ing, butt(o)n-ing, fidd([ə])l-er⟩, etc. The lexical representation of the morphological base in such cases, we may assume, contains an internal empty nucleus:[71]

(56)   (a)   ⟨fiddle⟩ fıdəl   (b)   ⟨fiddler⟩ fıdlə(r)

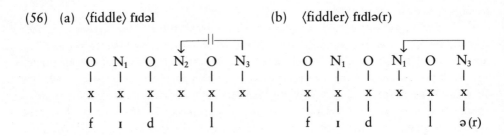

In (56a), N_2 fails to be properly governed (indicated by //) by the empty position N_3, since the latter is itself licensed (by parameter). N_2 must therefore be phonetically expressed, either as the latently present @ (yielding *fidəl*) or as a syllabic lateral (*fidl̩*, through spreading from the following onset). (56b), on the other hand, displays the same Proper Government configuration as ⟨fam(i)ly⟩ in (55). N_3 is filled (by the vowel of the suffix ⟨-er⟩) and is thus able to license N_2; the latter thus remains phonetically unexpressed.

Proper Government ensures that a syncopated vowel is always adjacent to an unsyncopated vowel. The constraint thereby derives the alternating . . . VCØCVCØ . . . pattern that is characteristic of languages in which syncope iterates across the word. A syncope 'lapse' in which adjacent vowels are both suppressed, for example in the sequence ... CØCØCV ..., is ruled out on the grounds that the second nucleus, being properly governed by the third, is unable to properly govern the first. One of the constraining effects of Proper Government is thus to debar adjacent empty nuclei from phonological representations.

In response to one of the questions raised at the beginning of 4.6.1, we may now conclude that an 'empty' nuclear position is not really empty at all. Rather it contains latently present melodic material in the shape of @, together with which it forms a potential autosegmental licensing domain. Whether the licensing potential is activated and thereby supplies an association between the position and the element depends on whether certain conditions are satisfied. In the case of syncope, this autosegmental licensing requirement is not met if the position is properly governed (as in an alternant such as ⟨def'nite⟩). But under different conditions, when the position is not properly governed (as in the alternant ⟨definitive⟩), it is empowered to license melodic material.

I have already mentioned the recognition of empty onsets as having set a phonological precedent for empty nuclei. It does not take much to think of analogues elsewhere in the grammar. Mention of the Projection Principle above suggests a parallel between empty nuclei in phonology and empty categories in syntax. Indeed, it has been proposed that the two are subject to the same universal constraint, the **Empty Category Principle (ECP)**, one sub-clause of which requires that a category or position must continue to be licensed by its head, even when it has been vacated as a result of syntactic movement or the delinking of melodic material.[72] We might say that an empty nucleus is properly governed by its head nucleus in the same way that, say, the trace of a noun-phrase complement which has been subject to WH-Movement is governed by its verb head.

We can develop this parallel further by picking up again on the theme that no systematic interactions will take place between superficially neighbouring positions if an empty position intervenes. A well-known example of this phenomenon in English syntax involves the alternation between ⟨want to⟩ and its contracted form ⟨wanna⟩. The contraction is sensitive to whether or not an empty category intervenes between ⟨want⟩ and ⟨to⟩.[73] As illustrated in (57a), contraction is an option if the two forms are strictly adjacent.

(57) (a) She's [the woman]$_i$ I want to talk to [e]$_i$
          She's the woman I wanna talk to.

     (b) She's [the woman]$_i$ I want [e]$_i$ to be president
          *She's the woman I wanna be president.

Compare (57a) with the sentence in (57b), where ⟨want⟩ is separated from ⟨to⟩ by the trace of its complement (co-indexed with ⟨the woman⟩); in this case, contraction is blocked. The failure of contraction here, reflecting a lack of adjacency between the categories occupied by ⟨want⟩ and ⟨to⟩, is strongly reminiscent of the failure of phonotactic dependencies to manifest themselves between onsets that are separated by an empty nucleus.

4.7 Lenition

4.7.1 Introduction

The remainder of this chapter is devoted to the analysis of consonantal lenition. In 3.4.2, we considered the melodic effects of this type of process. Now we turn our attention to the issues of where and why it occurs. This may seem an inordinate amount of space to devote to a single phenomenon. However, there is good reason to go into the matter in considerable detail. Our search for a non-arbitrary account of phonological processing has focused on establishing an intimate bond between the effects of a process and the context in which these make themselves felt. The first class of process to submit to analysis in these terms was that involving assimilation. The mechanism of spreading sets up a connection between the target and trigger of such processes in the most direct way possible – by having them associated to one and the same piece of melodic material.

Of the remaining process-types, a substantial proportion, perhaps the majority, fall under the rubric of lenition or weakening. Until recently, it had proved difficult to subject this class of phenomena to the same sort of non-arbitrary treatment as that successfully applied to assimilation. The particular challenge presented by lenition processes is that they lack an immediately obvious local cause.

Of course it has long been recognized that consonantal lenition, like vocalic reduction, characteristically takes place in 'weak' contexts. Nevertheless, the goal of formalizing this insight has turned out to be rather elusive. Informally, vowel reduction can be said to occur in metrically recessive nuclei, typically positions that are assigned weak stress or undergo harmony. The most-cited locations for consonantal lenition are codas, word-final contexts and foot-internal inter-vocalic contexts. It would be desirable to be able to subsume this apparently disparate range of contexts under a single dimension of prosodic weakness. In the rest of this chapter, we will consider a number of analyses of *t*-lenition in English which illustrate two fundamentally different ways of approaching this challenge.

We begin in the next section by reviewing the main contextual details of *t*-lenition in different types of English.

4.7.2 Four t-*lenition systems*

The data on which the discussion is based are drawn from four types of English, illustrating patterns of *t* realization which are distributed over relatively large geographical areas. As we will see, the conditions under which *t*-lenition manifests itself in these systems overlap to a significant extent. Nevertheless, they vary in interesting ways in a manner which, I hope to show, sheds light on the role played by autosegmental and prosodic licensing in conditioning phonological processes.

The four illustrative systems are as follows:[74]

(58) Lenition systems
    A: glottalling (restricted distribution)
    B: glottalling (wide distribution)
    C: tapping (unreleased stop in certain contexts)
    D: spirantization

Systems A and B exemplify glottalling as it operates in many areas of England and Scotland. The phonological distribution of the glottalled reflex in System A is more restricted than that in B. For example, while both systems show lenited *t* utterance-finally, as in ⟨pi[ʔ]⟩, only B shows it foot-internally, as in ⟨pi[ʔ]y⟩. A unidirectional implicational pattern reportedly exists in the geographical distribution of these two systems: in some areas, both systems exist side by side (with various patterns of social distribution); but, while the occurrence of B invariably implies that A is also present, the converse is not necessarily true. Viewed historically, the occurrence in certain areas of System A to the exclusion of B suggests that the latter is a more recent development of the former.[75]

C is a typical tapping system, showing a tapped reflex of *t* foot-internally (e.g. ⟨pi[ɾ]y⟩) and an unreleased, often pre-glottalized stop reflex in, for example, utterance-final position (e.g. ⟨pi[t⁻]⟩). The particular system from which the data given in this section are derived is one encountered in metropolitan New York. However, tapping is firmly established all over the United States, as well as in Canada, Australia, and some areas of England and Ireland.

System D displays the effects of spirantization to *s*, a process most characteristically associated with parts of southern Ireland and Merseyside in England. In the Irish English data supplied below, the spirantized reflex occurs both foot-internally and word-finally.

Lenition of *t* is by no means an isolated phenomenon in English. In terms of both realization and distribution, it is related to several other processes which considerations of space preclude us from discussing in detail here. Foot-internal tapping, for example, extends to *d*, with the result that the *t–d* contrast is potentially neutralized in this context in many dialects (so that ⟨ladder⟩ = ⟨latter⟩, for instance).[76] The distribution of pre-glottalized stop reflexes holds not just of *t* but of all voiceless plosives.[77] In some glottalling dialects, glottalling affects not only *t* but also *p* and *k*, albeit under a more restricted set of conditions.[78] And, as we saw in 3.4.2, spirantization can extend to other plosives and, in the case of *t*, can proceed as far as debuccalization to *h*.

In some areas where *t*-weakening is less firmly entrenched than in others, lenited reflexes typically alternate with unlenited reflexes under different social conditions. This variability will not concern us in the following discussion. Rather the focus will be on the phonological conditions under which the appearance of a lenited reflex is grammatical (even if optional) in each of the four illustrative systems.

I have selected the four systems described here on the basis of the way they point up differences in the conditioning of *t*-lenition by two main factors – the presence of a following licensed nucleus, and the immediate segmental context. The first of these relates to the occurrence of *t* inter-vocalically (as in ⟨pity⟩) and domain-finally (as in ⟨pity⟩), the second to the effect of surrounding consonants (as in ⟨mister⟩ and ⟨petrol⟩). A further conditioning factor, which we will not discuss, involves an inter-vocalic context in which the two nuclei occur in separate feet within the same word.[79] In some dialects, *t* can be lenited here if the second nucleus bears secondary stress, as in ⟨détàil, látèx⟩. This also applies to bipedal forms whose primary stress shifts according to the rhythmic context within the phrase. Forms of this shape which contain a lenition-prone *t* include ⟨thirteen, fourteen, eighteen⟩. (To see the effects of stress shift, compare ⟨éightèen wómen⟩ with ⟨èightéen banánas⟩.[80]) The manner in which this last dimension influences *t*-lenition cuts across the four-way classification of the systems to be discussed here.

As in previous chapters, the data are presented in word sets, each of which illustrates a particular configuration of phonological and morphological conditions. To start with, we will confine our attention to segmental contexts in which *t* is either inter-vocalic (as in ⟨pity⟩) or post-vocalic and word-final (as in ⟨pit⟩). We will consider the conditioning effects of neighbouring consonants later.

We begin our comparison by noting one context in which *t* is resistant to lenition in all four systems. As shown in (59), an unlenited plosive reflex occurs in a foot-initial onset, both word-initially (59a) and word-internally (59b). (Where a word contains more than one orthographic ⟨t⟩, the emboldened letter corresponds to the *t* which appears in the illustrated context.)

		A	B	C	D	
(59)						
	(a)	t	t	t	t	time, tin, trade
	(b)	t	t	t	t	pretend, boutique, politician, imitation

Inter-vocalically within a morpheme-internal foot, System B shows a glottal reflex, C a tap and D a spirant, while A retains an unlenited reflex. This pattern holds regardless of whether the dominant nucleus of the foot has primary (60a) or secondary word-stress (60b).

		A	B	C	D	
(60)						
	(a)	t	ʔ	ɾ	s	pretty, Peter, water, automatic
	(b)	t	ʔ	ɾ	s	photographic, automatic

As shown by the forms in (61), the same pattern manifests itself in an onset flanked by the two weak nuclei of a super-foot:

	A	B	C	D	
(61)	t	ʔ	ɾ	s	sanity, parity, political

As discussed in 4.6.2, this configuration contains two metrical domains: the dominant nucleus is bracketed with the following nucleus on the foot projection and with the third nucleus on the super-foot projection. In a form such as ⟨competitor⟩, both *t*s are susceptible to lenition in Systems B, C and D, the first by virtue of being foot-internal, the second by virtue of being internal to a super-foot.

Word-finally before a consonant or a pause (indicated in (62) by |), A joins B and D in showing a weakened reflex. It is in this context that the otherwise-tapping System C has an unreleased stop.

(62)
	A	B	C	D	
(a)	ʔ	ʔ	t⁻	s	let |, put |, light	
(b)	ʔ	ʔ	t⁻	s	let me, put by, light rain

Word-finally before a vowel, however, C again displays the tap:

(63)
	A	B	C	D	
(a)	t	ʔ	ɾ	s	let a, put it, light again,
(b)	t	ʔ	ɾ	s	let óff, put óver, light úp

Here, B and D also have lenited reflexes. Note that weakening occurs in this context irrespective of whether the following vowel is unstressed (63a) or stressed (63b). This means that, in System C, tapping before a stressed vowel may take place across a word boundary but not word-internally; compare the C data in (63b) and (59b).[81]

Based on the data presented so far, the main differences among the four systems with respect to the distribution of lenited *t* can be summarized informally as follows:

(64)
		A	B	C	D
(a)	Word-final before C or		ʔ	ʔ	t⁻	s
(b)	Word-final before V	t	ʔ	ɾ	s
(c)	Foot-internal	t	ʔ	ɾ	s

There are three main aspects of the data that any account has to get to grips with: (a) the unified behaviour of the domain-final and foot-internal contexts; (b) the relation between the tap and unreleased-stop alternants in System C; and (c) the apparent sensitivity to morpho-syntactic structure of the latter alternation, as well as of the alternation between *t* and *ʔ* in System A.

Note that the word-final context in (64a) contains the conjunction consonant or pause. In linear approaches, a conjunction such as this was directly incorporated into a rule's environment by means of brace ('curly-bracket') notation: {C, |}.[82] Couched in these terms, the glottalling rule for System A looks something like this:

(65)   t → ʔ/ ___ $\left\{\begin{matrix} C \\ I \end{matrix}\right\}$

Brace notation was originally introduced into the SPE-type framework to allow rules with overlapping structural descriptions to be collapsed. In (65), there are two sub-rules, one applying before C, the other before I. The notation is be interpreted in such a way that both subparts apply (a convention known as conjunctive rule ordering). The device was an early target for criticism of the rewrite-rule format, on the grounds that it vastly increases the expressive power of the model, to the extent that any grammar the model generates is in all likelihood unlearnable.[83] In principle, any two or more feature matrices or boundary symbols can be unified by means of the curly-bracket device. With this comes the prediction that, even if we restrict ourselves to combinations of two units, as in rule (65), each combination has an equal chance of being instantiated in rules characterizing processes in the world's languages. This is simply not correct. The vast majority of the expressible conjunctions are not attested in any natural language. And expanding the set of conjoined environments beyond two produces an exponential increase in the number of expressible permutations, again well nigh all of which correspond to nothing in the empirical record.

In contrast, the specific combination illustrated in (64a) is one that recurs with disturbing regularity in linear analyses of different languages and language families, although this fact remains no more than accidental within a theory which incorporates brace notation. This reflects a more general failure to evaluate a very small class of attested processes any differently from a vast array of unattested types.

For some time now, it has been recognized that the {C, I} conjunction is an inadequate circumlocution referring to a single context that can only be satisfactorily characterized in terms of constituent structure.[84] Indeed it was partly in response to this observation that linear representations were abandoned in favour of syllabically structured representations in the first place.

4.7.3 Coda analyses

We will now compare three constituent-based analyses of *t*-lenition, the first two of which were initially formulated exclusively to account for the process as it occurs in System-C dialects. Both of these illustrate a more general approach to consonantal weakening, one in which the coda is identified as the prime weak context. The main focus here will be on the formal machinery these analyses call on, specifically resyllabification, rule ordering and, in one case, **ambisyllabicity**. An ambisyllabic consonant is one that belongs simultaneously to a coda and a following onset. According to this type of approach, domain-final *t* in a form such as ⟨pit⟩ is syllabified in a coda. A further assumption is that, in line with onset maximization, a foot-internal *t* in a form such as ⟨pity⟩ is attached to an onset at the level of basic syllabification; subsequently, however, the consonant undergoes resyllabification into the preceding rhyme, an operation we may refer to as **Coda Capture.**

Under one such analysis, the rule by which a foot-internal consonant is captured into the coda of the dominant syllable on the left can be informally paraphrased as follows:[85]

(66) **Coda Capture**
 Within a foot, attach the consonant associated with the onset of the unstressed syllable to the coda of the stressed syllable.

Note that the way this operation is formulated leaves the initially established onset attachment undisturbed. The result is a foot-internal ambisyllabic consonant, as in the *t* of ⟨pity⟩:

(67)

```
O   R      O   R
|   | \   /    |
p   ɪ   t      i
```

A further resyllabification rule that has a bearing on *t*-lenition affects a word-final consonant in context (64b), as in ⟨get a⟩. Again paraphrasing, we may formulate this operation as follows:[86]

(68) **Onset Capture**
 Attach a word-final coda consonant to an unoccupied onset at the beginning of a following word.

As with (66), this rule creates ambisyllabic consonants, such as in ⟨{ge{t} a}⟩ (where {t} indicates the simultaneous occupation of a coda and an onset). Note that Coda Capture in (66) is stress-sensitive: *t* is ambisyllabic in ⟨{pí{t}y}⟩, where it is foot-internal, but not in ⟨{pre}{ténd}⟩, where it is foot-initial. Onset Capture in (68), on the other hand, is insensitive to stress: *t* is ambisyllabic in both ⟨gé{t} a}⟩ and ⟨{gè{t} óff}⟩.

Together, the two resyllabification rules set the scene for lenition, itself formulated as two sub-rules, one of which generates a tap, the other an unreleased stop:[87]

(69) **Lenition**
 (a) t → ɾ   if ambisyllabic
 (b) t → t⁻   if not syllable-initial

The derivation of the three forms in (70) illustrates the workings of this analysis (skeletal tier suppressed):[88]

(70)

⟨pity⟩	⟨get ɪ⟩	⟨get a⟩

```
          O R O R      O R         O R    R
          | | | |      | | \       | | \  |
          p ɪ t i      g ɛ  t      g ɛ  t ə
```

Coda Capture
```
    O  R    O  R
    |  |\ ⁄  |        —           —
    p  ɪ t   i
```

Onset Capture
```
                          O  R    O  R
             —            |  |\ ⁄  |
                          g  ɛ t   ə
```

Lenition (69)
```
    O R    R       O R          O  R    R
    | |\ ⁄|        | |\         |  |\ ⁄|
    p ɪ ɾ i        g ɛ t⁻       g  ɛ ɾ  ə
```

The following devices play a crucial role in this analysis: resyllabification, ambisyllabicity and rule ordering. In the case of Coda Capture and Lenition (69a), the ordering is **intrinsic**; that is, the latter cannot logically become operative until after the former has applied. However, in the case of Onset Capture and Lenition (69b), the ordering must be **extrinsically** imposed. These two rules could logically apply in either order. But were the operation of Lenition (69b) to precede that of Onset Capture, the *t* of a form such as ⟨get off⟩ could only be realized as an unreleased stop rather than as the attested tap. Thus, a System-C grammar has to contain a stipulation to the effect that Onset Capture must be ordered before Lenition (69b). Technically, the former rule **bleeds** the latter.

The device of ambisyllabicity has not been widely accepted in phonological theory.[89] The reason has to do with its anomalous status with respect to the bracketing of units in constituent structure. An otherwise uniform property of constituent structure in both phonology and syntax is that of **proper bracketing**, according to which no unit in a string may be simultaneously bracketed within two (or more) independent constituents. No word can simultaneously belong to, say, a verb phrase and an independent noun phrase (i.e. one that is not properly included in the former). To countenance the improper bracketing that is inherent in ambisyllabicity is to lose sight of this uniformity.

A second type of coda analysis dispenses with the need for ambisyllabicity. However, it retains the notion that the process operates in codas and thus also the need for resyllabification. The latter is reduced to a single operation in which the attachment of a foot-internal consonant to a preceding coda is accompanied by its detachment from its original onset position.[90] This may be informally stated as (71).[91]

(71) **Coda Capture II**
Within a foot, detach the consonant from the onset of the unstressed syllable and attach it to the coda of the stressed syllable.

As with the first analysis, resyllabification prepares the ground for *t*-lenition.

In order to characterize the relation between the tap and unreleased-stop reflexes of *t* in a type-C system, the following two-stage analysis of lenition, incorporating the binary feature [±release], has been proposed. First, a rule assigns values for the feature to *t* on the basis of the immediately following context. Specifically, if *t* is followed by a consonant or pause, it acquires a minus value; otherwise it is plus:[92]

(72) **Release**
A syllable-final oral stop is

    (a) [−release] before a consonant or a pause; and
    (b) [+release] elsewhere.

A syllable-final *t* will thus be [−release] in forms such as ⟨get by⟩ and ⟨get ∅⟩ (under (72a)) but [+release] in ⟨get a⟩ (under (72b)). A [−release] *t* subsequently yields *t⁻*. A [+release] *t* occurring in an onset is realized as a plosive (with aspiration if certain other conditions are met). In a coda, however, [+release] *t* is subject to tapping. The two lenited reflexes are derived by means of the following rules:[93]

(73) **Lenition II**
    (a)   t
          [+release] → ɾ in coda

    (b)   t
          [−release] → t⁻

The following derivations illustrate how these rules operate ([± release] abbreviated to [± r]):

(74)

	⟨pity⟩	⟨get ∅⟩	⟨get a⟩
	O R O R	O R	O R R
	p ɪ t i	g ɛ t	g ɛ t ə
Coda Capture II	O R R	—	—
	p ɪ t i		
Release (72)	O R R	O R	O R R
	p ɪ t i	g ɛ t	g ɛ t ə
	[+ r]	[− r]	[+ r]
Lenition II (73a)	O R R		O R R
	p ɪ ɾ i		g ɛ ɾ ə
Lenition II (73b)		O R	
		g ɛ t⁻	
	pɪɾi	gɛt⁻	gɛɾə

The main advantage this analysis enjoys over the first is its ability to account for the lenition facts without recourse to ambisyllabicity. It is also on the face of it simpler in that it dispenses with Onset Capture (68) (although, as we will see in a moment, this apparent saving may be illusory). Moreover, it dispenses with the need for extrinsic rule ordering. The tapping rule (73b) is intrinsically ordered after Coda Capture II (71); both lenition rules in (73) are intrinsically ordered after Release (72).

However, these savings do not come without costs being incurred elsewhere in the analysis. One price to be paid is the introduction of the *ad hoc* feature [release], for which there is little or no phonological motivation beyond this particular account, at least within an orthodox feature framework. Moreover, the sub-rule in (72a), which assigns [−release] to *t*, retains the problematical disjunction {C, l} that marred earlier linear analyses.

Taking stock of the formal devices just reviewed, we may note that each of the coda-based accounts invokes two or more of the following: extrinsic rule ordering, an ad hoc feature, ambisyllabicity and resyllabification. Each of these devices in its own way loosens the restrictiveness of the theory within which the analysis is framed. Resyllabification is incompatible with the most restrictive interpretation of the Structure Preservation Principle (53), according to which well-formedness conditions on prosodic structure remain in force throughout derivation. Coda Capture II (71), for example, creates a VC.V structure in which a coda position is unlicensed (in violation of Coda Licensing (16b)).

Underlying particular coda analyses of lenition is a more general assumption that melodic restrictions on domain-final consonants closely match or duplicate those operating in domain-internal codas. If this were true, it would provide some support for the view that both contexts are codas. It certainly is the case that there can be distributional overlap between the two positions, which co-occur in many classic examples of lenition and defective distribution.[94] However, this evidence cannot be considered sufficient to clinch the case for the coda assignment of final consonants. Even if we set aside the theoretical reasons we now have for rejecting this analysis, it is flatly contradicted by the substantial body of other empirical evidence reviewed in 2.4.4.

In any case, the distributional relationship between internal codas and final consonants is by no means as close as is often supposed. The evidence discussed in 2.4.4 shows that, in this respect, the two contexts are in fact quite different in English. Moreover, some of the best-known examples from other languages which supposedly demonstrate the relationship turn out, under close inspection, to be rather less than convincing.[95]

There is in fact a more fundamental flaw in the coda account of lenition: while it manages to shoe-horn the set of weak consonantal sites into a single constituent context, it provides no reason for why it should be the coda rather than any other syllabic context that particularly favours such processes. According to the theory within which the coda approach is formulated, lenition rules such as those in (69) and (73) would be no more highly valued than rules that weakened a consonant in, say, an onset or in the onset of a stressed syllable. Neither of the latter types coincides with the empirical record, at least not as an exhaustive characterization of a weakening context.

4.7.4 *Licensing analysis*

The question to be taken up in this and the following sections is whether an approach which has no recourse to resyllabification or indeed to any of the other machinery mentioned in the last section is up to the task of characterizing the same set of facts. I hope to show that a valid analysis of this type is available within a framework which incorporates independent principles of phonological licensing. Moreover, these same principles provide an answer not only to the question of why weakening occurs where it does but also to the even more fundamental question of why there exist distributional asymmetries at all.

We have already seen one respect in which an element-based approach is better equipped than one based on features (let alone *ad hoc* features) to represent weakening processes such as *t*-lenition in a constrained fashion (see 3.4.2). With binary features, lenition has to be expressed as the arbitrary substitution of one feature value by another. With univalent elements, on the other hand, all weakening processes are directly characterized as the suppression of melodic material that is present in lexical representation. The question now is whether the licensing framework outlined in this chapter is capable of capturing the conditions under which melodic decomposition takes place. I will try to show that an account of this type is indeed possible, not just for the System-C facts we have been concentrating on up to this point but for the other three illustrative systems as well.

Let us start by considering how to account for the selective conditioning of *t*-lenition by context (64a) (as in ⟨get by⟩) versus (64b) (⟨get a⟩). According to the first of the coda analyses above, this difference is attributable to the availability or otherwise of an onset position following the target segment. Specifically, a vacant onset is made available if, as in (64b), a vowel-initial word follows but not, as in (64a), if the target segment is succeeded by a consonant-initial word (in which the onset is already occupied) or a pause. The former case illustrates a recurring configuration in languages in which a word-final consonant is syllabified with a following word-initial vowel. Under a coda-based account, this effect is only achievable through resyllabification; specifically, an underlying word-final coda consonant is captured into a following onset if one becomes available during derivation. This aspect of the analysis is simply untranslatable into the licensing framework presented in this chapter. For one thing, the resyllabification operation is ruled out if Structure Preservation is assumed to persist throughout derivation. Moreover, we have seen sufficient evidence to support the view that a word-final consonant already occupies an onset position in any case.

If we assume that *t* in forms such as ⟨get by⟩ and ⟨get a⟩ in both instances occupies an onset slot, we must conclude that the distinction between contexts (64a) and (64b) resides in the nature of the following nucleus. In ⟨get by⟩, the position in question (a word-final parametrically licensed empty nucleus) is succeeded by an onset position:

(75)

```
O   N   O   N     O   N
|   |   |   |     |   | \
[x  x   x   x]   [x   x   x]
|   |   |         |   |   |
g   ɛ   t         b   a   y
```

⟨get a⟩, on the other hand, lacks a following onset position. The notion that the word-final consonant is syllabified with the following word-initial vowel can be implemented by assuming that an empty nucleus deletes next to a filled nucleus when no onset position intervenes:[96]

(76)   (a)

```
O₁  N₁  O₂  N₂      N₃               (b)  O₁  N₁  O₂      N₃
|   |   |   |       |                     |   |   |       |
x   x   x   x       x        →            x   x   x       x
|   |   |           |                     |   |   |       |
g   ɛ   t           ə                     g   ɛ   t       ə
```

The operation in (76) might be judged inadmissible under an extreme reading of the Structure Preservation Principle, since it results in the replacement of one specific licensing relation (that holding between N_2 and O_2 in (76a)) by another (between N_3 and O_2 in (76b)). It is, however, consistent with an interpretation under which **general** conditions on licensing remain in force throughout derivation. The relevant condition in (76) is the requirement (Onset Licensing (16a)) that O_2 be licensed by some nucleus, whatever the particular identity of that nucleus might be. To say that the onset is licensed by one nucleus in one domain and by a different nucleus in another implies no amendment to the set of prosodic templates defined over lexical representation by universal principles and parametric settings. The suppression of an empty position in (76) certainly does not entail the type of resyllabification whereby a position is reassigned from one constituent category to another, for example from a coda to an onset.

The operation whereby a nucleus deletes next to another nucleus is not just motivated to achieve the cross-word V.C] [V syllabification effect shown in (76). It can be viewed as part of a wider phenomenon, alluded to in 4.3.3, in which sequences of adjacent nuclei are disfavoured. Cross-linguistically, this manifests itself as a condition under which intra-morphemic sequences of filled nuclei tend to be absent from lexical representation. It also manifests itself in processes which serve to disengage potential nuclear sequences resulting from morphological concatenation. A process of this type demonstrates one of two strategies. One involves breaking up the sequence by supplying the intervening onset with melodic content. This frequently takes the form of a hiatus glide consisting of an element spread from one of the flanking nuclei. In some dialects of English, for example, a *w* glide appears in such contexts when the first vowel is round, as in ⟨too [w]early⟩. In this instance, the spreading element is U.[97] The other strategy for avoiding cross-word nuclear sequences is to suppress one of the nuclei. This is not widely employed in English (although it is evident in a handful of lexicalized contractions, such as ⟨I'm, you're⟩). However, it is firmly entrenched in many other languages. Witness, for example, the French apocope case briefly discussed in 4.6.1, with forms such as ⟨l'ami⟩ (from ⟨le/la ami⟩ 'the friend'), or the similar Yoruba pattern illustrated by forms such as *gba ɛrɔ̃* → *gbɛrɔ̃* ('receive meat').[98] The nucleus-suppressing strategy is the one that is formally related to the operation shown in (76).

The avoidance of consecutive nuclei is strongly reminiscent of the avoidance of consecutive identical melodic expressions that is embodied in the OCP (36). Indeed, it has been proposed that both phenomena are reflections of a more general version of the convention which applies not only to melodic expressions but also to constituents together with their positions.[99]

4.7.5 Licensing Inheritance

The next question is how to unify the word-final pre-vocalic context (64b) with the foot-internal context (64c). Both sites correspond to onsets, but on the face of it the licensing conditions in these lenition-favouring contexts are no different from those obtaining in other onset contexts in which lenition is disfavoured. For example, a foot-internal onset (occupied by *t* in, say, ⟨letter⟩) is inter-constituent-licensed by a following nucleus in the same way that a foot-initial onset is (as in ⟨time⟩). And the latter is precisely one of the contexts that is typically resistant to lenition. What turns out to be important, however, is that this identity only holds of licensing conditions obtaining in the immediate vicinity of the positions in question. Panning out to higher levels of projection, we discover that indirect licensing relations which contribute to the integration of foot-initial and foot-internal onsets into the prosodic hierarchy are significantly different. In particular, the licensing nucleus is itself unlicensed on the foot projection in the first instance (the *ɛ* in ⟨letter⟩) but licensed in the second (the *ə(r)* in ⟨letter⟩). This distinction, I will now try to show, has a crucial bearing on the varying abilities of different onset positions to support melodic material.

Consonantal lenition, viewed as melodic decomposition, can be taken as evidence of a position's diminished ability to support melodic content. Asymmetries in the capacity of different onset positions to sustain particular levels of melodic complexity are strongly reminiscent of the distributional inequalities obtaining within the governing domains in (29) (branching onsets, branching nuclei and coda-onset clusters). The Complexity Condition (32) is essentially a statement about the autosegmental licensing power of different positions within this type of domain, where greater power implies a greater toleration of melodic complexity. What the condition says is that a governed position can never have a greater capacity to license melodic material than its governor. By means of this constraint, we correctly derive the complexity gradients that are observable in these contexts. As it stands, however, the Condition has nothing to say about positions which, although not standing in a relation of direct licensing, nevertheless also display systematic discrepancies in melodic complexity. This is true of the two types of onsets that figure in the differential conditioning of lenition. The two sites in question, foot-internal and word-final, involve positions where the tendency towards low melodic complexity cannot be directly attributed to their status as licensees. Rather, as pointed out in the last paragraph, their weakness relative to foot-initial onsets seems to stem indirectly from relations involving the following nuclei that license them.

These observations suggest an intimate relationship between the prosodic and autosegmental aspects of licensing and further justify subsuming them under the single principle of Phonological Licensing in (8). A question worth pursuing is whether this relation is responsible for all asymmetries in melodic complexity, not just those involving direct licensing. This would mean that the Complexity Condition is reducible to some more fundamental principle which regulates the connection between the two mechanisms. The fundamental insight that initiates this line of enquiry is that the capacity of a position to support melodic contrasts is determined in large part by its place in the prosodic hierarchy.

To develop this idea, it will be convenient to be able to speak of a position's **autosegmental licensing potential**. This may be understood as the ability of a position either to directly license melodic content or to confer autosegmental licensing potential on another position. Viewed in these terms, distributional asymmetries reflect the fact that a prosodically unlicensed position has a greater degree of autosegmental licensing potential at its disposal than its licensee.

Two assumptions will help give this notion formal substance. First, as stated in (77), a licensed position acquires its ability to license melodic material from its licensor:[100]

(77) **Licensing Inheritance Principle**
　　　A prosodically licensed position inherits its autosegmental licensing potential from its licensor.

Second, the stock of autosegmental licensing potential invested in an unlicensed position is finite and is dissipated through transmission to licensed positions.

This is illustrated in the branching onset structure shown in (78) (where α stands for some melodic expression defining a consonant).

(78) (a) Direct autosegmental
           licensing

(b) Indirect autosegmental
     licensing

$[x_1 \quad x_2]O$
$\quad |$
$\quad \alpha_1$

$[x_1 \quad x_2]O$
$\qquad \quad |$
$\qquad \quad \alpha_2$

The immediate source of the autosegmental licensing potential available within the onset is the constituent head x_1. (As we will see presently, x_1 itself inherits this potential from outside the onset, specifically from the following nuclear head by which it is licensed.) Within the onset, as shown in (78a), the autosegmental licensing of the melodic expression α_1 by x_1 is direct. On the other hand, as shown in (78b), the licensing of α_2 by x_2 is indirect, since the position's licensing potential is acquired from x_1.

A licensed position can be thought of as a sort of resistor which attenuates the autosegmental licensing charge delivered by its licensor. This notion, together with the Licensing Inheritance Principle, allows us to derive the reduced distributional leeway of a licensed position *vis-à-vis* that of its licensor. The defective distributional characteristic of the right-hand slot of a branching onset is thus a reflection of the fact that its autosegmental licensing potential is diluted as a result of being inherited from another position, namely its licensor on the left.

All of the distributional inequalities derived by means of the Complexity Condition may now be viewed as instantiations of the more general principle of Licensing Inheritance. The downward complexity gradient enforced within branching onsets and favoured within branching nuclei can now be understood as reflecting the fact that the right-hand position in both cases acquires its autosegmental licensing potential from its constituent-governor on the left. Similarly, the upward complexity slope observable in coda-onset clusters results from the directionality of inter-constituent government: the coda inherits its autosegmental licensing potential from the following onset governor.

In fact, the autosegmental licensing power transmitted to the coda by the following onset is doubly diminished. As shown in (79), the onset x_2 which governs coda x_1 is itself licensed by the following nuclear head x_3.

(79) Coda C   R

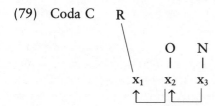

This means that the autosegmental licensing potential of the coda is inherited at two removes from its source; that is, it is depleted at two stages on a licensing path.[101]

Before extending this insight to the other lenition sites, it is worth making a brief excursus at this juncture to consider the relevance of the point just made to the distributional peculiarities of codas discussed in chapter 2. We are now in a better position to explain the fact that the coda of a heavy (two-position) rhyme has rather more distributional leeway than that in a super-heavy (three-position) rhyme. For example, as noted in 2.4.4, the former, unlike the latter, can support an oral stop; hence single-domain forms such as ⟨factor, apt⟩ but none on the lines of * *fiːktər* or * *eypt*. Or another example: a sonorant occupying the coda of a super-heavy rhyme must be place-linked to the following onset, as in ⟨mountain, shoulder⟩. In the case of a heavy rhyme, on the other hand, a coda sonorant can bear an independent place element. Thus we find forms such as ⟨dolphin, bulk⟩ but none of the shape * *duːlfn* or * *bowlk*.

Distributional discrepancies of this sort, we may surmise, are attributable to the relational distinction between the two types of coda pointed out in 4.3.5. As shown in (23a), the coda of a heavy rhyme is simultaneously licensed by the preceding nuclear head and by its governing onset. From the viewpoint of Licensing Inheritance, this means that it receives two injections of autosegmental licensing power. Compare this with the single transfusion received by the coda of a super-heavy rhyme, which is licensed only by the following onset (see (23b)). The second-hand quality of the licensing potential handed down by the governing onset in (79) means that neither type of coda makes a particularly strong autosegmental licensor. But the additional source of power available to the doubly licensed coda leaves it rather more distributional room to manoeuvre.

The two-stage nature of the licensing configuration in (79) provides the key to unifying the foot-internal and word-final sites where consonantal lenition takes place. The distributional disparity between foot-initial and foot-internal onsets is related to the different licensing potentials of the following nuclei. On the foot projection, the dominant nucleus is identified as a powerful autosegmental licensor by virtue of the fact that it is unlicensed within its domain. The licensed status of a recessive nucleus, on the other hand, marks it out as possessing correspondingly less autosegmental licensing potential. Hence the recurrent pattern whereby a maximal inventory of vocalic contrasts is to be found in dominant nuclei, whereas recessive nuclei frequently display reduced inventories. The phenomenon of vowel reduction, typical of recessive nuclei, is expressible as the suppression of elements when the autosegmental licensing power of the position to which they would otherwise be attached, inherited from the dominant nucleus, is insufficient to ensure their interpretation.[102]

The distributional asymmetry between the nuclei of a foot is potentially mirrored in the onsets they license at the inter-constituent level. Just as the distributional leeway of the dominant nucleus is less tightly restricted than that of its recessive sister, so the onset licensed by the former enjoys a greater distinctive potential than the onset licensed by the latter. Hence the widespread tendency for contrasts holding in foot-initial onsets to be neutralized foot-internally. This imbalance can be seen to follow from the Licensing Inheritance Principle, if we compare the different licensing paths involved in the two contexts, illustrated by the *t* in ⟨tunny⟩ (80a) and that in ⟨pity⟩ (80b). In the fragments of representations given on the right, the relevant licensing details are highlighted.

(80)   (a)   Foot-initial C

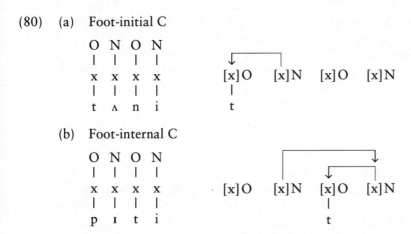

        (b)   Foot-internal C

From (80a) it can be seen that the source of a foot-initial onset's autosegmental licensing potential occurs at one remove from its prosodic licensor, the dominant nucleus of the foot. The diminished autosegmental licensing power of a foot-internal onset, by contrast, stems from the fact that it is inherited at two removes, as shown in (80b).

The word-final context can be identified as a weak autosegmental licensing site for similar reasons to those holding foot-internally. The onset position occupied by a final consonant is licensed by a following empty nucleus which is itself licensed, this time parametrically. This is illustrated in (81) for the *t* in ⟨get⟩ (again with the relevant licensing relations featured on the right).

(81)   Domain-final C   Final-empty nucleus parameter ON

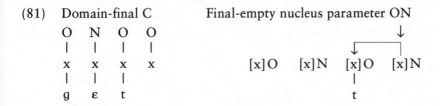

By invoking Licensing Inheritance, we have succeeded in unifying the three classic consonantal weakening contexts – coda, foot-internal, and domain-final. As depicted in (79), (80b) and (81), each involves a position whose autosegmental licensing potential is depleted at two stages on a licensing path. In short, the diminished ability of all three sites to support melodic contrasts stems from their relatively lowly status within the prosodic hierarchy. Under such circumstances, lenition results from the inability of a position to issue an autosegmental licence to particular elements.

Of course not all three contexts necessarily figure simultaneously as conditions on particular weakening processes. The differences between the foot-internal and domain-final sites, for instance, can be captured by referring to the status of the following licensed nucleus. A process that only occurs foot-internally is conditioned by the presence of a following nucleus that is licensed on the foot projection, as in (80a). A process that only occurs word-finally is triggered by the presence of a parametrically licensed empty nucleus, as in (81). For a process occurring in both contexts, we need only specify that the following nucleus is licensed. To illustrate these different conditions, let us briefly consider three weakening processes other than *t*-lenition.

An example of a lenition process that is confined to foot-internal contexts is provided by the suppression of *ð* that optionally occurs in some dialects (for example, those spoken in the north of Ireland). As a result of this weakening, forms such as ⟨mother, father, other, together, weather⟩ may lack the medial *ð* which appears in most other dialects. Hence a pronunciation such as *faər* ⟨father⟩. (In Dutch, a similar process has affected cognate *d* in the same position; cf. English ⟨brother⟩ and Dutch ⟨broer⟩.) Formally, this process can be expressed as the failure of a nucleus that is licensed on the foot projection to transmit sufficient autosegmental licensing power to enable the onset to support the relevant elements (head **R**, dependent **h**).

The widespread process of obstruent devoicing provides an example of weakening that occurs word-finally. Examples can be cited from a host of languages, including some of English's close West Germanic relatives such as Dutch and German. The version of the process that was once partially active in Old English is now more or less extinct in the modern language. Final devoicing has, however, developed independently in a few present-day dialects. It is found, for example, in certain types of African American English, where forms such as ⟨bi[t] = bid⟩, ⟨bi[k] = big⟩, ⟨li[ft] = lived⟩ are attested.[103] (While the distinction between the two series of obstruents is neutralized in this case, the original lexical contrast is preserved in the length of the preceding vowel, as in *bɪət* ⟨bid⟩ versus *bɪt* ⟨bit⟩, for example.) Devoicing consists in the suppression of the slack-vocal-cords element, an event that reflects the diminished autosegmental licensing power of a domain-final empty nucleus.[104]

The distributional properties of *h* in most dialects of English illustrate a weakening phenomenon that occurs both foot-internally and word-finally. The sound can appear in foot-initial onsets, both word-initially (as in (82a)) and word-internally (as in (82b)).

(82)   (a)   [h]it, [h]um, [h]ot
       (b)   be[h]alf, be[h]ind, appre[h]end
       (c)   ve[h]ícular   vé[h̷]icle
             pro[h]íbit   pro[h̷]ibítion

As shown in (82c), however, *h* is excluded from foot-internal onsets, a pattern which manifests itself in root-level alternations such as ⟨ve[h]ícular⟩ (foot-initial) versus ⟨véh̷icle⟩ (foot-internal). Furthermore, the sound is never found domain-finally in such dialects. (There are thus no words such as * *ræh*.) According to one approach, the unification of the two weakening contexts in this case is achieved by identifying both with coda position. This relies on the now-discredited assumptions that word-final consonants occupy a coda and that foot-internal onset consonants become resyllabified into a preceding coda.[105] The Licensing Inheritance proposal enables us to dispense with the latter device. All that has to be said in this case is that a licensed nucleus fails to bestow on a preceding onset the necessary capacity to license a lone **h** element.

4.7.6 Cyclic effects

We are now in a position to assess how the licensing proposal can be applied to the analysis of *t*-lenition contexts in our four illustrative dialects of English.[106] In tandem, the licensing configurations in (80b) and (81) define the conditions under which the various *t*-lenition processes operate:

(83)
N   O   N
| | | where x_3 is licensed either
x_1 x_2 x_3 (a) by x_1, or
|
t   (b) parametrically

Condition (83a) defines the foot-internal site represented by ⟨pity⟩ in (84a); condition (83b) defines the word-final site in ⟨pit⟩ (84b).

(84) (a)   (b) Parameter (19)   ON

O N O N   O N O N
| | | | | | | |
[x x x x]   [x x x x]
| | | | | | |
p ɪ t i   p ɪ t

Informally stated, the two glottalling systems, A and B, differ minimally with respect to whether lenition occurs pre-vocalically or not (see (64)). I have included these two systems in the comparative exercise for one express purpose – to show how the difference between them sheds light on the nature of the operation whereby the melodic content of a position is suppressed.

Although suppression of a melodic expression implies a withdrawal of its autosegmental licence, note that this does not necessarily imply that it is deleted. In principle, we can conceive of the delinking and deletion of melodic material as two independent operations. The simplest view would of course be that either but not both of these operations is a necessary part of the theory, or perhaps that deletion is no more than an automatic consequence of delinking. However, the conclusion that many phonologists have reached on the basis of the available evidence is that delinking and deletion are independent operations with different consequences. More accurately, delinking does not necessarily entail **immediate deletion**, although it is usually assumed that any melodic material not associated to a skeletal point at the end of a derivation is erased at that stage (one aspect of an operation known as **Stray Erasure**).[107]

One type of evidence supporting this view has to do with the manner in which phonological processes interact with morpho-syntactic structure. Let us remind ourselves of the assumption, outlined in 1.4.3, that processes occur cyclically: that is, their conditions are repeatedly checked through a succession of morpho-syntactic domains which are visible to the phonology. A given process which results in the suppression of melodic material is going to have quite different cyclic effects according to whether it is cast in terms of deletion of delinking without deletion. Any material that is deleted on a particular cycle will not be recoverable on a later cycle (one of the consequences of a principle known as the **Strict Cycle Condition**).[108] On the other hand, if melodic material is delinked but not deleted on a given cycle, it is potentially recoverable, should different licensing conditions become available on a subsequent cycle. That at least is the prediction which follows from the independence view of delinking and deletion; and it appears to be by and large correct, as we will now see.[109]

Let us now try to specify the precise conditions under which lenition occurs in each of our illustrative systems. As summarized in (64), the distributional difference between the two glottalling systems, A and B, resides in the fact that lenition in A only occurs domain-finally and then only if a consonant or pause follows. Under the ambisyllabicity approach, the latter conditions are implicitly identified as the context in which *t* fails to undergo resyllabification into a following onset (by rule (68)). Under the licensing account, since *t* already occupies an onset, the conditioning can only be expressed in terms of the nature of the following nucleus. In System B, glottalling occurs irrespective of whether the following nucleus is filled or empty. In System A, on the other hand, glottalling only occurs if the following nucleus is empty.

The initial representation of *t* in the lenition site contains the elements ?, **R** and **h**. Glottalling consists in the suppression of the elements **R** and **h** in the representation of *t* (see 3.4.2). In System B, these particular elements are unlicensed in context (83). In A, the same elements are unlicensed in context (83), but only if x_3 is empty. The manner in which this withdrawal of autosegmental licensing is implemented differs in the two systems. As will become clear, it is necessary to specify that the unlicensed elements are delinked in A but deleted in B:

(85) *t*-lenition A/B
      In context (83):

      (a) (System A) delink **R** and **h**, iff x_3 is empty;
      (b) (System B) delete **R** and **h**.

The System-A alternation between word-final *t* and *?* can now be shown to result from the selective manner in which the delinking conditions in (85a) are satisfied in different morphological domains. In a phrase such as ⟨get by⟩, word-final *t* is followed by an empty nucleus, both within the inner domain enclosing ⟨[get]⟩ and within the outer domain enclosing ⟨[get by]⟩. According to (85a) then, **R** and **h** remain unlicensed on both cycles, with the result that *t* manifests the glottalled reflex. This is shown in (86), where delinked elements are parenthesized.

(86)   ⟨get by⟩ *gɛʔbay* (System A)

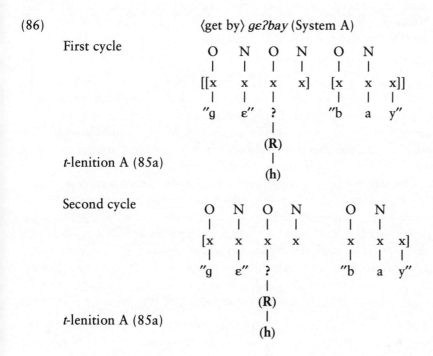

On the other hand, in a form such as ⟨get a⟩ *t* is followed by an empty nucleus only on the first cycle ⟨[get]⟩. Under the extended OCP, this nucleus is suppressed on the second cycle where it would otherwise stand next to the nucleus of the form ⟨a⟩. The result is that, within the phrasal domain ⟨[get a]⟩, *t* is followed by a filled nucleus:

(87)   ⟨get a⟩ *gɛt ə* (System A)

First cycle

      O   N   O   N   N
      | | | | |
    [[x   x   x   x] [x]]
      | | | |
     "g ɛ" ?   "ə"
               |
             (R)

t-lenition A (85a) |
               (h)

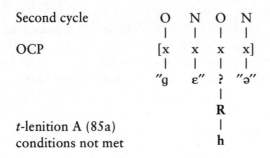

Second cycle

OCP

t-lenition A (85a)
conditions not met

On the second cycle, the presence of a filled nucleus following the *t* means that the conditions for *t*-lenition (85a) are no longer satisfied. The filled nucleus supplies the preceding onset position with the necessary capacity to license the elements **h** and **R**, with the result that an unweakened plosive reflex manifests itself. This account is in line with the view that delinking does not imply immediate deletion of melodic material. In (87), **h** and **R** are unlicensed in ⟨[get]⟩ and thus cannot receive phonetic interpretation on that cycle. They nevertheless remain present in the representation where they are potentially available for interpretation, should the required licensing conditions be met on a later cycle, as they are in ⟨[get a]⟩.

In the case of System B, the situation is quite straightforward. The deletion of **R** and **h** on an inner cycle correctly implies that these elements are not recoverable on subsequent cycles. Hence the retention of a glottalled reflex in both ⟨get by⟩ and ⟨get a⟩. The same state of affairs holds in spirantizing System D, with the difference that it is the element ? that fails to be licensed in context (83) and is deleted:

(88)   ***t*-lenition D**
        In context (83) delete ?.

We can now subject this analysis to a direct comparison with the coda accounts, by considering how it extends to System C. One aspect of the earlier accounts which can profitably be retained is the insight that the alternation between the tap and unreleased stop should be characterized in terms of two stages. The justification for this decision rests in the observation that the two stages are guided by different (though overlapping) conditions. In terms of their melodic composition, what the two reflexes have in common is an absence of noise release. Under an element-based account, this commonality is expressed as the deletion of a lexically present **h**. This constitutes one stage of lenition in System C and occurs in context (83), irrespective of whether x_3 is filled or empty. At this point, the weakened *t* is interpretable as an unreleased stop, the reflex that appears in a form such as ⟨get by⟩. The second stage of lenition takes this already weakened *t* and reduces it further by deleting ?, yielding a tap, but only if a phonetically interpreted nucleus follows. In summary:

(89) **t-lenition C**

    (a) In context (83) delete **h**;

    (b)

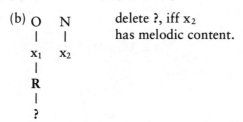

delete ?, iff x_2
has melodic content.

Note that the two stages are intrinsically ordered, which is fully in accord with the principle that phonological processes occur freely whenever their conditions are met. The tapping part of *t*-lenition (89b) is only free to apply once **h** has been suppressed by (89a). In other words, only a *t* without noise release is tapped.

    The derivations in (90) illustrate the two-stage aspect of this analysis. (Here and in subsequent derivations, deletion is represented by a slash through the relevant element(s).)

(90) (System C)   ⟨pity⟩   ⟨pit l⟩

                               O N O N   O N O N
                               | | | | | | | |
                               x   x   x   x   x   x   x   x
                               | | | | | | |
                             "p ɪ" R "ɪ"   "p ɪ" R
                                     | |
                                     ?   ?
                                     | |
t-lenition C (89a)   h̷   h̷

                               O N O N
                               | | | |
                               x   x   x   x
                               | | | |
                             "p ɪ" R "ɪ"
                                     |
t-lenition C (89b)   ʔ̷   conditions not met

                              pɪɾi   pɪt-

    Under this analysis, the alternation between the tap in ⟨get a⟩ and the unreleased stop in ⟨get by⟩ is attributable to the different ways in which the two lenition processes in (89) operate within different morpho-syntactic domains. In accordance with (89a), **h** fails to be licensed on the inner cycle ⟨[get]⟩. On the next cycle,

? continues to be licensed in ⟨[get by]⟩ but, in accordance with (89b), fails to be licensed in ⟨[get a]⟩. The following derivation demonstrates the resulting differences between the two forms:

(91) ⟨get by⟩ *gɛt‾bay*   ⟨get a⟩ *gɛɾə* (System C)
      Word cycle: *t*-lenition C (89a)

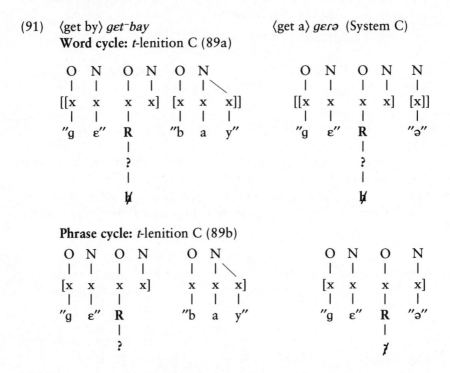

Phrase cycle: *t*-lenition C (89b)

    How does this analysis account for the observation that tapping in System C can take place before a stressed vowel word-finally (as in ⟨get óff⟩) but not word-medially (as in ⟨retáin⟩)? The difference resides in the fact that, as the dominant position within the foot and word domains, the stressed nucleus following the *t* in ⟨retáin⟩ is prosodically unlicensed, with the result that the conditions for h-loss, defined in (89a), are never met. In ⟨get óff⟩, on the other hand, the *t*, being domain-final, is followed by a parametrically licensed empty nucleus on the first cycle ⟨[get]⟩, where the conditions for suppression of h (89a) are met. Within the phrasal domain ⟨[get off]⟩, the presence of a following filled nucleus satisfies the conditions for the deletion of ? (89b), resulting in a tapped reflex.
    The analysis presented in this and the previous sections draws on principles of licensing which are motivated by a diverse range of phenomena apparently unrelated to English *t*-lenition. I have tried to show that, within this framework, the facts of *t*-lenition can be treated without resorting to any of the following devices relied on by previous analyses: resyllabification, ambisyllabicity, extrinsic rule ordering, and ad hoc features. Moreover, the question of why lenition occurs where it does is answered by identifying particular positions in the prosodic hierarchy as weak autosegmental licensors.

4.7.7 *Preceding consonants*

So far, our examination of the *t*-lenition facts has been confined to vocalic contexts. We now turn our attention to the influence that neighbouring consonants can exert on the process. Here too, licensing relations between adjacent positions can be shown to play a decisive conditioning role.

The consonantal sites in question involve the constituent configurations in (92). (As before, α indicates some melodic expression corresponding to a consonant.)

(92)   (a)   (b)

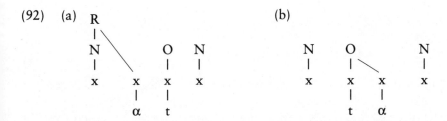

It will prove significant that these constitute a subset of the governing domains in (29). In (92a), *t* is preceded by a coda consonant (as in ⟨mist, mister⟩); in (92b), *t* forms part of a branching onset (as in ⟨petrol⟩). In each of these contexts, *t* is at least potentially susceptible to lenition, provided the second nucleus is licensed. It turns out, however, that the process is liable to be blocked in both instances, an observation that has led to such contexts sometimes being referred to as 'protected environments'.[110] Let us first examine condition (92a).

In none of our illustrative systems is lenition grammatical if the preceding consonant is an obstruent. This goes for both foot-internal (93a) and domain-final (93b) positions:

(93)   A   B   C   D
     (a)   t   t   t   t   after, mister, pistol, chapter, doctor
     (b)   t   t   t   t   left, fist, bust, act, apt, adopt

(Domain-finally in this context *t* (and, after sonorants, *d*) is subject to the independent process of total suppression discussed in 1.1. In some types of English, this is restricted to casual speech styles and is triggered when a consonant-initial word follows, as in ⟨best do, mind the⟩. In other dialects, the lexical representations of such words have apparently been restructured to exclude the final coronal altogether.[111])

A preceding resonant does not have the same categorical blocking effect. Forms which historically contained *r* in this context show lenition, irrespective of whether the modern reflex has consonantal constriction (rhotic pronunciation) or has been vocalized (non-rhotic). Each of the four lenition systems is attested in both rhotic and non-rhotic versions, and in every case the lenition facts are identical to those associated with historically vocalic contexts. Compare the following results with those in (93):

(94)
	A	B	C	D	
(a)	t	ʔ	ɾ	s	party, quarter, forty
(b)	ʔ	ʔ	t⁻	s	hurt l, court l, part l

The presence of a preceding lateral, on the other hand, exerts an inhibiting influence on lenition. As shown in (95), tapping and spirantization are blocked in this context.

(95)
	A	B	C	D	
(a)	t	ʔ	t	t	filter, shelter
(b)	ʔ	ʔ	t⁻	t	fault, belt

It is possible to get a stop reflex with no noise release here, but in this case the homorganicity of the coronal *lt* cluster results in a merger of ʔ and t⁻. That is, while an unreleased stop component realizes the *t*, coronality manifests itself over the cluster as a whole. In Systems A and B, however, historically dark *l* in this context is susceptible to vocalization to w; in this event, the debuccalization that results from glottalling removes the coronal gesture altogether, producing realizations such as *bɛwʔ* ⟨belt⟩.

The effect of a preceding nasal also varies from system to system, as demonstrated in (96).

(96)
	A	B	C	D	
(a)	ʔ	ʔ	t⁻	t	hint, sent, rant
(b)	t	ʔ	Ø	t	winter, twenty, plenty

In parallel with the post-*l* context, both spirantization and tapping are blocked here. In tapping dialects, *t* is either retained after *n* or lost altogether; in the event of the latter, a form such as ⟨plenty⟩ rhymes with ⟨penny⟩. Another parallel with *lt* concerns the homorganicity of *nt*, which results in a suspension of the ʔ–t⁻ difference. Moreover, the resonant can undergo vocalization, leaving nasality as a secondary characteristic on the preceding vowel, as in *bɛ̃t⁻* ⟨bent⟩.

In rule-based treatments of these facts, the conditioning effect of a preceding consonant is specified in the environment of the lenition rule. For example, the tapping sub-rule applies if the target *t* is immediately preceded by a [−consonantal] segment, where the latter is understood as designating the class of vowels, glides and *r*. In the glottalling version of the rule, the relevant specification is [+sonorant].[112] The inherent arbitrariness of rewrite rules is revealed in the fact that the theory provides no reason why these particular features or their values should favour the operation of lenition rather than others.

According to the alternative analysis to be presented here, the consonantal conditioning of lenition follows directly from the role played by melodic complexity in phonological licensing. The consonantal context in (92a) involves a relation of inter-constituent government between the onset occupied by *t* and a preceding coda. (In what follows, **governing consonant** is used as shorthand for the technically more accurate term **consonant occupying a governing position.**) The enforcement of the Complexity Condition at this level of structure requires that the consonant in the governed coda be no more complex than the governing onset *t*. This requirement is met as long as the *t* is not subject to radical reduction. As shown in (97a), a full plosive *t*, with at least three elements (four, if the laryngeal element **H** is included), is more complex than a preceding obstruent with two.

(97) (a)   (b)

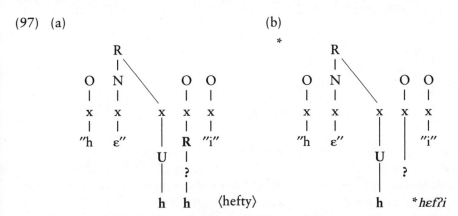

However, as illustrated by the ungrammatical glottalling in (97b), any weakening of the *t* to a single element, as occurs in tapping and glottalling, would fall foul of the Complexity Condition by reversing the direction of the complexity slope between the two positions. In other words, the immunity of *t* to lenition in this context stems from the governing responsibilities it discharges in relation to a preceding coda obstruent.

A consonant occurring in a protected location is thus subject to two contradictory pressures. Occupying a position with relatively weak autosegmental licensing capacity, it is susceptible to reduction. At the same time, it is required by the Complexity Condition to retain a certain minimum level of melodic content in order to be able to fulfil the governing obligations it has towards an adjacent position. That the former pressure is no more than a predisposition which may or may not be realized is confirmed by the fact that lenition does not obligatorily occur in every system which presents the relevant conditions. After all, not all dialects of English display *t*-lenition. What the licensing account sets out to tell us is **where** and **why** melodic reduction can take place. The individual grammar is then free to take up the option of actuating the process or not. The Complexity Condition is, by contrast, an inviolable principle of universal phonology. Wherever a predisposition and an irresistible force come into conflict, there is of course no real contest. It is for this reason that the governing duties of a sound overrule whatever propensity it might have to lenite.

This account extends to *lt* clusters. The failure of tapping in this context can be attributed to the fact that reduction to **R** would rob the governing *t* of the melodic material necessary to maintain the complexity differential *vis-à-vis* the governed lateral (which, recall, consists of two elements, ? and **R**). However, vocalization of a dark *l* to *w* in this context has two historical outcomes which render a following onset *t* liable to lenition. First, it results in the loss of the stop and coronality elements. What appears in its stead is the **U** element, a reflex of the lateral's originally secondary gesture. Second, the vocalized reflex has been historically reanalysed as belonging to the preceding nucleus, with the consequent creation of a new set of *w*-gliding diphthongs (see exercise 3 at the end of chapter 5). The upshot, as shown in (98), is that forms such as ⟨belt⟩ now lack the coda position that was once occupied by *l*:

(98)

bɛw? ⟨belt⟩

In this configuration, the original relation of inter-constituent government, which is retained in non-vocalizing dialects, is no longer present. Thus relieved of its former licensing responsibilities, *t* is given a free hand to decompose. Hence the glottalled reflexes in the vocalizing systems A and B listed in (95).

The facility with which *t* lenites after historical *r* indicates that here too we are dealing with the absence of a coda position. This is more obviously true of dialects in which original *r* has been reduced to schwa or some other vocalic reflex. But there is a good deal of evidence, which is quite independent of the lenition facts, to suggest that the modern pre-consonantal reflex of historical *r* occupies a nuclear position in both non-rhotic and rhotic dialects. The evidence, to be reviewed in the next chapter, relates to the manner in which the contrastive potential of a nucleus is greatly curtailed by the presence of a following *r*. This effect is explained if the latter is assumed to be absorbed directly into the nucleus. This state of affairs is illustrated in the following representations of non-rhotic and rhotic variants of ⟨party⟩:

(99)　(a)　*parti*　　　　　　　　(b)　*paːti*

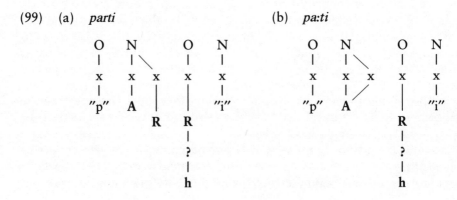

The widespread lenition of *t* shown in (94) can then be attributed to the absence of a coda position in both non-rhotic and rhotic pronunciations of forms such as ⟨party⟩. Under such circumstances, the onset *t* has no governing duties to discharge, with the result that it is at liberty to reduce without contravening the Complexity Condition.

As regards *nt* clusters, we should bear in mind that the place identity of a coda nasal is dependent on an element that is distinctively lodged in the following onset. As illustrated in the representation of ⟨twenty⟩ with unlenited *t* shown in (100a), this asymmetry contributes to the existence of an upward inter-constituent complexity slope.

(100)　(a) *twɛnti*　　　　　(b) *twɛnʔi*

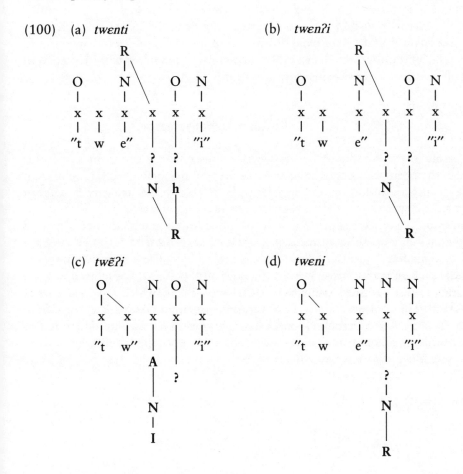

(c) *twɛ̃ʔi*　　　　(d) *twɛni*

One spin-off of this is that reduction of an onset *t* in such a context will not jeopardize the complexity differential as long as the process is only partial. For example, suppression of the noise element **h** will have the effect of flattening but not reversing the incline. This is shown in (100b) where this version of lenition results in the optional realization *twɛnʔi*, encountered in System B. (100c) and (100d) show historically restructured forms in which the coda position, formerly occupied by the nasal, has been lost altogether. In (100c), another System-B variant, the nasal element has migrated to the preceding nucleus, producing a nasalized vowel; in (100d) the medial onset retains ʔ and R from the original cluster and N from the original nasal consonant.

4.7.8 *Following consonants*

The pre-consonantal onset context shown in (92b) is restricted to foot-internal position, as in ⟨petrol, sentry⟩. This is because English does not sanction word-final branching onsets (unlike French where we find forms such as *vitr* 'window pane'). Forms with medial *ty*, as in ⟨statue⟩, only occur in dialects in which this sequence has not undergone palatalization to č (see exercise 2 of chapter 2). In forms which retain *ty*, as well as in the much more common forms with medial *tr*, none of our illustrative systems shows lenition:

(101) A   B   C   D
       t   t   t   t   petrol, patrimony, mattress

This result is attributable to the relation of constituent government that holds between the position occupied by *t* and its onset complement. The failure of even partial reduction in this context appears to be related to the stringent manner in which a downward complexity gradient is enforced in onsets.

That said, it may seem something of a contradiction to note that some System-B speakers actually do show forms which contrast with those in (101) in having a superficial medial sequence of glottalled *t* followed by *r*. The lenited reflex occurs in words such as *pɒʔri* ⟨pottery⟩, *bæʔri* ⟨(assault and) battery⟩. For many speakers, the latter is distinguished from *bætri* ⟨(car) battery⟩ in which the medial *tr* is categorical. The contradiction is, however, only apparent. The lenited *ʔr* configuration involves not a branching onset but the vowel-syncope site illustrated in (51). That is, the *t* and *r* of a form such as ⟨batt(e)ry⟩ occupy independent onsets which straddle a syncope-prone nucleus:

(102)   O   N   O   N   O   N
          | | | | | |
          x   x   x   x   x   x
          | | | | |
         ʺb   æ   tʺ   ʺr   iʺ
                      @

In forms such as this, recall, two conditions are present which permit the melodic content of the licensed second nucleus to be suppressed. The nucleus in question is followed (a) by the weak nucleus of a super-foot; and (b) by an onset resonant. In the event of syncope occurring in this context, *t* finds itself succeeded by an empty nucleus (which itself is licensed by virtue of being properly governed by the final nucleus occupied by *i*). Under these circumstances, we expect it to display precisely the same propensity to lenite as when it is followed by domain-final empty nucleus. A comparison of the facts in (103a) (repeated from (62)) and (103b) show that this prediction is borne out.

(103)

	A	B	C	D	
(a)	ʔ	ʔ	t⁻	s	let me, put by, light rain
(b)	ʔ	ʔ	t⁻	s	batt'ry, pott'ry

For those speakers who have the contrast between *bæʔri* and *bætri* ⟨battery⟩ mentioned above, we must assume that the latter item has been reanalysed as having an internal *tr* onset; in other words, it has the same foot structure as a form such as ⟨petrol⟩. This conclusion is bolstered by the observation that the *bætri* variant contains a voiceless *r*, the usual realization of a liquid occurring in the same onset as a voiceless stop (cf. the *l* and *r* realizations in ⟨pray, play, crew, clue⟩).

In a similar vein, a form such as ⟨watery⟩ in some System-C dialects can have three different variants, each of which reflects a particular set of conditions, including the two just mentioned: ⟨wa[rə]ry⟩ (foot-internal, cf. ⟨water⟩ (60)), ⟨wa[t⁻r]y⟩ (the empty-nuclear context, cf. ⟨batt'ry⟩ (103b)), and ⟨wa[tr]y⟩ (branching onset, cf. ⟨petrol⟩ (101)).

This treatment of medial *tør* has a bearing on the analysis of other apparent clusters of *t* plus resonant occurring in this context, as in ⟨atlas, cutlass, chutney, atmosphere⟩. As already mentioned in 2.4.4, there is reason to doubt that medial strings of this type form genuine clusters. For one thing, they do not constitute well-formed branching onsets. Moreover, there are theory-internal grounds for rejecting the assumption that they are coda-onset sequences.

First, such a conclusion would entail a laryngeal contrast between *t* and *d* in this position, as in ⟨chutney⟩ versus ⟨kidney⟩. Anomalously, this would be the sole example of such a distinction among coda obstruents. Under these circumstances, the presence of laryngeal element would mean that *t* contained at least three elements, rendering it too complex to be governed by a following onset *l*.

Second, for *t* to be in a coda in forms such as ⟨atlas⟩ would present the only instance of that particular consonant occurring in a governed position. The general pattern is that *t* cannot be licensed by any other consonant, not even by a relatively complex obstruent. And this is no less true of the coda-onset context than of any other. Hence the asymmetry between occurring -*pt*-, -*kt*- clusters (as in ⟨chapter, doctor⟩) and non-occurring * -*tp*-, *-*tk*-. The anomaly here then would be a situation in which a resonant such as in ⟨chutney⟩ possessed a degree of licensing power denied to obstruents.

Third, a vowel-length contrast is possible before *t* when followed by *l*, *n* or *m*; compare the short nucleus in ⟨chutney, litmus, cutlery⟩ with the long in ⟨lightning⟩. In the latter instance, the preceding rhyme is already occupied by a branching nucleus. This means that a coda, were one present, would be only singly licensed (by the following onset). In that case, we would expect it to be subject to the set of restrictions that hold of codas in super-heavy rhymes (summarized in 2.4.4). Most relevantly, it would be unable to support a plosive of any sort. In short, *t* cannot occupy a coda position in such forms.

The conclusion that is forced on us by these considerations is that the consonants of *tn, tl* and *tm* strings occupy independent onsets separated by an intervening empty nucleus. In other words, forms such as ⟨chutney, atlas, litmus⟩ have the same super-foot structure as syncope-prone forms such as ⟨fatt(e)ning, battling, dec(i)mal⟩ and indeed as *tr* forms such as ⟨batt(e)ry⟩. The only difference is that syncope is obligatory in the former case and optional in the latter.[113] With this conclusion comes the prediction that the lenition facts in *tø̸n, tø̸l* and *tø̸m* contexts should line up with those attested in contexts where *t* occurs before a domain-final empty nucleus.

This is by and large true, provided we make allowances for the independent effects of homorganicity already mentioned in connection with *lt* and *nt* clusters. The fact that *t* shares the elements **R** and **?** with both *l* and *n* means that the contrast between *?* and unreleased *t⁻* is suspended in *tø̸l* and *tø̸n* sequences. That is, while the element **h** can be suppressed under these conditions (as stated in (85) and (89)), the retention of both **R** and **?** can be accounted for as resulting from melodic coalescence triggered by the OCP. This is shown in the following relevant portion of the representation of *tø̸n*:

(104)

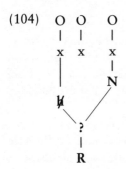

Retention of **R** blocks debuccalization and produces the neutralization of the *?–t⁻* contrast; retention of **?** blocks spirantization and tapping. The upshot is that all four of our lenition systems show an unreleased stop reflex in the *tø̸l/tø̸n* context.

This last point also explains the nature of lenited *t* reflexes before potentially syllabic resonants. Take for example the final portion of a form such as ⟨button⟩. Here, the latent vocalic content of the post-*t* nucleus is generally only realized in very careful speech. In this event, *t* occurs foot-internally before a filled nucleus, and the lenition facts line up exactly like those in (60). That is, we find variants such as *bʌɾən* (System C) and *bʌʔən* (System B). This is also the pattern we find in dialects which retain the vocalic content of the unstressed nucleus in final *təm* and *təl* sequences (as in *barəm* ⟨bottom⟩ and *barəl* ⟨bottle⟩, both System C). In the more usual variant of forms such as ⟨button⟩, the one that occurs most frequently in casual speech, the vocalic content of the nucleus is usurped by the *n* spreading from the following onset, resulting in a syllabic nasal. Under these circumstances, the OCP coalescence of the elements **R** and ?, shared by the contiguous oral and nasal coronal consonants, is responsible for an unreleased stop appearing as the neutralized reflex of lenited *t* in all four systems:

(105)   A   B   C   D
     t⁻ t⁻ t⁻ t⁻   button, frighten, cotton

4.8 Summary

In this chapter, we have examined the pivotal role played by phonological licensing in the organization of phonological representations. An apparently disparate range of processes and representational properties can be derived by reference to the fundamental notions of locality and directionality, in terms of which the principle is defined. Properties of the prosodic hierarchy that are accounted for in this way include the maximal binarity of branching constituent structure and the headed nature of relations holding between adjacent positions both within and across constituents, as well as between the projections of nuclear heads.

The local aspect of licensing defines the conditions under which the necessary adjacency between the trigger and target of a phonological process is established. Headedness meanwhile determines the directionality of the process. An intimate connection can be shown to exist between the autosegmental licensing power of a position and the prosodic licensing relations it contracts with other positions in the string. In this way, we account for a range of melodic phenomena, including vowel and consonant reduction, syncope, and phonotactic asymmetries traditionally described in terms of sonority sequencing.

Exercises

1 Four coda analyses

The data Below appear four sets of data presented in terms of one type of analysis proposed in the phonological literature. According to the analysis, the crucial context in which the phenomena in question operate is the coda.[114] This approach is founded on two assumptions which, in the light of arguments presented in this chapter and in chapter 2, must be regarded as unsound: (a) a word-final consonant occupies a coda; and (b) a consonant occupying an onset in core syllabification can under certain circumstances be captured into a preceding coda. Where necessary, these syllabifications are indicated below by means of full-stop notation (VC.C, for example).

The task Ignoring the melodic consequences of the processes, focus on the contexts in which they take place. We may take it that the reported analyses are right in assuming that some aspect of phonological constituent structure is involved. Restate the conditions under which each process occurs, without resorting to either of the coda assumptions just mentioned. In some cases, it will be necessary to spell out the morpho-syntactic domains within which the relevant contexts are located.

I PRE-FORTIS CLIPPING

In most types of English, vowels under certain conditions display significantly shorter duration before fortis than before non-fortis consonants (see 3.6). The process is described by some writers as **clipping**, to indicate that it is independent of the lexical short–long distinction involved in root-level phenomena such as closed-rhyme shortness and trisyllabic laxing. Thus the lexically short vowel *ɪ* is clipped in a form such as ⟨bit⟩ but not in ⟨bid⟩, just as the lexically long vowel *iː* of ⟨beat⟩ is clipped in relation to that in ⟨bead⟩. The process also affects vowel-resonant clusters before a fortis consonant; the *ɛl* sequence is clipped in ⟨shelf⟩, for instance, but not in ⟨shelve⟩.

For clipping to operate, the vowel-consonant sequence has to occur in a certain context which, according to one account, involves tautosyllabicity. In other words, the consonant is assumed to occupy a coda, either word-finally as in (a) or pre-vocalically as in (b).

	Clipped	Unclipped
(a)	bleat.	bleed.
	lap.	slab.
	face.	phase.
	slant.	band.
	pulp.	bulb.
(b)	peop.le	feeb.le
	fick.le	wigg.le
	sof.a	ov.er
	wint.er	cind.er
	hamp.er	clamb.er

II TAPPED *r*

In the conservative standard pronunciation of the south of England, it is common to find tapped and approximant realizations of *r* being used under complementary sets of conditions. According to one view, the tap occurs in coda position and the approximant elsewhere. As we will see in the next chapter, the dialect is **non-rhotic**: historical *r* is suppressed before a consonant or pause. The alleged coda *r* therefore only shows up pre-vocalically, as in (a).

(a)	Tap	(b)	Approximant
	ver.y		red
	sorr.y		trod
	fear.ing		key.ring

III STOP EPENTHESIS

In 3.5, we briefly examined the melodic consequences of stop epenthesis in resonant-fricative sequences. This produces, for example, *n^{t}s* from *ns* in ⟨prince⟩ and *l^{t}s* from *ls* in ⟨else⟩. The focus here is on the context in which this phenomenon operates. According to one view, it occurs when the relevant cluster is contained within a coda:

Stop epenthesis	No stop epenthesis
n^{t}s.	*n.s*
fence	rain-soaked
dance	unsuitable
l^{t}s.	*l.s*
else	hillside
pulse	Alsatian

IV ELISION OF *t/d*

As briefly discussed in 1.1, word-final *t* and *d* are subject to elision when they occur in a cluster. The most favourable context is one where *t/d* is sandwiched between two other consonants, i.e. where a consonant-initial word follows, as in ⟨send me, best part⟩. Under one analysis, the *t/d*-final cluster under such circumstances occurs in a coda:

t/d elision	No elision
CC.C	C.CC
bes*t* part	mistrial
sen*d* me	androgenous
tol*d* Rory	children

2 Saramaccan

The data Saramaccan is a creole language spoken in Surinam. The bulk of its lexicon is historically drawn from English, although it also displays substantial input from various West African languages, Dutch and Portuguese. The following list of English-derived words provides a reasonably representative sample of the segmental and syllabic characteristics of the language, many of which are traceable to a West African base.[115]

The task

(a) Establish in what ways Saramaccan differs from English with respect to the phonological constituent parameters discussed in this chapter, specifically those relating to onsets, nuclei, rhymes and the status of word-final consonants.

(b) Detail the melodic composition of the vowel and consonant systems. Discuss the manner in which these diverge from the corresponding English systems.

mb, nd and *ŋg* are pre-nasalized stops (see 2.2.3). *kp* and *gb* are co-articulated labial-velar stops.

1	léi	'learn'		11	si	'see'
2	lέi	'ride'		12	púu	'pull'
3	kóti	'cut'		13	lútu	'root'
4	kɔ́tɔ	'cold'		14	fósu	'first'
5	sitónu	'stone'		15	sákpi	'shake'
6	góni	'gun'		16	dédε	'dead'
7	bígi	'begin'		17	áti	'hurt'
8	fási	'fashion'		18	wéfi	'wife'
9	ko	'come'		19	béti	'bite'
10	te	'time'		20	óso	'house'
21	mófo	'mouth'		31	tɔ́fɔ	'tough'
22	bói	'boil'		32	sísa	'sister'
23	bédi	'bed'		33	léti	'right'
24	koósu	'clothes'		34	wéi	'weary'
25	bέε	'belly'		35	buúu	'blood'
26	dɔ́ɔ	'door'		36	baáka	'black'
27	gɔ́ɔ	'grow'		37	boóko	'break'
28	ópo	'up'		38	fuútu	'fruit'
29	dɔɔ́ŋgɔ	'drunk'		39	kεέ	'cry'
30	hɔ́ndɔ	'hundred'		40	pεέ	'play'
41	kaábu	'crab'		51	sikísi	'six'
42	kiíki	'creek'		52	mókisi	'mix'
43	woóko	'work'		53	gbóto	'boat'
44	sáti	'short'		54	kónde	'country'
45	ǰári	'yard'		55	mbéi	'make'
46	máta	'mortar'		56	ndéti	'night'
47	heépi	'help'		57	sindéki	'snake'
48	gólu	'gourd'		58	ndófu	'enough'

49	sáfu	'soft'		59	lóŋgi	'long'
50	éside	'yesterday'		60	taáŋga	'strong'
61	ékisi	'egg'		71	físi	'fish'
62	diíŋgi	'drink'		72	lóbi	'rub'
63	ǰómbo	'jump'		73	kíi	'kill'
64	sómbɛ	'someone'		74	fúu	'full'
65	féndi	'find'		75	bói	'boil'
66	paándi	'plant'		76	hói	'hold'
67	paandási	'plantation'		77	baáa	'brother'
68	líŋga	'(ear-)ring'		78	wáka	'walk'
69	ála	'all'		79	féndi	'find'
70	saápu	'sharp'		80	láfu	'laugh'

81	mbéti	'animal, meat'
82	ǰéni	'(sugar) cane'
83	édi	'head'
84	sátu	'salt'
85	pɔ́tɔ	pot'
86	sumáa	'small'
87	kpéti-kpéti	'altogether' (cf. quite)
88	kpókpóosu	'knock-knee' (cf. cross)

5 Floating Sounds

5.1 Introduction

One of the structural innovations of non-linear phonology that figured prominently in the last chapter is the notion of empty positions, skeletal slots without any manifest melodic content.[1] Recognition of this situation leads to the possibility of contemplating its converse – a melodic unit without its own skeletal point. Under the autosegmental aspect of licensing, such a unit would be phonetically uninterpretable as long as it remained in this unattached state. On the other hand, suppose during the course of derivation licensing conditions were made available which enabled such a 'floating' segment to acquire attachment to a vacant position. Under such circumstances, the melody unit would be rescued from its unattached limbo, and its phonetic identity could be made manifest. In this chapter, we will consider evidence supporting just such an analysis of English *r*.

5.2 English *r*-systems

5.2.1 *The most imperfect of consonants*

> As this letter is but a jar of the tongue, sometimes against the roof of the mouth, and sometimes at the orifice of the throat, it is the most imperfect of all the consonants.

This remark on the sound *r* appears in John Walker's *Critical Pronouncing Dictionary and Expositor of the English Language,* first published in 1791. In the chapter entitled 'Principles of English pronunciation', the author elaborates on the claim that there are two types of *r*-sound:

> There is a distinction in the sound of this letter, never noticed by any of our writers on the subject, which is, in my opinion, of no small importance; and that is, the rough and smooth *r*. The rough *r* is formed by jarring the tip of the tongue against the roof of the mouth near the fore teeth: the smooth *r* is

a vibration of the lower part of the tongue, near the root, against the inward region of the palate, near the entrance of the throat.[2]

In order to avoid 'producing any harshness to the ear', Walker recommends that the rough variant be used in one set of phonological contexts, illustrated by such words as ⟨Rome, rage⟩, and the smooth variant in another set, illustrated by ⟨bar, bard⟩.

Walker refers to two other patterns of *r*-pronunciation which fail to meet with his approval. In the 'harsh' Irish accent, the rough variant is erroneously used in all phonological contexts. 'But if this letter is too forcibly pronounced in Ireland, it is often too feebly sounded in England, and particularly in London, where it is sometimes entirely sunk.'[3]

Our knowledge of the present-day descendants of the dialects described by Walker confirms that he had put his finger on what was to become one of the most salient pronunciation variables in English. The rough–smooth difference has to do with whether historical *r* is pronounced with or without some degree of consonantal constriction, typically involving the tip or blade of the tongue. The **rhotic** pattern is one in which consonantal (rough) *r* appears in all of the phonological contexts in which the sound appeared historically. Orthographic ⟨r⟩ provides a reasonably accurate guide to the original distribution, since the English spelling system was formalized at a time when all dialects were rhotic. In the **non-rhotic** pattern, historical *r* fails to show up consonantally in certain positions. Instead what we find is a vocalic ('smooth') reflex or, in some cases, zero (Walker's 'sunk' variant).

In order to be able to make sense of the basic distributional differences between rhotic and non-rhotic systems, it is necessary to take into account a further range of related phenomena. One of these concerns a set of *r*–zero alternations that widely occur in non-rhotic dialects. What we find is that some originally *r*-ful words never contain consonantal *r*, while others alternate between an *r*-less and an *r*-ful variant. The alternation takes the form of a **sandhi** (cross-morpheme) phenomenon which is dependent on whether a vowel or consonant follows; compare ⟨ba*ɾ* the⟩ with ⟨ba[ɾ] a⟩. The constricted reflex under such circumstances is sometimes referred to as **linking r**. In some dialects, we encounter an extension of the sandhi process whereby a so-called **intrusive r** crops up in alternating words which originally lacked it, e.g. ⟨saw[∅] them⟩ versus ⟨saw[ɾ] it⟩.

Another phenomenon related to rhoticity concerns the nature of vowels that occur before historical *r*. In most dialects, the set of vocalic contrasts in this context is radically different from those encountered before other consonants, from the viewpoint of both length and quality.

In this chapter, we will take a detailed look at this apparently disparate range of phenomena and see how they might be accounted for in a unified manner. Questions raised by these phenomena include the following. What is the phonological distribution of smooth *r*? In non-rhotic systems, is *r* lexically present in alternating *r*–zero forms? If so, how is it represented, what is its lexical incidence, and how is the zero alternant derived? Is 'unetymological' intrusive *r* phonologically any different from the etymological type of linking *r*? How do we account for the characteristic interaction between *r* and a preceding nucleus?

We can start by comparing the distributional properties of *r* in four types of dialect. Then we will discuss competing proposals for characterizing the distributions in terms of segmental or syllabic context. Next we will compare deletion and insertion analyses of the *r*–zero alternation and reject both in favour of a third alternative, one in which sandhi *r* is treated as a lexically 'floating' segment bereft of any attachment to a syllabic position. Discussion of the conditions under which sandhi *r* appears leads on to a consideration of vowel–*r* interactions and a proposal that these reflect the occurrence of post-vocalic *r* within the nucleus. At various points, it will be instructive to consider some of the historical issues that arise when we compare different reflexes of original *r* in present-day dialects.

5.2.2 Four ɾ-systems

To gain a picture of the range of dialect differences we encounter in the distribution of consonantal *r*, let us consider four illustrative systems. System A is the basic rhotic type that is recessive in England but is well-established in Canada, Ireland, Scotland, most of the United States and parts of the Caribbean.[4] The other three patterns are all non-rhotic in some sense, although we will see that they differ in rather interesting ways. System B displays the linking-*r* pattern described in classic textbook accounts of the standard pronunciation associated with southern England.[5] C, exhibiting intrusive *r*, is the basic system in non-rhotic England, although versions of it also occur in some parts of the eastern and southern United States and in the southern hemisphere.[6] D is characteristic of certain conservative dialects spoken in the Upper South of the United States.[7]

In many geographical areas, the patterns we are going to examine are categorical for large numbers of speakers. In others, however, the realization of historical *r* is subject to different degrees of variability, typically involving competition between rhotic and non-rhotic norms of pronunciation. This kind of situation prevails in parts of England (Lancashire, the West Country and the rural south), parts of the United States (some areas of the eastern seaboard and the South) and some Caribbean territories (for example, Guyana and Jamaica).[8]

Each of the categories **rhotic** and **non-rhotic** covers a range of phonetic manifestations. A rhotic variant is one in which historical *r* retains some kind of constricted realization. This may either take the form of a tap, as in some Scottish and Irish varieties, or more generally an approximant. The latter usually involves some degree of tongue-tip curl or high front bunching of the tongue blade, although uvular *r* is attested in a couple of enclaves in Scotland and the north of England.[9] In certain phonological contexts, rhotacism can consist in the superimposition of *r*-colouring on a preceding vowel. This is most frequently associated with the central rhotacized quality symbolized as ɚ, as in fɚst ⟨first⟩. (In what follows, I will simply use the broad transcription V*r* for rhotacized vowels and only employ the symbol ɚ where the context so demands.) Later in the chapter,

we will consider how each of these variants should be represented. A pronunciation which lacks constriction as understood in any of the senses just described is
non-rhotic. Under such circumstances, historical *r* shows up as some form of
vocalic reflex – either as the lengthened portion of a preceding non-high vowel (as
in *ka:d* ⟨card⟩, *dɔ:* ⟨door⟩) or as a post-vocalic glide. The glide reflex is most
usually of the in-gliding type (as in *fiə* ⟨fear⟩, *dɔə* ⟨door⟩), although up-gliding
patterns are also attested in certain eastern and southern United States dialects
(typically though not exclusively System D).[10] Hence pronunciations such as in
pow ⟨poor⟩, *bəyd* ⟨bird⟩.

In the material to be presented below, each system displays one set of positive
data, designated by plus marks, and one set of negative data, designated by
asterisks. The positive data indicate a constricted reflex of historical *r*, the
negative a zero or vocalic reflex. As in previous chapters, the presentation is in the
form of word sets, each of which illustrates a particular configuration of phonological and morphological conditions. For instance, the words in the following set
exemplify the manifestation of historical *r* before a consonant within the same
morpheme:

(1) A   B   C   D
     +   *   *   *   beard, cart, warn, source

This example shows that, in morpheme-internal pre-consonantal position, constricted *r* is grammatical in System A but not in the other three systems. In
recognition of the potential for variability that exists in some parts of the data to
be presented, at certain points a plus mark is to be taken to indicate that
consonantal *r* is optionally as opposed to categorically present in a particular
system.

We begin our comparison of the different systems by identifying one of the
contexts in which consonantal *r* always appears:

(2)   A   B   C   D
    (a)   +   +   +   +   red, rack, rude
    (b)   +   +   +   +   tray, dread, prime, fry

That is, in all four of our illustrative systems constricted *r* occurs in foot-initial
onsets, whether these be non-branching as in (2a), or branching as in (2b).[11]

Some type of consonantal *r* also appears in foot-internal onsets in Systems A, B
and C. In D, on the other hand, constricted *r* fails to show up in this context,
where we find instead a vocalic glide reflex or zero:

(3) A   B   C   D
     +   +   +   *   very, carry, dairy

Further differences among the systems emerge as soon as we examine contexts
in which historical *r* is not followed by a vowel. The distinction between rhotic A

and non-rhotic B, C, and D is evident in the word-internal pre-consonantal position already illustrated in (1). The same distributional divergence manifests itself pre-consonantally whenever historical *r* occurs word-finally:

(4)   A   B   C   D
    (a)   +   *   *   *   bear to, star sign, poor man, clear view, alter the
    (b)   +   *   *   *   after you, before one

Note that the informal term **pre-consonantal** here refers to the syllabic position of a following sound rather than to its phonetic quality. (4a) and (4b) illustrate the same syllabic context, namely one in which the word following historical *r* begins with an onset. As the data here confirm, it makes no difference whether the sound occupying the onset is characterized by some kind of consonantal constriction, as in (4a), or is a (non-consonantal) glide, as in (4b).

   The pattern illustrated in (4) is also found whenever historical *r* occurs word-finally before a pause (|):

(5)   A   B   C   D
      +   *   *   *   bear |, star |, poor |, clear |, alter |

   Turning now to morpheme-final historical *r* when followed by a vowel, we find constricted reflexes appearing in Systems A, B and C but not in D. This pattern is evident both word-internally (6a) and across words (6b). In B and C, the *r*-ful variant is obligatory in the former context and optional (though preferred) in the latter.

(6)   A   B   C   D
    (a)   +   +   +   *   bearing, starry, altering
    (b)   +   +   +   *   bear up, star of, poor Eva, clear up, alter a, after all,
                              before eight

In non-rhotic B and C, we now see an alternation between *r* and zero in words such as ⟨bear, star, poor⟩; linking *r* shows up pre-vocalically, as in (6), while the zero alternant appears pre-consonantally or pre-pausally, as in (4) and (5). On the face of it, the distribution in (6) appears to be identical to that of pre-vocalic *r* in a morpheme-internal context (cf. the forms in (3)). However, as we will see later, there can be quite striking discrepancies in the range of vocalic distinctions that hold before *r* in V*r*]V as opposed to V*r*V sequences.

   Taking stock of the distributional facts reviewed so far, we can say that rhotic System A displays consonantal *r* in the full range of contexts examined so far. The non-rhotic systems, on the other hand, only show constricted reflexes in some or all pre-vocalic positions. In Systems B and C, we find *r*–zero alternations in morpheme-final position, with the consonantal alternant appearing pre-vocalically. System D, in contrast, shows no such alternation; constricted *r* fails to appear morpheme-finally and is confined to foot-initial onsets.

5.2.3 *Intrusive* r

One question that arises at this point is whether loss of post-vocalic constricted *r* in the non-rhotic systems has resulted in mergers with nuclei from other historical sources. In some instances, this is indeed what has happened. Consider first the morpheme-internal pre-consonantal context illustrated in (1). The nucleus of words which historically contained *ar* (⟨barn, cart, lard⟩, etc.) is in most non-rhotic dialects identical to the long low vowel that comes from various non-rhotic sources, such as in ⟨calm, palm⟩ (containing a vocalized development of historical *al*) and ⟨father, Rajah⟩. On the other hand, in many non-rhotic systems the in-gliding diphthong in the BEARD word class is the exclusive reflex of historical V*r* in this context; it remains distinct from diphthongs and long vowels which have no rhotic source, such as those in BADE or BEAD.[12]

The synchronic relevance of the merger issue should become clear when we consider whether there is any evidence to support the presence of a lexical *r* in forms which are superficially *r*-less. On the face of it, there seems nothing to suggest that a child learning a categorically non-rhotic system should have any more reason to reconstruct a post-vocalic *r* in a form such as *fa:m* ⟨farm⟩ (historically *r*-ful) than in a form such as *ka:m* ⟨calm⟩ (historically *r*-less). The question becomes less straightforward when we consider morpheme-final position where the *r*–zero alternation comes into play in Systems B and C. Here there would seem to be a prima facie case for contemplating the existence of an underlying *r* which gets deleted under certain circumstances.[13] In order to be able to get to grips with this issue, we need to extend our comparison of the four illustrative systems by examining whether the historical distinction between V*r*] and V] sequences is maintained.

First consider what happens with schwa in word-final position. In particular, compare forms such as ⟨after, fear⟩ (etymologically *r*-ful), with those such as ⟨sofa, idea⟩ (etymologically *r*-less):

(7)	A	B	C	D	
(a)	+	*	*	*	after ten, better not, fear them
(b)	*	*	*	*	sofa by, Sheena Kelly, idea to

In the pre-consonantal context illustrated in (7), the *r*-less pattern of the three non-rhotic systems results in a merger of the V*r*] versus V] contrast. In rhotic A, the contrast is retained. However, the non-rhotic systems diverge when we consider the occurrence of the same forms in pre-vocalic position:

(8)	A	B	C	D,	
(a)	+	+	+	*	after all, better apple, fear of
(b)	*	*	+	*	sofa and, Sheena Easton, idea of

In (8a), B and C optionally display the linking *r* already illustrated in (6). D is not expected to show linking *r* in this position, given the total absence of morpheme-final *r* from this system. Note that, in the pre-vocalic context, non-rhotic B joins rhotic A in retaining the contrast between V*r*] and V]. What is striking about non-rhotic C here is that it actually exhibits a wider incidence of constricted *r* than rhotic A. That is, *r* shows up not only in the etymologically *r*-ful forms in (8a) but also in the etymologically *r*-less forms in (8b), as in ⟨Sheena[ɹ] Easton⟩. In the latter case, the *r* is, from a diachronic point of view, unetymological or 'intrusive'.

The domain within which optional *r*-sandhi operates in Systems B and C is apparently not syntactically circumscribed. All that is required is that no pause intervene after the word-final context. The following examples illustrate how intrusive *r* in C can occur phrase-internally (9a), across a phrase boundary (9b), across a clause boundary within a root sentence (9c), and even across sentences (9d).[14]

(9) (a) All that's left is a vast area [ɹ] of debris.
     (b) Honda[r] own this circuit.
     (c) This could be a problem for Villa[ɹ] as he floats one in for Klinsmann.
     (d) You can see Senna[ɹ]. I can't hear him.

A pattern similar to that evident in (7) and (8) emerges when we extend our comparison of historical V*r*] versus V] sequences to other vowels. Pre-consonantally, only A contrasts PAW with PORE and PA with PAR:

(10)   A   B   C   D
     (a)   +   *   *   *   lore to, sore knee
                                   far too, star turn

     (b)   *   *   *   *   law takes, saw them
                                   ma said, Shah can

Pre-vocalically across a word boundary, B and C show linking *r* (11a), while C also shows intrusive *r* (11b):

(11)   A   B   C   D
     (a)   +   +   +   *   lore of, sore eye
                                   far off, star of

     (b)   *   *   +   *   law of, saw it
                                   ma and, Shah of

In C and D, ⟨lore of⟩ and ⟨law of⟩ are homophones. In D, neither form contains *r*, as a result of ⟨lore of⟩ lacking linking *r*. In C, both phrases contain *r*, the etymological variety in ⟨lore of⟩ and the intrusive variety in ⟨law of⟩. Pre-vocalic intrusive *r* is also possible word-internally in PAW forms in C, as in ⟨saw[r]ing wood⟩, ⟨draw[r]ing a picture⟩ (even if this particular pronunciation touches a raw nerve with – to borrow again from John Walker – 'the learned and the polite').[15]

Superficially at least, there is a restriction on the sandhi patterns illustrated in (6), (8) and (11): they only hold if the vowel involved in the final Vɹ] versus V] contrast is non-high. The sound in question may be schwa, in which case it occurs either alone in an unstressed nucleus (as in the second syllable of ⟨better⟩) or as the off-glide of a stressed diphthong (as in ⟨fear⟩). Otherwise, the segment is a full vowel of low or mid quality (as in PAW–PORE, PA–PAR). Intrusive *r* never appears pre-vocalically if the morpheme-final vowel is high or up-gliding:

(12)   A   B   C   D
       *   *   *   *   fee of, me and
                               pity it, plenty of
                               two and, lieu of
                               day off, say it
                               so on, go away

Stating the restriction in these terms might give the impression that independent vowel-quality conditions exert an influence on the distribution of consonantal *r*. If so, the nature of the conditioning might seem somewhat arbitrary: why should high rather than, say, front vowels disfavour the occurrence of *r*? Or preceding rather than, say, following vowels, for that matter? There is another possibility: that the restriction reflects the opposite effect, one in which *r* itself exerts an influence on the quality of a preceding vowel. This is a question we will take up in a later section.

The main distributional differences among our four illustrative systems can be now be summarized as follows:

(13) | | A | B | C | D |
|---|---|---|---|---|
| Morpheme-internal | | | | |
| __stressed V | + | + | + | + |
| __unstressed V | + | + | + | * |
| _C | + | * | * | * |
| _] | + | * | * | * |
| Cross-morpheme | | | | |
| __] V | + | + | + | * |
| __] C | + | * | * | * |

5.3 A linear analysis of smooth *r*

Proceeding now to an account of the facts outlined in the last section, let us begin by considering how an orthodox SPE-style rule approach captures the conditions under which constricted *r* **fails** to occur in non-rhotic systems. According to the best established analysis within this framework, non-rhoticity is characterized as the deletion of *r* under certain conditions. A first draft of such a rule might look something like this:[16]

(14)   r → ∅/___ $\left\{\begin{matrix} C \\ | \end{matrix}\right\}$

That is, *r* is deleted before either a consonant or a pause. The rule, some have suggested, characterizes what may be described as a 'proto-non-rhotic' system, one in which historical *r* is lexically recoverable in all contexts, for example through continued exposure to the original rhotic model.[17] Whether it accurately captures the state of affairs in our illustrative non-rhotic systems is, however, another matter. For example, adapting the rule to account for System D would at the very least involve building in a further condition referring to whether a following vowel bears stress and occurs in the same morpheme as the target *r*. As it stands, the rule begs a number of questions, some of which have quite fundamental implications for phonological theory.

One question concerns the status of the rule's input. At least in the case of Systems B and C, there are good grounds for wanting to construct an underlying *r* in morphemes such as ⟨star⟩ which show the *r*–zero alternation. Underlying *r* can be posited on the basis of the pre-vocalic alternant (e.g. ⟨starry⟩ with medial *r*), even though the consonant fails to appear in the pre-consonantal or pre-pausal alternant (e.g. ⟨sta𝑟 struck⟩). Forms in which *r* originally occurred pre-consonantally within morphemes, as in ⟨farther, farm⟩, are a different kettle of fish. Here there are no alternations to support the retention of underlying *r* in categorically non-rhotic systems. Moreover, if *r* were assumed to be underlyingly present in such forms, then this would also have to be true of historically *r*-less forms, such as ⟨father, calm⟩. Given the historical merger, the learner has no way of recovering the original contrast between V*r* and V in these contexts.

It has, however, been argued from a phonemically oriented perspective that underlying *r* in this context can be extrapolated from certain quality effects it allegedly conditions in a preceding vowel.[18] Below I will present an autosegmental adaptation of this view, in which approximant *r* is composed of independent vocalic and tongue-constriction elements. Given such a representation, it is possible to assume that the vocalic element can be lexically retained as a reflex of historical *r* in a non-rhotic system even after the constriction has been lost.

If it is assumed that historical *r* is lexically absent from the morpheme-internal pre-consonantal environment in non-rhotic systems, rule (14) can be taken to operate vacuously in this context. That is, in such systems the lexical shape of all forms containing this context already conforms to the rule's output.

In System D, the zero reflex of historical *r* never alternates with constricted *r* in any context. The form ⟨starry⟩, for example, lacks an *r*-ful alternant, not just pre-pausally (⟨sta[𝑟]|⟩) and pre-consonantally (⟨sta[𝑟] struck⟩) but pre-vocalically as well (⟨sta[𝑟]y⟩, ⟨sta[𝑟] of⟩). An initial reaction to these observations would be to conclude that the lexical representations of such forms, along with those containing the internal pre-consonantal context, have been historically restructured so that they now lack *r*. The validity of this conclusion would depend largely on whether or not *r* could still be recoverable on the basis of any qualitative traces it might have left on preceding vowels. In fact, in dialects of this type, etymological V*r* has typically undergone merger with V; hence homophones such as ⟨whore–hoe, sore–so, lord–load⟩, all with *ow*.[19] A System-D grammar still needs to make some provision for the generalization that constricted *r* is not sanctioned domain-finally or pre-consonantally. Unlike in the case of the other two non-rhotic systems, however, the regularity is a purely static distributional one.

The main problem with rule (14) stems from the same basic flaw in the rewrite-rule model as the one that confronted us in 4.7.2 – the failure of the brace notation to explain why this familiar combination of contexts, {C, |}, should keep recurring to the exclusion of virtually every other permutation of contexts defined by the model. More recent treatments of non-rhoticity have responded to this problem by recognizing that this phenomenon, no less than others previously treated in terms of the notorious conjunction, is more appropriately characterized in terms of syllabic conditions. Precisely what aspect of constituent structure might be involved in this instance is the issue we now turn to.

5.4 A coda analysis

5.4.1 R-Dropping

Viewed as a deletion process, non-rhoticity can be considered a type of weakening. It is therefore not surprising that early non-linear analyses of the phenomenon identified the coda as the target site, the same context as that widely believed to favour other types of lenition. Ultimately, this account is unsatisfactory for some of the same reasons as those discussed in relation to *t*-lenition in 4.7.3. Nevertheless, the coda analysis of non-rhoticity is worth considering, given the soundness of the original insight upon which it is founded, namely that weakening processes are primarily triggered not by segmental or boundary conditions but by aspects of constituent structure. Moreover, it helps point up certain interesting properties of the data that are perhaps not quite so obvious when viewed from an orthodox linear perspective.

The coda account of non-rhoticity actually comes in a number of guises. However, for our immediate purposes, it will be sufficient to take a single stripped-down version and assume that it can be translated fairly straightforwardly into terms appropriate to the various formats. Since we can postpone discussion of the special length effects which are evident in V*r* rhymes, we may temporarily suppress representational details relating to the nucleus and the skeletal tier.

According to the coda proposal, the pre-consonantal and pre-pausal conditions under which constricted *r* fails to appear in non-rhotic dialects can be unified under the single context of the rhyme, as shown in (15).

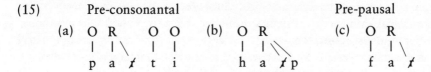

(15)   Pre-consonantal   Pre-pausal

Note that the unification of contexts is achieved by making the assumption that word-final consonants, including *r*, are syllabified in coda position; see (15b) and (15c). This view is of course at variance with the model of constituent structure defended in chapters 2 and 4, but let us accept it for the moment for the sake of argument.

Putting the coda and *r*-deletion accounts together, we can now formalize non-rhoticity in Systems B and C in terms of rule (16).[20]

(16)   **R-Dropping**

R
|
=
|
r

That is, *r* is delinked whenever it occurs in a rhyme; see (17a). As depicted in (17b), an onset *r* in Systems B and C remains unaffected:

(17)   R-Dropping

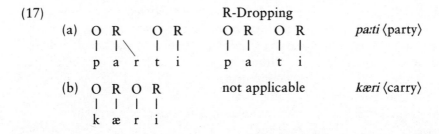

The distinction then between rhotic and non-rhotic dialects is that the latter but not the former have some version of rule (16) in their grammars. The rule is responsible for a surface distributional difference in which rhotic systems show constricted *r* in both onsets and rhymes, while non-rhotic systems have the potential to show the consonant only in onsets.

Now consider how this account can be extended to deal with the *r*–zero alternation, confining our attention for the time being to System B. Recall that, in this system, there is a contrast between morphemes such as ⟨bar⟩, which show the alternation, and those such as ⟨Shah⟩, which invariably end in a vowel; see the data in (6), (8) and (11). This sort of situation is classically dealt with under the criterion of **surface predictability**.[21] Given a set of morphemes which shows an alternation between segments X and Y and another set which only ever contains X, we assume that Y is underlyingly present in the alternating set. The X alternant in the latter set is then derived by process. If we were to choose X as underlying in the alternating cases, the process necessary to derive the Y alternant would be unable to distinguish between the alternating and non-alternating forms (unless we resorted to arbitrary diacritics). So it would incorrectly change underlying Xs in the non-alternating morphemes into Ys.

Applying this criterion to the System B case at hand, we can take *r* to be underlyingly present in forms which show the *r*–zero alternation. The zero alternant can then be derived by means of the R-Dropping rule (16) already formulated on the basis of distributional evidence; thus *ba:r* → *ba:* ⟨bar⟩.

The question now arises as to how we ensure that the *r* alternant in forms such as ⟨bar⟩ is preserved in pre-vocalic contexts. A solution that springs to mind is to suggest that such *r*s are not syllabified in rhymal position at the time R-Dropping applies. Since they are immediately followed by a nucleus, we can take it that they occur in an onset, where they fail to meet the structural description of the R-Dropping rule. This is illustrated in (18), where we can compare the fate of pre-consonantal *r* in ⟨barred⟩ with that of pre-vocalic *r* in ⟨barring⟩.

(18)

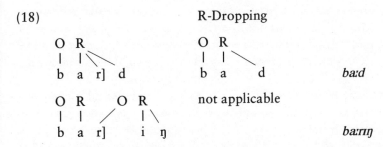

One requirement of this analysis is that an unoccupied onset be made available for pre-vocalic *r* to be syllabified into. This involves resyllabification, a version of the Onset Capture rule in 4.7.3.[22] Initially, stem-final *r* is attached to a rhymal position on the inner cycle where the form ⟨bar⟩ is syllabified. Then the consonant is re-attached to a following onset when this becomes available on the next cycle in the form ⟨barring⟩. This is more fully illustrated in (19).

(19) Inner cycle   Outer cycle
                           Onset Capture   R-Dropping

(a) ⟨barred⟩

       O   R   not applicable   O   R
       | | \ | | \
      [[b a r] d]   [b a   d]

(b) ⟨barring⟩

       O R   R   O R   O R   not applicable
       | | \ | \ | | / | \
      [[b a r] i ŋ]   [b a   r   i ŋ]

In ⟨barring⟩, the vacant onset happens to be supplied by a word-level suffix. But the position can also be provided by a following word in a phrasal or larger domain, as the following derivation of ⟨bar of⟩ illustrates:

(20)   Word cycle   Phrasal cycle
                                                 Onset Capture   R-Dropping

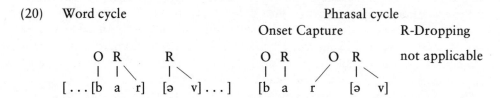

Implicit in the derivations in (19) and (20) is the assumption that phonological strings contain syllable structure on all cycles. In order to dispense with resyllabification under the coda analysis, it would be necessary to take the alternative view that strings are syllabified once only and 'last thing'. That is, syllable structure would not be present on inner cycles but would be constructed post-cyclically after all morpho-syntactic operations had been completed. This would mean that *r* would only ever appear in onset position in ⟨barring⟩ and in coda position in ⟨barred⟩. However, this alternative is not open to us. As we saw in 2.3.4, syllable structure has to be made available from the outset of derivation, since it provides the backdrop against which phonotactic relations in non-analytic domains are defined.

A further requirement of the coda analysis is that the deletion of morpheme-final *r* must somehow be held at bay until the consonant has had a chance to become syllabified into a following onset, if one is available. Deletion must not be allowed to apply on the inner cycle; otherwise, *r* would be erroneously erased in ⟨barring⟩ at a stage when the consonant is still in the rhyme:

(21)   Inner cycle   Outer cycle
                          R-Dropping   Onset Capture

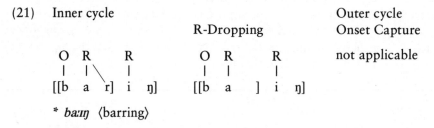

This undesired result could of course be prevented by the brute-force expedient of extrinsically ordering the two rules.[23] However, a rather more attractive alternative, which dispenses with rule ordering, is to assume (a) that the delinking of *r* occurs freely wherever its structural description is met; and (b) that it does not entail immediate deletion. This would allow *r* to be delinked on the inner cycle (⟨bar⟩ in (18)) and then subsequently relinked should a vacant onset become available on a later cycle, as in ⟨barring⟩. Any delinked *r* which failed to find sanctuary in an onset on any cycle would then be erased at the end of derivation, as in the case of ⟨barred⟩.

One striking consequence of the coda analysis, as formulated to this point, is that the phonological distribution of *r* in underlying representations in rhotic System A and non-rhotic B is very similar. In both cases, underlying *r* can appear in rhymes as well as onsets. Moreover, the lexical incidence of the consonant is also identical in onsets and in morpheme-final position and differs only in that *r* occurs before a morpheme-internal consonant in A but not in B. The main distinction between the dialects is relatively superficial and has to do with whether or not R-Dropping is present in the grammar.

5.4.2 R-Epenthesis

Now we can consider where System C fits into this classification. The C group of dialects, recall, displays the so-called intrusive-*r* pattern, one symptom of which is the absence of a contrast between alternating V*r*]–V] and non-alternating V] words.[24] All words ending in a particular class of vowels in pre-consonantal or pre-pausal position show a variant containing constricted *r* in pre-vocalic position. The immediate question is whether or not an *r* is lexically present in these forms. If there is one, we need some kind of deletion rule by which to derive the zero variants. If there is not, we need some kind of insertion rule. Either way, the lexical incidence of *r* is going to differ from the patterns found in Systems A and B.[25] If there is an underlying *r* in these cases, it will appear not only in those morphemes which have it in A and B (the etymologically 'correct' ones such as ⟨car, lore⟩, etc.) but also in many forms which lack it in the other systems (the etymologically 'incorrect' ones such as ⟨pa, law, idea⟩, etc.). If there is no underlying *r*, it will be missing from both historically *r*-less and *r*-ful forms.

The particular class of vowels which precedes alternating *r* in System C is in principle identical to that preceding historical *r* in both Systems A and B. (D has its own special developments, on which more presently.) In most dialects, whether rhotic or non-rhotic, the sub-system of vowels in this context is quite unlike that occurring in other contexts. For one thing, the set of contrasts holding before historical *r* is much reduced from the maximal inventory, as found say before *t*. This is illustrated in the following comparison of the two stressed sub-systems in a typical southern English non-rhotic system (B or C):

(22)   Maximal inventory   Inventory before historical *r*

BIT	ɪ	FEAR	ɪə	
BEAT	iː			
BET	ɛ	BEAR	ɛə	
BAIT	ey			
BITE	ay	WIRE	æə	
BAT	æ			
CART	aː	BAR ⎤	aə	
SHOUT	aw	HOUR ⎦		
COT	ɒ			

CAUGHT	ɔː			
CUT	ʌ			
BOAT	ow		FOUR	ɔə
PUT	ʊ		POOR	
BOOT	uː			

The collapse of distinctions before historical *r* is evidently due to a number of qualitative and quantitative developments, some of which we will examine later in the chapter. The fact that similar developments show up in most rhotic dialects confirms that, at least historically speaking, these various effects can be attributed directly to *r* itself. For the moment, it will be sufficient to speak of a general lowering influence that historical *r* exerts on a preceding vowel.

A standard rule-based approach to the *r*–zero alternation in C-type dialects is to treat it in terms of segment insertion.[26] The relevant rule turns out to be more or less an inverted form of R-Dropping. The main justification for this analysis is that the surface distribution of morpheme-final *r* is allegedly fully predictable in a type-C system. Given this predictability, so the argument goes, the segment is not distinctive in the alternating site and thus does not need to be represented underlyingly.[27] This account is founded on the assumption that the appearance of *r* in this context is dependent on the quality of a preceding vowel rather than vice versa – an inversion of the historical pattern just outlined. In other words, the special set of vowels before historical *r* now supposedly forms an independent sub-system which is represented in the lexicon and constitutes the right-hand portion of the environment into which *r* is inserted.

An orthodox linear formulation of the insertion rule looks something like this:[28]

(23)
$$\emptyset \ \rightarrow \ r/[-high] \underline{\quad} V$$

The initial portion of the rule's environment refers to the generalization that the *r* alternant in System C only appears after non-high vowels; compare the data in (6), (8) and (11) with those in (12). It is not necessary for the insertion site to be specified as morpheme-final position; the rule can be assumed to apply vacuously in morpheme-internal contexts, where *r* is already present underlyingly (as in ⟨dairy⟩).[29]

Reinterpreting (23) in syllabic terms, we can state that *r* is inserted into an unoccupied onset, provided that it is preceded by a non-high vowel:[30]

(24)   **R-Epenthesis**

$$\emptyset \ \rightarrow \ r/ \quad \begin{matrix} N & O \\ | & | \\ [-high] & - \end{matrix}$$

(The horizontal bar under the onset indicates the insertion site.) The operation of the rule is illustrated in the following derivations of ⟨saw = soar⟩ in System C (in those dialects which have a mid round nucleus in this class of words):

(25) R-Epenthesis

```
O R  O R                            sɔː tu ⟨saw/sore to⟩
|  |  |  |        not applicable
[[s ɔ] [t u]]

O R  R              O R      O R     sɔːr ɪn ⟨saw/sore in⟩
|  |  |\            |  |    /   |  \
[[s ɔ] [i n]]       s  ɔ   r    i   n

O R                                 sɔːd ⟨sawed/soared⟩
|  |\            not applicable
[[s ɔ] d]

O R  R              O R      O R     sɔːrɪŋ ⟨sawing/soaring⟩
|  |  |\            |  |    /   |  \
[[s ɔ ] [i ŋ]       s  ɔ   r    i   ŋ
```

5.4.3 Non-Rhoticity

Let us take it that the coda analyses just outlined are correct at least in so far as they identify constituent structure as the conditioning factor in non-rhoticity. To be in a position to assess the validity of the remaining aspects of the analyses, it will be useful for us to have some theory-neutral bench mark which couches the statement of non-rhoticity solely in terms of distributions that are observable in the data. Any statement formulated in terms of R-Dropping fails to fit this bill, since it incorporates certain assumptions about the nature of the rule's lexical input which may or may not be justified. Specifically, it presupposes a mismatch between the incidence of *r* at the initial and final stages of derivation. What is required is a statement formulated as an **output condition** on derivation – one which specifies the distributional goal that a successful derivation must target but which is neutral on the question of how that goal is achieved. That is, it makes no claims about the lexical status or derivational history of *r* in non-rhotic systems.

R-Dropping focuses on the conditions under which lexical *r* **fails** to surface in non-rhotic systems. Suppose we now switch the perspective and reformulate our bench-mark statement in terms of where *r* **does** appear. Based on the observed distribution of *r* in constituent contexts, an output condition for both Systems B and C might be expressed as follows:

(26) **Non-Rhoticity**
      r appears exclusively in onsets.

Any analysis of non-rhoticity must capture this generalization in some way. The simplest analysis is one which requires only one statement to do so. A deletion analysis of System B can in principle meet this criterion by specifying the complement set of contexts. Whether the particular deletion account offered by the R-Dropping rule in (16) can be judged successful in this respect depends on whether the coda environment in its structural description correctly characterizes this complement set. As we will now see, there are grounds for concluding that it does not.

One aspect of the deletion account of non-rhoticity that is common to both the SPE and coda formulations of the process concerns the point made earlier about vacuous application. Under the coda view, there are two contexts where deletion operates vacuously – in morpheme-internal rhymes (as in the first syllables of ⟨farther, party⟩) and in final rhymes closed by some other consonant (as in ⟨farm, harp⟩). As a dynamic process which produces an active *r*–zero alternation, the rule has a relatively restricted domain of application. Although the formulation of the rule in (24) might give the impression that deletion affects any syllable rhyme, all of the observable alternation action actually only takes place in what, under this analysis, constitutes a word-final rhyme – and even then only when this is not closed by some other consonant. This is of itself not necessarily a bad thing, since the rule succeeds in subsuming the alternating and non-alternating contexts under a single generalization about the surface distribution of non-rhoticity. What is peculiar, however, is that the dynamic aspect of the coda analysis boils down to an account of what happens in absolute domain-final position – the very position whose supposed rhymal status we now have good reason to reject. In short, the coda context referred to in R-Dropping (16) does not accurately identify the set of contexts that complements the onset site referred to in (26).

What then of the epenthesis account of System C? In expressing a significant generalization about the surface distribution of *r*, the Non-Rhoticity condition (26) is as much true of the System-C grammar as it is of B. R-Epenthesis (24) on it own is not sufficient to capture the full distributional facts of *r* in this type of dialect. In other words, the insertion analysis requires two statements regulating the surface distribution of *r* – R-Epenthesis and Non-Rhoticity. A simpler and therefore preferable account would be one in which the distribution of the consonant in intrusive-*r* dialects is reduced to a single statement.

In any case, there are additional reasons for questioning the validity of R-Epenthesis. The rule is potentially arbitrary in two respects. First, the process itself must be considered arbitrary, unless grounds can be provided for assuming that it must be *r* that is inserted rather than any other randomly selectable sound. There is no obvious local source in the surrounding vowels. The potential damage of this criticism might be mitigated by invoking the universally unmarked status of coronals. That is, it might be argued that the coronality of *r* is specified by a universal default rule which, by virtue of being supplied by Universal Grammar, comes cost-free to the System-C grammar. There are certainly other examples of languages which make use of what looks like a spontaneously appearing *r* in certain contexts. The question remains, however, as to why it is *r* that epenthesizes rather than some other coronal such as *t* or *d*, particularly since obstruents such as the latter are considered less marked than sonorants.

There is another respect in which R-Epenthesis is in need of justification. Why should it take place in the context it does, between vowels as long as the first is non-high? Would we have been surprised if it had applied in any other environment? The inter-vocalic aspect of the context may seem to be motivated by a universal preference for syllables with filled onsets. That is, the epenthetic segment supplies a realized onset which breaks up a potential sequence of nuclei.[31] But if the rule were an instantiation of this preference, we would expect it to split up any potential V-V sequence. The puzzle is why it should only fulfil this function when the preceding vowel is non-high. Epenthesis, recall, fails to apply after high vowels in sequences such as ⟨fee of, two and, day of, bow and⟩ (see the forms in (12)).

To counter this criticism, we might note that this is the very context where we find hiatus-breaking *y* and *w* glides; hence ⟨fee [y]of, two [w]and⟩. As mentioned in 4.7.4, this phenomenon is straightforwardly treated as the spreading of I or U from a nucleus into a following vacant onset. What unifies the set of vowels preceding the intrusive-*r* context, it might be argued, is that they lack either of these elements; *r* then is the default hiatus-breaker which appears in the absence of a locally available high glide.[32]

These arguments in defence of R-Epenthesis are based on the assumption that the rule accurately captures a surface-true generalization about intrusive-*r* systems. The force of this claim is, however, undermined by the observation made above that *r* exerts a lowering influence on a preceding vowel. This tendency, which is attested cross-linguistically, is sometimes invoked as an explanation for the occurrence of [–high] in the left-hand environment of the rule. But, if anything, the observation actually constitutes an argument **against** R-Epenthesis. At stake is the question of which segment is influencing which. Is the appearance of intrusive *r* dependent on the quality of the vowel, or is the quality of the vowel dependent on the *r*? The R-Epenthesis analysis implies the former answer. But the latter answer is implicit in the claim that *r* has a lowering effect on a preceding vowel. This effect has to be accounted for in any event. That is, there has to be some independent provision in the grammars of all our illustrative systems which accounts for the reduced set of vowel contrasts found in this context. The epenthesis account of intrusive *r* fails in this respect.

A preferable analysis of non-rhoticity would be one which meets the following criteria. First, is should be consistent with the view that domain-final *r* no more occupies a final coda than does any other consonant. Second, it should if possible derive each of the observed patterns of *r*-distribution by means of a single statement. Third, it should account for the qualitative influence that *r* exerts on a preceding vowel. In the following sections, we will consider an alternative account which comes closer to fulfilling these goals than those discussed so far.

5.5 Floating *r*

Expressed in terms of autosegmental licensing, (26) might provisionally be reformulated as follows:

(27) **Non-Rhoticity'**
Only an onset position licenses *r*.

The condition in (27) correctly allows for the appearance of *r* in word-initial and internal onsets, as in ⟨red, carry⟩. What of *r* in other positions? Let us accept the argument that the only other context in which *r* is lexically present in non-rhotic System B is domain-finally in forms which show the *r*–zero alternation, as in ⟨bar⟩. The question now is what syllabic position such occurrences of domain-final *r* occupy, if it is denied that they are syllabified in the rhyme. In line with the conclusions reached in chapters 2 and 4, a reasonable first assumption would be that lexical *r* in this context occupies an onset licensed by an empty nucleus, as in:

(28)
```
   O  N        O  N
   |  | \      |  |
   x  x  x     x  x
   |  |  /     |
   b  a        r
```

This analysis seems attractive, since it would permit us to unify *r* loss with the various sorts of weakening discussed in the last chapter. Non-Rhoticity could thus be understood as reflecting the weak licensing capacity of the final empty nucleus. More specifically, the parametrically licensed nuclear position could be viewed as failing to supply the preceding onset with sufficient autosegmental licensing power to support the melodic expression defining *r*. However, as we will see below, there are grounds for considering the representation in (28) to be appropriate only for one quite specific type of system but not for others.

Enquiring into the syllabic position occupied by *r* begs another question, namely whether it is necessary to assume that a consonant in this context occupies **any** kind of position at all. In fact, phonological theory makes available another possibility – that domain-final *r* is lexically a 'floating' segment with no syllabic position of its own. The sort of configuration envisaged here is illustrated by the following lexical representation of ⟨bar⟩:[33]

(29)
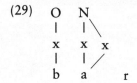

In (29), we have an *r* which is not attached to any syllabic position. As long as the melodic expression remains in this detached state, it is autosegmentally unlicensed and thus unrealizable. For it to be phonetically expressed, it must acquire some attachment to an available position. In (29), the only available position is the nearest point dominated by the nucleus. However, according to condition (26), *r* can only be licensed by an onset in non-rhotic systems. A candidate position does become available, if we continue with the assumption, already made in the coda account of non-rhoticity, that an unoccupied onset is supplied by a following vowel-initial morpheme. The association of a floating segment to an available onset, we may assume, automatically triggers the creation of a skeletal point.[34] In a form such as ⟨bar a⟩ (30a), the floating *r* can thus 'dock' on to a position which is able to license it:[35]

(30) (a) ⟨bar a⟩

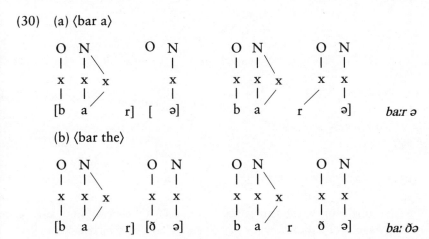

(b) ⟨bar the⟩

The difference between a docked and an unlicensed *r* is the difference between *r*-ful and *r*-less alternants in the non-rhotic B system. In ⟨bar the⟩ (30b), the onset following the floating *r* is already occupied. Since there is nowhere for the segment to dock, it remains unlicensed and hence unrealized.

Under the floating-segment analysis, the rule of R-Dropping in System B is replaced by a condition requiring *r* to be licensed by an onset position. Where does this leave the rule of R-Epenthesis which characterizes the pattern of intrusive *r* in System C? In B, the lexical representations of alternating V*r*]–V] morphemes such as ⟨bar⟩ are distinguished from those of non-alternating V] morphemes such as ⟨Shah⟩ by the presence of a domain-final floating *r*:

(31) System B

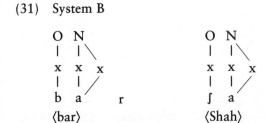

The Non-Rhoticity condition in (27) correctly characterizes the surface distribution of *r* in System C no less than in B. But what consequences does this observation have for the lexical representation of morphemes which show the *r*–zero alternation in C? Given that the historical distinction between *r*-final and *r*-less forms has been obliterated in this system, there are in principle two possible ways of representing forms such as ⟨bar⟩ and ⟨Shah⟩ under the floating-segment account: either both contain domain-final floating *r* (32a), or neither does (32b).

(32)   System C

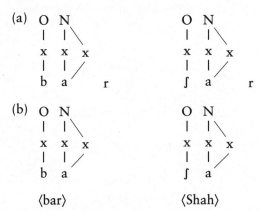

(bar)   (Shah)

With representations such as those in (32a), the *r*–zero alternation in System C can be derived in exactly the same way as in B, i.e. in terms of the Non-Rhoticity' condition (27). No additional rules or conditions are required. The difference between B and C is thus purely a matter of lexical incidence; floating *r* is present in the lexical representation of a greater number of forms in C than in B (and than in A, for that matter).[36]

It might be surmised that the lexical incidence of floating *r* in System C is restricted to those forms in which the consonant is preceded by a non-high vowel. If this were true, the analysis would then be open to criticism on the grounds that it failed to capture this clear generalization. However, this objection presupposes one of the assumptions underpinning the epenthetic-*r* analysis alluded to above, namely that it is the quality of a preceding vowel which determines the appearance of *r*, rather than vice versa. This analysis, as we saw, is itself vulnerable to criticism on the grounds that it fails to account for the general lowering influence of *r*.

On the other hand, if the alternating *r* is lexically present, as in (32a), it is available as a lowering trigger. (Precisely what it is about *r* that has this effect is a question to be addressed in 5.7.2.) Under this analysis, the absence from the data of sequences of a high vowel followed by intrusive *r* is not the reflection of some mysterious lexical lacuna. In principle, floating *r* is free to occur after any vowel in lexical representation. The distributional gap is a reflection of a process

which lowers vowels in this context. Thus there are lexical contrasts such as *fiː*
⟨fee⟩ versus *fiːr* (→ *fiər*) ⟨fear⟩.

Let us summarize the floating-segment analysis of non-rhotic Systems B and C.
In both systems, as expressed in the Non-Rhoticity′ condition (27), the surface
distribution of constricted *r* is limited to onset position – see (33a) (where α
indicates some vocalic expression).

(33)   (a)   O N   (b)   N
             | | |
             x x   x
             | | |
             r α   α r

In lexical representation, *r* occurs either in onset position (33a) (as in ⟨red, carry⟩)
or domain-finally as a floating consonant (33b) (as in ⟨bar⟩). The phenomenon of
r-sandhi is formally expressed as follows: the licensing of a lexically floating *r* is
contingent on an unoccupied onset being made made available for it to dock on
to; otherwise it fails to surface.

Amongst the non-rhotic systems, D is distinguished from B and C both in terms
of the lexical incidence of *r* and in terms of the manner in which *r* is licensed by
onsets. In the absence of alternations motivating the lexical construction of
morpheme-final *r*, it must be assumed that D lacks floating *r*. Thus D possesses
r-less lexical representations such as those in (32b).

As it stands, the Non-Rhoticity′ condition (27) is inadequate for System D.
While any onset is capable of licensing *r* in B and C, only foot-initial onsets can
do so in D (see (3)). This in fact renders the distribution of *r* in D identical to that
of *h* in most dialects of English, as discussed in 4.7.5:

(34)   General English *h*   System D *r*
        Foot-initial   [h]ead   [r]ed
        Foot-internal   ve[h̸]icle   ve[ɾ]y
        Domain-final   *kah   ca[ɾ]

The same kind of licensing conditions can be assumed to apply in each case. That
is, in line with the Licensing Inheritance Principle, the ability of an onset to
autosegmentally license *r* varies according to whether the following nucleus from
which that ability is acquired is itself licensed. The licensing charge delivered by
the dominant nucleus of a foot, unlicensed within that domain, is passed relatively
directly on to the preceding onset. The autosegmental licensing power of a
foot-internal onset, on the other hand, is attenuated as a result of being acquired
via the licensed nucleus on the foot projection. In D at least, this diminished
potential manifests itself as an inability to support not only *h* but also *r*. In
Systems B and C, any nucleus can empower its onset to license *r*; in D, by contrast,
only an unlicensed nucleus has the capacity to do so.

5.6 Historical interlude

By way of a brief detour, let us at this point consider some historical evidence which seems to favour the floating-*r* analysis over one incorporating rewrite rules such as R-Dropping and R-Epenthesis. The sequence of events leading up to the present pattern of dialect divergence among *r*-systems looks quite different when viewed in terms of the two types of analysis. Before examining what the main differences are, let us establish in what respects the historical perspectives of the two accounts converge. We can start from the assumption that the main innovations involving *r* occurred in the ancestors of modern non-rhotic dialects. According to both accounts, the development of non-rhoticity has produced at least some restructuring of lexical representations. Specifically, it has resulted in the loss of constricted *r* from morpheme-internal pre-consonantal positions, as in ⟨party, harp⟩.

The stories start to diverge as soon as we compare their versions of how the domain-final *r*–zero alternation came into being. In the rewrite-rule tradition, the latter development is characterized in terms of rule change. In the case of non-rhotic systems such as B which lack intrusive *r*, the specific change allegedly took the form of the addition of R-Dropping to their grammars. Intrusive *r*, it has been claimed, results from a further innovation, whereby the output of an R-Dropping grammar is reanalysed in terms of insertion. The emergence of the new rule, R-Epenthesis (24), is said to reflect a process of **rule inversion**.[37] With this change comes a further restructuring of lexical representations – the loss of domain-final constricted *r*.

The mechanisms of rule addition and inversion have no direct translations in the floating-*r* account. From the latter perspective, the primary non-rhotic innovation is the failure of any position other than an onset to license *r*. The emergence of the Non-Rhoticity′ condition in (27) is only weakly equivalent to the addition of an R-Dropping rule. The account makes no provision for anything resembling rule inversion. Not having the same formal properties as a rule, the Non-Rhoticity′ condition cannot be inverted; there is no input and no output to invert. The two types of account thus make quite different claims about how intrusive *r* came into existence. The rule-inversion account locates the change in the phonological component as a regular phonological process. According to the floating-*r* account, the change is essentially a lexical one: specifically, it is an extension of the lexical incidence of domain-final *r* to morphemes which were etymologically *r*-less. What it is that could have triggered this restructuring is a question to be taken up presently.

The two accounts also make quite different claims about the relative chronology of the changes that produced intrusive *r*. Rule inversion firmly implies that the intrusive C-system pattern is an off-shoot of an older non-intrusive B.[38] By contrast, the floating-*r* account is entirely neutral on the question of historical precedence. It would be entirely consistent with the latter analysis if intrusive *r* arose independently of etymological linking *r*. In fact, given that domain-final *r* is potentially present in lexical representation in any system, it would not be surprising to discover cases of intrusive *r* in **rhotic** dialects.

The historical documentary record supports the independent development of intrusive *r*. Evidence of its existence is as old as the evidence for *r*-loss itself. A generation before John Walker's description of smooth versus rough *r*, Thomas Sheridan was castigating Londoners for inserting *r* after the final ⟨-a⟩-vowel of words such as ⟨Belinda⟩ and ⟨Dorlinda⟩.[39] Moreover, there is plenty of evidence of intrusive *r* in rhotic dialects, past and present, where it is most widely reported in final unstressed position.[40] The significance of the latter context is bound up with the peculiar status of final unstressed schwa in the history of English.

The final unstressed reflex of Old English full vowels was lost by the end of the Middle English period (e.g. Old English ⟨butan⟩, Middle English ⟨but[ə]⟩, modern ⟨but⟩). Since that time, final *ə* has been something of an outcast in English phonology. At various times when it might have been expected to appear as a result of more recent developments, some other reflex has often elbowed its way in. The innovations in question include the non-standard reduction of unstressed final *o* in forms such as ⟨window, shadow⟩ and the by-now extensive borrowing or coining of words with ⟨a⟩-final spellings (⟨sofa, Sheena, NASA⟩, etc.). When these developments first took off, *ə* was by no means the only attested reflex. Alternat-ive outcomes which survive to this day include front vowels (reflected in dialect spellings such as ⟨Americkay, windy⟩ for ⟨America, window⟩). Significant-ly, another reflex found in some present-day conservative rhotic dialects is *ər* (or *ɚ*) with unetymological *r*, demonstrated in spellings such as ⟨yeller, feller, swaller⟩ for ⟨yellow, fellow, swallow⟩.

Why should final schwa be disfavoured in this way? The relevant context, note, is one in which the element @ potentially occupies a domain-final nucleus (as in ⟨Dinah⟩). This overlaps with the context of a parametrically licensed final empty nucleus (as in ⟨dine⟩), which latently contains @ as well. As suggested in 4.6.1, the contrast can be characterized in terms of whether or not @ occurs as the head of the relevant vocalic expression.

(35) (a) Final schwa   (b) Final empty nucleus

       N   N
       | |
      x]   x]
       |
      <u>@</u>   @

We might speculate that this contrast is marked in some way and fails to be sustained in all systems.

Viewed in these terms, System C is subject to a word-level ban on the occurrence of final schwa.[41] The equivalent context is in fact *r*-final, even though the consonant is lexically floating and thus not always phonetically interpreted:

(36)

The occurrence of intrusive *r* in forms such as ⟨NASA[r] is⟩ in dialects of this type implies that the stricture against true final schwa has continued to shape the integration of incoming borrowings or neologisms. The constraint might reasonably be expected to have extended to all cases of final schwa, including those occurring in a stressed nucleus. This would not only have affected the vowel in FIR but also the schwa portion of in-gliding diphthongs such as *ɪə* (FEAR) and *ɔə* (FOUR). Originally, these vowels were the exclusive reflexes of historical V*r* sequences. But later mergers with vowels from other sources (such as PAW = PORE) would have resulted in the extension of floating *r* to etymologically *r*-less forms.

The historical evidence suggests that intrusive *r* has been around for a long time and that its emergence was originally motivated by a disfavouring of final schwa. To the extent that this conclusion is at variance with the rule-inversion account of the phenomenon, it also serves to undermine further the rewrite-rule approach to *r*-sandhi. It also puts paid to the notion that intrusive-*r* dialects are the direct descendants of a non-rhotic B-type system which lacks the phenomenon. The germ of this idea seems to be buried in a prescriptive myth, according to which non-standard dialects are deviant outgrowths from a central standard stem whose phonology somehow faithfully mirrors the orthography.

5.7 Vowels before *r*

5.7.1 Rhotic systems

As we have seen, what sets rhotic dialects apart from non-rhotic is the surface occurrence of constricted *r* in other than onset position. Exactly what these other positions are is something we now have to determine. Valuable clues bearing on the issue are provided by the pre-*r* vocalic developments touched on in 5.4.2.

Considering morpheme-internal environments first, we might take the view that constricted *r* in rhotic variants of forms such as ⟨party⟩ occupies a coda position in exactly the same way as, say, the *p* of ⟨chapter⟩ or the *f* of ⟨hefty⟩:

(37) (a)   (b)

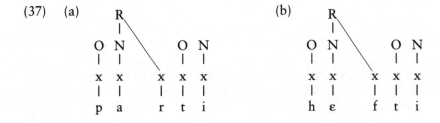

Likewise, coda *r* might be considered to occur before a domain-final consonant, as in ⟨harp, beard, fern⟩, on a par with, for example, the *s* of ⟨lisp⟩ or the *k* of ⟨fact⟩.

As for domain-final constricted *r* in forms such as ⟨fear, far⟩, we might suppose that it has the same constituent status as other final consonants. As already mentioned in 5.4.5, this would imply a syllabification in which the *r* of ⟨far⟩ occupies an onset followed by an empty nucleus in exactly the same way as, say, the *t* of ⟨feet⟩:

(38) (a)
```
     O   N        O   N            (b)   O   N        O   N
     |   |\ |   | |                      |   |\       |   |
     x   x  x   x x                      x   x  x     x   x
     |   | /    |                        |   | /      |
     f   a      r                        f   i        t
```

As we saw in 2.4.4, the extra-rhymal status of a domain-final consonant allows a preceding stressed nucleus to display the full gamut of vocalic contrasts.[42] If the syllabification in (38a) is correct, we should expect to find exactly the same state of affairs before final *r* in rhotic dialects.

The prediction is in fact borne out only in a subset of rhotic systems, namely those of Scots and Scottish English. The inventory of vocalic contrasts before final *r* in a typical Scottish English system is shown in column (c) of (39).

(39) Scottish English

(a)		(b)		(c)	
BEAT	i	SEIZE	iː	FEAR	iː
BIT	ɪ	FIZZ	ɪ	FIR	ɪː
CUT	ʌ	FUZZ	ʌ	FUR	ʌ
BET	ɛ	FEZ	ɛː	PER	ɛː
BAIT	e	DAZE	eː	FAIR	eː
BITE	əy	RISE	ay	WIRE	ay
BAT	a	JAZZ	aː	FAR	aː
SHOUT	əw	BLOUSE	əw	HOUR	əw
POT/CAUGHT	ɒ	ROS/CAUSE	ɒː	FOR	ɒː
BOAT	o	ROSE	oː	FOUR	oː
PUT/BOOT	u	LOSE	uː	POOR	uː

A brief mention of some of the characteristically Scottish features illustrated in (39) will help fill in the background to the vocalic inventories in the different contexts. The system lacks the COT–CAUGHT and PUT–BOOT vowel contrasts found in other dialects. Vowel-length differences, such as that between short *i* in BEAT and long *iː* in SEIZE and FEAR are entirely conditioned by the following consonant. (Vowels with variable length are long word-finally or before *r*, *v*, *ð* or *z* and short elsewhere.[43]) This pattern (which also underlies the difference between *əy* in BITE and *ay* in RISE and FIRE) explains the regular length correspondences between the vowel set in (39a) on the one hand and that in (39b) and (39c) on the other.

The main point to emerge from (39) is that there is a one-to-one match between the vowel inventory found before *r* and that found before other consonants. In other words, domain-final *r* in Scottish English is just like any other final consonant in that it exerts no distributional influence on a preceding vowel. The conclusion must thus be that final *r* in this type of system has exactly the same constituent status as other consonants in this context, namely that shown in (38a).

The situation in virtually all other rhotic dialects is strikingly different. In these systems, the sets of vowel contrasts before final *r* are typically quite unlike those found before other consonants. This goes hand in hand with varying patterns of merger that are similar or identical to those illustrated in (22) for non-rhotic dialects. Some idea of the special developments in this context can be gained by comparing the three Scottish sub-systems in (40) with those found in various other rhotic dialects:[44]

(40)	(a)	Scottish	(i)	(ii)
	FIR	ɪ	⎱ ⎰	⎱ ⎰
	PER	ɛ	ə:	ə:
	FUR	ʌ	ʌ	

	(b)	Scottish	(i)	(ii)	(iii)
	WIRE	ay	ayə		ayə
	FAR	aː	aə	aə	
	HOUR	əw	awə	awə	aə

	(c)	Scottish	(i)	(ii)	(iii)
	POOR	uː	uə		uə
	FOUR	oː	oə	oə	
	FOR	ɔː	ɔə	ɔə	oə

(Pre-*r* neutralizations are also evident in contexts where the consonant appears in domain-internal onsets; thus there are potential mergers in the MERRY–MARRY–MARY series as well as in SPIRIT–EERIE, on which more below.)

As illustrated in (40), the qualitative adjustments that accompany the shrinking of the distinctive space inhabited by pre-*r* vowels include a widespread lowering, the disfavouring of tenseness and the presence of an off-glide. For the sake of brevity, we may focus only on the last of these effects, one which results from a process sometimes known as **breaking**.[45] Dialects which have up-gliding diphthongs such as *ow, ey* in contexts which display the maximal system of contrasts tend to lack these before *r*. A typical instantiation of this pattern is to have the up-glide replaced by a schwa in-glide, a development which is usually accompanied by a lowering of the first portion of the diphthong; compare, say, *ɛə* in ⟨care⟩ with *ey* in ⟨fade⟩. In another development, we find the up-glide being retained and serving simultaneously as the onset of a separate syllable containing *ər*, e.g. *key.yər* ⟨care⟩, *fay.yər* ⟨fire⟩.

A lot of ink has been spilt in debates about how the restricted set of vowels before historical *r* should be assigned to phonemic categories set up on the basis of the maximal inventory found in other contexts.[46] The phonemic assignment problem is essentially a transcriptional one; it involves taking each of the pre-*r* vowels and relating it to one of the vowels in the maximal inventory. This problem simply does not come up for discussion within a non-phonemic phonology, particularly if we are not wedded to the assumption that the same system of phonological distinctions necessarily holds in all contexts. What does need to be explained, however, is the observation that the set of vocalic contrasts is severely reduced before *r* in other than Scottish systems. Why should we find such a defective pattern in this context and not before other consonants? (Actually, something similar is to be found before the vocalized reflex of *l* in some dialects. See exercise 3 at the end of this chapter.)

5.7.2 *Nuclear* r

The idea we want to be able to capture formally is that post-vocalic *r* in other than Scottish systems somehow constricts the potential for vocalic distinctions to manifest themselves. As noted above, the relative freedom of vowel contrasts to hold independently of following domain-final consonants other than *r* can be taken to reflect the syllabification of such VC sequences into separate constituents (see (38b)). Suppose we take the vocalic restrictions that obtain before domain-final *r* to reflect a closer relationship between segments in a V*r* sequence. Specifically, let us make the assumption that *r* in these contexts is syllabified in the nucleus itself. The presence of *r* within a nucleus would then be expected to result in a compression of the distinctive space available to vocalic elements. By way of a first draft of this proposal, the representation in (41) illustrates the occurrence of nuclear *r* in the rhotic form of ⟨bar⟩. The branching nucleus here takes the form of a diphthong with a rhotic off-glide:

(41)
```
O   N
|   |\
x   x  x
|   |  |
b   a  r
```

In rhotic systems other than Scottish, the defective distribution of pre-*r* vowels is not restricted to contexts where the consonant occurs domain-finally. Similar merger patterns to those illustrated in (40) are to be found domain-internally before a consonant. Compare, for example, the vocalic sub-systems found before -*nt* and -*rt* clusters, shown in (42). Again we can use the unmerged Scottish English pattern as a reference point.

(42)

				Scottish	Other rhotic
FLINT	ɪ	SKIRT	ɪ	ɪ	
TENT	ɛ	PERT	ɛ	ɛ	{ɚ}
BLUNT	ʌ	HURT	ʌ	ʌ	

This suggests that the type of syllabification shown in (41) should be extended to domain-internal contexts, as in the following representation of ⟨part⟩.

(43)
```
    O  N       O  N
    |  |\      |  |
    x  x  x    x  x
    |  |  |    |
    p  a  r    t
```

(On the representation of ɚ, more presently.) In this way, the defective distribution of vowels before *r*C clusters can be attributed to the fact that some of the contrastive space available within the nucleus is taken up by *r*.

The nuclear status of non-onset *r* is further supported by the behaviour of pre-consonantal *r* in *t*-lenition, discussed in 4.7.7. Recall that glottalling, for example, can occur if *t* is directly preceded by a nucleus, as in ⟨bit, city⟩, but is generally blocked if *t* is preceded by a consonant occupying a coda position, as in ⟨fist, apt, mister, chapter⟩. What is significant in the context of the present discussion is that *rt* sequences pattern exactly like V*t* sequences in permitting lenition to take place. This fact is explained if *r* is assumed to be nuclear in such contexts; the absence of a coda consonant in a form such as ⟨part⟩ (43) means that *t* is free to lenite.

External evidence bearing on the nuclear status of *r* is to be found in slips of the tongue. A common type of speech error involves the substitution or transposition of entire nuclei, as in ⟨pope smiker = pipe smoker⟩, ⟨bud begs = bed bugs⟩, ⟨Biv and Bell = Bev and Bill⟩, *fuːt miːving* = ⟨feet moving⟩.[47] If V*r* really does constitute a nuclear unit in forms such as ⟨bar, part⟩, then we should expect it to pair with *r*-less nuclei in slips of the tongue perpetrated by rhotic speakers. This is indeed exactly what we find. Some attested examples: ⟨serp is souved = soup is served⟩, ⟨the shirt didn't hot much = the shot didn't hurt much⟩, ⟨par p[ay]ty = pie party⟩, ⟨fart very hide = fight very hard⟩.[48]

There is plenty of evidence from English and other languages that liquids and indeed resonant consonants in general can have nuclear status under certain conditions. In English, the existence of nuclear laterals and nasals is already well established and is reflected in the term 'syllabic' frequently applied to the final segments of forms such as ⟨kitten⟩ and ⟨kettle⟩. The practice of extending this description to final unstressed *r*-ful syllables in rhotic dialects (as in ⟨letter⟩) also has a long history. (John Hart was already treating final unstressed *r* along these lines in 1570.[49]) In terms of constituent structure, this suggests representations such as the following:

(44)   (a)
```
    O  N  O  N
    |  |  |  |
    x  x  x  x
    |  |  |  |
    k  ɪ  t  n
```
(b)
```
    O  N  O  N
    |  |  |  |
    x  x  x  x
    |  |  |  |
    k  ɛ  t  l
```
(c)
```
    O  N  O  N
    |  |  |  |
    x  x  x  x
    |  |  |  |
    l  ɛ  t  r
```

In order to explore the idea that the presence of an *r* in a nucleus somehow crowds out certain vocalic contrasts, we need now to take into consideration the melodic make-up of nuclear segments.

The ability of resonants to occupy nuclei is sometimes attributed to their vowel-like phonetic properties. In the case of *r*, the relationship with full vowels is particularly clear in most types of English where the segment is realized as an approximant. Of all the coronal sonorants, approximant *r* is the one with the most vowel-like resonance characteristics. One way of viewing this sound is as a combination of one component whose articulatory execution calls for an apical (tongue-tip) or laminal (blade) gesture and another which manifests itself as a vocalic dorsal (tongue-body) gesture. This implies some kind of vowel-coloured *r* or an *r*-coloured vowel. The vowel colouring is typically 'dark' (velarized or pharyngealized).[50] But 'clear' or palatal colouring is reported in a few dialects; hence the palatal which occurs in the glide reflex of vocalized *r* in a pronunciation such as *bəyd* ⟨bird⟩.[51]

The representational difference between approximant and tap *r* can be defined in terms of whether or not the phonological expression which characterizes each of the segments contains a vocalic element. As we saw in 3.4.2, a tap is a simplex expression containing the coronal element **R**. Approximant *r* can then be considered a compound of **R** and either **I** or **@**. These differences are shown in (45).[52]

(45) (a) Tap *r*   (b) Dark approximant *r*   (c) Clear approximant *r*

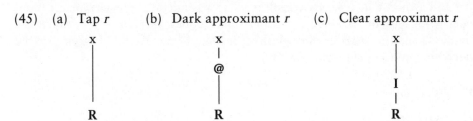

(45b) can now be taken as the representation that nuclear approximant *r* assumes in most rhotic dialects (significantly, though, not in the Scottish system illustrated in (39), as we will see below). In a branching nucleus such as that found in ⟨fear⟩, the approximant occupies the right-hand position. As shown in (46a), this yields an in-gliding diphthong, one that has been subject to breaking.

(46) (a) ⟨fear⟩   (b) ⟨fir = fur⟩

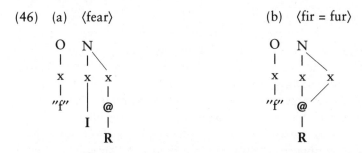

In a form such as ⟨fur⟩ (46b), where the entire nucleus is usually described as having coronal constriction, the approximant occupies both nuclear positions.[53]

The squeezing effect that nuclear *r* exerts on the distinctive space available to vowels, as we have seen, has both a vowel-quality and a length aspect. The qualitative aspect can be accounted for in terms of the non-occurrence of incompatible elements within the same position. The failure of up-gliding diphthongs such as *ay, ey* to appear in direct contact with approximant *r* is due to the impossibility of having a segment that simultaneously possesses palatal and non-palatal primary constrictions. To resolve the conflict between I and @, one of two options is taken up. Either the I fails to appear, in which case we find a diphthong such as *aər*. Compare ⟨tie⟩ with ⟨tire⟩:

(47)   tay ⟨tie⟩   taər ⟨tire⟩

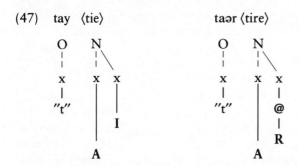

Or I and @ occur in separate constituents as a result of the approximant occupying a nucleus of its own, as in (48). The appearance of a *y* between the diphthong and the *ər* arises through the spreading of the palatal off-glide into the intervening unoccupied onset position.

(48)   ⟨tire⟩ *tay.yər*

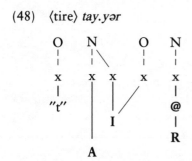

In the same way, we can treat the parallel patterns that affect diphthongs with *w* off-glides, as in such variant pronunciations of ⟨flour⟩ as *flaər, flaw.wər*.

Now consider the impact that nuclear *r* has on historical vowel-length contrasts. It is characteristic of rhotic dialects other than Scottish ones that the distinction between long and short vowels is suspended before domain-final *r*. The distinction holds freely before all other single consonants in this position. Thus, although we can have a contrast between, say, *i:* and *ɪ* before final *d* (as in ⟨bead⟩ versus ⟨bid⟩), there is no equivalent contrast before final *r*. All stressed nuclei in the latter position are long; we can have, say, *bɪər* ⟨beer⟩ but not **bɪr*. This exceptional behaviour is entirely puzzling, if we assume that final *r* is syllabified in exactly the same way as other consonants. However, it is accounted for, if *r* in this position is considered to occupy the same nucleus as the preceding vowel. In this way, the existence of only long nuclei before final *r* is related to an independently statable fact about English (and other Germanic languages):

(49)   Domain-final stressed nuclei must branch.

The condition in (49) is responsible for the fact that the contrast between long and short stressed vowels in English is suspended domain-finally in favour of the long series. It helps define the notion of minimal word in English; a monosyllabic word must contain two nuclear positions.[54] Hence the grammaticality of forms such as *fi:* ⟨fee⟩, *fey* ⟨fay⟩, *fow* ⟨foe⟩ but not of **fi, *fæ, *fɔ*.

According to the nuclear-*r* analysis, an ungrammatical form such as ** bɪr* would contain a single nuclear position occupied by the melodic expression defining an *r*-coloured *ɪ*. Under (49), the non-branching structure of the nucleus rules this form out for exactly the same reason as, say, ** bɪ*.

Unlike the rhotic dialects just discussed, Scottish English does exhibit a vowel-length difference before domain-final *r*. As indicated in (39), vowels in this context can be either long (as in *fi:r* ⟨fear⟩, *fo:r* ⟨four⟩) or short (as in *fɪr* ⟨fir⟩, *fʌr* ⟨fur⟩). This pattern is entirely to be expected, if final *r* in this type of system is considered to be syllabified in an onset just like other consonants (see (38)). Under these circumstances, a preceding nucleus is free to branch or not. It is also significant that Scottish dialects tend to have a characteristically consonantal tap realization of *r* in this context and that pre-*r* vowels show an absence of the breaking pattern found in other rhotic systems. This is consistent with our conception of a tap as an expression containing **R** but no vocalic element which could spread into the preceding nucleus. Compare the following Scottish representations of ⟨fear⟩ and ⟨fir⟩ with the nuclear-*r* representations in (46):

(50)   Scottish English

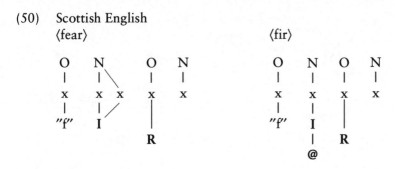

The Scottish system of vowel contrasts before domain-final *r* is probably the closest we get to the historical system among modern dialects. It is thus reasonable to assume that the syllabification in (50) represents the original pattern. So the absorption of final *r* into a preceding nucleus that has occurred in other rhotic dialects is an innovation. And, as we have seen, this historical restructuring has had the effect of destroying the original distinction between branching and non-branching nuclei in this environment. Previously, the distinctive burden in this context was borne by both length and quality contrasts. With the loss of distinctive length, the load shifts entirely onto the qualitative dimension. Any changes which, under the influence of nuclear *r*, then affect vowel quality are liable to place the historical contrasts in further jeopardy and in some instances lead to full-scale merger. The different stages in this historical series of events are recapitulated in different present-day merger patterns, including those shown in (40).

5.7.3 *Non-rhotic systems*

The compression of pre-*r* vocalic contrasts illustrated in (40) is also evident in non-rhotic dialects. This suggests that these systems have undergone a process that is similar to the nuclear incorporation of *r* that has affected non-Scottish rhotic systems. At first sight, the floating-segment analysis proposed for domain-final linking *r* in non-rhotic dialects might appear to exclude this possibility. That is, it is not immediately obvious how final *r* can be simultaneously floating and yet be incorporated in a preceding nucleus. However, this apparent contradiction is resolved, if we pursue the idea that approximant *r* is composed of both a coronal and a vocalic element, as shown in (45). It is not necessary to think of a process such as nuclear incorporation as affecting the segmental content of *r in toto*. Let us assume that, in non-rhotic systems, the vocalic element, but not **R**, undergoes absorption into the nucleus.

As before, we may assume that an *r* which is floating on the innermost cycle anchors to a following vacant onset on the next cycle, as illustrated in ⟨fea[r] a⟩ (51a). If no such onset is available, the stranded **R** remains unlicensed and unrealized, as in ⟨fea͜r the⟩ (51b).

(51) (a) *fɪər ə* ⟨fear a⟩

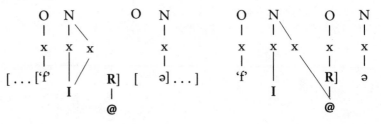

(b) *fɪə ðə* ⟨fear the⟩

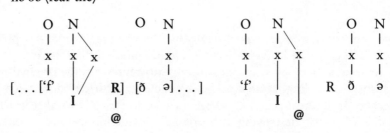

Thus in non-rhotic systems, it is only one element of the lexical content of floating *r* that gets incorporated into the nucleus, namely **@**. The non-rhoticity of such systems stems from the failure of **R** to participate in this absorption. It is now necessary to adjust the Non-Rhoticity condition given in (26), such that it refers only to the element **R** rather than to the whole melodic expression defining *r*.

As for historical *r* in non-final nuclei (as in ⟨party, harp⟩), we can now refine our assumption that it has been lost from lexical representations in non-rhotic systems. The effects of breaking are still in evidence in these contexts, for example in *bɪəd* ⟨beard⟩. This indicates that it is the coronal element **R** alone that has been lost. As in pre-consonantal domain-final position, what remains is the vocalic reflex of historical *r* – the element **@**.

In non-rhotic systems, the range of vowels that display breaking effects in environments where the vocalic content of historical *r* has undergone nuclear incorporation varies from dialect to dialect. The widest distribution of breaking is found in systems which have in-gliding reflexes in BEER, CARE, BAR, FOR, FOUR and POOR (for example, *ɪə, ɛə, aə, ɔə, oə, ʊə* respectively). Elsewhere, however, the incidence of breaking is reduced, partly through mergers involving the POOR, FOUR and FOR nuclei (see (22)), and partly through a tendency for the in-gliding pattern to be replaced by a long monophthongal one, for example *aə > aː*. The latter development, which (as we saw in 4.4.3) consists in the rightward spreading of melodic material from the first nuclear position into the second, preferentially affects relatively lower vowels. The most extreme outcome of this development occurs in dialects in which *ɪə* in BEER remains as the only in-gliding diphthong; otherwise we find monophthongal *aː* in BAR, *ɔː* in FOR = FOUR = POOR and *ɛː* in CARE.

5.7.4 MERRY-MARY-MARRY

Another site where breaking effects are to be observed in some dialects is before onset *r* within morphemes, as in ⟨carry, spirit, sorry⟩. Once again the result is varying degrees of merger, which suggests that the nuclear incorporation account can be extended to this position. Since medial onset *r* is lexically present in both rhotic System A and non-rhotic B/C, the distribution of the merger patterns cuts right across the classification of the three systems. It is worth comparing such dialects with those in which the generalization of breaking has failed to take place, because the latter provide further evidence of a systematic phonological difference between lexically floating and anchored *r*.

As in domain-final position, breaking in medial position has had the effect of neutralizing the historical distinction between long and short vowels in favour of long. In cases where breaking has affected the domain-final but not the domain-internal context, we get contrasts such as *hʌri* ⟨hurry⟩ (short vowel before medial *r*) versus *fəːr]i* ⟨furr-y⟩ (long before domain-final *r*). The extension of breaking to medial environments can lead to large-scale merger of V*r*V versus Vː*r*(])V contrasts, so that ⟨hurry⟩ and ⟨furry⟩, for example, become perfect rhymes. (52) shows main historical distinctions that can be affected in this way, together with some representative vocalic realizations. The mergers affect different dialects to differing extents.[55]

(52) spirit   ɪ   }
       spear]ing   iə   } ɪə

       Mary   ɛə   }
       merry   ɛ   } ɛə   }
       marry   æ   æə   } ɛə
                                                          }

       hurry   ʌ   }
       furr]y   ə: } ə:

       sorry   ɔ   }
       story   oə   } oə

The operation of breaking in medial contexts indicates that the nuclear incorporation of @ can affect *r* not only when it is floating, as shown in (51), but also when it is lexically anchored to an onset. An originally short nucleus affected by this change undergoes historical restructuring, resulting in potential merger with an originally long vowel. Compare the following unbroken (53a) and broken (53b) variants of ⟨merry⟩:

(53)   (a) mɛri ⟨merry⟩   (b) mɛəri ⟨merry (= Mary)⟩

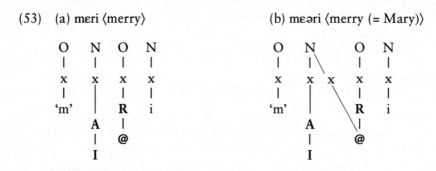

5.7.5 Summary

In 5.7, we have examined the special length and quality effects that appear in vowels preceding historical *r* in other than Scottish systems. Under the deletion and epenthesis accounts of non-rhoticity discussed in 5.4, the nature of these patterns remains mysterious. The effects can, however, be explained if we assume that *r*, or at least some part of its melodic make-up, has invaded the nuclear space inhabited by the vowels in question. Breaking, for example, can be attributed to the presence of the vocalic component of approximant *r* in a nucleus. The main distinction between non-Scottish rhotic systems on the one hand and non-rhotic systems on the other is that the element **R** has been absorbed into the nucleus in the former case but not in the latter.

5.8 Conclusion

In this chapter, we have seen how the distributional peculiarities of *r* in English reflect the rather special status it has in various dialects. Its nearest relatives in the system are *y* and *w*. Like them, it can occur in nuclei as well as in onsets. Its appearance in nuclei accounts for the squeezing of the space that is available to vocalic distinctions in V*r* contexts. In non-rhotic systems, *r* in sandhi environments is represented as a lexically floating segment which attaches itself to an unoccupied onset when this is made available during the course of a derivation.

The glide-like status of *r* is reflected not only in its distributional but also its phonetic properties. In terms of its coronal constriction and ability to occur in onsets, it lines up with the true consonants. In terms of its secondary vocalic characteristic and its ability to occur in nuclei, it lines up with the true vowels. In non-rhotic dialects where it is the sole participant in sandhi, its floating representation makes it unlike any other segment in the system. John Walker was surely not wide of the mark when he described *r* as the most imperfect of the consonants.

Exercises

1 *Other r-systems*

The data Get your own. There are various *r*-systems which do not correspond exactly to any of the four described in this chapter. If you have access to speakers of such a system (yourself, for example), collect data that you can draw on in considering the following questions.

The task

  (a) Precisely in what respects does the system differ from those discussed in this chapter?
  (b) To what extent is the divergence attributable to differences in the lexical incidence of *r*?
  (c) If the system exhibits an *r*–zero alternation, can the floating-*r* analysis account for it? If not, how might the analysis be modified so that it does?
  (d) Determine the set of vowel contrasts before historical *r*. If it is not identical to those found in other contexts, account for the differences.

2 Breaking and the southern drawl

The data   The data below illustrate the front vowel series before historical *r* in a particular non-rhotic southern dialect of United States English.[56] The range of vowel qualities and their lexical incidence are not directly equivalent to anything described in the standard textbooks, but this point can be set on one side for the purposes of this exercise.

The system exhibits a version of the in-gliding pattern discussed in this chapter. Note, however, that breaking only occurs in a specific subset of historical-*r* contexts. This results in superficial contrasts between broken and unbroken reflexes; compare, say, the $\varepsilon\partial$ of ⟨caring⟩ with the *e:* of ⟨Mary⟩.

The task

(a) Provide a full analysis both of the *r*–zero alternation and of breaking in this system.
(b) How are the breaking and non-breaking contexts distinguished under the floating-*r* analysis?
(c) Determine the morpho-syntactic domains within which the different vocalic variants occur.
(d) What is the elemental make-up the various vowels represented in the data, and how is this affected by breaking?

1	ɪə̯	beer, fear, jeer
2	ɪər . . .	beery, fearing, jeering
3	iːr . . .	Erie, hero, series
4	ɛə̯	care, hear, scare
5	ɛər . . .	caring, hearing, scaring
6	eːr . . .	dairy, hilarious, Mary
7	ɛr . . .	berry, heron, merry
8	æə̯	air, bear, dare
9	æər . . .	airy, bearer, daring
10	ær . . .	carrot, sparrow, marry

3 London laterals

The data   In many dialects of English, *l* is vocalized to *w* in certain phonological contexts. In some cases, this results in *l-w* alternations rather similar to those involving *r* and zero; for example, ⟨pee[l]ing-pee[w]⟩. Moreover, like the *r* pattern, *l*-vocalization can have quite significant effects on the quality of a preceding vowel. Perhaps not surprisingly then, the lateral pattern raises issues very similar to those discussed in this chapter.

The particular vocalizing pattern illustrated here is one that is firmly established in London and is apparently gaining ground throughout the southeast of England. The data in I provide information about the conditions under which the vocalized reflex occurs. As usual, the data are arranged in word rows, each of which represents a particular configuration of phonological and morphological conditions. The data in II show the influence vocalized *l* exerts on the quality and length of a preceding vowel. Note that the system is non-rhotic, a point that is of relevance in rows II.4(b) and II.5. For comparative purposes, the system's maximal vocalic inventory, as found for example before *t*, is given in III. For ease of reference, the row numbers in II and III indicate rough correspondences between the two inventories.

The task

(a) Determine the conditions under which the vocalized reflex appears.
(b) Account for the *l–w* alternation. What is the lexical representation of forms that show the alternation?
(c) Compare the reduced vowel inventory in II, which occurs before the vocalized reflex of *l*, with the maximal inventory given in III. Account for the effect that *l*-vocalization has on preceding vowels.

I *l* VERSUS *w*

1	l	live, loud
2	l	play, glow
3	l	trolley, tally, yellow
4	w	belt, fold, help, bulge
5	w	tell l, pull l, feel l, goal l
6	w	tell Joe, pull through, feel bad, goal down
7	w	felled, bowled, sealed
8	l	telling, pulling, feeler, goalie
9	l	tell us, pull over, feel it, goal up

II VOWELS BEFORE VOCALIZED *l*

1	ɪw	(a) fill, still, build, guilt
		(b) feel, steal, field
2	ɛw	tell, bell, else, weld
3	æw	(a) pal, Val
		(b) tail, pale, mail
		(c) owl, fowl, growl
4	aw	(a) tile, pile, smile
		(b) snarl, Charles

5   əw   twirl, girl, hurl
6   ɒw   (a) doll, solve
              (b) goal, pole, bold
              (c) dull, gull, bulb
7   ow   (a) full, pull, bull
              (b) fool, pool, school
              (c) fall, crawl, fault

III MAXIMAL VOWEL INVENTORY

1	ɪ	BIT	əy	BEAT		
2	ɛ	BET				
3	æ	BAT	æy	BAIT	æː	BOUT
4	ɒy	BITE	aː	CART		
5	əː	SHIRT				
6	ɒ	POT	aw	BOAT	a	BUT
7	ʊ	PUT	əw	LOOT	oː	CAUGHT

Epilogue

What makes English sound English? The question can be approached from two angles. Looking at it from the outside in, as it were, we might ask whether anything distinguishes English phonology from the phonologies of other languages. That is, can we put our finger on a collection of phonological properties that will uniquely identify English to the exclusion of other languages, especially its close Germanic relatives? Or, bearing in mind the considerable phonological diversity that accompanies the wide geographical dispersal of the language, we might consider the issue from the inside out: what if anything unites different dialects of English at the phonological level? Put concretely, is there something specifically 'English' about the phonologies of, say, Sydney, Detroit or Glasgow English that immediately sets them apart from dialects of, say, Frisian, Dutch or German?

Viewed from a classical SPE perspective, the relation between the phonological systems of cognate dialects involves the two areas of the grammar where pronunciation facts are accommodated in this model – the lexicon and the phonological component. Although either or both of these might be expected to be implicated in dialect differentiation, the emphasis in the relevant literature has been placed firmly on the phonological component. This leads to an apparently straightforward interpretation of the view that related dialects share some kind of underlying structural identity. Panlectal unity is supposedly manifested in a shared set of phonological representations in the lexicon and, possibly, a shared core of phonological rules. Dialect divergence is then deemed to involve discrepancies in the organization of phonological rules. These arise historically from the selective manner in which such rules undergo addition, loss, reordering or restructuring in individual grammars.

Even taken on its own terms, an extreme interpretation of this view – that all dialect variation is expressible in terms of rule differences – does not stand up to scrutiny. At stake here is the question of whether the phonological non-uniformity of related dialects is in principle any different from cross-language diversity. Most research which has specifically addressed this issue has come up with a consistent answer – a resounding no. As is by now well known, the distinction between **language** and **dialect** has no basis in linguistic reality but is defined in purely social, political or cultural terms. This may seem a rather disappointing conclusion, because it would appear to undermine the intuitively appealing notion that purely linguistic criteria can be used to group together particular systems as 'dialects of the same language'. The abiding attraction of this assumption is reflected in the way it has continued to figure with varying degrees of explicitness in the phonological literature. However, all the evidence suggests that no neat cutoff point exists at which 'dialects', distinguished purely by the contents of their phonological rule components, give way to 'languages', distinguished by differing lexical representations.

In any event, the whole question of dialect and language variation takes on a quite different complexion once we begin to move away from a rule-oriented approach to phonological phenomena. Indeed, it is now reasonable to ask whether it is even appropriate to think of **phonology** as identifying an independent module in the grammar.

The response to the equivalent question in relation to syntax is now no. **Syntax**, on current understanding, no longer refers to an autonomous grammatical component, as it did in earlier generative theory. It is instead an informal term applied to the mapping between LF and PF, a relation that is governed by quite general constraints rather than by grammar-specific rules.

In the light of the theoretical developments outlined in the preceding chapters, it is reasonable to suggest that **phonology** is on the way to achieving something of the same status. The term can still be applied to the derivational function whereby one set of phonological representations is mapped onto another. But the scope of activity attributed to this function has shrivelled quite dramatically from what was countenanced in the heyday of SPE. The notion that there exists an independent phonological module, chock-full of language-specific rules, is now obsolescent. The explanatory burden previously borne by the phonological rule component has gradually been taken over by the enriched model of representations that has emerged during the last twenty years or so. Thus when we nowadays speak of the 'phonology of language X', we are referring primarily to the phonological structure of its lexical entries.

So is the phonological structure of English in any way peculiarly English? We can ask the question again, this time from the viewpoint of a theory which dispenses with rewrite rules. Taking the 'external' perspective first, we might set out to identify a combination of settings on particular phonological parameters that occurs in English but in no other language. This is a highly unlikely result, in view of the small number of such parameters and the comparatively large number of natural languages. Particularly when we narrow the focus to exclude all but its West Germanic sisters, it becomes clear that English is anything but special. Take, for example, the English settings on five major parameters controlling prosodic structure: branching onsets (ON), branching rhymes (ON), branching nuclei (ON), foot-level licensing (HEAD-INITIAL), and licensing of final empty nuclei (ON). In terms of these settings, English looks just like any other West Germanic language, not to mention a considerable number of its more distant Indo-European cousins.

Switching to the 'internal' perspective, by asking what unifies different phonological grammars of English, begs the question of what qualifies as a dialect of English. It is probably true that the parametric settings just mentioned hold for the vast majority of systems to which the label **English** might uncontroversially be attached. Rather less certain is the status of systems which have predominantly English lexical stock but whose genetic affiliation to the language is at best obscure. These are precisely the cases with divergent settings on the parameters in question. Many anglophone creoles and pidgins, for example, display an absence of one or more of the following characteristics: complex onsets, contrastive vowel length, closed rhymes, and word-final consonants. Each of these reflects an OFF setting on the relevant parameter.

The main role of phonological representations is to provide addresses for lexical storage and retrieval. Much of the phonological content of individual lexical entries is perforce idiosyncratic, affirming the arbitrariness of the sound–meaning pairing. However, the overall design of the representations in terms of which entries are structured reflects quite general properties of the human language faculty. In other words, these properties define the set of possible lexical addresses. Each language exploits a subset of these addresses, the selection being circumscribed by the particular combination of settings the system opts for on a small number of phonological parameters.

As to the matter of derivation, the null hypothesis is that it is constrained by the same principles as shape the design of lexical representations. Within an authentically generative model of grammar, phonological derivation does no more than define the distributional and alternation regularities that hold over phonological representations, both in the lexicon and in larger syntactic frames. It does not, for example, serve the extra-grammatical function of preparing representations for submission to articulation and perception.

Within a full-blooded principle-based approach, phonological derivation is in large part automatic. An automatic derivational effect is one that, in response to universal constraints, is the inevitable consequence of some combination of conditions obtaining within a representation. The conditions are primarily prosodic, the effects primarily melodic. Each of the latter takes the form of a decision about whether the prosodic licensing status of a particular position enables it to support the phonetic interpretation of a given element α. In short, all phonological processing can be distilled into the universal schema **license** α. The massive over-generation that flows from this generalization is stemmed by the intervention of general constraints which, among other things, ensure that there is a host of prosodic conditions under which α cannot be licensed.

That said, it needs to be stressed that the emerging model stops short of being fully deterministic. It still possesses a certain degree of 'slack', permitting situations in which more than one derivational outcome is well-formed. This is as it should be. For example, any analysis of *t*-lenition in English has to make allowances for the fact that different dialects opt for different weakened reflexes. Nevertheless, the number of melodic options that are attested in such cases amounts to no more than a handful. The challenge is to ensure that the set of possible derivations defined by our model matches this observation as closely as possible.

In sum, phonological differences between grammars come in three forms. Some are systematic and reflect divergent permutations of parametric settings. Others may take the form of differing choices from a limited set of derivational outcomes allowed for by particular combinations of parametric settings and universal constraints. The remainder are a matter of idiosyncratic distinctions in the phonological content of individual lexical entries. None of these differences is the preserve of specifically 'dialect' as opposed to 'language' variation. The main value of focusing on the former lies in the opportunity it affords us of investigating the scope of cross-grammar differences in laboratory-like conditions.

Notes

Chapter 1 Sounds and Words

1 For an overview of developments in this model, in the tradition of Chomsky (1965, 1981), see van Riemsdijk and Williams (1986: 170ff).

2 The overall semantic interpretation of a sentence, when uttered in context, of course depends on more than the purely grammar-internal factors mentioned here. Extra-grammatical factors relating to the real-world setting in which the sentence is uttered naturally have a significant role to play in this regard. For one approach to the 'real-semantics' issue, see Sperber and Wilson (1986) and Kempson (1988).

3 This insight is perhaps most commonly associated with de Saussure (1916).

4 In the phonological literature of this century, the 'item-and-process' model described here has been associated with generative phonology since its earliest days (e.g. Halle 1959). Earlier precedents are to be found in the writing of, amongst others, Bloomfield (1933).

5 An alternative analysis under which the lexical representation of ⟨send⟩ is *sɛn*, with the *d* then being inserted pre-vocalically, is ruled out for the reason that it would insert *d* after all *n*-final morphemes. This would result in a very large number of erroneous derivations, such as **sʌnd* for ⟨sun⟩.

6 For a more detailed look at dialect differences relating to Cy clusters, see exercise 2 at the end of chapter 2.

7 See van der Hulst and Smith (1982a) for discussion of this development.

8 For an excellent summary of the ordered-rule approach, see Kenstowicz and Kisseberth (1979).

9 See van Riemsdijk and Williams (1986) for a summary of early rule-oriented work in generative syntax and for a discussion of more recent reactions against it. Textbook presentations of the classic SPE model of phonology include those of Schane (1973), Hyman (1975), Kenstowicz and Kisseberth (1979), Katamba (1988), Durand (1990) and Carr (1993).

10 Again see van Riemsdijk and Williams (1986).

11 See for example Chomsky (1992) and Brody (1992).

12 See especially Bromberger and Halle (1988).

13 See in particular Kaye, Lowenstamm and Vergnaud (1985, 1990).

14 One of the earliest explicit declarations of this view is that of Kaye, Lowenstamm and Vergnaud (1985). See now also, for example, Kaye, Lowenstamm and Vergnaud (1990), Prince and Smolensky (1993) and the papers in Goldsmith (1993).

15 See Anderson (1982), Levin (1985) and the discussion in chapter 4.

16 Full explications of the formal devices of the rewrite-rule model in phonology are to be found for example in Schane (1973) and Hyman (1975).

17 For discussion of this point, see for example Kaye (1989: 58ff).
18 SPE (ch. 9), Kean (1975).
19 Kaye, Lowenstamm and Vergnaud (1990).
20 Haegeman (1991: 167ff), Manzini (1992).
21 On the notion of locality in phonology, see for example Itô (1986) and Archangeli and Pulleyblank (1992: ch. 1).
22 This is the **autosegmental** view of phonological representation, pioneered by Goldsmith (1976) and to be discussed in some detail in chapter 3.
23 See, for example, Kaye, Lowenstamm and Vergnaud (1985), Mascaró (1987), Yip (1988a), Piggott (1988), Avery and Rice (1989) and Archangeli and Pulleyblank (1992).
24 Kaye (1989: 89ff).
25 See for example Chomsky (1981: ch. 1; 1986a).
26 Chomsky (1964: 64).
27 For an extensive critique of the over-generating properties of rule ordering in phonology, see Pullum (1976).
28 On this point, see for example Kaye (1989: ch. 5).
29 Chomsky (1981).
30 Parametric variation in phonology is one of the main themes of chapter 4. For explicit discussions of the topic in the phonological literature, see for example Hayes (1980), Itô (1986), Kaye, Lowenstamm and Vergnaud (1990) and Archangeli and Pulleyblank (1992: ch. 4).
31 Halle and Vergnaud (1987).
32 See especially the collection of articles in Benincà (1989).
33 The **root** and **word** terminology is traditional. See Selkirk (1982a) for detailed discussion and analysis. Roughly equivalent classifications use such terms as **primary** and **secondary** affixation (Bloomfield 1933) and **Class-I** and **Class-II** morphology (Siegel 1974).
34 Allen (1978).
35 See for example Siegel (1974).
36 Siegel (1974).
37 Sproat (1985), Fabb (1988).
38 Borowsky (1989).
39 Myers (1987).
40 That is, such alternations are **structure-preserving** in the sense of Kiparsky (1985). More on this notion in chapter 4.
41 See, for example, Halle and Mohanan (1985) and Borowsky (1986: 232ff).
42 The facts in (24) are true of the majority of dialects. Other patterns of ŋ distribution are attested, some of which we will consider in exercise 1 at the end of chapter 2.
43 The use of the term **analytic** in this specific sense is attributable to Kaye and Vergnaud (1990).
44 On the non-independence of domains created by affixation, see for example Kiparsky (1982a).
45 For example, Kiparsky (1982a, 1985), Halle and Mohanan (1985), Mohanan (1986), Pulleyblank (1986), Booij and Rubach (1987). For a summary and references, see Kaisse and Shaw (1985).
46 For example, Kaye and Vergnaud (1990).
47 For non-derivational approaches to root-level alternations, see for example Lieber (1982), Marantz (1982) and Kaye and Vergnaud (1990).

48 For discussion of external evidence bearing on the representation of root-level alternations in English, see for example Jaeger (1986), McCawley (1986) and Wang and
Derwing (1986).
49 On this point, see Kahn (1976: 8ff).
50 Wells (1982: 310–13).
51 Wells (1982: 312ff).
52 Harris (1990a).
53 As well as summarizing the main developments, Harris (1989) provides references to
the relevant data sources.
54 For detailed descriptions of these particular systems, see Labov, Yaeger and Steiner
(1972) (New York City) and Harris (1985) (Belfast).
55 For the details of Aitken's Law, see Aitken (1981) and Lass (1974).
   Lowland Scots, a Germanic relative of English, has a long history of independent
development in Scotland. Scottish English refers to those dialects that have emerged as
a result of the more recent importation of English. For a discussion of the relationship
between the two languages, see Aitken (1984a).
56 On the morphological sensitivity of Aitken's Law, see for example Harris (1990a) and
McMahon (1991).

Chapter 2   Constituency

1 Jones (1989: 15 ff) provides a discussion of the historical details as well as references to
the classic literature on the topic.
2 Technically, deletion would be said to **bleed** lengthening if it applied first. To derive the
correct result, the opposite order has to be imposed, in which case the rules are said to
stand in a **counter-bleeding** relation. The best discussion of rule-ordering relations is
probably that of Kenstowicz and Kisseberth (1979: ch. 8).
3 The literature contains various proposals for establishing pair-wise relations between
linear rules, such as those described here, which evidently conspire to create a given
outcome. According to one suggestion, a particular principle of rule ordering favours
counter-bleeding relations (as outlined in note 2) over bleeding relations. See Kiparsky
(1982b: ch. 4) for discussion and references.
4 In its original incarnation, the skeletal or timing tier was represented as a sequence of
C and V slots (McCarthy 1979, Clements and Keyser 1983). Under this proposal, each
slot contained a value for the feature [syllabic]: minus for C, plus for V. Before long, it
was acknowledged that this mode of representation contained a degree of unwarranted
redundancy, since the syllabic status of a position was coded twice – once in the value
for [syllabic], and again in constituent structure. Since, as we will see presently, there
are independent grounds for retaining constituency, the conclusion was reached that a
featural characterization of syllabicity could be dispensed with altogether. Thus shorn
of all featural content, the positions on the timing tier come to be viewed as nothing
more than place-holders in phonological structure. This insight is originally due to Kaye
and Lowenstamm (1984) and was taken up in Levin (1985) and subsequent work.
5 This non-linear arrangement, incorporating association lines, is an extension of the
classic autosegmental treatment of tone originally developed by Leben (1973) and
Goldsmith (1976).
6 McCarthy (1979), Halle and Vergnaud (1980), Clements and Keyser (1983).
7 For skeletal treatments of compensatory lengthening in other languages, see for
example Steriade (1982), Clements and Keyser (1983: 77ff) and the papers in

Wetzels and Sezer (1985). More recent treatments of the phenomenon, based on the **mora** rather than the skeletal point as the fundamental unit of timing, include that of Hayes (1989).

8 The terms and their associated concepts are originally due to Goldsmith (1976).

9 This is the Linkage Condition discussed by, among others, McCarthy (1979), James Harris (1980) and Goldsmith (1990: 52–3).

10 De Chene and Anderson (1987).

11 The no-crossing effect was originally obtained by means of a phonological constraint, the Well-Formedness Condition of Goldsmith (1976: 48). Sagey (1988), however, shows that it can be derived from the more general logical principles referred to here (see also Bird and Klein 1990).

12 These examples illustrate primary final stress. The same pattern is evident in final open syllables with secondary stress, e.g. *mæroː/mærow* ⟨marrow⟩, *bæleː/bæley* ⟨ballet⟩.

13 Kaye, Lowenstamm and Vergnaud (1990).

14 Thanks to Neil Smith for the ⟨catch it⟩–⟨cat shit⟩ minimal pair.

15 The term is due to Hayes (1982). For discussion and further references, see Hogg and McCully (1987: 106ff).

16 There are apparent counterexamples in, for instance, ⟨detách, attách, allége⟩. However, these forms have final stress for the same reason as, say, ⟨detér, abút, permít, concúr, compél⟩: the initial syllable coincides with an unstressable prefix. On this point, see SPE (p. 94).

17 For an early non-linear analysis of contour tones, see Leben (1973). Other dynamic segment-types which can be treated in the same contour terms include short diphthongs (e.g. *ya, wa*, as in (a)) and pre-nasalized stops (*nd, mb*, etc., as in (b)).

$$
\begin{array}{cccc}
\text{(a)} & x & \text{(b)} & x \\
& / \ \backslash & & / \ \backslash \\
& y \quad a & & n \quad d
\end{array}
$$

Type (a) occurs, for example, in French (e.g. *trwa* ⟨trois⟩ 'three'), type (b) in, for example, Venda (southern Bantu, South Africa, e.g. *mbudzi* 'goat'). Neither structure is attested in English.

18 For discussion, see van der Hulst and Smith (1982a).

19 Early attempts to integrate syllable structure into generative phonology include those of Vennemann (1972a), Hooper (1972) and Kahn (1976).

20 These facts have been widely discussed in the literature on word stress. See, for example, SPE (pp. 71 ff), Liberman and Prince (1977) and Kaye (1989: 79 ff).

21 See SPE (ch. 3).

22 On the evidence for the onset–rhyme split, see for example Pike and Pike (1947), Kuryłowicz (1948), Pike (1967), Fudge (1969, 1987), Selkirk (1982b) and James Harris (1983).

23 It is sometimes claimed that a certain type of reduplication process targets ('circumscribes') a syllable-sized constituent. A typical example is provided by Tagalog, where the recent perfective prefix is a CV template in which the segmental material is a copy of the initial CV portion of the base to which it is attached. The inflected form of the base *galit* 'get mad', for instance, is *ka-ga-galit* 'just got mad' (the reduplicative prefix emboldened). McCarthy and Prince (1986) treat this as the prefixation of a syllable (1986). However, see now Kaye (1991) for an alternative analysis which dispenses with all reference to the syllable node and makes use of the notion of licensing (to be discussed in chapter 4).

24 Reasons for dispensing with an independent syllable node are discussed by Aoun (1979) and Kaye, Lowenstamm and Vergnaud (1990).

25 This tradition is evident in a number of writing systems. These include the various Brāhamī-derived scripts of India, used for writing a wide range of Indo-European, Dravidian and other languages. One example is the Devanagari script, the system used for Sanskrit and various modern languages such as Hindi, Nepali and Marwari. The same basic principle underlies the Ethiopic script, the original Ge'ez system which has since been adapted for Amharic, Oromo, Tigr, Tirginā, and other modern languages of Ethiopia. (For a useful summary, see Coulmas 1989.)

26 An example from a widely used typists' manual: 'words should be divided between syllables, e.g. ⟨win-dow, pic-ture⟩. Many words can be divided in a number of ways. For example, the word ⟨qualifying⟩ could be divided: ⟨qual-ifying, quali-fying⟩' (Mackay 1982: 33).

27 See the references in note 22.

28 On the phonotactic evidence for the onset–rhyme split, see Fudge (1969, 1987), Selkirk (1982b) and Kaye (1985).

29 For reasons be discussed presently, forms such as ⟨catkin⟩ cannot be considered counterexamples to this generalization.

30 Such a uniform characterization is impossible if positions are assumed not to be syllabic skeletal slots but rather **morae** assigned solely on the basis of rhyme weight (Hyman 1985). In moraic theory, onset segments are adjoined either to the first mora of a syllable (e.g. Zec 1988) or directly to the syllable node (e.g. Hayes 1989). The exclusive concentration on rhyme-internal quantity in this approach precludes a unified account of phonotactic dependencies, since these also involve extra-rhymal relations, namely those illustrated in (21a) and (21c). There is thus no single dimension with reference to which phonotactic restrictions can be stated. The relations involved can be (a) between non-moraic melody units (within the onset); or (b) between morae (within the nucleus); or (c) between moraic and non-moraic material (coda-onset clusters).

31 These assumptions are rarely made explicit. On the reasons for doubting their validity, see Kaye, Lowenstamm and Vergnaud (1990).

32 On this point, see especially Selkirk (1982b).

33 Chomsky (1964).

34 For example O'Connor and Trim (1953), Abercrombie (1967: ch. 3), Kreidler (1989: 77 ff.) and Giegerich (1992: 137 ff.).

35 This formulation adapted from Clements and Keyser (1983: 37). See also Selkirk (1982b: 359).

36 The relevance of Italian vowel length to the syllabification of medial *s*C clusters is discussed by Kaye, Lowenstamm and Vergnaud (1990).

37 The notion of sonority, under various guises, has a long history in phonological scholarship. See for example Jespersen (1913), Saussure (1916), Jakobson and Halle (1956), Vennemann (1972a), Steriade (1982), Selkirk (1984).

38 However, various proposals have been made to the effect that language-specific sub-hierarchies exist within each of the classes defined in (26), e.g. Steriade (1982), Levin (1985).

39 Jakobson and Halle (1956), Selkirk (1984: 116), Vennemann (1988).

40 Selkirk (1984), Levin (1985).

41 Steriade (1982), Levin (1985), Vennemann (1988).

42 For a reanalysis of the Polish clusters just mentioned, see Gussmann and Kaye (1993).

43 Cf. Clements and Keyser (1983: 41).

44 The cluster *sr* appears in some types of African American English (Wells 1982: 558) and in some rural areas of England (see the entries under ⟨shrew⟩ (item IV. 5.2) in the *Survey of English Dialects* (Orton and Barry 1969, Orton and Tilling 1969)).

45 Cross-constituent voice assimilation only operates within the **foot**. For present purposes, a foot may be defined informally as a rhythmic group composed either of (a) a single stressed syllable; or (b) a stressed syllable followed by an unstressed syllable. (More on this in chapter 4.) The word ⟨bask⟩ contains one example of a foot of type (a); ⟨basket⟩ contains one of type (b). The generalization about voice assimilation between constituents does not hold when they occur in separate feet. This is illustrated by the *k-d* sequence in ⟨ánecdòte⟩, a form composed of two feet: *ænək* and *dowt*. There are a few apparent counterexamples to the foot-internal pattern, such as ⟨Hodgkin⟩. These involve consonants which, as explained in 2.3.4, must be considered non-adjacent, due to the presence of an intervening analytic morpheme boundary.

46 As noted by, among others, Selkirk (1982b: 347) and Clements and Keyser (1983: 47).

47 On the constituent-based distinction between vowels and glides, see for example Kaye and Lowenstamm (1984), Selkirk (1984) and Borowsky (1986: 274 ff).

48 For discussion of *Cy* phonotactics in English, see Borowsky (1986: 278 ff).

49 The following arguments are based on Kaye (1992), whose analysis of these data is partially anticipated by Borowsky (1984).

50 Levin (1985: 159 ff).

51 Kaye, Lowenstamm and Vergnaud (1990), Kaye (1992).

52 There is one VC pattern that is sometimes cited as an example of a phonotactic restriction holding between a nucleus and a coda. In general English, only a coronal consonant can occur after the diphthong *aw*, as in ⟨mouth, pout, proud, house, crown, foul⟩ (Anderson 1986). There are no examples of labials or velars occurring in this context: **plawm*, **rawb*, **tawg*. As we will see below, however, there is every reason to reject the assumption that final VC sequences of this type constitute nucleus-coda clusters.

53 Transcriptions such as *ia* and *uo* are sometimes employed to represent long diphthongs in certain regional dialects of English. However, on closer inspection, these turn out to be no more than quasi-phonemic symbolizations (usually devised for typographical convenience) of diphthongs which conform to the restricted pattern being discussed here. In the representation of certain Caribbean Englishes, for instance, the transcription ⟨ia⟩ is often used to represent a diphthong of the type *iə* (e.g. Cassidy and LePage 1967).

54 Some languages, such as Icelandic (Einarsson 1945), show a contrast between long and short diphthongs. As indicated in the text, the representational difference is one between a two-position nucleus (a) and a single nuclear position occupied by a contour segment (b) (see note 11):

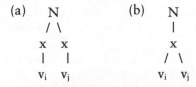

55 One of the most frequently cited examples of a language supposedly exhibiting a three-way vowel-length contrast is Estonian. The so-called over-long vowels, however,

involve bi-nuclear sequences (see Lehiste 1978). For discussion of other cases of falsely reported over-long nuclei, see Levin (1985: 106 ff).

56 The notion that a binary limit is imposed on branching structure in phonological representations was originally applied to higher-level constituents such as the foot and the word, particularly as these function in stress assignment (Liberman and Prince 1977, Hayes 1980). On the idea that syllabic constituency is structured in parallel fashion, see Pike (1967), McCarthy (1979), Kiparsky (1979, 1981) and Selkirk (1982b). The most restrictive interpretation of binarity is probably that of Kaye, Lowenstamm and Vergnaud (1990), who propose that all syllabic constituents are subject to a limit of two **positions**. This excludes the configuration in (39d), since the nested branching structure it contains results in a three-position rhyme.

57 Borowsky provides one of the most detailed discussions of English rhyme phonotactics (1986, 1989).

58 See for example Vennemann (1988: 40 ff).

59 As mentioned in note 45, this generalization does not hold across separate feet. Thus it is possible to find obstruent clusters with unlike voice in two-foot forms such as ⟨Aztec, anecdote⟩.

60 ⟨Cambridge⟩ can be set aside as a compound name with a historical word-level internal boundary. The *b* in both ⟨chamber⟩ and ⟨cambric⟩ represents a historical excrescence. This is probably related to a more general historical process whereby an epenthetic stop appears between a nasal and a following liquid, cf. ⟨bramble⟩ (from Old Saxon *brāmal*), ⟨Henry/Hendry⟩. As the first of these examples suggests, the juxtaposition of the nasal and liquid typically results from vowel syncope. This is also true of ⟨chamber⟩ (from late Latin ⟨camera⟩ 'room') and ⟨cambric⟩ (from Flemish ⟨Kamerijk⟩).

61 Prince (1984), Kaye, Lowenstamm and Vergnaud (1990).

62 In chapter 4, we will consider yet another interpretation of these facts, one which combines aspects the two positions outlined here. According to the third view, there is more than one level at which syllabification is established. At a basic level, where systematic phonotactic restrictions are stated, a consonant-only suffix is not incorporated into syllabic structure. At this stage, it is said to be **extra-syllabic** (on which more presently). At a more superficial level, however, basic phonotactic constraints are relaxed and the final consonant becomes syllabified along with the stem.

63 McCarthy (1979), Itô (1986), Myers (1987).

64 The term **contingent extra-syllabicity** is Goldsmith's (1990: 108).

65 McCarthy (1979), Itô (198b), Myers (1987).

66 For discussion of the notion of degenerate syllable, see for example McCarthy (1979) and Selkirk (1981). The most forthright defence of the onset analysis of word-final consonant position is probably that of Kaye (1990a). See also Borowsky (1986: 197 ff.).

67 The same point can be made in relation to languages which, unlike English, display word-final obstruent-sonorant clusters. An example is French, which has final clusters such as those in (a).

(a)			(b)		
vitr	'window pane'		*trɛ*	'very'	
propr	'clean'		*aprɛ*	'after'	
sabl	'sand'		*ble*	'corn'	
sabr	'sabre'		*bra*	'arm'	
sufl	'breath'		*sufle*	'breathe'	
sakr	'consecration'		*sakre*	'holy'	
sɛrkl	'circle'		*kle*	'key'	

Final clusters of this type are identical to those found in pre-vocalic branching onsets, such as in (b). The parallel distribution is straightforwardly explained if we follow Charette (1991, 1992) in recognizing final branching onsets, as in

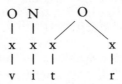

68 James Harris (1983: 83 ff).
69 This is essentially the traditional notion of **catalexis**, recently integrated into metrical theory by Giegerich (1985), Kiparsky (1992) and others.
70 Fudge (1969), Selkirk (1982b).
71 Fudge (1969), Selkirk (1982b). Clause (b) of (57) is reminiscent of the Coda Conditions proposed by It (1986) and adapted for English by Borowsky (1986) and Yip (1991).
72 We now need to reappraise the generalization that only coronal consonants can follow the diphthong of the SHOUT class; compare ⟨mouth, pout, proud, house, crown, foul⟩ with, say, *plawm, *rawb, *tawg. As remarked on in note 52, this is sometimes cited as evidence supporting the rhymal status of final VC sequences. As we now know, this syllabification is contradicted by the much more substantial body of evidence reviewed in this section.
    Nevertheless, since a final consonant occupies a separate constituent from a preceding nucleus, we would expect the two positions to be more or less phonotactically independent of one another. At first sight, this sits uneasily with the generalization regarding SHOUT. The distributional restriction should, however, probably be considered a historical accident. This view is bolstered by the fact that certain regionally restricted dialects retain forms reflecting an earlier distributional pattern in which *aw* (or some cognate reflex) occurred freely before non-coronals. Hence examples such as ⟨cowp⟩ 'overturn', ⟨howf⟩ 'burial ground' and ⟨howk⟩ 'dig into' found in Scotland and parts of northern England and Ireland (*Concise Scots Dictionary*).
73 The paucity of forms with *u* in closed syllables in the southern-type system cannot be considered significant. The short six-vowel sub-system arose as a result of historical *u* developing a lowered reflex, ʌ. The original pattern is retained in the north of England, where *u* is to be found in closed-syllable forms such as ⟨gulp, bulk, tusk, tuft, thunder⟩. The conditions under which southern lowering initially took place were in fact quite independent of the closed-syllable context. (Surrounding labial consonants disfavoured the change. For details and references, see Harris 1992a.) So the paucity of *u* forms such as ⟨pulpit⟩ in the southern system reflects the fact that lowering had the overall effect of bleeding *u* from a whole range of contexts.
74 For a full description and analysis of closed-syllable shortening in English, see Myers (1987).
75 We may assume here that the *p* cannot occur in the onset of a degenerate syllable, in the way that the *v* of ⟨receive⟩ does. If it did, we would have a cluster of adjacent onsets, one occupied by *p*, the other by *t*. At this point we may simply accept that such a configuration is ill-formed, but in chapter 4 we will see how this result can be derived by general principle.
76 This discussion of the significance of closed-rhyme shortness to the determination of domain structure in forms such as ⟨wept⟩ versus ⟨seeped⟩ is based on Kaye and Vergnaud (1990).

77 Or, to use Fudge's (1969) term, a **termination**. See also Fujimura and Lovins (1978), Kiparsky (1979) and Halle and Vergnaud (1980). For some of these writers, the notion of **appendix** extends to a coronal subset of final consonants which, according to the view advanced in this chapter, are better analysed as belonging to an onset.
78 Selkirk (1982b), Goldsmith (1990: 147).
79 A similar point can be made with respect to the unusual form ⟨mulct⟩. The complex final cluster in this word lends it the appearance of containing the word-level suffix ⟨-ed⟩ (cf. ⟨bulk-ed⟩). The source of the *k* in ⟨mulct⟩ is something of a mystery; the cognate Latin form is *multa* 'a fine'.
80 *Oxford English Dictionary*. The origins of ⟨traipse⟩ remain shrouded in mystery.
81 Rule-driven treatments of syllabification are to be found in the work of such as Kahn (1976), Steriade (1982), Clements and Keyser (1983), Archangeli (1984) and Levin (1985).
82 Lowenstamm (1979), Selkirk (1981), Kaye and Lowenstamm (1984), Itô (1986).
83 Thanks to Aled Jones for providing and discussing the south Wales data.

Chapter 3 Melody

1 The concept of subsegmental primes goes back at least as far as the early grammarians of the Indian subcontinent. It is to some extent implicit in familiar labels such as **labial, nasal** and **voiced**; however, these have traditionally been viewed as classifications of the dimensions along which systems of sounds are structured, rather than as independent entities which inhere in segments. (On this point, see Anderson (1985: 117 ff).) Rigorous attempts to formalize the notion in modern phonology do not really begin until the Prague School of the 1930s. See, for example, Trubetzkoy (1939) and Jakobson (1939). For an overview of Prague School phonology, see Fischer-Jørgensen (1975: ch. 3) and Anderson (1985: chs 4, 5).
2 van der Hulst (in press), for example, attempts to reduce all phonological expressions to different combinations of two fundamental building blocks.
3 This general approach is represented in frameworks such as Glossematics and Stratificational Theory (see Fischer-Jørgensen 1975 for discussion and references), as well as in the work of, for example, Fudge (1967) and Foley (1977).
4 Jakobson (1939) was one of the first to insist on the binary nature of phonological oppositions.
5 See especially Trubetzkoy (1939). Partially or wholly privative characterizations of phonological oppositions figure in such frameworks as Firthian Prosodic Analysis (see Palmer 1970 for references), Dependency Phonology (Anderson and Jones 1974) and Feature Geometry (Clements 1985).
6 Some current feature approaches recognize both single-valued and two-valued primes. See, for example, Itô and Mester (1986) and Pulleyblank (in press).
7 On this point, see for example den Dikken and van der Hulst (1988).
8 SPE (ch. 9).
9 For expositions of Underspecification Theory, see Archangeli (1984, 1988), Archangeli and Pulleyblank (1992) and the papers in *Phonology* 5:2.
10 This approach, known as Radical Underspecification, has two main variants. In one, termed Context-Sensitive Radical Underspecification by Mohanan (1991), underlyingly unspecified values are universally unmarked (e.g. Kiparsky 1982a). In another, Context-Free Radical Underspecification, languages are free to leave either marked or unmarked values underlyingly blank (e.g. Archangeli 1984). Mohanan (1991) provides a critique of the observational and explanatory shortcomings of both approaches.

11 For more detailed argumentation on this issue, see den Dikken and van der Hulst (1988).

12 Anderson and Ewen (1980).

13 The discussion in this section is based on Harris and Lindsey (in press).

14 For discussion of an example of this type, see Archangeli (1984: 29 ff).

15 The notion of a systematic phonetic level pre-dates SPE (see Halle 1959 and Chomsky 1964) and continues to be widely assumed in current underspecification approaches.

16 On this point, see Lass (1984: 205) and Mohanan (1991).

17 Braine (1974).

18 For an explicit statement of this view, see Bromberger and Halle (1988).

19 The notion that at least some primes are independently interpretable is implicit in early work in Dependency Phonology (Anderson and Jones 1974).

20 The term **element** is the one suggested by Kaye, Lowenstamm and Vergnaud (1985).

21 My own first exposure to this view came in the form of early Dependency Phonology (Anderson and Jones 1974, 1977). (See now also Anderson and Ewen 1987 and the papers in Anderson and Durand 1987.) More recent incarnations of the idea are to be found in Particle Phonology (Schane 1984a), Government Phonology (Kaye, Lowenstamm and Vergnaud 1985), the extended Dependency approach of van der Hulst, Smith and others (e.g. van der Hulst and Smith 1985, van der Hulst 1989), as well as in the work of Rennison (1984, 1990) and Goldsmith (1985).

22 The term **fusion** used in this sense (together with its opposite **fission**, on which more presently) is due to Schane (1984a).

23 Below we will discuss the formal implementation of these operations in terms of spreading and delinking. Explicit proposals that phonological processes are reducible to fundamental operations of this sort are to be found, for example, in Kaye, Lowenstamm and Vergnaud (1985), Mascaró (1987), Yip (1988a), Piggott (1988), Avery and Rice (1989) and Archangeli and Pulleyblank (1992).

24 For the historical details of the Great Vowel Shift, see for example Jespersen (1909) and Ekwall (1975). Analyses of the phenomenon in terms of features are provided by SPE and Wolfe (1972). For a Particle analysis, see Schane (1984b); for Dependency analyses, see and Anderson and Ewen (1987) and Jones (1989).

25 A detailed historical description of these processes is provided by Dobson (1968: 765 ff, 783 ff).

26 The southeastern English development of the BOAT vowel to *aw* has not resulted in merger with the vowel of BOUT, since this has shifted to *æw* or *æː*.

27 This insight is already present in Firthian Prosodic Analysis (see Palmer 1970 for an anthology).

28 In generative phonology, the non-linear mode of representation was originally developed for dealing with tonal phenomena. See especially Goldsmith (1976), to whom the term **autosegmental** is originally due. The model was soon extended to the treatment of vowel harmony (Clements (1981)) and thence to other phenomena.

29 The bottle-brush metaphor is (as far as I know) originally due to Halle and Vergnaud (1980).

30 On the representation of dominance versus co-indexing within melody units, see Hayes (1990) and Ewen (in press).

31 This use of tier conflation is proposed by Kaye, Lowenstamm and Vergnaud (1985).

32 As an example of I-loss, we may cite the historical backing of original *æ* to *a* in southern English and derivative dialects (discussed in 2.4.4). The effects of this development are evident in the 'broad-*a*' pronunciation of words such as ⟨pass, path, dance⟩. The

representation of *æ*, as we will see in 3.3.3, involves both **I** and **A** (although arranged differently to how they appear in *e*). Backing of *æ* takes the form of I-loss, the remaining **A** defining *a*.

33   The representation of intra-segmental asymmetries varies to some extent from one element-based framework to another. In Dependency Phonology, a pair of atoms α and β can enter into one of three relations: (a) α dependent on β; (b) β dependent on α; and (c) mutual dependency. In the framework presented in this chapter, only relations (a) and (b) are recognized. This is the arrangement assumed in, for example, Kaye, Lowenstamm and Vergnaud (1985) and van der Hulst (1989). In Schane's (1984a) Particle Phonology, preponderance is formalized by allowing multiple occurrences of the same element to be stacked within a single expression.

34   The *e/ɛ* and *æ* realizations resulting from the asymmetrical fusion of **A** and **I** are the outputs assumed by Kaye, Lowenstamm and Vergnaud (1985) and van der Hulst (1989).

35   The use of this term is due to Kaye, Lowenstamm and Vergnaud (1985).

36   For an expansion of the discussion in this section, see Harris and Lindsey (in press).

37   Acoustic definitions of the Jakobsonian features are provided by Jakobson, Fant and Halle (1962).

38   For a recent account of how representations containing articulatory features might be mapped onto the acoustic signal, see Clements and Hertz (1991).

39   On the lack of articulatory invariance in vowel production, see Ladefoged et al. (1972), Lieberman and Blumstein (1988: 162 ff) and the references therein.

40   Broadly speaking, this vowel of neutral quality corresponds to the centrality element in Dependency Phonology (Lass 1984: 277 ff, Anderson and Ewen 1987), to the 'cold' vowel of Government Phonology (Kaye, Lowenstamm and Vergnaud (1985), and to an 'empty' segment lacking any active vocalic prime in Particle Phonology (Schane 1984a) as well as in van der Hulst's (1989) 'extended' Dependency approach.

41   See Archangeli (1984: 57 ff) for a survey of some of the default vowels that appear in various languages. In her Underspecification approach, these vowels are analysed as segments which are devoid of all featural content in lexical representation.

42   For a review and discussion of the literature on vocal settings, see Laver (1980).

43   This idea is due to Kaye, Lowenstamm and Vergnaud (1985).

44   The notion that non-peripheral vowels are compounds containing the neutral element is originally due to Lass (1984: 277 ff). Adaptations of this idea are discussed in Harris and Lindsey (in press) and Charette and Kaye (1993).

45   Petterson and Wood (1987).

46   Palmada (1991: ch. 2).

47   For analyses of the Bantu harmony pattern in A-I-U terms, see Goldsmith (1985) and Rennison (1987). A related analysis of height harmony in the Pasiego dialect of Spanish is provided by Harris (1990b).

48   Lass (1976: ch. 1) provides a summary and extensive discussion of the relevant literature.

49   Halle and Clements (1983).

50   See the references to early English phoneticians in, for example, Dobson (1968); the short–long dichotomy is also implicit in the work of Trager and Smith (1951).

51   For example, Lass (1976) and Halle and Mohanan (1985).

52   This is the solution preferred by Kaye, Lowenstamm and Vergnaud (1985) and Rennison (1990).

53 Anderson and Ewen's (1987) proposal is a mixture of the two outlined here. For them, ATR is represented both as an independent element and in terms of intra-segmental dependencies. Yet another approach is to allow multiple occurrences of the same element to appear simultaneously within the same expression. According to one implementation of this idea, ATR *i*, for example, contains two instances of **I**, while non-ATR *ɪ* contains only one (Schane 1984a).

54 The original system, containing five vowels, survives in the north of England. Scots, together with its derivative dialects, has its own special developments (Aitken 1984b).

55 For the details, see Wells (1982).

56 The avoidance of merger that is characteristic of 'chain shifts' of this type is discussed by, among others, Jespersen (1909) and Luick (1921).

57 For the details, see Kurath and McDavid ((1961: 7–8) and Wells (1982: 168 ff).

58 The one-mouth principle (the term is Anderson's (1985: 121)), already present in Jakobson's work, has more recently been taken up by, for example, Anderson and Ewen (1987), Smith (1988) and Clements (1991a).

59 For the details, see Harris (1985: 195 ff).

60 Hyman (1975: 165).

61 Harris (1985: ch. 2) provides a survey and discussion of work in which the position of consonants on weakening paths is formalized in terms of scales of relative phonological strength.

62 See Lass and Anderson (1975) for a discussion of opening trajectories.

63 It has sometimes been assumed (for example by McCarthy 1988) that glottalling only affects consonants which already contain a glottalized component. There are certainly cases of languages in which glottalic stops lenite to *ʔ*. In Arbore, for example, we find alternations such as *hid'e* (1st sing.)–*hiʔte* (2nd sing.) 'gird on' and *hiik'e* –*hiiʔte* 'grind' (Hayward (1984); *d'* and *k'* indicate glottalic consonants). However, there are plenty of other cases where the correlation does not hold. In Malay, non-glottalized *k* in, say, *masak-an* ('the cooking') alternates with *ʔ* in *masaʔ* ('to cook') (Farid 1980). Both types of pattern are encountered in glottalling dialects of English. In London, for example, *ʔ* occurs in the same contexts as pre-glottalized variants of all voiceless stops. In West Yorkshire, on the other hand, the equivalent consonants, when not subject to glottalling, are not only non-glottalized but are also often pre-aspirated.

64 For a detailed exposition of this approach, see Harris (1990c).

65 An early formalization of the insight that *h* and *ʔ* belong to the class of reduction consonants is to be found in Lass (1976). The elements **ʔ**, **h** and **R** are proposed by Kaye, Lowenstamm and Vergnaud (1990).

66 For a more detailed discussion of the signal characteristics of **ʔ**, **h** and **R**, see Lindsey and Harris (1990) and Harris and Lindsey (in press).

67 The notion that the relation among plosives, fricatives and *h* involves a progressive loss of closure is inherent in the account of opening proposed by Lass and Anderson (1975).

68 Glottalised consonants, such as occur in some dialects of English as reflexes of voiceless plosives, can be represented as contour segments, i.e. two melodic expressions linked to a single skeletal point. The glottalic component corresponds to an expression containing only **ʔ**, while the supralaryngeal identity of the segment is defined by whatever elements are present in the other expression.

69 Free combination of the elements for consonants generates one melodic compound not represented in (42) or (44), namely **ʔ** fused with **h**. In the absence of a place-defining element, this expression defines a glottal stop with noise release, a reflex that is, to the best of my knowledge, unattested in English. Before concluding that the model needs to

be amended to exclude the generation of such a compound, it is necessary to investigate thoroughly reports that a contrast between released and unreleased glottal stops does indeed exist in some languages, such as Burmese (Cornyn 1964).

70 This is, for example, the Philadelphia pattern described by Ferguson (1972). For further discussion and references, see Harris (1989).

71 See Kaye, Lowenstamm and Vergnaud (1990).

72 The existence of an independent nasality component is widely assumed in feature-based frameworks; it also figures in some privative approaches, e.g. Anderson and Ewen (1987) and Kaye, Lowenstamm and Vergnaud (1990).

73 Hyman's (1982) analysis of Gokana is a particularly convincing example.

74 This isomeric relation between labial-velar and labial stops is proposed by Kaye, Lowenstamm and Vergnaud (1990).

75 There is no necessary connection between coronal palatalization and stridency, as the reflexes t^y/d^y mentioned in 3.4.1. indicate. Nevertheless, it is true that the two effects do frequently go hand in hand. Whether and how this connection should be captured in melodic structure remain open questions.

76 Clements (1985), Clements and Hume (in press).

77 On the functional unity of primes defining place, see for example Goldsmith (1981), Steriade (1982), Mohanan (1983).

78 Processes conventionally referred to as metathesis also fall into this category. As the term suggests, these are traditionally understood as the transposition of two adjacent segments. However, more recent work has shown that they can be treated as a particular combination of simple delinking and spreading. For an example of the latter kind of analysis, see van der Hulst and van Engelenhoven (1993).

79 The geometric model was initially developed by Mascaró (1983), Clements (1985) and Sagey (1986). McCarthy (1988) and Clements and Hume (in press) present further proposals within this framework, together with summaries and discussion of the relevant literature.

80 Clements (1985), Sagey (1986).

81 For conflicting views on this matter, see for example Clements (1985), Sagey (1986), McCarthy (1988), Avery and Rice (1989) and the articles in Paradis and Prunet (1991).

82 The view that primes defining manner contrasts are directly attached to the ROOT node is to be found in the work of, among others, McCarthy (1988).

83 It has been argued that the primes involved in vocalic contrasts have their own internal organization under PLACE, which in articulatory terms reflects differing degrees of aperture (e.g. Clements 1991b). There is some evidence that I and U can function as a class to the exclusion of A. Ewen and van der Hulst (1988) propose the following type of arrangement to accommodate this patterning:

Access to I and U as a class is then gained via the intermediate node which immediately dominates both elements to the exclusion of A.

84 For the proposal that affricates consist of a sequence of ROOT nodes, see Clements (1987). According to an opposing view, they involve sequences of differently valued terminal features (Sagey 1986).

85   Affrication is particularly prevalent in urban England, including London (Wells 1982: 323).

86   The High German Consonant Shift is one of the best known examples (see for example König 1978: 62 ff).

87   The term is due to Hayes (1986). According to his account of the phenomenon, a rule which explicitly makes reference to a single association line (a non-geminate structure) does not apply to a structure containing two lines (such as found in a geminate). For an alternative suggestion, framed in terms the notion of licensing to be introduced in the next chapter, see Harris (1990c).

88   Fourakis and Port (1986).

89   For a related geometric analysis of intrusive stops, see Clements (1987).

90   Ladefoged (1982: 130 ff).

91   Ibid.

92   Ladefoged (1971: ch. 2).

93   Halle and Stevens (1971).

94   Haudricourt (1961), Matisoff (1973).

95   The idea that the three-way laryngeal contrast (H–L–zero) holds both for consonant phonation types and for tone is proposed by Kaye, Lowenstamm and Vergnaud (1990).

96   The view that tone and phonation type involve the same primes has been challenged by, for example, Anderson (1978).

97   For example Kahn (1976), Selkirk (1982b).

98   Ladefoged (1971: 12–13).

99   See for example Hayes's (1984) treatment of this phenomenon in Russian.

100 SPE (300 ff), Halle and Stevens (1971).

101 For example, Lodge (1984: 9, 58).

102 One extension of this phenomenon is illustrated by the tensing data in exercise IV at the end of chapter 1.

103 *Pace* Zwicky (1975).

104 See Kerswill (1987) for discussion of this phenomenon in Durham (England). The same pattern is mentioned by Wells as occurring in Trinidad and the Caribbean Windward Islands (1982: 580).

105 The presentation in 3.8 is based heavily on collaborative work with Geoff Lindsey (Lindsey and Harris 1990, Harris and Lindsey 1992, in press). I am very happy to acknowledge the hefty contribution Geoff has made to my thinking on the matters summarized in this appendix.

106 The Scots data are adapted from Mather and Speitel (1986).

107 The system illustrated here is found in south and west Yorkshire (Wells 1982: 366–7). It is distinct from the more northerly pattern exemplified in (58).

108 Data based on Luelsdorff (1975: 66 ff).

Chapter 4   Licensing

1   On the headedness of phonological constituents, see for example Kiparsky (1979), Levin (1985), Lowenstamm and Kaye (1985), Kaye, Lowenstamm and Vergnaud (1990).

2   For a survey of the unequal distribution of syllable structure types, see Kaye and Lowenstamm (1981).

3   Ibid.

4   On the prosodic hierarchy, see for example Selkirk (1980), Nespor and Vogel (1986) and McCarthy and Prince (1986).

5 Kiparsky (1979, 1981).
6 Halle and Vergnaud (1987). For a summary of proposals relating to tree and/or grid representations of metrical structure, see Goldsmith (1990: ch. 4).
7 For the Dependency Phonology approach, see for example Anderson and Jones (1977), Anderson and Ewen (1987) and the references therein. On government or prosodic government, see Lowenstamm and Kaye (1985), Kaye, Lowenstamm and Vergnaud (1990) and further references to be supplied below.
8 Discussions of the X-bar properties of the prosodic hierarchy are provided by, for example, Anderson (1982), Levin (1985), Uriagereka (1986) and Lowenstamm (1989).
9 Nespor and Vogel (1986), Anderson and Ewen (1987).
10 An early formalization of this notion is the Principle of Exhaustive Syllabification (McCarthy 1979, Selkirk 1981).
11 On the mechanism of Prosodic Licensing, see McCarthy (1979), Selkirk (1981) and Itô (1986), among others.
12 On the mechanism of Autosegmental Licensing, see Goldsmith (1989).
13 On the stray erasure of extra-syllabic positions, see Steriade (1982) and Itô (1986).
14 On the role of directionality in licensing relations, expressed in terms of the notion government, see Kaye, Lowenstamm and Vergnaud (1990). I will reserve the term **government** for a quite restricted set of licensing contexts to be described below.
15 This formulation from Kaye (1990a).
16 In fact, x_2 also licenses the onset position x_1, a matter to be taken up in 4.3.3.
17 The ultimate head is equivalent to the Designated Terminal Element within the metrical realm of phonological structure (Liberman and Prince 1977).
18 On the role of locality in licensing relations, see Itô (1986) and Kaye, Lowenstamm and Vergnaud (1990).
19 On the use of these terms, see respectively Kaye, Lowenstamm and Vergnaud (1990) and Archangeli and Pulleyblank (1992).
20 Kaye (1990a).
21 The following discussion of licensing at different levels of the prosodic hierarchy follows in its essential outlines the theory presented in Kaye, Lowenstamm and Vergnaud (1990) and developed in works such as Kaye (1990a, 1990b) and Charette (1991). See Brockhaus (in press) for a useful summary and further references.
22 This is not the place to recount the vagaries of the English stress system. Whole volumes have been devoted to the subject. (A useful description is provided by Fudge 1984.) There are numerous deviations from the general word-level pattern of right dominance alluded to here. Examples of bipedal words which exhibit left-dominance include ⟨váricòse, gládiàtor, fántasìse⟩. Some such forms can be accounted for by various sub-regularities. Others are truly exceptional.
23 Parametric accounts of a wide variety of stress systems are provided by, for example, Hayes (1980) and Halle and Vergnaud (1987).
24 This phenomenon, sometimes known as Pre-vocalic Tensing (SPE: 74–5), shows up in root-level alternations such as ⟨formula–formulaic, impious–pious⟩. For discussion of the dialect differences, see Halle and Mohanan (1985: 80 ff).
25 See also Aoun (1979).
26 Vergnaud (1982).
27 The formulation in (16b) is based on Kaye (1990a).
28 The other effect of onset maximization is to ensure that the first C of a VCCV sequence is only syllabified in a coda if it cannot form a branching onset with the second C; hence ⟨taw.dry⟩ as opposed to* ⟨tawd.ry⟩. This effect is derivable, not by Coda Licensing, but

by means of a principle, to be discussed below, which regulates the ability of different segment-types to occur in inter-constituent (and other) contexts.

29　The following discussion of domain-final consonants and syllable-structure typology draws heavily on Kaye (1990a).

30　The proposal that a final onset consonant is licensed by a following empty nucleus is due to Kaye, Lowenstamm and Vergnaud (1990).

31　Cf. Kaye (1990a: 324).

32　On the derivation of maximal binarity of constituents from the principles of strict directionality and locality, see Kaye, Lowenstamm and Vergnaud (1990).

33　Kaye, Lowenstamm and Vergnaud (1990) deny the existence of three-position rhymes. Thus for them the locality requirement must be satisfied within the constituent; it is not sufficient for a coda position to be licensed by a following onset.

34　See Myers (1991a) for recent discussion of this topic.

35　The notion that particular phonological properties can be unplaced with respect to other aspects of a representation is one of the major features of Firthian Prosodic Phonology. See Robins (1957) for a discussion of the relevant literature.

36　This is a more restricted application of the term **government** than that usually associated with Government Phonology (Kaye, Lowenstamm and Vergnaud 1990, Charette 1991). It coincides to some extent with the use of Rice (1992).

37　The proposal to extend Minimality to governing relations in phonology is due to Charette (1989). The relevant clause of the Minimality Condition, as first formulated by Chomsky (1986b: 42), is as follows:

In the configuration . . . α . . . [γ . . . δ . . . B . . .], α does not govern β if γ is the **immediate projection** of δ excluding α.

The other clause of the Condition prevents α in the above configuration from governing β, irrespective of the level of projection of γ. This cannot be allowed to apply to phonological relations, since it would forbid an onset head from governing a preceding coda.

38　The notion that melodic complexity determines occupancy of particular syllabic positions is explored by, among others, Kaye, Lowenstamm and Vergnaud (1990), Harris (1990c) and Rice (1992). The formulation and implementation of the Complexity Condition given here is from Harris (1990c), on which the following discussion is based.

39　As already noted in 2.4.2, reported counterexamples to the generalization that branching onsets consist of an obstruent plus liquid or glide reflect misanalyses based on the unfounded assumption that any word-initial consonant sequence automatically constitutes a well-formed onset. Such cases submit to alternative analyses in which the first of two consonants is either preceded or followed by an empty nuclear position (on which more in 4.7.8). Some supposed onsets can be shown to syllabify as coda-onset clusters, on a par with the *s*C pattern discussed at length in 2.4.2. One set of examples involves the word-initial *pt-* and *kt-* sequences of Ancient Greek (Kaye 1992). Others take the form of bogus clusters containing an intervening empty nucleus, such as in the word-initial sonorant-obstruent sequences of Polish (Gussmann and Kaye 1993) and the alleged onset geminates of Berber (Guerssel 1990).

40　Some languages, such as those of the southern Bantu group, do have onset *tl/dl*, but these are lateral affricates. That is, rather than occupying two positions, these sounds are contour segments consisting of two melodic expressions attached to a single skeletal point.

41 The fundamental insight behind the OCP is already present in the work of Bendor-Samuel (1960) and Leben (1973). The formulation of the principle, first proposed by Goldsmith (1976), has appeared in several versions, including the one given here based on McCarthy (1986). For other interpretations, see for example, Odden (1988) and Yip (1988b).

42 On this point, see now Goldsmith (1990: 309 ff).

43 The Complexity Condition on its own is unable to account for the non-occurrence of *ua* and *ia* in branching nuclei. We would expect these to be well-formed, since their level complexity profiles place them on a par with, say, *aw* and *ay*. (As noted in 2.4.3, the same melodic sequences do appear as contour segments within a non-branching nucleus, in which case they are often transcribed *wa*, *ya*.) A solution to this problem is offered by Kaye, Lowenstamm and Vergnaud (1985, 1990), who propose that each element possesses a value of a property known as **charm**. Among other things, this determines whether or not an element can appear in a governed position. The values are assigned in such a way that a lone **A** is ungovernable, while **I** and **U** are governable. One effect of this is to bar **A** from appearing in the complement position of a branching nucleus.

44 The term is Goldsmith's (1989), in recognition of Prince's (1984) observations on such languages.

45 The stop contrast, recall, is restricted to heavy rhymes, i.e. those in which the coda is doubly licensed, as in (23). More on this below.

46 It is still necessary to account for the distributional asymmetry whereby coronal plosives are excluded from coda position (*-tk-*, *-tp-*, etc.). According to a feature-based proposal by Yip (1991), this effect can be derived by assuming that coronals are underspecified for place at the point in derivation at which phonotactic constraints operate. One of these constraints takes the form of a rule which associates a lexical place value to the first segment in a stop-C cluster. Since coronals are unspecified at this point, the relevant value can only be labial or velar – hence *p*C or *k*C. If the following C is unspecified for place, it receives a coronal value by a later default rule – hence *pt* or *pk*.

The rule referring to stop-C clusters is of course arbitrary, but the basic insight – that coronals in some sense lack an active place component – is worthy of serious consideration. Carrying the notion over to element theory would result in the radical move of dispensing with the coronal element **R** altogether. This would of course require a thoroughgoing reappraisal of how melodic contrasts should be represented in the theory. (For some preliminary suggestions along these lines, see Backley 1993.) Such a revision would, however, offer a possible solution to the distributional asymmetry in question.

Lacking a place element would mean that coronals would be less complex and hence more governable than other place-types. At first sight, this might seem to yield the wrong result. Being of relatively low complexity, coronals might be expected to be **more** likely to occur in codas than other types – the opposite of the attested pattern. However, their very placelessness in such a position would render them susceptible to place-sharing with the following governing onset. In other words, we would never encounter an independent *t* in a coda, for the reason that such a segment would always be submerged under a geminate. According to this analysis, noting that English lacks *tk*/*tp* clusters is just another way of saying that the language lacks geminates. The implications of this speculative account remain to be thoroughly investigated.

47 Kaye, Lowenstamm and Vergnaud (1990) express this restriction in terms of the notion of charm alluded to in note 43. According to their proposal, the particular charm value

associated with laryngeally specified segments excludes them from governed positions, including codas and onset complements.

48 As least in terms of its templatic orientation, this view of syllabification is in line with the work of McCarthy (1979), Selkirk (1982b), Itô (1986) and others, discussed in 2.5.

49 Clements and Keyser (1983: 107 ff).

50 In fact, according to one earlier linear analysis, the historical *h* is lexically retained in *h-aspiré* words and deleted once it has fulfilled its function of blocking vowel deletion (Selkirk and Vergnaud 1973).

51 For an example of this analysis, see Keyser and O'Neill (1985: ch. 4).

52 The idea that a lexically empty position can be phonetically interpreted as the neutral element is due to Kaye (1990b).

53 This particular OCP-based constraint evidently only operates within as opposed to across independent analytic domains. Thus it blocks consecutive occurrences of a segment-type α from appearing within the same word-level domain, whether this comprises (a) a single domain (*[. . . α α . . .]); or (b) a domain that includes a bound morpheme (as in *[[. . . α] α . . .]). (See 1.4.3 for discussion of the different bracketing patterns.) (b) corresponds to the configuration in forms of the ⟨voted⟩ type. The purview of the constraint does not extend to consecutive occurrences of α which appear in separate independent domains: [. . . α] [α . . .]. Thus, there is no restriction against identical or similar segments appearing on both sides of a word boundary, as illustrated by collocations such as ⟨bad dog, bad timing, toss some, phase six⟩.

54 Data from Hoijer (1946) and Kenstowicz and Kisseberth (1979).

55 The sensitivity of this type of vowel syncope to word frequency has been investigated by Hooper (1976).

56 The term **super-foot** is due to Selkirk (1980).

57 This is, for example, the southern English pattern (Wells 1982: 165 ff).

58 Hooper (1978), for example, claims that resyllabification in all of these cases produces syllable-initial clusters.

59 See Barry and Grice (1991) on the difficulty of distinguishing the different variants in the acoustic signal.

60 The data are from Hooper (1978), supplemented by some of my own. Hooper proposes a resyllabification analysis in which vowel syncope is sensitive to the sonority relations between the flanking consonants.

   Of the forms in (50c), those containing a fricative in either of the flanking positions seem rather more likely to permit syncope. In at least one case, ⟨med(i)cine⟩, the syncopated variant of is quite usual for many speakers.

61 Kahn (1976), Selkirk (1982b), Borowsky (1986).

62 The literature abounds with examples, including the resyllabification analysis of vowel syncope discussed above and several other analyses to be reviewed below.

   T. Mohanan's (1989) analysis of Malayalam syllable structure might seem to be exceptional in this respect. According to her proposal, codas are permitted underlyingly in the language but are then disallowed at later stages of derivation. The discrepancy, she claims, is motivated to account for different sets of facts which call for apparently contradictory syllabification. The changeover from one type of syllabification to another is signalled by a transformation which moves underlying coda consonants into a following onset. This does seem to imply a situation in which constraints increase in restrictiveness during derivation. In our terms, the parameter which permits branching rhymes is switched from the marked ON setting to OFF.

However, the proposal turns out to resemble the familiar type of analysis in which constraints become progressively relaxed in the course of derivation. Allowing consonants to be resyllabified into onsets in Malayalam can only be achieved at the expense of completely overturning otherwise universal sonority-sequencing constraints (complexity effects in our terms). This is illustrated by putative restructurings such as *cam.pa* → *ca.mpa* 'jasmine', *bʰak.t/i* → *bʰa.kt/i* 'devotion', *ḍab.ba* → *ḍa.bba* 'tin can'. In other words, after resyllabification there are essentially no restrictions on what constitutes an onset in the language. A principle-based approach to the same set of facts would call for a radically different analysis.

63 Kiparsky (1985), Borowsky (1986: 12 ff), Myers (1991b).
64 On this point, see Kaye (1990a) and Harris (1992b).
65 See for example van Riemsdijk and Williams (1986: 251 ff).
66 The application of the Structure Preservation Principle to prosodic licensing is originally due to Selkirk (1982b). Kaye, Lowenstamm and Vergnaud (1990) express the notion in terms of the phonological instantiation of the Projection Principle. In the phonological literature, the term **structure preservation** has also been used in the rather different sense of imposing restrictions on the combinability of feature values within a single melodic expression, without regard to sequential position (e.g. Kiparsky 1985). We touched on this notion in 1.4.2.
67 This view is explicitly espoused by, for example, Itô (1986).
68 Other examples include Moroccan Arabic (Kaye 1990b), French (Charette 1991) and Polish (Gussmann and Kaye 1993).
69 Kaye (1990b), Charette (1991).
70 Mohanan (1985).
71 This is essentially the analysis proposed by Brockhaus (1992) for the same general pattern in standard German.
72 For a useful summary and discussion of the ECP, see Haegeman (1991: ch. 8). On the phonological implementation of the principle, see especially Kaye (1990b) and Charette (1991).
73 More accurately, it is a particular type of empty category that blocks contraction, namely PRO. For discussion and analysis of this phenomenon, see van Riemsdijk and Williams (1986: 149 ff).
74 Data on Systems A and B are drawn from Leslie (1983) and Harris and Kaye (1990). Material relating to System C is widely available in the literature (e.g. Kahn 1976, Kiparsky 1979, Selkirk 1982b, Harris and Kaye 1990). System-D data are from Harris (1990c).
75 See Leslie (1989) on this point.
76 The merger is by no means complete, since in some cases a durational difference in the preceding vowel provides evidence of the original distinction. This is illustrated by the famous ⟨rider–writer⟩ example; in most tapping dialects, the former word retains a relatively longer stressed vowel than does the latter.
77 See for example Wells (1982: 260 ff).
78 This is true of London Vernacular English (Sivertsen 1960).
79 For discussions of how *t*-lenition operates differently within foot-level and word-level prosodic domains, see Leslie (1983) and Harris and Kaye (1990).
80 On this pattern of stress shift, see for example Liberman and Prince (1977).
81 Some System-A dialects show the effects of a special development whereby word-final *t* alternates with approximant *r* (identical to that in ⟨berry⟩) after a short vowel, e.g. ⟨ge[ɹ] off⟩. See Wells (1982: 370).

82 The use of this conjunction is typical of a large number of linear analyses of various phenomena. For examples, see the references in James Harris (1983: ch. 3).

83 For the arguments, see for example Kahn (1976) and James Harris (1983).

84 ibid.

85 Coda Capture is in all essential details equivalent to Kahn's Rule III (1976: 48), which forms part of his analysis of tapping in a system of type C. Adaptations of his approach include Leslie's (1983) account of glottalling systems. Gussenhoven (1986) treats English oral stop allophony in similar terms.

86 This is equivalent to Kahn's Rule V (1976: 53).

87 Kahn's versions of these rules are respectively Flap and Glottalization (1976: 99–100).

88 Although Kahn's (1976) characterization of syllable structure is not identical to that given here, the differences do not materially affect the presentation of his analysis. For example, his representations contain syllable nodes lacking internal constituency.

89 For arguments against ambisyllabicity, see for example Selkirk (1982b).

90 The spirit of this analysis is already present in Stampe (1973). The execution of the analysis, as well as its extension to other aspects of English plosive allophony, is essentially the work of Selkirk (1982b), subsequently adopted by others including Borowsky (1986).

91 In its essentials, this is the version formulated by Borowsky (1986: 265).

92 This rule is not actually formalized by Selkirk (1982b) but can be extrapolated from her discussion.

93 Selkirk (1982b: 373).

94 See Harris (1992b) for a summary and discussion of some of the classic examples.

95 A case in point is Lardil (Australia), frequently cited as a language in which non-coronal consonants fail to appear in either internal codas or final position. This, it has been proposed, can be accounted for by a single condition which bars the feature [- coronal] from associating to a coda position (Itô 1986: 84 ff). In fact, the sets of consonants permitted in each context are not identical. Internal codas are restricted to (coronal) liquids (as in *piṇen* 'woman', *relka* 'head') or nasals which, if not coronal, must be place-linked to a following onset (e.g. *kuŋka* 'groin', *tjempe* 'mother's father') (data from Kenstowicz and Kisseberth 1979: 109ff). Final position also only permits coronals; however, this set includes not only liquids and nasals (e.g. *yalul* 'flame', *yaraman* 'horse') but also, unlike internal codas, plosives (e.g. *yarput* 'snake, bird'). This pattern certainly demonstrates the special status of coronals as well as the special autosegmental licensing properties of the two contexts. However, it fails to indicate that the contexts necessarily have the same constituent status.

96 See Vergnaud (1982) and Gussmann and Kaye (1993) for discussion. Formally, this operation is somewhat akin to a notion made available in other frameworks, in which a consonant is extra-metrical whenever it occurs domain-finally (as in ⟨get⟩) but loses its extra-metrical status once it appears domain-internally (in this case within the phrase containing ⟨get a⟩). See for example Itô (1986).

97 Another widespread hiatus-filler is the glottal stop, as in ⟨too [ʔ]early. This example belongs to a class of phenomena, referred to in 3.3.5, which present a challenge to the view that all processes have a local cause. Specifically, they involve the apparently spontaneous appearance of melodic material which has no obvious local source. Why it should be ʔ rather than some other element that emerges in the onset context is something of a mystery.

98 Thanks to Nikee Ola for the Yoruba data.

99 See for example Charette (1991: 90).

100 This discussion of Licensing Inheritance is based on Harris (1992b).

101 For a somewhat similar use of the notion licensing path, see Goldsmith (1990: 113 ff).
102 It seems reasonable to consider vowel syncope an extreme form of reduction. This suggests that Proper Government, which defines the conditions under which syncope occurs, must be viewed as independent of licensing between nuclei on the foot and word projections. Proper Government may be thought of as a mechanism which completely guts a position of its ability to license melodic material.
103 Luelsdorff (1975: 67–8).
104 This analysis is proposed by Brockhaus (1992), with exemplification from German, Polish and Catalan.
105 This is the proposal advanced, for example, by Borowsky (1986).
106 The following analysis develops the accounts proposed in Harris (1990c) and Harris and Kaye (1990).
107 On Stray Erasure and the question of where it operates in derivation, see for example Steriade (1982) and Itô (1986).
108 For discussions of this principle, see for example Mascaró (1976), Kiparsky (1982a) and Halle and Mohanan (1985).
109 The mechanism by which Itô (1986) derives the independence of failure to link and Stray Erasure is rather different to what is presented here. For her, the question of whether a segment is erased or retained on a given cycle depends on whether or not it is licensed by extra-prosodicity within that domain.
110 Lass and Anderson (1975: ch. 5).
111 Fasold (1972), Neu (1980).
112 Kahn (1976: 99 ff), Selkirk (1982b: 373), Leslie (1983).
113 The choice between optional and obligatory syncope is not peculiar to the context under discussion here, i.e. one where the consonant on the left of the syncope site is *t/d*, while that on the right is a resonant. The same pattern is also evident in a form such as ⟨ev(e)ry⟩, in which syncope is obligatory for some speakers and optional for others.
114 These are four of seven phenomena which Wells (1990) analyses in coda terms.
115 Data from Alleyne (1980).

Chapter 5 Floating Sounds

1 A 1990 draft of this chapter circulated under the title 'The most imperfect of consonants'.
2 Walker (1791: 50).
3 Ibid (p. 50).
4 Accounts of A (my own native system) have been around in various forms for as long as there has been a scholarly tradition of English phonetics.
5 B is the standard southern British system recommended in the classic pronunciation guides such as Jones (1956) and Gimson (1962). However, as these authors acknowledge, most if not all native speakers of southern British standard actually use some version of System C.
6 I have collected the System-C data myself, but they can easily be verified in any number of works, including Wells (1982: 222 ff). For reports on intrusive *r* in the United States, see Kurath and McDavid (1961: ch. 2) and McCarthy (1991).
7 Non-rhotic System D lies at the 'deep vernacular' end of the Southern United States dialect continuum. The data are based primarily on my own observations, supported by reports by, among others, Bailey (1969) and Wells (1982).

8 Detailed information regarding the social distribution of competing rhotic and non-rhotic variants is available for several areas. See especially Labov's (1966) study of New York City. For summaries of the regional distribution of this variable in the eastern United States, see Kurath and McDavid (1961); for England, see Wells 1982 (vol. 2).

9 Wells (1982: 367 ff).

10 Sledd (1966).

11 In some dialects, *r* fails to show up in onsets occupied by *θ*. Hence forms such as ⟨th⟨ee, th⟨ow. This is true, for instance, of some otherwise System-D dialects in the southern United States (Bailey 1969: 189) as well of some (System-A) dialects in Ireland.

12 This is by no means true of all non-rhotic dialects. In some Caribbean varieties, the in-gliding *iə* vowel of BEARD can merge with that in BADE. This is the pattern in, for example, non-rhotic Jamaican English (Cassidy and LePage 1967). In some north-eastern United States dialects, there is a potential merger between the BEARD nucleus and the in-gliding reflex of historical short *æ* in BAD (Labov, Yaeger and Steiner 1972).

13 For early discussion of this issue, see Sledd (1966).

14 The type of case illustrated in (9d) is apparently only possible when a close pragmatic or stylistic relationship holds between the two sentences. For discussion of the prosodic domains within which *r*-sandhi operates, see Nespor and Vogel (1986: 234 ff).

15 According to Wells, the appearance of intrusive *r* after the PAW vowel is more likely to raise hackles than it does in other contexts (1982: 225). It may be necessary to recognize a variant of System C in which intrusive *r* occurs after *æ* (⟨ma[r] and pa⟩) or schwa (⟨idea[r] of⟩) but not after the PAW vowel (*⟨saw[r] it⟩). On this point, see Gimson (1962: 204).

16 In its essential details, this is the rule proposed by, among others, Kahn (1976: 23), Wells (1982: 218 ff) and Gussmann (1980: 38).

17 Kahn (1976: 23).

18 For example, Sledd (1966).

19 Wells (1982: 557).

20 This is essentially the rule proposed for System-B dialects by, among others, Kahn (1976: 109) and Mohanan (1986: 36).

21 Kenstowicz and Kisseberth (1979: ch. 3).

22 Mohanan adopts a more restricted form of Onset Capture which applies only to *r* (1986: 36).

23 The wrong result here is due to the **counter-bleeding** order of R-Dropping and Onset Capture. The desired ordering relation would be one of **bleeding**; in applying first, Onset Capture would remove forms such as ⟨barring⟩ from the purview of R-Dropping.

24 C is, however, like B in displaying the contrast at the end of certain **roots**; compare ⟨sphe⟨e–sphe[r]ical⟩ with ⟨formula–formula[∅]ic⟩. More on this anon.

25 Nespor and Vogel seem to ignore this point when they claim that *r*-sandhi in both System B and C can be treated as *r*-insertion (1986: 228). Such an arrangement derives intrusive *r*, correctly in C but erroneously in B.

26 Some have argued that deletion and insertion co-exist within an intrusive-*r* grammar. According to one version of this view, these take the form of independent rules – R-Dropping, which derives the zero variant of etymological linking *r*, and *r*-insertion, which derives unetymological intrusive *r* (e.g. Gussmann 1980: 34 ff, Lodge 1984: 12 ff). This proposal seems to be founded on the erroneous assumption that linking *r* is obligatory, while intrusive *r* is optional. In fact, speakers who variably suppress unetymological *r* are also observed to suppress the etymological variant. This indicates that the two reflexes are non-distinct for such speakers.

According to an alternative proposal (McCarthy 1991), deletion and epenthesis co-occur in intrusive-*r* dialects not as autonomous rules but as different effects of a single symmetrical rule ('*r* alternates with ∅'). The selection of alternants is guided by separate output constraints. One of these filters out coda *r*; another, which amounts to a bar on hiatus, is satisfied by the appearance of sandhi *r*. The etymological provenance of the latter is irrelevant under this analysis. The formulation of the anti-hiatus constraint is, however, somewhat problematical (see note 41).

27 This argument is widely repeated in the literature; see, for example, Wells (1982: 222 ff) and Trudgill (1986: 71 ff).
28 This is essentially the formulation given by, for example, Wells (1982: 226) and Nespor and Vogel (1986: 228–9).
29 In intrusive-*r* dialects, the contrast between historically *r*-ful and *r*-less forms survives in a number of root-level alternations. Thus *r* occurs in one alternant of pairs such as ⟨sphere–sphe[r]ical, explore–explo[r]ation, clear–clea[r]ance⟩ but not in, say, ⟨formula–formulaic, algebra–algebraic⟩. The insertion analysis runs into trouble, if it assumed that root-level alternations are derived by phonological process. As formulated in (23) or (24), the *r*-insertion rule would be unable to deal with alternations such as ⟨satire–sati[r]ical, admire–admi[r]ation, aspire–aspi[r]ation⟩. In these cases, discussed by Gussmann (1980: 34 ff), the vowel preceding the supposedly epenthetic *r* is high, not non-high as required by the rule.
30 A version of this rule is provided by Kahn (1976: 111).
31 Broadbent (1991), McCarthy (1991).
32 A rather more appealing alternative is to assume that sandhi *r* has its source in the preceding non-high vowel itself. According to one such proposal, *r* is the onset manifestation of an expression consisting of head @ and dependent **A**, the latter spreading from a preceding nucleus (Broadbent 1991).
33 The floating treatment of English *r*-sandhi is in the spirit of related analyses proposed for other languages. The idea that a melodic unit can lack association to a skeletal point was originally applied to the phenomenon of floating tones (see, for example, Goldsmith 1976). Closer precedents for the analysis to be presented here are the treatments of French liaison consonants developed by Vergnaud (1982), Piggott and Singh (1985), Prunet (1986), Encrevé (1988) and Charette (1991). In Charette's analysis, for example, the form *kaʃe* ⟨chachet⟩ 'seal (noun)' contains a final floating *t* which is audible when it attaches to a following onset, as in *kaʃte* ⟨cacheter⟩ 'to seal' (1991: 188 ff).
34 As proposed by Vergnaud (1982).
35 The autosegmental docking metaphor is originally due to Goldsmith (1976).
36 The notion that, in non-rhotic systems, etymologically *r*-less forms have assimilated to the lexically *r*-ful pattern (rather than vice versa) is to be found, for example, in Gimson (1962: 92), Lindsey (1990) and Scobbie (1992).
37 Vennemann (1972b), Wells (1982: 222 ff), Trudgill (1986: 71 ff), McMahon (1992). For a critique of historical rule inversion, see McCarthy (1991) and Scobbie (1992).
38 There is certainly a widespread impression among the general public that intrusive *r* is a recent (and mostly unwelcome) innovation. An example: 'there is one recent development which needs hitting on the head. It is the revanchist expansion of our old enemy, the intrusive "r", . . . now pitching for end-vowels. This gives us most hideously the perversion of "draw" into "dror" and the subsequent scream-inducing "droring"' (Edward Pearce, 'Unspoken shifts in the spoken word', *The Guardian* (Manchester and London), 3 October 1990). The notion that System C is a recent off-shoot of B is taken for granted in much of the phonological literature; see for example the references in the previous note.

39 Sheridan (1762: 34).

40 The phenomenon is sometimes referred to as **hyper-rhoticity** (Wells 1982: 221–2, Trudgill 1986: 74 ff). In such systems, the appearance of *r* in, say, ⟨comma[r]⟩ is not restricted to sandhi contexts, which indicates that it has a lexical source (as opposed to being inserted). In this respect, hyper-rhotic dialects are similar to non-rhotic intrusive-*r* dialects, as will become clear below.

41 The proposal that System C is subject to some kind of word-structure constraint is also made by McCarthy (1991). His solution takes the form of a filter which places an embargo on final 'vowels' in intrusive-*r* dialects. The term **vowel** in his formulation (*V]$_{\text{word}}$) is an informal reference to a nuclear position occupied by other than a high vocalic segment. In other words, it is a re-statement of the left-hand environment of the R-Epenthesis rule in (24). Words ending in *i/y* or *u/w* are licit, as in ⟨see, day, too, go⟩. The constraint triggers *r*-insertion in words ending in non-high vowels such as *ə, a:* or *ɔ:*. This analysis is only valid for dialects with up-gliding diphthongs in DAY (e.g. *ey*) and GO (e.g. *ow*). It cannot account for intrusive-*r* dialects in which the corresponding nuclei are occupied by the mid monophthongs *e:* and *o:* (such as the northern English varieties described in 3.3.6). The second portion of these monophthongs, being non-high, qualifies as a 'vowel' in McCarthy's sense. It should thus be expected to give rise to intrusive *r*. This is not the case. As noted in 3.3.2, *e:* and *o:* behave like *ey* and *ow* in yielding respectively *y* and *w* glides in hiatus; hence *de: yəv* ⟨day of⟩, *so: wə* ⟨so a⟩.

42 The contrastive possibilities diminish to one or two vocalic contrasts in unstressed contexts, as in the final vowels of words such as ⟨rapid, abbot, ribbon⟩. But this is a function of the prosodic weakness of the nucleus within the foot and has nothing to do with the presence or absence of a following consonant.

43 For the details of this regularity, which figures in exercise V of chapter 1, see Aitken (1981) and Lass (1974).

44 Surveys of pre-*r* vocalic systems, including those illustrated here, include Kurath and McDavid (1961: ch. 4), Wells (1982: 153 ff) and Kreidler (1989: 52 ff). Some very approximate examples of the geographical spread of the different sub-systems in (40): (40a) (i) Ireland, (ii) England, North America; (40b) (i) eastern New England, metropolitan New York, the Upper South, rural Ireland, (ii) some central areas of the eastern United States, (iii) western Pennsylvania and points west; (40c) (i) Ireland, (ii) parts of the southern United States, (iii) most of the northeastern United States apart from New England.

45 Sledd (1966), Wells (1982: 213 ff).

46 Wells's (1982) survey of different vocalic systems before historical *r* includes a particularly clear discussion of this issue.

47 Fromkin (1973: 251–2).

48 Ibid.

49 More recent proposals for nuclear *r* include those of Selkirk (1982b) and Mohanan (1986: 37 ff).

50 Ladefoged (1982: 78).

51 Sledd (1966).

52 The neutral element must be assumed to be the head of the expression defining dark approximant *r*. This follows from the element's inability to contribute to the phonetic interpretation of any expression in which it occurs as a dependent (see 3.3.5).

53 This is a formalization of an observation made, for example, by Kenyon and Knott (1953: xix–xx). For a related analysis, see Clements and Keyser (1983: 32). In non-

rhotic dialects, the cognate vowel in non-alternating contexts (as in *bəːn* ⟨burn⟩, where historical *r* is unrecoverable) should presumably be represented as follows:

54 The idea that the minimal word can be prosodically defined is due to McCarthy and Prince (1986). According to the interpretation of the notion given here, both CVV and CVC forms satisfy the requirement that words in English minimally contain two nuclear positions. In a CVV word such as ⟨see⟩, the two positions occur within the same nucleus. A CVC word such as ⟨pit⟩ is well-formed for the same reason that disyllabic ⟨pity⟩ is. Both these words contain two nuclear positions, the first of which is occupied by the short vowel *ɪ*. In the case of ⟨pity⟩, the second nuclear position is the one occupied by the unstressed vowel. In the case of ⟨pit⟩, the relevant position is the parametrically licensed final empty nucleus.

55 Again see the surveys in Kurath and McDavid (1961) and Wells (1982).

56 The dialect in question is the Atlanta system described by Sledd (1958), to whom I also owe the title of this exercise (1966).

References

Abercrombie, David (1967). *Elements of General Phonetics*. Edinburgh: Edinburgh University Press.

Aitken, A. J. (1981). The Scottish vowel-length rule. In M. Benskin and M.L. Samuels (eds), *So Mony People Longages and Tonges: philological essays in Scots and mediaeval English presented to Angus McIntosh*, 131–57. Edinburgh: Middle English Dialect Project.

Aitken, A. J. (1984a). Scots and English in Scotland. In Trudgill 1984, 517–32.

Aitken, A. J. (1984b). Scottish dialects and accents. In Trudgill 1984, 94–114.

Allen, Margaret (1978). Morphological investigations. Ph.D. dissertation, University of Connecticut.

Alleyne, Mervyn C. (1980). *Comparative Afro-American: an historical-comparative study of English-based Afro-American dialects of the New World*. Ann Arbor: Karoma.

Anderson, John M. (1986). Suprasegmental dependencies. In Durand 1986, 55–133.

Anderson, John M. and Jacques Durand (eds) (1987). *Explorations in Dependency Phonology*. Foris: Dordrecht.

Anderson, John M. and Colin J. Ewen (1980). Introduction: a sketch of Dependency Phonology. In John M. Anderson and Colin J. Ewen (eds), *Studies in Dependency Phonology*. Ludwigsburg Studies in Language and Linguistics 4. Ludwigsburg: University of Ludwigsburg.

Anderson, John M. and Colin J. Ewen (1987). *Principles of Dependency Phonology*. Cambridge: Cambridge University Press.

Anderson, John M. and Charles Jones (1974). Three theses concerning phonological representations. *Journal of Linguistics* 10. 1–26.

Anderson, John M. and Charles Jones (1977). *Phonological Structure and the History of English*. Amsterdam: North-Holland.

Anderson, Stephen R. (1978). Tone features. In Victoria Fromkin (ed.), *Tone: a linguistic anthology*, 133–75. New York: Academic Press.

Anderson, Stephen R. (1982). The analysis of French schwa; or, how to get something from nothing. *Language* 58. 534–73.

Anderson, Stephen R. (1985). *Phonology in the Twentieth Century*. Chicago: University of Chicago Press.

Aoun, Joseph (1979). Is the syllable or the supersyllable a constituent? *MIT Working Papers in Linguistics* 1. 140–8.

Archangeli, Diana (1984). *Underspecification in Yawelmani Phonology and Morphology*. PhD dissertation, MIT. Published 1988, New York: Garland.

Archangeli, Diana (1988). Aspects of Underspecification Theory. *Phonology* 5. 183–205.

Archangeli, Diana and Douglas Pulleyblank (1992). Grounded phonology. MS. University of Arizona and University of British Columbia.

Aronoff, Mark and Richard T. Oerhle (eds) (1984). *Language and Sound Structure: studies in phonology presented to Morris Halle by his teacher and students*. Cambridge, MA: MIT Press.

Avery, Peter and Keren Rice (1989). Segment structure and coronal underspecification. *Phonology* 6. 179–200.

Backley, Phillip (1993). Coronal: the undesirable element. *UCL Working Papers in Linguistics* 5. 301–23.

Bailey, Charles-James N. (1969). Introduction to Southern States phonetics: chapters 5 and 6. *University of Hawaii Working Papers in Linguistics* 6. 105–203.

Barry, William and Martine Grice (1991). Auditory and visual factors in speech database analysis. *Speech, Hearing and Language: Work in Progress* 5. 9–32. London: Department of Phonetics and Linguistics, University College London.

Bell, A. and J. B. Hooper (eds) (1978). *Syllables and Segments*. Amsterdam: North-Holland.

Bendor-Samuel, J. T. (1960). Some problems of segmentation in the phonological analysis of Terena. *Word* 16. 348–55. Reprinted in Palmer 1970, 214–21.

Benincà, Paola (ed.) (1989). *Dialect Variation and the Theory of Grammar*. Dordrecht: Foris.

Bird, Steven and Ewan Klein (1990). Phonological events. *Journal of Linguistics* 26. 33–56.

Bloomfield, Leonard (1933). *Language*. New York: Holt.

Booij, Geert and Jerzy Rubach (1987). Postcyclic versus postlexical rules in lexical phonology. *Linguistic Inquiry* 18. 1–44.

Borowsky, Toni J. (1984). On resyllabification in English. In M. Wescoat (ed.), *Proceedings of the West Coast Conference on Formal Linguistics* 3, 1–15. Stanford, CA: Stanford Linguistics Association.

Borowsky, Toni J. (1986). Topics in the lexical phonology of English. PhD dissertation, University of Massachusetts.

Borowsky, Toni J. (1989). Structure Preservation and the syllable coda in English. *Natural Language and Linguistic Theory* 7. 145–66.

Braine, Martin D.S. (1974). On what might constitute learnable phonology. *Language* 50. 270–99.

Broadbent, Judith (1991). Linking and intrusive *r* in English. *UCL Working Papers in Linguistics* 3. 281–302.

Brockhaus, Wiebke G. (1992). Final devoicing: principles and parameters. PhD dissertation, University College London.

Brockhaus, Wiebke G. (in press). Skeleton and suprasegmental structure within Government Phonology. To appear in Durand and Katamba, in press.

Brody, Michael (1992). A note on the organization of grammar. *UCL Working Papers in Linguistics* 4. 3–9.

Bromberger, Sylvain and Morris Halle (1988). Why phonology is different. *Linguistic Inquiry* 20. 51–70.

Carr, Philip (1993). *Phonology*. London: Macmillan.

Cassidy, F. G. and R. B. LePage (1967). *Dictionary of Jamaican English*. Cambridge: Cambridge University Press.

Charette, Monik (1989). The minimality condition in phonology. *Journal of Linguistics* 25. 159–87.

Charette, Monik (1991). *Conditions on Phonological Government*. Cambridge: Cambridge University Press.

Charette, Monik (1992). Mongolian and Polish meet Government Licensing. *SOAS Working Papers in Linguistics and Phonetics* 2. 275–92.

Charette, Monik and Jonathan Kaye (1993). The death of ATR. Ms. School of Oriental and African Languages, University of London.

Chene, E. B. de and S. R. Anderson (1987). Compensatory lengthening. *Language* 55. 505–35.

Chomsky, Noam (1964). *Current Issues in Linguistic Theory*. The Hague: Mouton.

Chomsky, Noam (1965). *Aspects of the Theory of Syntax*. Cambridge, MA: MIT Press.

Chomsky, Noam (1981). *Lectures on Government and Binding*. Dordrecht: Foris.

Chomsky, Noam (1986a). *Knowledge of Language: its nature, origin and use*. New York: Praeger.

Chomsky, Noam (1986b). *Barriers*. Cambridge, MA: MIT Press.

Chomsky, Noam (1992). A minimalist program for linguistic theory. *MIT Occasional Papers in Linguistics* 1.

Chomsky, Noam and Morris Halle (1968). *The Sound Pattern of English*. New York: Harper and Row.

Clements, George N. (1981). Akan vowel harmony: a nonlinear analysis. In George N. Clements (ed.), *Harvard Studies in Phonology* 2, 108–77.

Clements, George N. (1985). The geometry of phonological features. *Phonology Yearbook* 2. 223–50.

Clements, George N. (1987). Phonological feature representation and the description of intrusive stops. *CLS 23, Part 2: parasession on autosegmental and metrical phonology*, 29–50.

Clements, George N. (1991a). Place of articulation in consonants and vowels: a unified theory. *Working Papers of the Cornell Phonetics Laboratory* 5. 77–123.

Clements, George N. (1991b). Vowel height assimilation in Bantu languages. *Working Papers of the Cornell Phonetics Laboratory* 5. 37–76.

Clements, George N. and Susan R. Hertz (1991). Nonlinear phonology and acoustic interpretation. *Proceedings of the XIIth International Congress of Phonetic Sciences*, vol. 1/5, 364–73. Provence: Université de Provence.

Clements, George N. and Elizabeth V. Hume (in press). Segment structure. To appear in Goldsmith, in press.

Clements, George N. and Samuel Jay Keyser (1983). *CV Phonology: a generative theory of the syllable*. Cambridge, MA: MIT Press.

Cornyn, William S. (1964). Outline of Burmese grammar. *Language* 20, Supplement: Language Dissertations, vol. 38.

Coulmas, Florian (1989). *The Writing Systems of the World*. Oxford: Blackwell.

den Dikken, Marcel and Harry van der Hulst (1988). Segmental hierarchitecture. In van der Hulst and Smith 1988, Part I, 1–78.

Dobson, E. J. (1968). *English Pronunciation 1500–1700*. vol. 2, 2nd edn. Oxford: Clarendon Press.

Durand, Jacques (ed.) (1986). *Dependency and Non-Linear Phonology*. London: Croom Helm.

Durand, Jacques (1990). *Generative and Non-Linear Phonology*. Harlow, Essex: Longman.

Durand, Jacques and Francis Katamba (eds) (in press). *Frontiers of Phonology Atoms, structures and derivations. Harlow*, Essex: Longman.

Einarsson, S. (1945). *Icelandic Grammar, Texts, Glossary*. Baltimore: John Hopkins Press.

Ekwall, Eilert (1975). *A History of Modern English Sounds and Morphology*. Translated and edited by Alan Ward. Oxford: Blackwell.

Encrevé, P. (1988). *La Liaison avec et sans enchaînement: phonologie tridimensionnelle et usages du français*. Paris: Editions du Seuil.

Ewen, Colin J. (in press). Dependency relations in phonology. To appear in Goldsmith, in press.

Ewen, Colin J. and Harry van der Hulst (1988). [high], [low] and [back] or [I], [A] and [U]. In P. Coopmans and A. Hulk (eds), *Linguistics in the Netherlands 1988*, 51-60. Dordrecht: Foris.

Fabb, Nigel (1988). English suffixation is constrained only by selectional restrictions. *Natural Language and Linguistic Theory* 6. 527–39.

Farid, M. Onn (1980). *Aspects of Malay Phonology and Morphology: a generative approach*. Bangi: Universiti Kebangsaan Malaysia.

Fasold, Ralph (1972). *Tense Marking in Black English*. Arlington, VA: Center for Applied Linguistics.

Ferguson, Charles (1972). 'Short *a*' in Philadelphia English. In M. E. Smith (ed.), *Studies in Linguistics in Honor of George L. Trager*, 259–74. The Hague: Mouton.

Fischer-Jørgensen, Eli (1975). *Trends in Phonological Theory*. Copenhagen: Academisk Forlag.

Foley, James (1977). *Foundations of Theoretical Phonology*. Cambridge: Cambridge University Press.

Fourakis, M. and R. Port (1986). Stop epenthesis in English. *Research in Phonetics and Computational Linguistics* 5, 37–71. Bloomington, IN: Indiana University.

Fromkin, Victoria A. (1973). A sample of speech errors. In Victoria A. Fromkin (ed.), *Speech Errors as Linguistic Evidence*, 243–69. The Hague: Mouton.

Fudge, Eric C. (1967). The nature of phonological primes. *Journal of Linguistics* 3. 1–36.

Fudge, Eric C. (1969). Syllables. *Journal of Linguistics* 5. 253–86.

Fudge, Eric C. (1984). *English Word-Stress*. London: Allen and Unwin.

Fudge, Eric C. (1987). Branching structure within the syllable. *Journal of Linguistics* 23. 359–77.

Fujimura, Osamu and Julie Lovins (1978). Syllables as concatenative phonetic units. In Bell and Hooper 1978, 107-20.

Giegerich, Heinz J. (1985). *Metrical Phonology and Phonological Structure: German and English*. Cambridge: Cambridge University Press.

Giegerich, Heinz J. (1992). *English Phonology: an introduction*. Cambridge: Cambridge University Press.

Gimson, A.C. (1962). *An Introduction to the Pronunciation of English*. London: Arnold.

Goldsmith, John A. (1976). *Autosegmental Phonology*. PhD dissertation, MIT. Published 1979, New York: Garland.

Goldsmith, John A. (1981). Subsegmentals in Spanish phonology: an autosegmental approach. In W. W. Cressey and D. J. Napoli (eds), *Linguistic Symposium on Romance Languages* 9, 1–16. Washington, DC: Georgetown University Press.

Goldsmith, John A. (1985). Vowel harmony in Khalkha Mongolian, Yaka, Finnish and Hungarian. *Phonology* 2. 251–74.

Goldsmith, John A. (1989). Licensing, inalterability and harmonic rule application. *CLS* 25. 145–56.

Goldsmith, John A. (1990). *Autosegmental and Metrical Phonology*. Oxford: Blackwell.

Goldsmith, John A. (ed.) (1993). *The Last Phonological Rule*. Chicago: University of Chicago Press.

Goldsmith, John (ed.) (in press). *A Handbook of Phonology*. Oxford: Blackwell.

Guerssel, Mohand (1990). On the syllabification pattern of Berber. Ms. Université du Québec à Montréal.

Gussenhoven, Carlos (1986). English plosive allophones and ambisyllabicity. *Gramma* 10. 119–41.

Gussmann, Edmund (1980). *Introduction to Phonological Analysis*. Warsaw: Państwowe Wydawnictwo Naukowe.

Gussmann, Edmund and Jonathan Kaye (1993). Polish notes from a Dubrovnik café. Ms. School of Oriental and African Studies, University of London.

Haegeman, Liliane (1991). *Introduction to Government and Binding Theory*. Oxford: Blackwell.

Halle, Morris (1959). *The Sound Pattern of Russian*. The Hague: Mouton.

Halle, Morris and G.N. Clements (1983). *Problem Book in Phonology*. Cambridge, MA: MIT Press.

Halle, Morris and K. P. Mohanan (1985). The segmental phonology of modern English. *Linguistic Inquiry* 16. 57-116.

Halle, Morris and Kenneth N. Stevens (1971). A note on laryngeal features. *Quarterly Progress Report of the Research Laboratory of Electronics* (MIT) 101. 198-213.

Halle, Morris and Jean-Roger Vergnaud (1980). Three-dimensional phonology. *Journal of Linguistic Research* 1. 83-105.

Halle, Morris and Jean-Roger Vergnaud (1987). *An Essay on Stress*. Cambridge, MA: MIT Press.

Harris, James (1980). Nonconcatenative morphology and Spanish plurals. *Journal of Linguistic Research* 1. 15-31.

Harris, James (1983). *Syllable Structure and Stress in Spanish*. Cambridge, MA: MIT Press.

Harris, John (1985). *Phonological Variation and Change*. Cambridge: Cambridge University Press.

Harris, John (1989). Towards a lexical analysis of sound change in progress. *Journal of Linguistics* 25. 35-56.

Harris, John (1990a). Derived phonological contrasts. In Ramsaran 1990, 87-105.

Harris, John (1990b). Reduction harmony. Paper presented at the 13th GLOW Phonology Workshop, London.

Harris, John (1990c). Segmental complexity and phonological government. *Phonology* 7. 255-300.

Harris, John (1992a). English goes west: on the trail of short *u*. Ms. University College London.

Harris, John (1992b). Licensing Inheritance. *UCL Working Papers in Linguistics* 4. 359-406.

Harris, John and Jonathan Kaye (1990). A tale of two cities: London glottalling and New York City tapping. *The Linguistic Review* 7. 251–74.

Harris, John and Geoff Lindsey (1992). Segmental decomposition and the signal. Paper presented at the 7th International Phonology Meeting, Krems, July 1992.

Harris, John and Geoff Lindsey (in press). The elements of phonological representation. To appear in Durand and Katamba, in press.

Hart, John (1569). *An Orthographie, Conteyning the Due Order and Reason Howe to Paint Thimage of Mannes Voice, Most Like to the Life or Nature*. Reprinted 1969, *English Linguistics 1500–1800*. Menston: Scholar Press.

Haudricourt, A.-G. (1961). Bipartition et tripartition des systèmes de tons dans quelques langues d'Extrême-Orient. *Bulletin de la Société de Linguistique de Paris* 56. 163–80.

Hayes, Bruce (1980). *A Metrical Theory of Stress Rules*. PhD dissertation, MIT. Published 1981, New York: Garland.

Hayes, Bruce (1982). Extrametricality and English stress. *Linguistic Inquiry* 13. 227–76.

Hayes, Bruce (1984). The phonetics and phonology of Russian voicing assimilation. In Aronoff and Oehrle 1984, 318–28.

Hayes, Bruce (1986). Inalterability in CV phonology. *Language* 62. 321–51.

Hayes, Bruce (1989). Compensatory lengthening in moraic phonology. *Linguistic Inquiry* 20. 253–306.

Hayes, Bruce (1990). Diphthongisation and coindexing. *Phonology* 7. 31–72.

Hayward, Dick (1984). *The Arbore Language: a first investigation*. Hamburg: Helmut Buske.

Hogg, Richard and C.B. McCully (1987). *Metrical Phonology: a coursebook*. Cambridge: Cambridge University Press.

Hoijer, H. (1946). Tonkawa. In *Linguistic Structures of Native America*. New York: Viking Fund Publications in Anthropology.

Hooper, Joan B. (1972). The syllable in phonological theory. *Language* 48. 525–40.

Hooper, Joan B. (1976). Word frequency in lexical diffusion and the source of morpho-phonological change. In W. Christie Jr (ed.), *Current Progress in Historical Linguistics*, 95–105. Amsterdam: North-Holland.

Hooper, Joan B. (1978). Constraints on schwa-deletion in American English. In Jacek Fisiak (ed.), *Recent Developments in Historical Phonology*, 183–207. The Hague: Mouton.

Hulst, Harry van der (1989). Atoms of segmental structure: components, gestures and dependency. *Phonology* 6. 253-84.

Hulst, Harry van der (in press). Radical CV phonology. To appear in Durand and Katamba, in press.

Hulst, Harry van der and Aone van Engelenhoven (1993). Metathesis effects in Tutukeian-Letinese. Paper presented at the First Holland Institute of Linguistics Conference in Phonology, January 1993.

Hulst, Harry van der and Norval Smith (1982a). An overview of autosegmental and metrical phonology. In van der Hulst and Smith 1982b, Part I, 1–46.

Hulst, Harry van der and Norval Smith (eds) (1982b). *The Structure of Phonological Representations*. Two parts. Dordrecht: Foris.

Hulst, Harry van der and Norval Smith (1985). Vowel features and umlaut in Djingili, Nyangumarda and Warlpiri. *Phonology* 2. 275–302.

Hulst, Harry van der and Norval Smith (eds) (1988). *Features, Segmental Structure and Harmony Processes*. Two parts. Dordrecht: Foris.

Hyman, Larry M. (1975). *Phonology: theory and analysis*. New York: Holt, Rinehart and Winston.

Hyman, Larry M. (1982). The representation of nasality in Gokana. In van der Hulst and Smith 1982b, Part I, 111–30.

Hyman, Larry M. (1985). *A Theory of Phonological Weight*. Dordrecht: Foris.

Itô, Junko (1986). *Syllabic Theory in Prosodic Phonology*. PhD dissertation, University of Massachussetts. Published 1988, New York: Garland.

Itô, Junko and R. Armin Mester (1986). The phonology of voicing in Japanese. *Linguistic Inquiry* 17. 49–73.

Jaeger, Jeri J. (1986). On the acquisition of abstract representations for English vowels. *Phonology* 3. 71–98.

Jakobson, Roman (1939). Observations sur le classement phonologique des consonnes. *Proceedings of the Third International Congress of Phonetic Sciences*. 31–41.

Jakobson, Roman and Morris Halle (1956). *Fundamentals of Language*. The Hague: Mouton.

Jakobson, Roman, Gunnar M. Fant and Morris Halle (1962). *Preliminaries to Speech Analysis*. Cambridge, MA: MIT Press.

Jespersen, Otto (1909). *A Modern English Grammar on Historical Principles, Part 1: sounds and spellings*. London: Allen and Unwin.

Jespersen, Otto (1913). *Lehrbuch der Phonetik*. Leipzig: Teubner.

Jones, Charles (1989). *A History of English Phonology*. Harlow, Essex: Longman.

Jones, Daniel (1956). *An Outline of English Phonetics*. 8th edn. Cambridge: Heffer.

Kahn, Daniel (1976). *Syllable-Based Generalizations in English Phonology*. PhD dissertation, MIT. Published 1980, New York: Garland.

Kaisse, Ellen M. and Patricia A. Shaw (1985). On the theory of Lexical Phonology. *Phonology Yearbook* 2. 1–30.

Katamba, Francis (1988). *An Introduction to Phonology*. Harlow, Essex: Longman.

Kaye, Jonathan (1985). On the syllable structure of certain West African languages. In Didier Goyvaerts (ed.), *African Linguistics: essays in memory of M.W.K. Semikenke*, 285–308. Amsterdam: John Benjamins.

Kaye, Jonathan (1989). *Phonology: a cognitive view*. Hillsdale, NJ: Lawrence Erlbaum.

Kaye, Jonathan (1990a). 'Coda' Licensing. *Phonology* 7. 301–30.

Kaye, Jonathan (1990b). Government in phonology: the case of Moroccan Arabic. *The Linguistic Review* 7. 131–59.

Kaye, Jonathan (1991). Head projection and indexation: a theory of reduplication. Paper presented at the 14th GLOW Colloquium, Leiden.

Kaye, Jonathan (1992). Do you believe in magic? The story of s+C sequences. *SOAS Working Papers in Linguistics and Phonetics* 2. 293–314.

Kaye, Jonathan and Jean Lowenstamm (1981). Syllable structure and markedness theory. In A. Belletti, L. Brandi and L. Rizzi (eds), *Theory of Markedness in Generative Grammar*, 287-316. Pisa: Scuola Normale Superiore.

Kaye, Jonathan and Jean Lowenstamm (1984). De la syllabicité. In François Dell, Daniel Hirst and Jean-Roger Vergnaud (eds), *Forme sonore du langage*, 123–59. Paris: Hermann.

Kaye, Jonathan, Jean Lowenstamm and Jean-Roger Vergnaud (1985). The internal structure of phonological elements: a theory of charm and government. *Phonology Yearbook* 2. 305–28.

Kaye, Jonathan, Jean Lowenstamm and Jean-Roger Vergnaud (1990). Constituent structure and government in phonology. *Phonology* 7. 193–232. Originally published 1989 as Konstituentenstruktur und Rektion in der Phonologie, *Linguistische Berichte* 114. 31–75.

Kaye, Jonathan and Jean-Roger Vergnaud (1990). Phonology, morphology and the lexicon. Paper presented at the 13th GLOW Colloquium, Cambridge, England.

Kean, Marie Louise (1975). The theory of markedness in generative grammar. PhD dissertation, MIT.

Kempson, Ruth (1988). Logical form: the grammar–cognition interface. *Journal of Linguistics* 24. 393–431.

Kenstowicz, Michael and Charles Kisseberth (1979). *Generative Phonology: description and theory*. New York: Academic Press.

Kenyon, J. S. (1958). *American Pronunciation*. 10th edn. Ann Arbor, MI: George Wahr.

Kenyon, J. S. and T. A. Knott (1953). *A Pronouncing Dictionary of American English*. Springfield, MA: Merriam.

Keyser, Samuel J. and Wayne O'Neill (1985). *Rule Generalization and Optionality in Language Change*. Dordrecht: Foris.

Kerswill, Paul E. (1987). Levels of linguistic variation in Durham. *Journal of Linguistics* 23. 25–49.

Kiparsky, Paul (1979). Metrical structure is cyclic. *Linguistic Inquiry* 8. 421–42.

Kiparsky, Paul (1981). Remarks on the metrical structure of the syllable. In W. U. Dressler, O. E. Pfeiffer and J. R. Rennison (eds), *Phonologica 1980: Akten aus den Vierten Internationalen Phonologie-Tagung, Wien*, 245–56. Innsbruck: Innsbrucker Beiträge zur Sprachwissenschaft.

Kiparsky, Paul (1982a). From Cyclic Phonology to Lexical Phonology. In van der Hulst and Smith 1982b, Part I, 131–75.

Kiparsky, Paul (1982b). *Explanation in Phonology*. Dordrecht: Foris.

Kiparsky, Paul (1985). Some consequences of Lexical Phonology. *Phonology* 2. 85–138.

Kiparsky, Paul (1992). Catalexis. Ms. Stanford University.

König, Werner (1978). *dtv-Atlas zur deutschen Sprache*. Munichn: Deutscher Taschenbuch Verlag.

Kreidler, Charles W. (1989). *The Pronunciation of English*. Oxford: Blackwell.

Kurath, Hans and Raven I. McDavid Jr (1961). *The Pronunciation of English in the Atlantic States*. Ann Arbor: University of Michigan Press.

Kuryłowicz, Jerzy (1948). Contributions à la théorie de la syllabe. *Bulletin de la société polonaise de linguistique* 8. 80–114.

Labov, William (1966). *The Social Stratification of English in New York City*. Washington, DC: Center for Applied Linguistics.

Labov, William, Malcah Yaeger and R. Steiner (1972). *A Quantitative Study of Sound Change in Progress*. Philadelphia, PA: US Regional Survey.

Ladefoged, Peter (1971). *Preliminaries to Linguistic Phonetics*. Chicago: University of Chicago Press.

Ladefoged, Peter (1982). *A Course in Phonetics*. 2nd edn. New York: Harcourt, Brace and Jovanovich.

Ladefoged, Peter, J. DeClerk, M. Lindau and G. Papcun (1972). An auditory motor theory of speech production. *UCLA Phonetics Laboratory Working Papers in Phonetics* 22. 48-76.

Lass, Roger (1974). Linguistic orthogenesis? Scots vowel quantity and the English length conspiracy. In John Anderson and Charles Jones (eds), *Historical Linguistics II: theory and description in phonology, Proceedings of the First International Conference on Historical Linguistics, Edinburgh, September 1973*, 311-52. Amsterdam: North-Holland.

Lass, Roger (1976). *English Phonology and Phonological Theory*. Cambridge: Cambridge University Press.

Lass, Roger (1984). *Phonology: an introduction to basic concepts*. Cambridge: Cambridge University Press.

Lass, Roger and John M. Anderson (1975). *Old English Phonology*. Cambridge: Cambridge University Press.

Laver, John (1980). *The Phonetic Description of Voice Quality*. Cambridge: Cambridge University Press.

Leben, William (1973). Suprasegmental phonology. PhD dissertation, MIT.

Lehiste, Ilse (1978). The syllable as a structural unit in Estonian. In Bell and Hooper 1978, 73–83.

Leslie, David (1983). Left capture and British voiceless stop allophony. Paper presented at the 19th Congress of the International Association of Logopaedics and Phoniatrics, University of Edinburgh, August 1983.

Leslie, David (1989). Lenition systems. Paper presented at the London Phonology Seminar, University of London.

Levin, Juliette (1985). A metrical theory of syllabicity. PhD dissertation, MIT.

Liberman, Mark and Alan Prince (1977). On stress and linguistic rhythm. *Linguistic Inquiry* 8. 249–336.

Lieber, Rochelle (1982). Allomorphy. *Linguistic Analysis* 10. 27–52.

Lieberman, Philip and Sheila E. Blumstein (1988). *Speech Physiology, Speech Perception, and Acoustic Phonetics*. Cambridge: Cambridge University Press.

Lindsey, Geoff (1990). Quantity and quality in British and American vowel systems. In Ramsaran 1990, 106–18.

Lindsey, Geoff and John Harris (1990). Phonetic interpretation in generative grammar. *UCL Working Papers in Linguistics* 2. 355–69.

Lodge, K. R. (1984). *Studies in the Phonology of Colloquial English*. London: Croom Helm.

Lowenstamm, Jean (1979). Topics in Prosodic Phonology. PhD dissertation, University of Massachussetts.

Lowenstamm, Jean (1989). Prosodic government. *Langues orientales anciennes: philologie et linguistique* 2. 221–3

Lowenstamm, Jean and Jonathan Kaye (1985). Compensatory lengthening in Tiberian Hebrew. In Wetzels and Sezer 1985, 97–132.

Luelsdorff, Philip (1975). *A Segmental Phonology of Black English*. The Hague: Mouton.

Luick, Karl (1921). *Historische Grammatik der englischen Sprache*. Leipzig: Tauchnitz.

McCarthy, John J. (1979). Formal problems in Semitic morphology and phonology. PhD dissertation, MIT. Distributed by Indiana University Linguistics Club.

McCarthy, John J. (1986). OCP effects: gemination and antigemination. *Linguistic Inquiry* 17. 207-63.

McCarthy, John J. (1988). Feature geometry and dependency: a review. *Phonetica* 45. 84-108.

McCarthy, John J. (1991). Synchronic rule inversion. *Proceedings of the Seventeenth Annual Meeting of the Berkeley Linguistics Society*. 192–207.

McCarthy, John J. and Alan Prince (1986). Prosodic morphology. Ms. University of Massachusetts.

McCawley, James D. (1986). Today the world, tomorrow phonology. *Phonology* 3. 27–44.

Mackay, Edith (1982). *Universal Typing: advanced level*. London: Pitman.

McMahon, April (1991). Lexical phonology and sound change: the case of the Scottish Vowel Length Rule. *Journal of Linguistics* 27. 29–53.

McMahon, April (1992). Rule inversion: a lexicalist reanalysis. Ms. University of Cambridge.

Manzini, M. Rita (1992). *Locality: a theory and some of its empirical consequences*. Cambridge, MA: MIT Press.

Marantz, Alec (1982). Re reduplication. *Linguistic Inquiry* 13. 435–82.

Mascaró, Joan (1976). Catalan phonology and the phonological cycle. PhD dissertation, MIT. Distributed by Indiana University Linguistics Club.

Mascaró, Joan (1983). Phonological levels and assimilatory processes. Ms. Universitat Autònoma de Barcelona.

Mascaró, Joan (1987). A reduction theory of voicing and other sound effects. Ms. Universitat Autònoma de Barcelona.

Mather, J. Y and H.H Speitel (1986). *The Linguistic Atlas of Scotland, Scots Section, Volume III: phonology*. London: Croom Helm.

Matisoff, J. A. (1973). Tonogenesis in southeast Asia. In Larry M. Hyman (ed.), *Consonant Types and Tone*, 71–95. Los Angeles: University of Southern California.

Mohanan, K. P. (1983). The structure of the melody. Ms. MIT.

Mohanan, K. P. (1985). Syllable structure and lexical strata in English. *Phonology Year-book* 2. 137–54.

Mohanan, K. P. (1986). *The Theory of Lexical Phonology*. Dordrecht: Reidel.

Mohanan, K. P. (1991). On the bases of Radical Underspecification Theory. *Natural Language and Linguistic Theory* 9. 285–325.

Mohanan, Tara (1989). Syllable structure in Malayalam. *Linguistic Inquiry* 20. 589–625.

Myers, Scott (1987). Vowel shortening in English. *Natural Language and Linguistic Theory* 5. 485–518.

Myers, Scott (1991a). Persistent rules. *Linguistic Inquiry* 22. 315–44.

Myers, Scott (1991b). Structure Preservation and the Strong Domain Hypothesis. *Linguistic Inquiry* 22. 379–85.

Nespor, Marina and Irene Vogel (1986). *Prosodic Phonology*. Dordrecht: Foris.

Neu, H. (1980). Ranking of constraints on /t,d/ deletion in American English: a statistical analysis. In William Labov (ed.), *Locating Language in Time and Space*, 37–54. New York: Academic Press.

O'Connor, J. D and J. L. M. Trim (1953). Vowel, consonant and syllable: a phonological definition. *Word* 9. 103–22.

Odden, David (1988). Anti-antigemination and the OCP. *Linguistic Inquiry* 19. 451-74.

Orton, Harold and Michael V. Barry (1969). *Survey of English Dialects, Basic Material: the West Midland counties*. Leeds: Arnold.

Orton, Harold and Philip M. Tilling (1969). *Survey of English Dialects, Basic Material: the East Midland counties and East Anglia*. Leeds: Arnold.

Palmada Félez, Blanca. 1991. La fonologia del català i els principis actius. Doctoral dissertation, Universitat Autònoma de Barcelona.

Palmer, Frank (ed.) (1970). *Prosodic Analysis*. London: Oxford University Press.

Paradis, Carole and Jean-François Prunet (eds) (1991). *The Special Status of Coronals: internal and external evidence. Phonetics and Phonology* 2. San Diego, CA: Academic Press.

Petterson, Thore and Sidney Wood (1987). Vowel reduction in Bulgarian and its implications for theories of vowel reduction: a review of the problem. *Folia Linguistica* 21. 261–79.

Piggott, Glynne (1988). The parameters of nasalisation. Ms. McGill University.

Piggott, Glynne and R. Singh (1985). The phonology of epenthetic segments. *Revue Canadienne de Linguistique* 30. 415-53.

Pike, Kenneth (1967). *Language in Relation to a Unified Theory of Human Behaviour*. The Hague: Mouton.

Pike, Kenneth and Eunice Victoria Pike (1947). Immediate constituents of Mazateco syllables. *International Journal of American Linguistics* 13. 78–91.

Prince, Alan S. (1984). Phonology with tiers. In Aronoff and Oehrle 1984, 234–44.

Prince, Alan S. and Paul Smolensky (1993). Optimality theory: constraint interaction in generative grammar. *Technical Report # 2 of the Rutgers Center for Cognitive Science*, Rutgers University.

Prunet, Jean-François (1986). Spreading and locality domains in phonology. PhD dissertation, McGill University.

Pulleyblank, Douglas (1986). *Tone in Lexical Phonology*. Dordrecht: Reidel.

Pulleyblank, Douglas (in press). Feature geometry and underspecification. To appear in Durand and Katamba, in press.

Pullum, Geoff K. (1976). *Rule Interaction and the Organization of a Grammar*. PhD dissertation, University College London. Published 1978, New York: Garland.

Ramsaran, Susan (ed.) (1990). *Studies in the Pronunciation of English: a commemorative volume in honour of A.C. Gimson*. London: Routledge.

Rennison, John (1984). On tridirectional feature systems for vowels. *Wiener linguistische Gazette*. 33-4, 69-93. Reprinted in Durand 1986, 281–303.

Rennison, John (1987). Vowel harmony and tridirectional vowel features. *Folia Linguistica* 21. 337-54.

Rennison, John (1990). On the elements of phonological representations: the evidence from vowel systems and vowel processes. *Folia Linguistica* 24. 175–244.

Rice, Keren D. (1992). On deriving sonority: a structural account of sonority relationships. *Phonology* 9. 61–100.

van Riemsdijk, Henk and Edwin Williams (1986). *Theory of Grammar*. Cambridge, MA: MIT Press.

Robins, R. H. (1957). Aspects of prosodic analysis. *Proceedings of the University of Durham Philosophical Society* 1. 1–12. Reprinted in Palmer 1970, 157–73.

Sagey, Elizabeth (1986). The representation of features and relations in non-linear phonology. PhD dissertation, MIT.

Sagey, Elizabeth (1988). On the ill-formedness of crossing association lines. *Linguistic Inquiry* 19. 109–18.

Saussure, Ferdinand de (1916). *Cours de linguistique générale*. Paris: Payot.

Schane, Sanford S. (1973). *Generative Phonology*. Englewood Cliffs, NJ: Prentice-Hall.

Schane, Sanford S. (1984a). The fundamentals of Particle Phonology. *Phonology* 1. 129–56.

Schane, Sanford S. (1984b). Two English vowel movements: a particle analysis. In Aronoff and Oehrle 1984, 32–51.

Scobbie, James M. (1992). Against rule inversion: the development of English [r]-sandhi. Poster paper, 7th International Phonology Meeting, Krems.

Selkirk, Elizabeth O. (1980). The role of prosodic categories in English word stress. *Linguistic Inquiry* 11. 563–605.

Selkirk, Elizabeth O. (1981). Epenthesis and degenerate syllables in Cairene Arabic. In Hagit Borer and Joseph Aoun (eds), *MIT Working Papers in Linguistics* 3. 209–32.

Selkirk, Elizabeth O. (1982a). *The Syntax of Words*. Cambridge, MA: MIT Press.

Selkirk, Elizabeth O. (1982b). The syllable. In van der Hulst and Smith 1982b, Part II, 337–84.

Selkirk, Elizabeth O. (1984). On the major class features and syllable theory. In Aronoff and Oehrle 1984, 107-36.

Selkirk, Elizabeth O. and Jean-Roger Vergnaud (1973). How abstract is French phonology? *Foundations of Language* 10. 249–54.

Sheridan, Thomas (1762). *A Course of Lectures on Elocution*. Reprinted 1968, Menston: Scholar Press.

Siegel, Dorothy (1974). Topics in English morphology. PhD dissertation, MIT.

Sivertsen, E. (1960). *Cockney Phonology*. Oslo: Oslo University Press.

Sledd, James H. (1958). Some questions of English phonology. *Language* 34. 252–60.

Sledd, James H. (1966). Breaking, umlaut, and the Southern drawl. *Language* 42. 18-41.

Smith, Norval. (1988). Consonant place features. In van der Hulst and Smith 1988, Part I, 209–36.

Sperber, Dan and Deirdre Wilson (1986). *Relevance: communication and cognition.* Oxford: Blackwell.

Sproat, R. (1985). On deriving the lexicon. PhD dissertation, MIT.

Stampe, David (1973). A dissertation on Natural Phonology. PhD dissertation, University of Chicago.

Steriade, Donca (1982). Greek prosodies and the nature of syllabification. PhD dissertation, MIT.

Trager, G. L. and H. L. Smith (1951). *An Outline of English Structure. Studies in Linguistics, Occasional Papers* 3. Norman, OK: Battenburg Press.

Trubetzkoy, N. (1939). *Grundzüge der Phonologie. Travaux du cercle linguistique de Prague* 7.

Trudgill, Peter (ed.) (1984). *Language in the British Isles.* Cambridge: Cambridge University Press.

Trudgill, Peter (1986). *Dialects in Contact.* Oxford: Blackwell.

Uriagereka, Juan (1986). Government functions and the Classical Arabic verb paradigm. Paper presented at the 9th GLOW Colloquium, Barcelona/Girona.

Vennemann, Theo (1972a). On the theory of syllabic phonology. *Linguistische Berichte* 18. 1–18.

Vennemann, Theo (1972b). Rule inversion. *Lingua* 29. 209–42.

Vennemann, Theo (1988). *Preference Laws for Syllable Structure and the Explanation of Sound Change.* Berlin: Mouton de Gruyter.

Vergnaud, Jean-Roger (1982). On the theoretical bases of phonology. Paper presented at the 5th GLOW Colloquium, Paris.

Walker, John (1791). *A Critical Pronouncing Dictionary and Expositor of the English Language.* London: Robinson and Cadell. Reprinted 1968, *English Linguistics 1500–1800* 117. Menston: Scholar Press.

Wang, H. Samuel and Bruce L. Derwing (1986). More on English vowel shift: the back vowel question. *Phonology* 3. 99–116.

Wells, J. C. (1982). *Accents of English.* 3 vols. Cambridge: Cambridge University Press.

Wells, J. C. (1990). Syllabification and allophony. In Ramsaran 1990, 76–86.

Wetzels, Leo and Engin Sezer (eds) (1985). *Studies in Compensatory Lengthening.* Dordrecht: Foris.

Wolfe, Patricia M. (1972). *Linguistic Change and the Great Vowel Shift in English.* Berkeley and Los Angeles: University of California Press.

Yip, Moira (1988a). Template morphology and the direction of association. *Natural Language and Linguistic Theory* 6. 551–77.

Yip, Moira (1988b). The Obligatory Contour Principle and phonological rules: a loss of identity. *Linguistic Inquiry* 19. 65–100.

Yip, Moira (1991). Coronals, consonant clusters, and the coda condition. In Paradis and Prunet 1991, 61–78.

Zec, Draga (1988). Sonority constraints on prosodic structure. PhD dissertation, Stanford University.

Zwicky, Arnold M. (1975). Settling on an underlying form: the English inflectional ending. In D. Cohen and J. R. Wirth (eds), *Testing Linguistic Hypotheses*, 129–85. New York: Wiley.

Subject index

⟨a/an⟩ 60
adjacency 12, 14, 48–51, 156, 163, 182,
    187–8, 191–3
    string 156–9
adjunct position 153, 158, 160, 163–4,
    168–9
advanced tongue root *see* tense vs. lax
affricate 39–41, 131
African American English
    final devoicing in 210
    nasals in 147
    sr clusters in 278 n.44
Aitken's Law 30–1, 255
alternation 3, 60–1, 63, 125, 165–6,
    180, 182, 192–3, 197, 240–1, 266–7
    of *r* and zero 231, 234–5, 238,
    240–52, 266
    see also root-level alternation
ambisyllabicity 198–200, 202
analytic morphology 25, 50–1, 70–1,
    82, 182
appendix 81–2
Arabic
    onsets in 150
Arbore
    glottalling in 284 n.63
assimilation
    of manner 132
    of place 2, 9, 14, 18, 72, 118–19,
    165
    of voice 23, 58–9, 136–8, 145–6, 278
    n.45
association line 13–14, 35, 37, 101, 128,
    165–6
    no crossing constraint on 37
æ-tensing/lengthening 29–30, 69, 77–8,
    125
ATR *see* tense vs. lax
Australia

tapping in 121, 195
autosegmental licensing *see* licensing
autosegmental representation 101–2,
    105, 127–8

Belfast
    æ-tensing in 30
Berber
    geminates in 288 n.39
binary branching 63, 65, 82–3, 163,
    178, 279 n.56
bleeding order *see* rule
bogus consonant cluster 67, 182, 187,
    222–3, 288 n.39
bound morpheme 19, 290 n.53
brace notation 197–8, 202, 238–9
breaking *see* vowel
breathy voice 135
broad *a* 282–3 n.32
    see also æ-tensing/lengthening
Bulgarian
    vowel reduction in 112

Canada
    rhoticity in 232
    tapping in 115, 195
Caribbean
    breaking in 116, 278 n.53, 294 n.12
    rhoticity in 232
Catalan
    devoicing in 135
    vowel reduction in 110, 112–13
charm 289 n.43, 289 n.47
class node 128–9
closed-rhyme shortness 20, 55, 78–80,
    149, 161, 168–9, 226
closed-syllable shortening *see*
    closed-rhyme shortness
Coda Capture 198–202, 225

Index of vowel word-classes

Following the practice adopted in the text, vowel contrasts are identified here according to the classes of words in which they occur, indicated by means of capitalized head-words. Rather than being listed alphabetically, the indexed head-words are grouped according to the following rough historical-phonological criteria: (a) short versus (b) long/diphthongal versus (c) pre- *r*.

Short
BIT 115, 243, 255, 268
BET 115, 243, 255, 268
BAD/BAT 115, 117, 243, 255, 268, 294 n.12
COT/POT 106, 115, 117, 243, 255, 268
BUT/CUT 109, 115, 243, 255, 268
PUT 115, 243, 255, 268
Long/diphthongal
BEAD/BEAT/MEET 103, 115, 235, 243, 255, 268
BADE/BAIT/DAY/MATE 99, 100, 106, 116, 235, 243, 255, 268, 294 n.12, 296 n.41
BOAT/GO 100, 106, 116, 244, 255, 268, 296 n.41
BOOT/LOOT 103, 115, 244, 255, 268
BITE 115–16, 243, 255, 268
BOUT/SHOUT 115–16, 243, 255, 268, 280 n.12
TOY 117
CAUGHT/PAW 99, 117, 236–7, 244, 254–5, 268, 294 n.15

CALM/PA 117, 236–7
Before historical *r*
BEARD/BEER/FEAR 235, 243, 254–5, 263, 294 n.12
EERIE 256
SPIRIT 256
BEAR/CARE/FAIR 243, 255, 263
MARY 256, 263–4
MERRY 256, 263–4
MARRY 256, 263–4
BAR/CART/FAR/FARM/PAR 117, 236–7, 243, 255–6, 263, 268
COURT/FOUR/PORE 117, 236–7, 244, 254–6, 263
FOR 255–6, 263
POOR 244, 255–6, 263
FIR/SHIRT/SKIRT/ THIRD 109, 254–7, 268
FUR/HURT 255–7
PER/PERT 255–7
WIRE 243, 255, 256
HOUR 243, 255–6